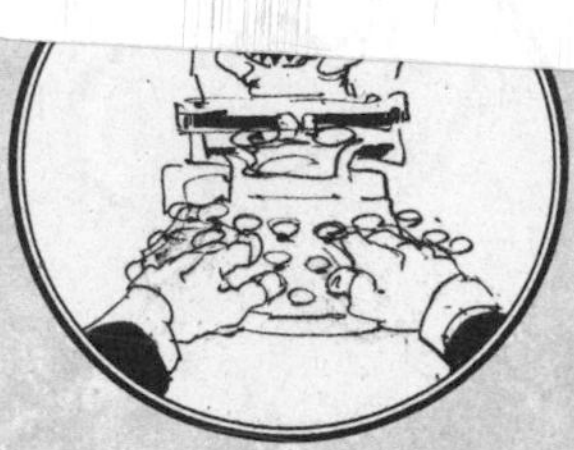

POSUKA DEMIZU

I was told that the anime would start around the time this volume went on sale in Japan.

Even though the days pass by so quickly, the progress of the anime gradually getting made is more fun than I ever dreamed.

By the way, in the next volume, a certain someone is finally going to make a move!!

The puzzle pieces are getting placed, and the day they form a full picture is drawing near.

I'll see you in the next volume!

KAIU SHIRAI

Writer Shirai's interesting tidbits for *The Promised Neverland* fanatics, part 4!

I love the notes that Demizu Sensei wrote with the character designs.

Nigel and Yvette make Team Artisan. Gillian and Alicia are Team Gillian's High School. And then...Thoma, Lanni and Sandy are Team Broccoli.

(Broccoli!!)

Please enjoy this volume!

Posuka Demizu debuted as a manga artist with the 2013 *CoroCoro* series *Oreca Monster Bouken Retsuden*. A collection of illustrations, *The Art of Posuka Demizu,* was released in 2016 by PIE International.

Kaiu Shirai debuted in 2015 with *Ashley Gate no Yukue* on the *Shonen Jump+* website. Shirai first worked with Posuka Demizu on the two-shot *Poppy no Negai*, which was released in February 2016.

VOLUME 12
SHONEN JUMP Manga Edition

STORY BY KAIU SHIRAI
ART BY POSUKA DEMIZU

Translation/Satsuki Yamashita
Touch-Up Art & Lettering/Mark McMurray
Design/Julian [JR] Robinson
Editor/Alexis Kirsch

YAKUSOKU NO NEVERLAND © 2016 by Kaiu Shirai, Posuka Demizu
All rights reserved.
First published in Japan in 2016 by SHUEISHA Inc., Tokyo.
English translation rights arranged by SHUEISHA Inc.

The stories, characters and incidents mentioned in this publication are
entirely fictional.

Printed in Canada

Published by VIZ Media, LLC
P.O. Box 77010
San Francisco, CA 94107

10 9 8 7 6 5 4 3 2
First printing, October 2019
Second printing, February 2021

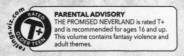

viz.com

THE PROMISED NEVERLAND

12

Starting Sound

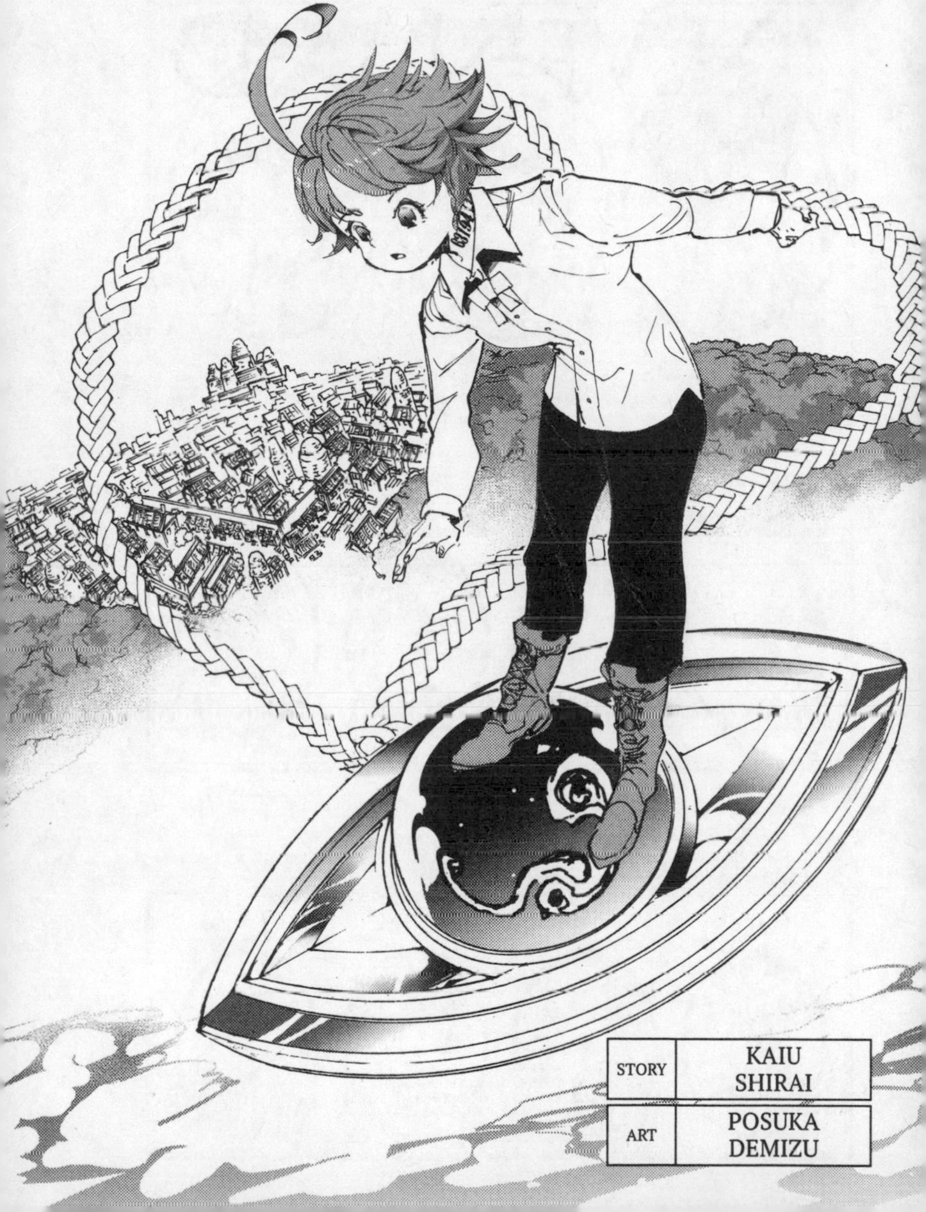

STORY	KAIU SHIRAI
ART	POSUKA DEMIZU

CHARACTERS

The Children of Grace Field House

They aim to free all of the children who are trapped in Grace Field House within two years.

RAY	EMMA	NORMAN
On the Run	On the Run	In New Farm Lambda

RAY

On the Run

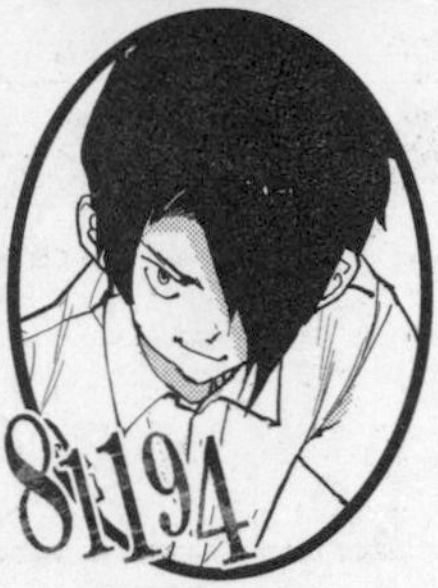
81194

The only one among the Grace Field House children who can match wits with Norman.

EMMA

On the Run

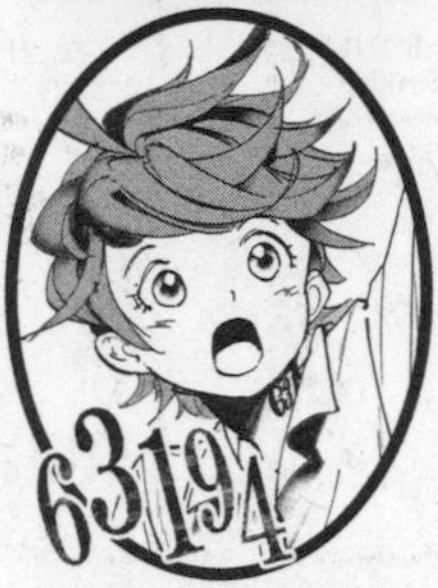
63194

An enthusiastic and optimistic girl with superb athletic and learning abilities.

NORMAN

In New Farm Lambda

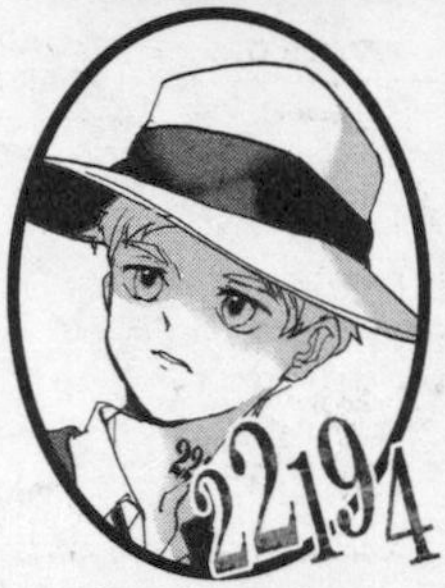
22194

A boy with excellent analytical and decision-making capabilities. He is the smartest of the children from Grace Field House.

CAROL

In Grace Field House

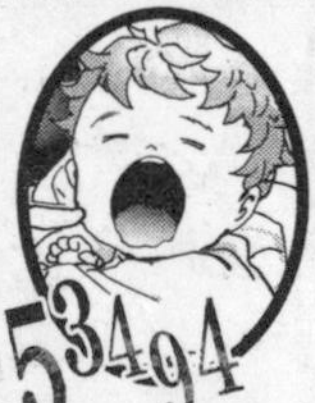
53494

PHIL

In Grace Field House

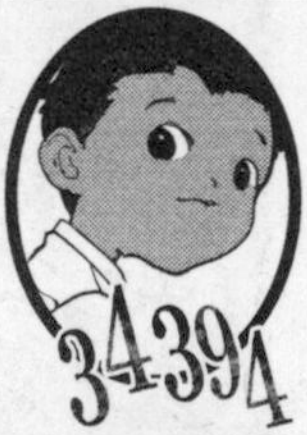
34394

GILDA

On the Run

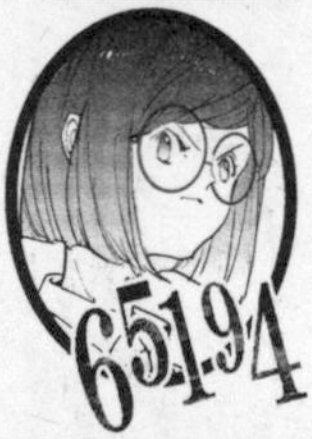
65194

DON

On the Run

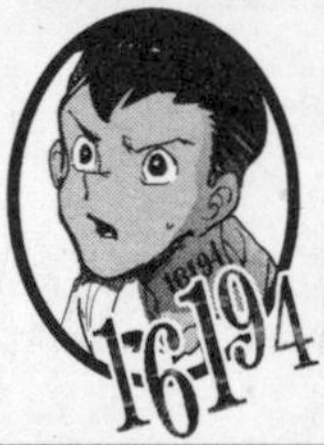
16194

The Children of Grand Valley

The children who were trapped in Goldy Pond, a hunting ground for demons. They started a rebellion and won the battle against the demons.

ZACK

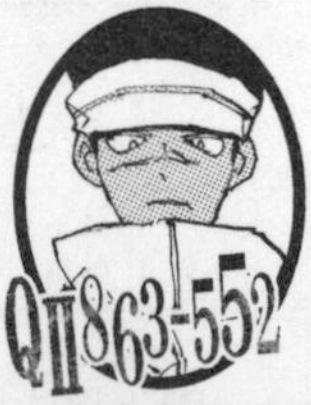
QII 863-552

VIOLET

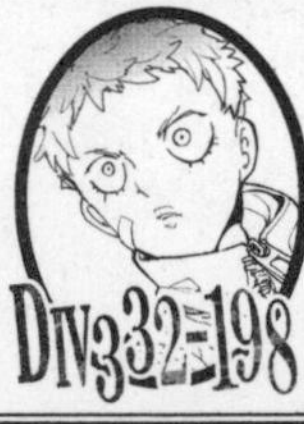
DIV 332-198

SONYA

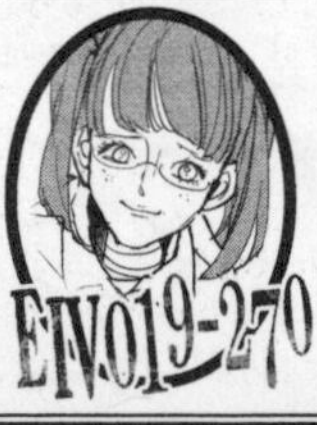
EIV 019-270

OLIVER

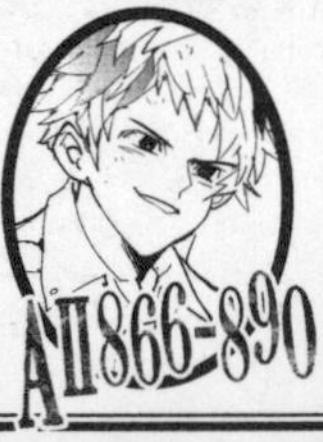
AII 866-890

The Ratri Clan

The descendants of the human who made a promise with the demons 1,000 years ago. They work as mediators between the two worlds.

PETER RATRI

Younger Brother

WILLIAM MINERVA (JAMES RATRI)

Older Brother

 ### The Escapees from Glory Bell

Just like Emma's group, they escaped from the farm with their friends. But they became the last two survivors when they were attacked by demons at Goldy Pond 13 years ago.

YUGO

LUCAS

ETR3M8

KGX2A7

 ### ? ? ?

Nomadic demons. They are forbidden by their religion to eat humans raised in farms.

MUJIKA

SONJU

 ### The Demons of Goldy Pond

They hunted humans secretly, which was forbidden, at Goldy Pond. They were killed when the humans rebelled.

GRAND DUKE LEUVIS

LORD BAYON

The Story So Far

Emma is living happily at Grace Field House with her foster siblings. One day, she realizes that they are being bred as food for demons and decides to escape with a group of other children. At a safe shelter, she meets a man who guides her and Ray to Goldy Pond, a location Minerva indicated in a letter. But Emma is kidnapped on the way and suddenly finds herself inside Goldy Pond. There she meets other humans and joins their fight to annihilate the demons and escape. After they return to the shelter, Emma reveals to everyone her intention to free all of the children in the farms using the information she obtained at Goldy Pond. Meanwhile, Peter Ratri finds out about the incident at Goldy Pond and makes a move.

THE PROMISED NEVERLAND 12

Starting Sound

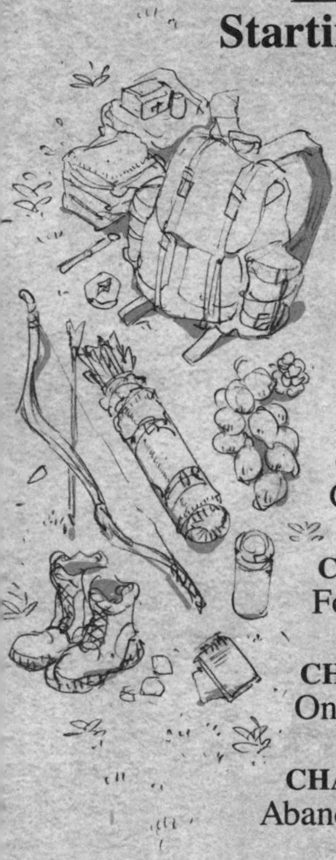

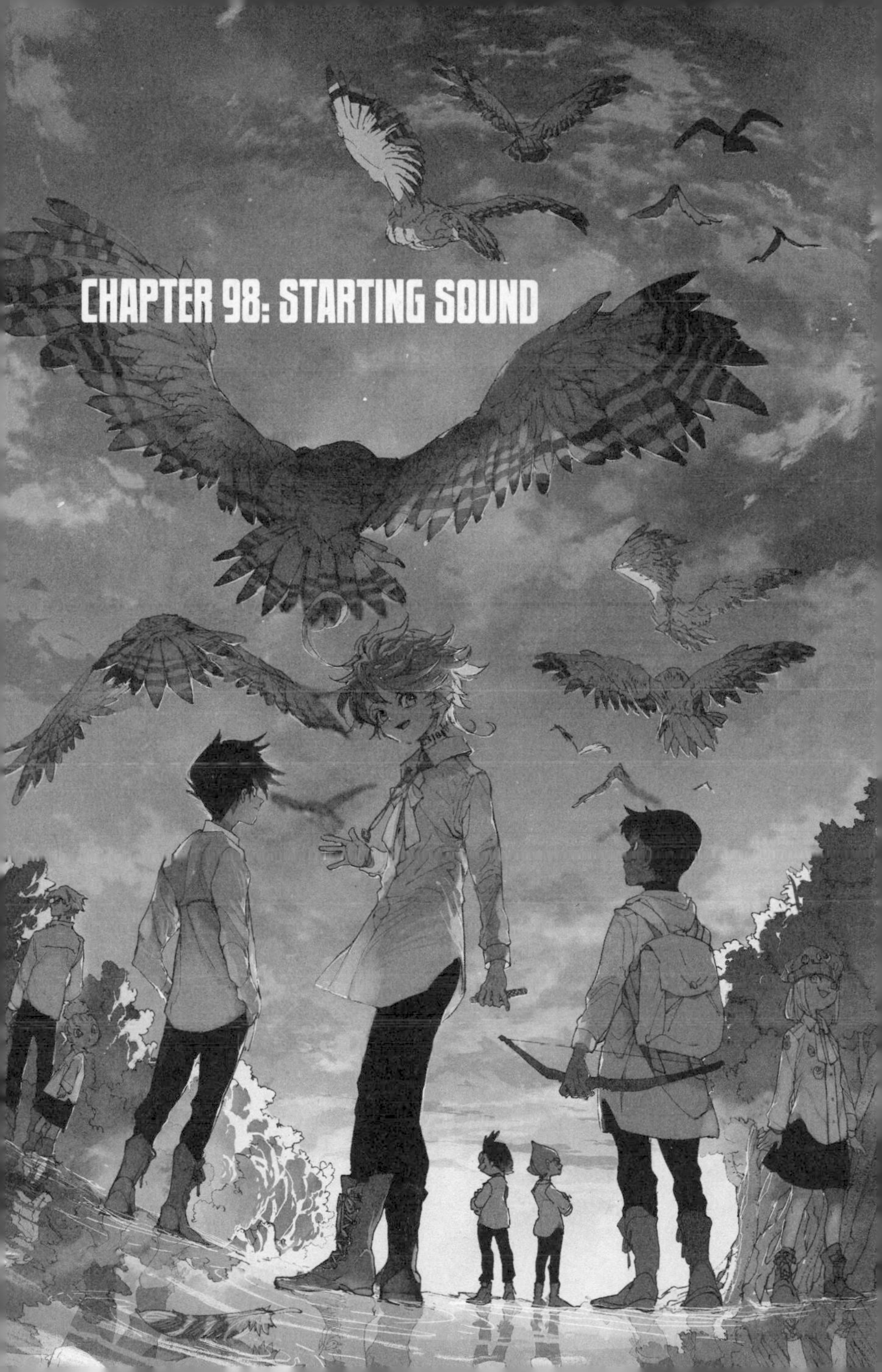
CHAPTER 98: STARTING SOUND

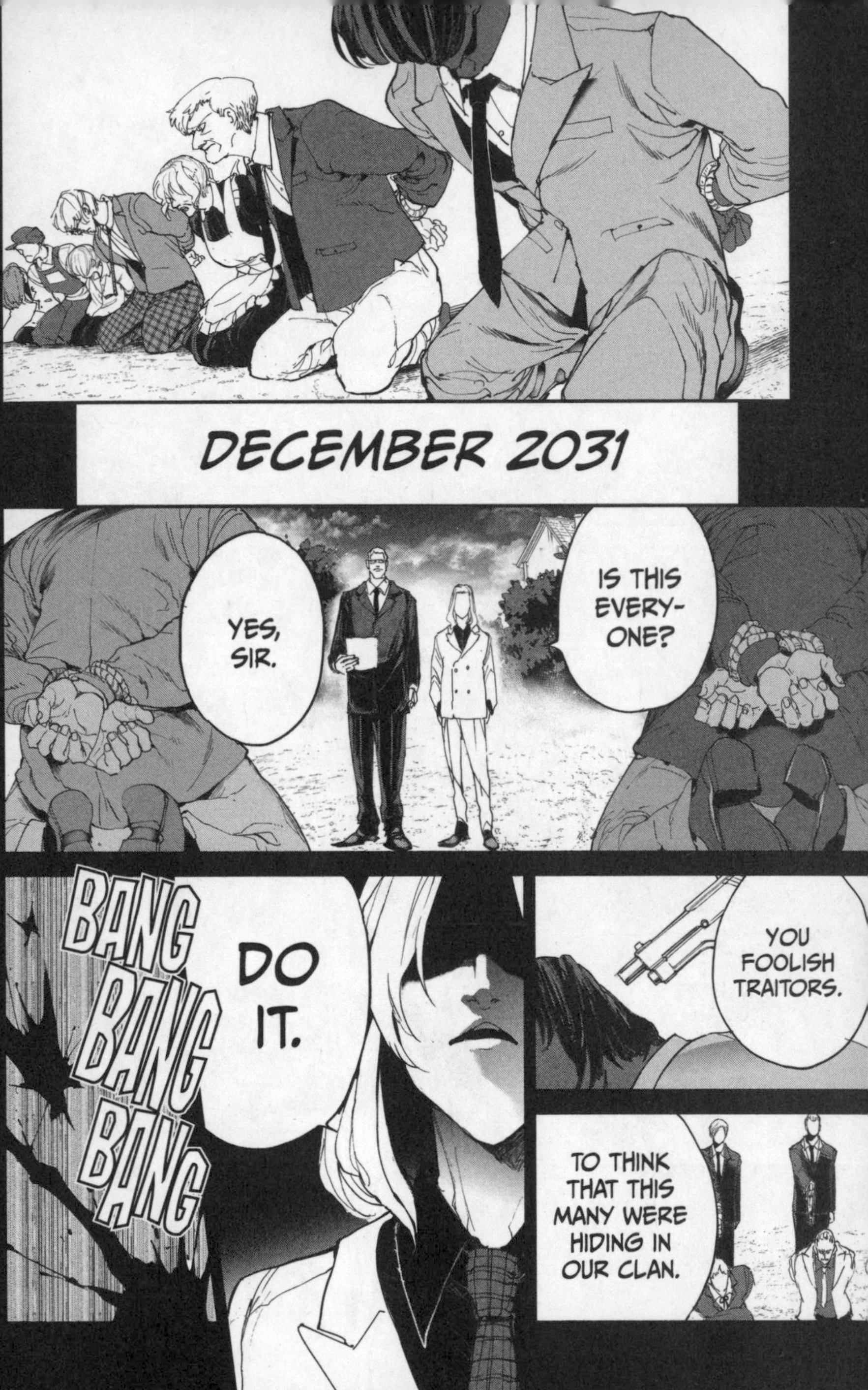
DECEMBER 2031
IS THIS EVERY-ONE?
YES, SIR.
YOU FOOLISH TRAITORS.
TO THINK THAT THIS MANY WERE HIDING IN OUR CLAN.
DO IT.
BANG BANG BANG

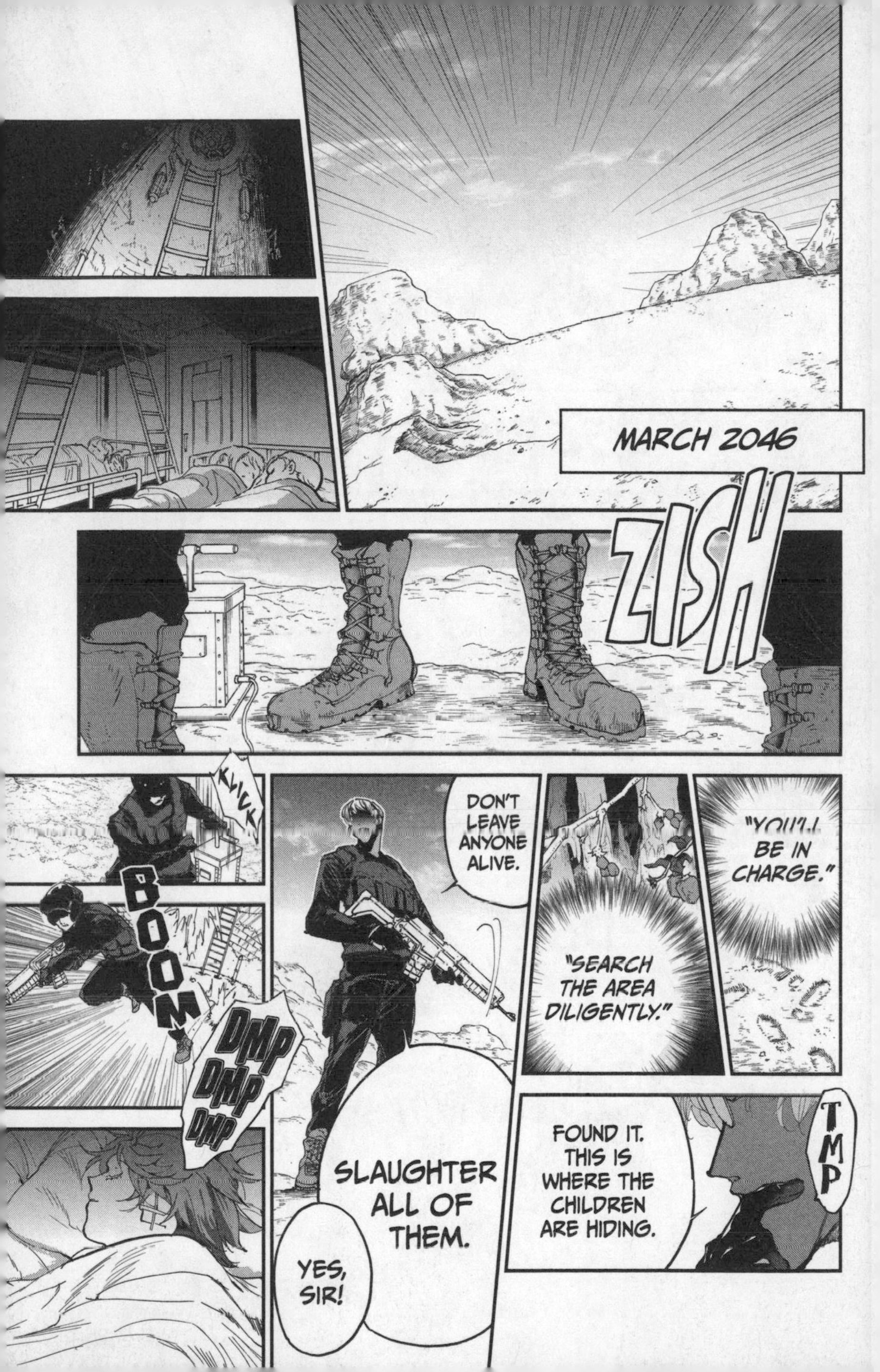
MARCH 2046
ZISH
"YOU'LL BE IN CHARGE."
"SEARCH THE AREA DILIGENTLY."
FOUND IT. THIS IS WHERE THE CHILDREN ARE HIDING.
TMP
DON'T LEAVE ANYONE ALIVE.
SLAUGHTER ALL OF THEM.
YES, SIR!
KLICK
BOOM
DMP DMP DMP

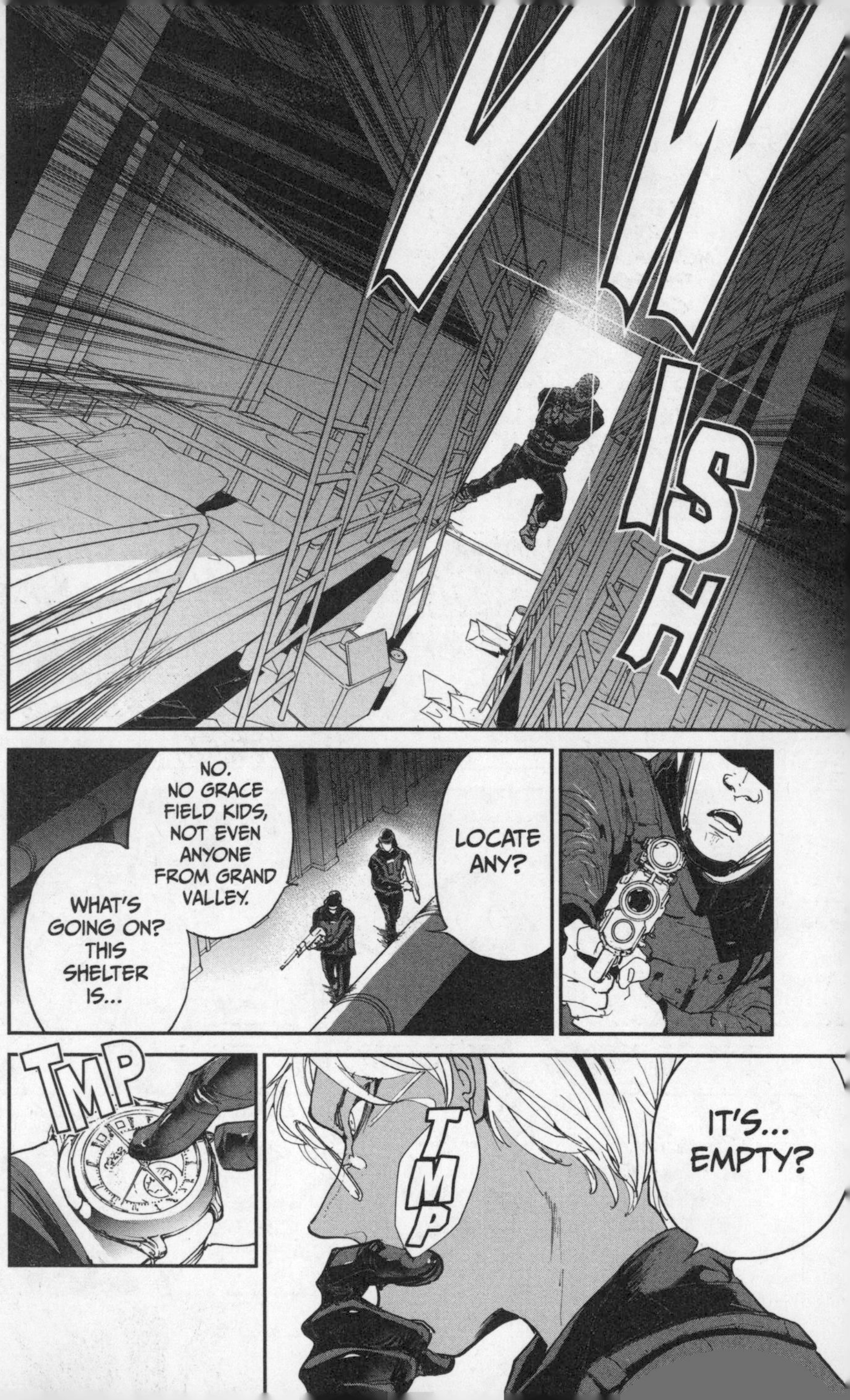
VWISH
LOCATE ANY?
NO. NO GRACE FIELD KIDS, NOT EVEN ANYONE FROM GRAND VALLEY.
WHAT'S GOING ON? THIS SHELTER IS...
IT'S... EMPTY?
TMP
TMP

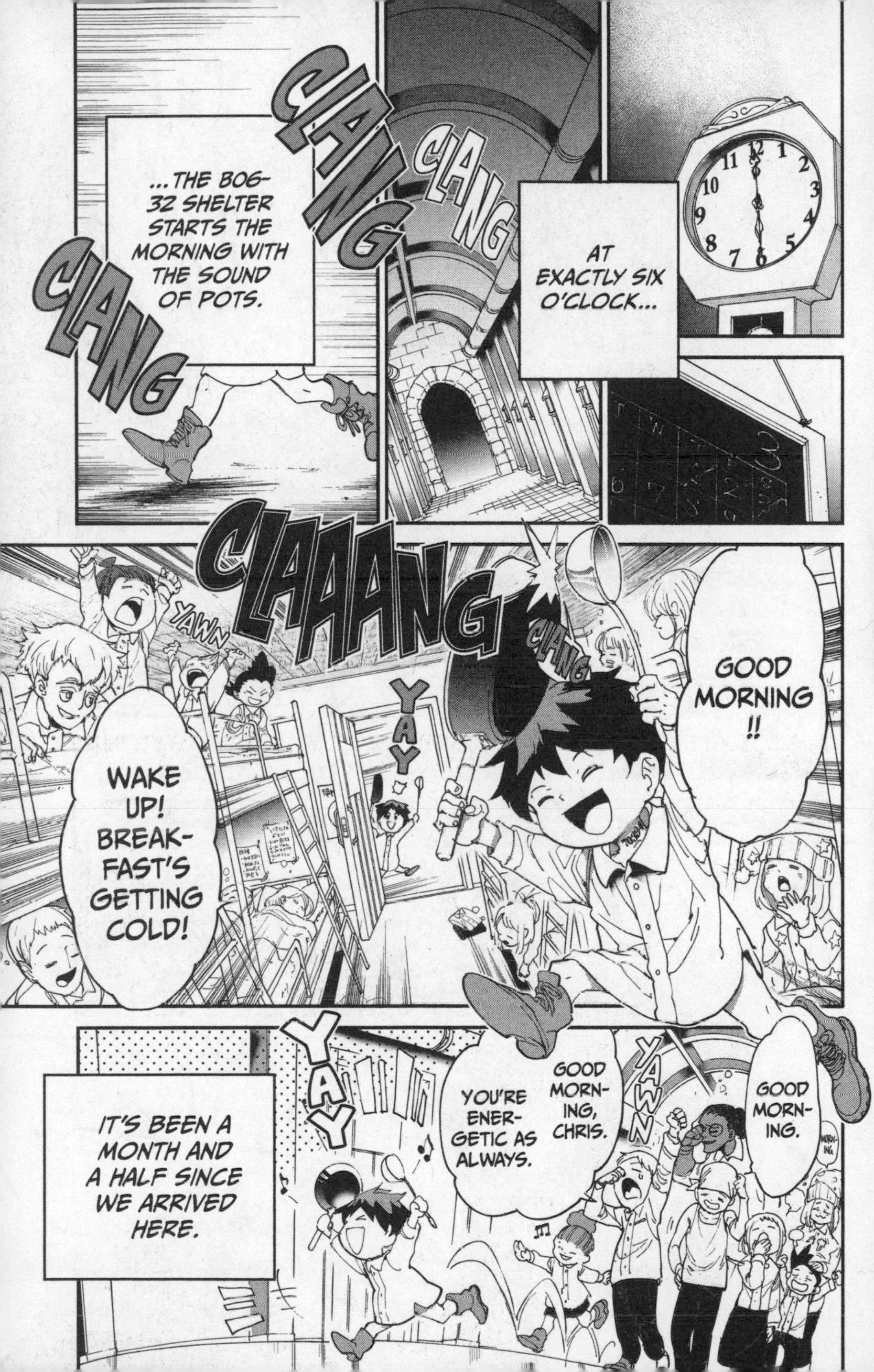
AT EXACTLY SIX O'CLOCK...
CLANG
CLANG
...THE B06-32 SHELTER STARTS THE MORNING WITH THE SOUND OF POTS.
CLANG
GOOD MORNING!!
CLANG
CLAAANG
YAY
YAWN
WAKE UP! BREAK-FAST'S GETTING COLD!
GOOD MORN-ING.
MORN-ING.
YAWN
GOOD MORN-ING, CHRIS.
YOU'RE ENER-GETIC AS ALWAYS.
YAY
IT'S BEEN A MONTH AND A HALF SINCE WE ARRIVED HERE.

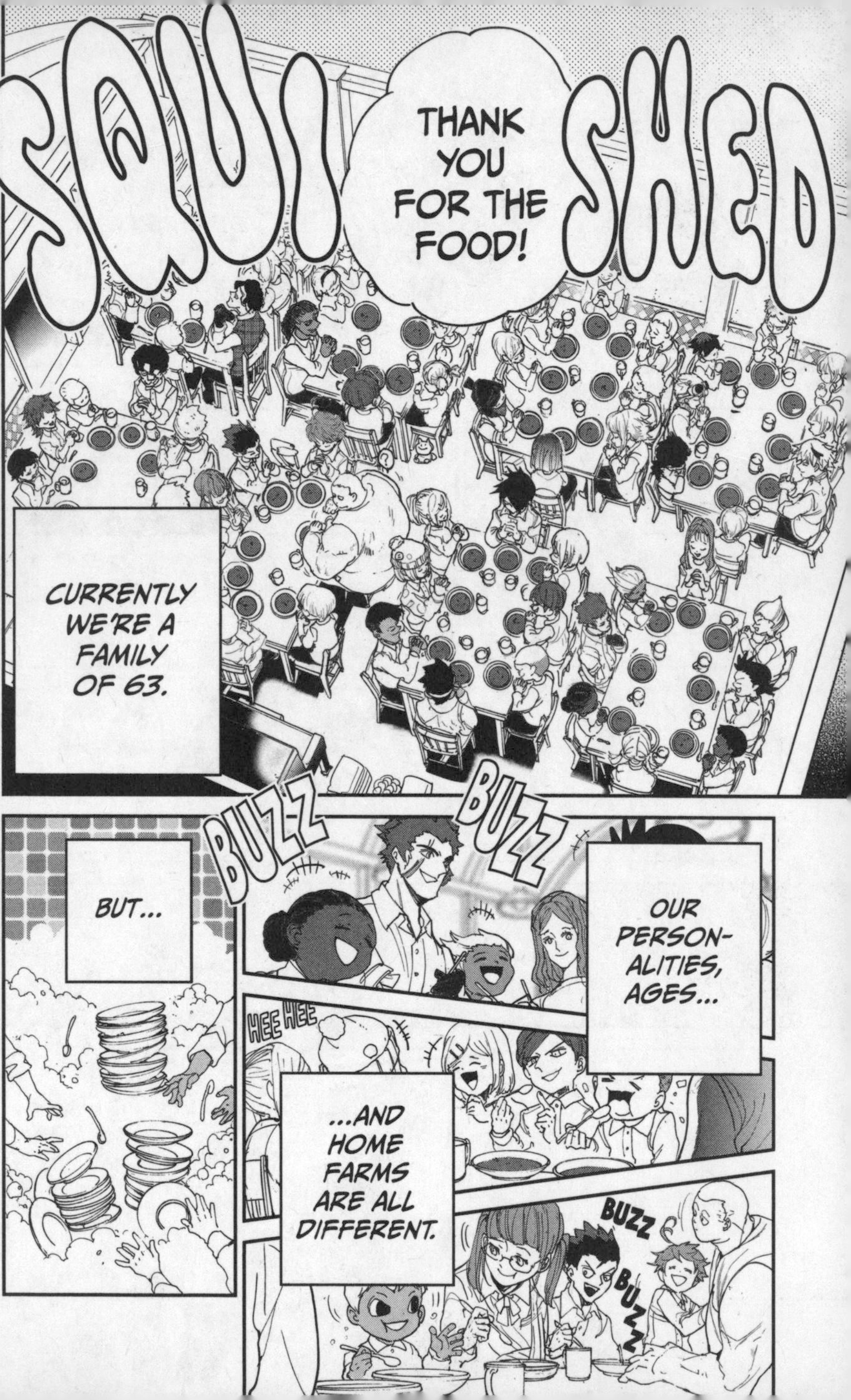
SQUISHED
THANK YOU FOR THE FOOD!
CURRENTLY WE'RE A FAMILY OF 63.
BUT...
BUZZ BUZZ
OUR PERSON-ALITIES, AGES...
HEE HEE
...AND HOME FARMS ARE ALL DIFFERENT.
BUZZ BUZZ

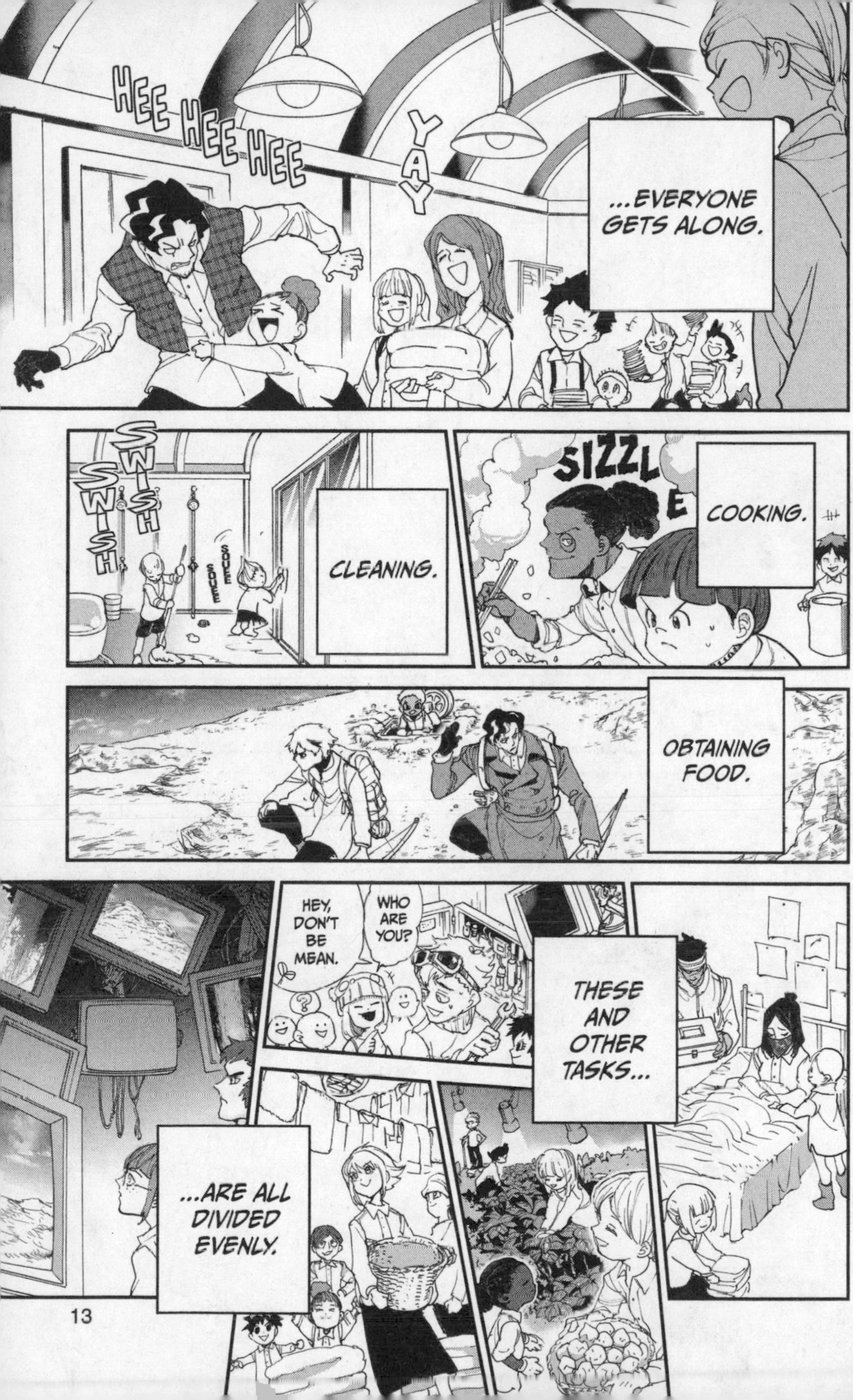
HEE HEE HEE
YAY
...EVERYONE GETS ALONG.
SIZZLE
COOKING.
SWISH SWISH
SQUEE SQUEE
CLEANING.
OBTAINING FOOD.
THESE AND OTHER TASKS...
WHO ARE YOU?
HEY, DON'T BE MEAN.
...ARE ALL DIVIDED EVENLY.

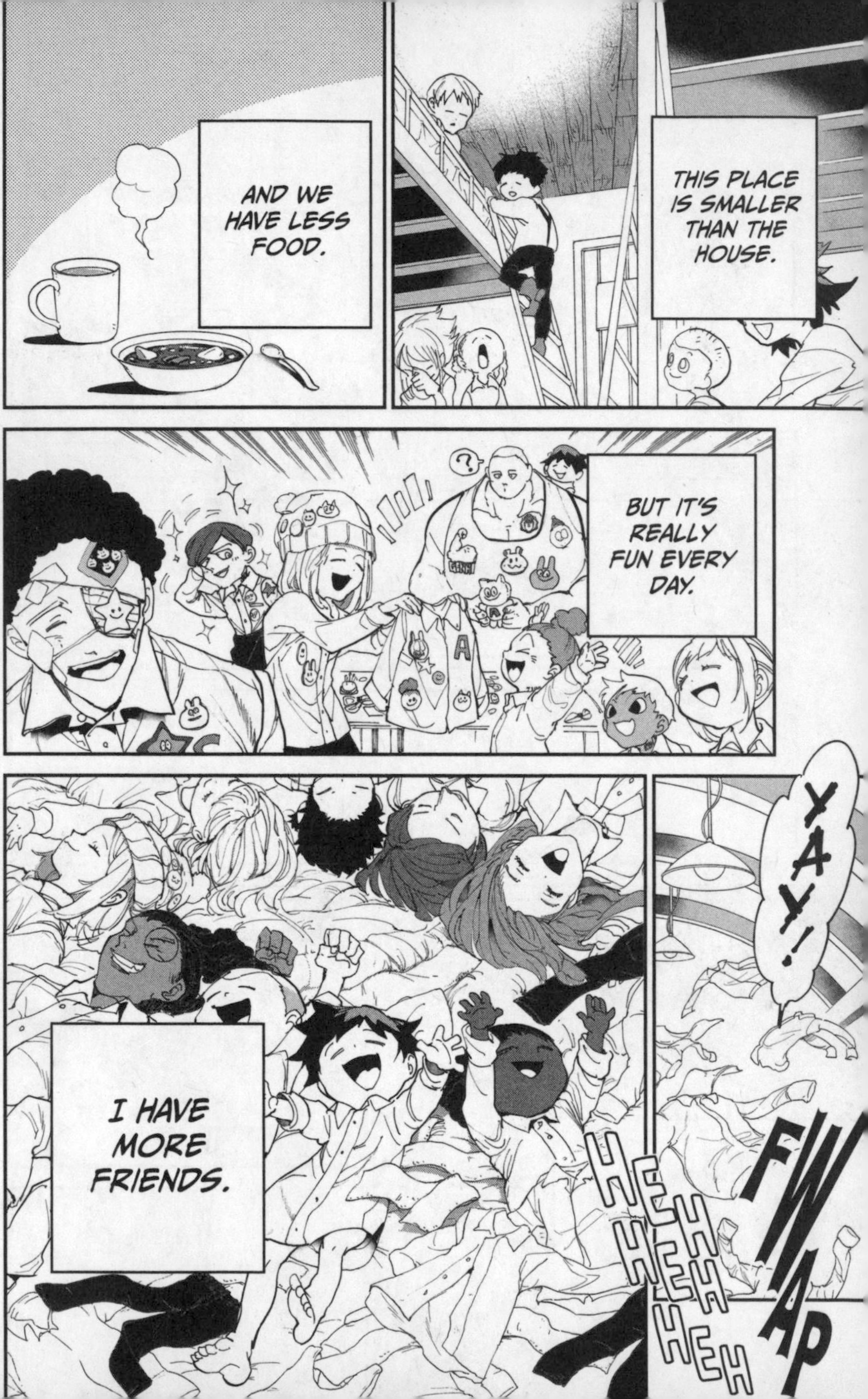

THIS PLACE IS SMALLER THAN THE HOUSE.
AND WE HAVE LESS FOOD.
BUT IT'S REALLY FUN EVERY DAY.
YAY!
FWAP
HEH HEH HEH HEH HEH HEH
I HAVE MORE FRIENDS.

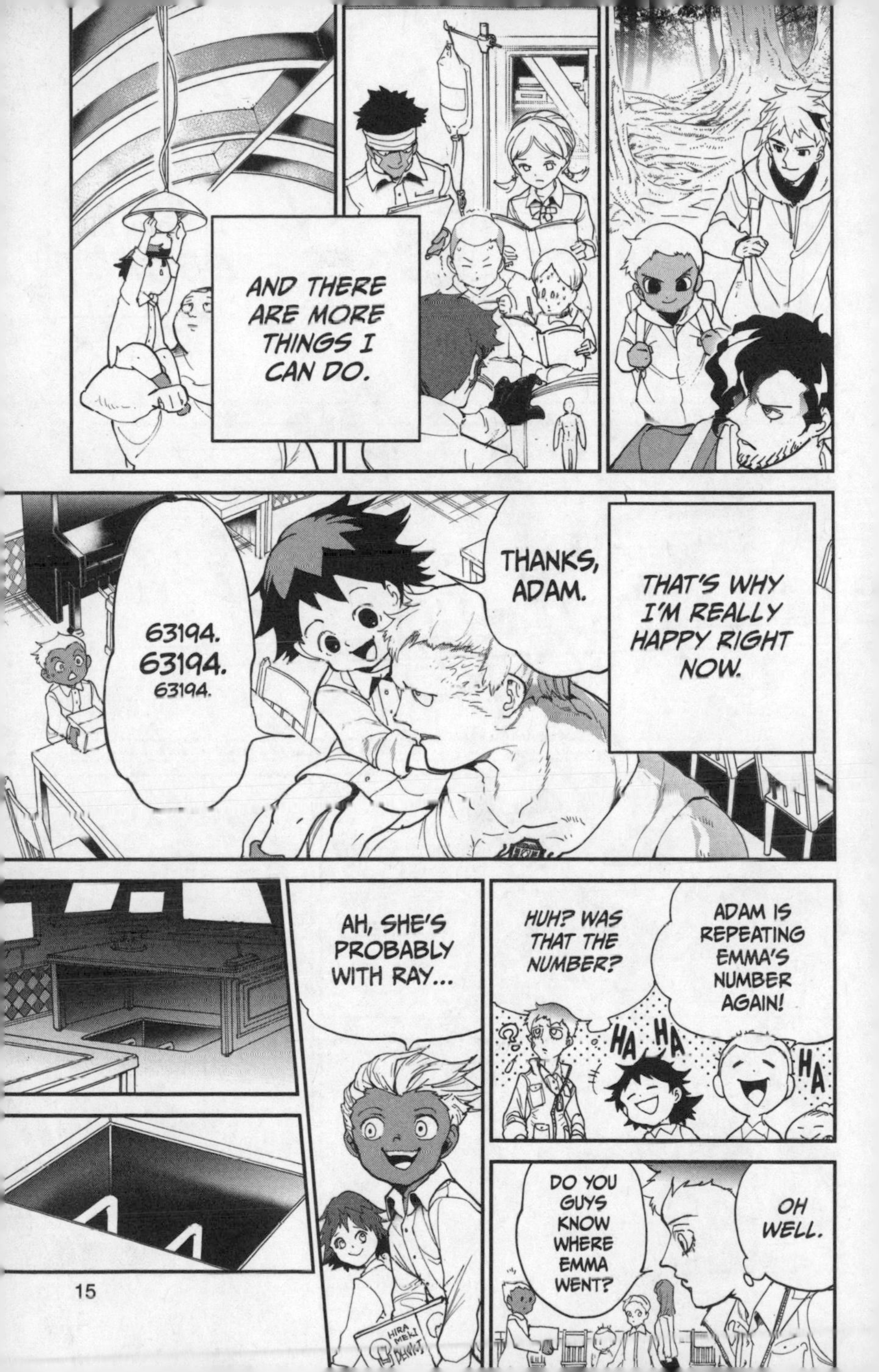
AND THERE ARE MORE THINGS I CAN DO.
THAT'S WHY I'M REALLY HAPPY RIGHT NOW.
THANKS, ADAM.
63194. 63194. 63194.
ADAM IS REPEATING EMMA'S NUMBER AGAIN!
HUH? WAS THAT THE NUMBER?
HA HA HA
OH WELL.
DO YOU GUYS KNOW WHERE EMMA WENT?
AH, SHE'S PROBABLY WITH RAY...

...IN THE SECRET ROOM.

GWUNG

ANY WORD FROM THE SUP-PORTERS?

STILL NO CONTACT FROM THEM.

NOPE.

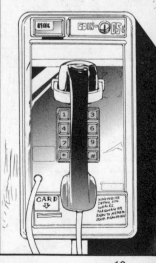

16

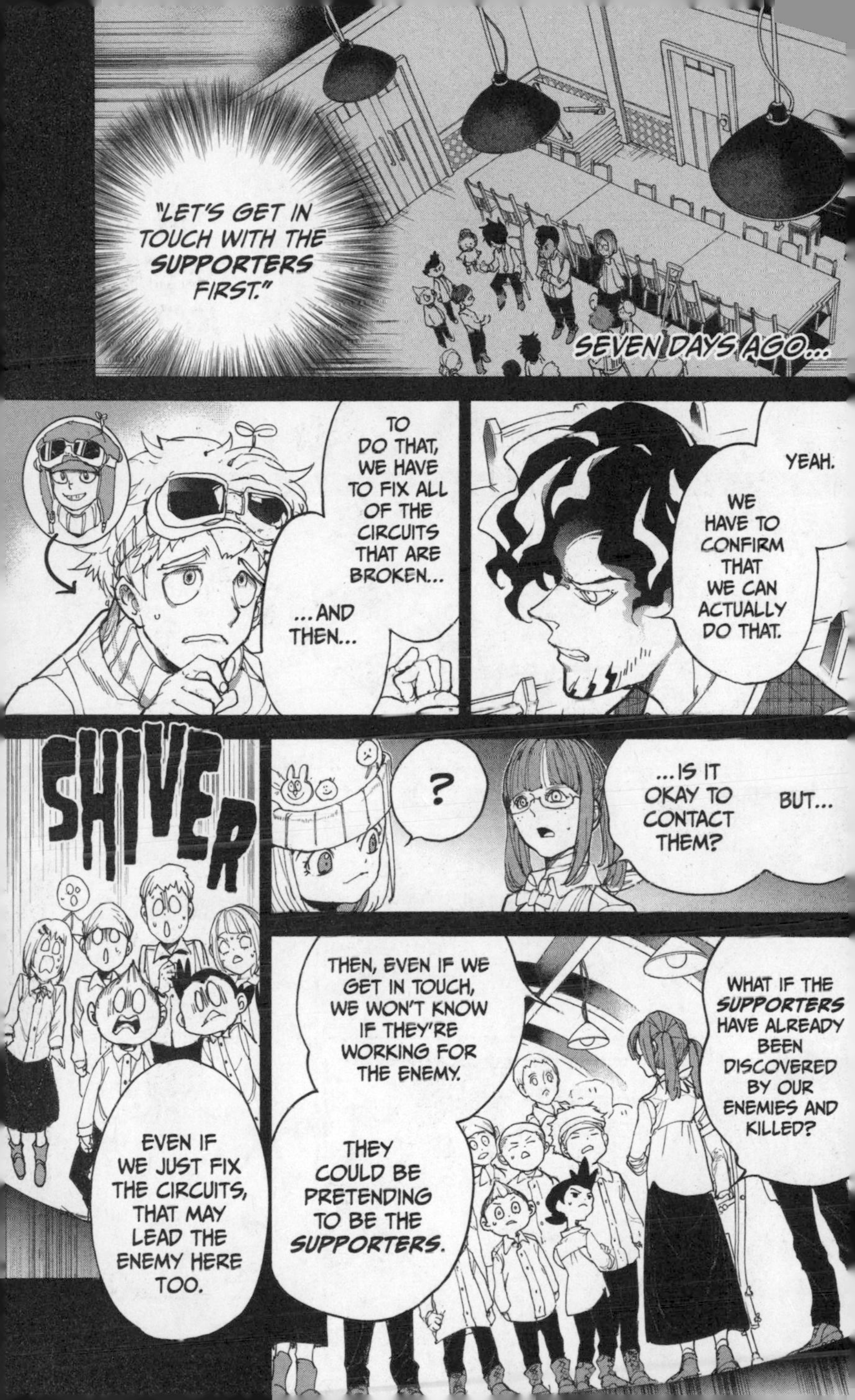
"LET'S GET IN TOUCH WITH THE SUPPORTERS FIRST."
SEVEN DAYS AGO...
YEAH.
WE HAVE TO CONFIRM THAT WE CAN ACTUALLY DO THAT.
TO DO THAT, WE HAVE TO FIX ALL OF THE CIRCUITS THAT ARE BROKEN...
...AND THEN...
BUT...
...IS IT OKAY TO CONTACT THEM?
?
WHAT IF THE SUPPORTERS HAVE ALREADY BEEN DISCOVERED BY OUR ENEMIES AND KILLED?
THEN, EVEN IF WE GET IN TOUCH, WE WON'T KNOW IF THEY'RE WORKING FOR THE ENEMY.
THEY COULD BE PRETENDING TO BE THE SUPPORTERS.
SHIVER
EVEN IF WE JUST FIX THE CIRCUITS, THAT MAY LEAD THE ENEMY HERE TOO.

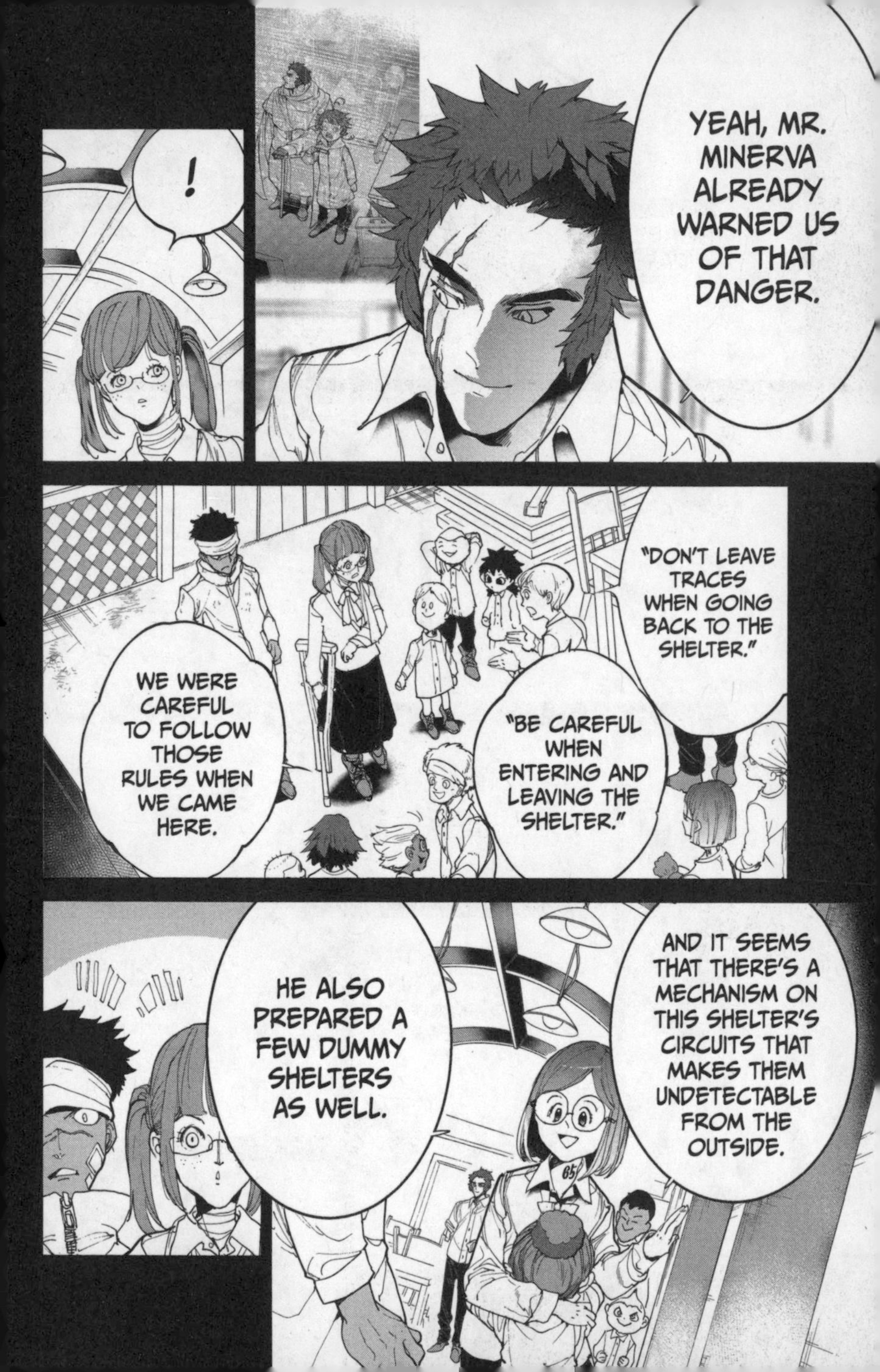
YEAH, MR. MINERVA ALREADY WARNED US OF THAT DANGER.
!
"DON'T LEAVE TRACES WHEN GOING BACK TO THE SHELTER."
"BE CAREFUL WHEN ENTERING AND LEAVING THE SHELTER."
WE WERE CAREFUL TO FOLLOW THOSE RULES WHEN WE CAME HERE.
AND IT SEEMS THAT THERE'S A MECHANISM ON THIS SHELTER'S CIRCUITS THAT MAKES THEM UNDETECTABLE FROM THE OUTSIDE.
HE ALSO PREPARED A FEW DUMMY SHELTERS AS WELL.

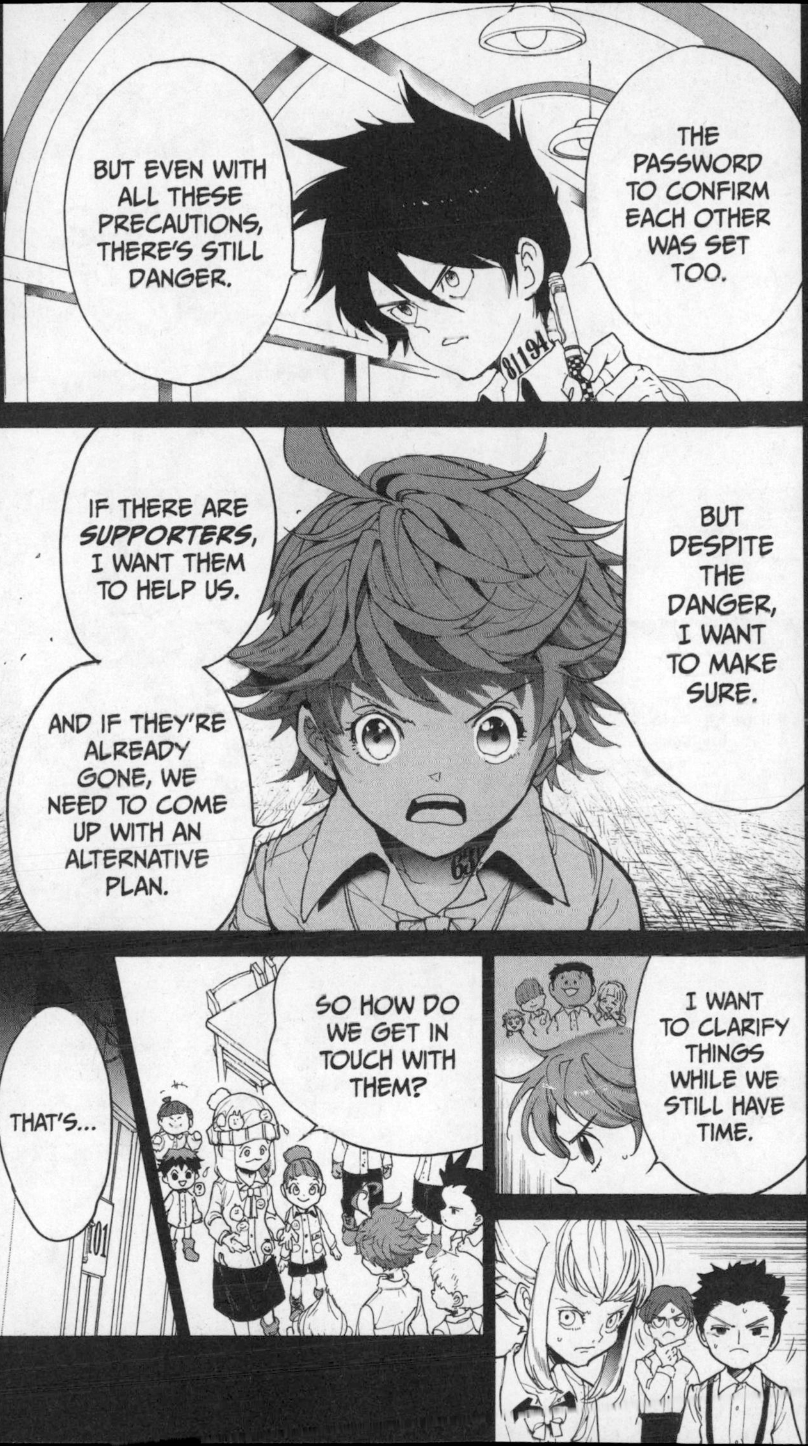
THE PASSWORD TO CONFIRM EACH OTHER WAS SET TOO.
BUT EVEN WITH ALL THESE PRECAUTIONS, THERE'S STILL DANGER.
BUT DESPITE THE DANGER, I WANT TO MAKE SURE.
IF THERE ARE *SUPPORTERS*, I WANT THEM TO HELP US.
AND IF THEY'RE ALREADY GONE, WE NEED TO COME UP WITH AN ALTERNATIVE PLAN.
I WANT TO CLARIFY THINGS WHILE WE STILL HAVE TIME.
SO HOW DO WE GET IN TOUCH WITH THEM?
THAT'S...

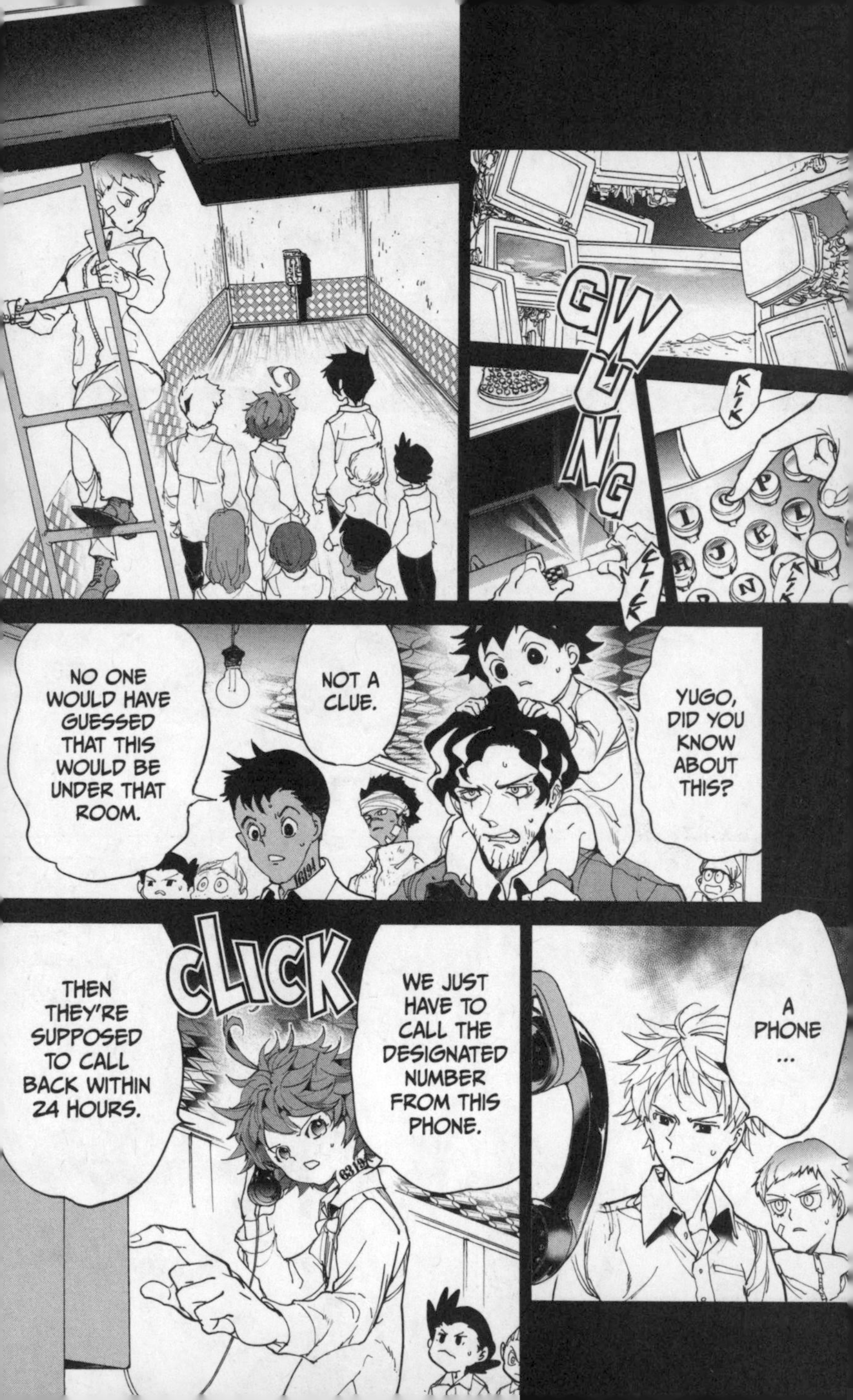
GWUNG
KLIK
CLIK
KLIK
YUGO, DID YOU KNOW ABOUT THIS?
NOT A CLUE.
NO ONE WOULD HAVE GUESSED THAT THIS WOULD BE UNDER THAT ROOM.
A PHONE ...
CLICK
WE JUST HAVE TO CALL THE DESIGNATED NUMBER FROM THIS PHONE.
THEN THEY'RE SUPPOSED TO CALL BACK WITHIN 24 HOURS.

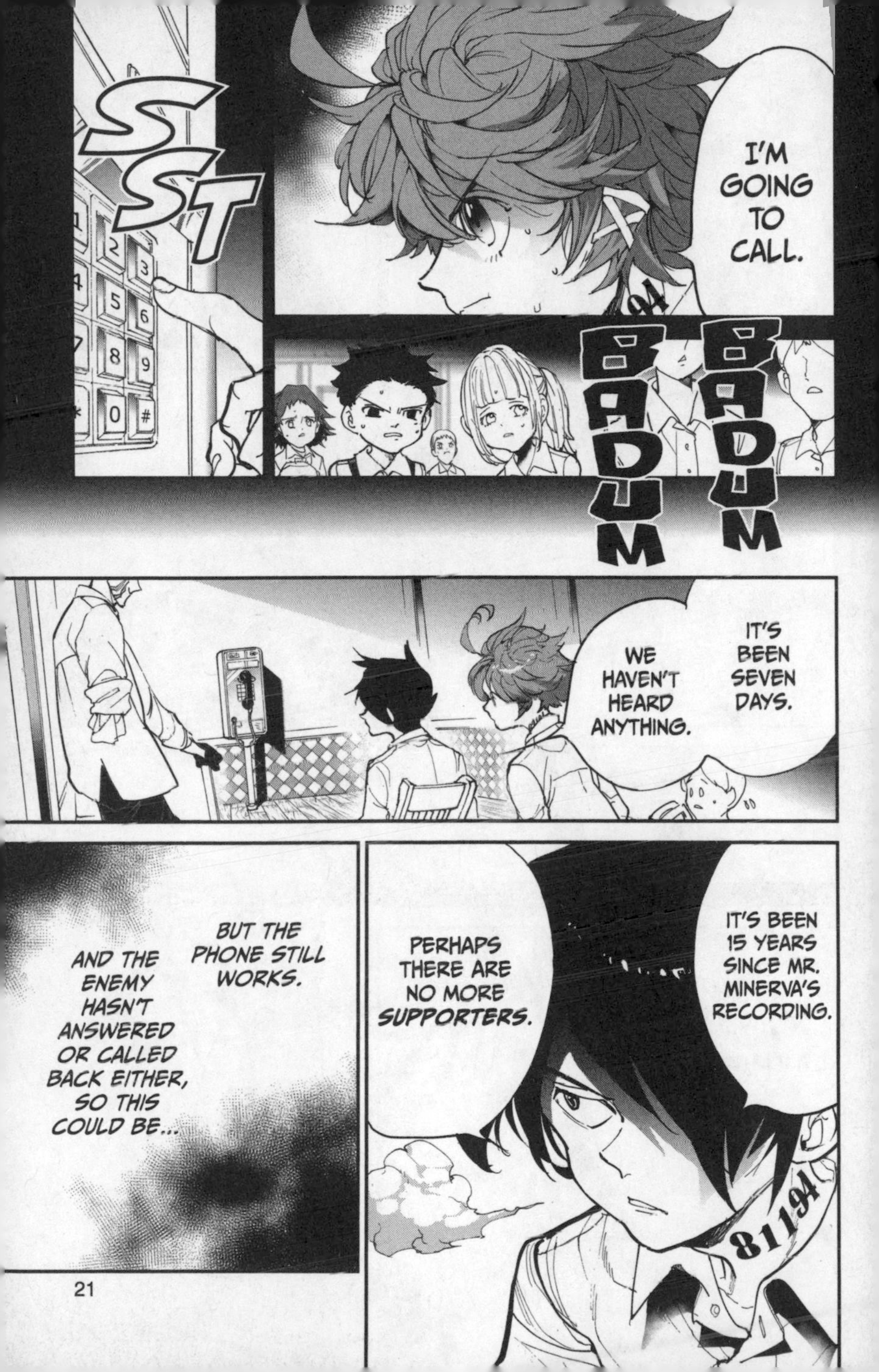

I'M GOING TO CALL.
BADUM BADUM
SST
IT'S BEEN SEVEN DAYS.
WE HAVEN'T HEARD ANYTHING.
IT'S BEEN 15 YEARS SINCE MR. MINERVA'S RECORDING.
PERHAPS THERE ARE NO MORE SUPPORTERS.
BUT THE PHONE STILL WORKS.
AND THE ENEMY HASN'T ANSWERED OR CALLED BACK EITHER, SO THIS COULD BE...

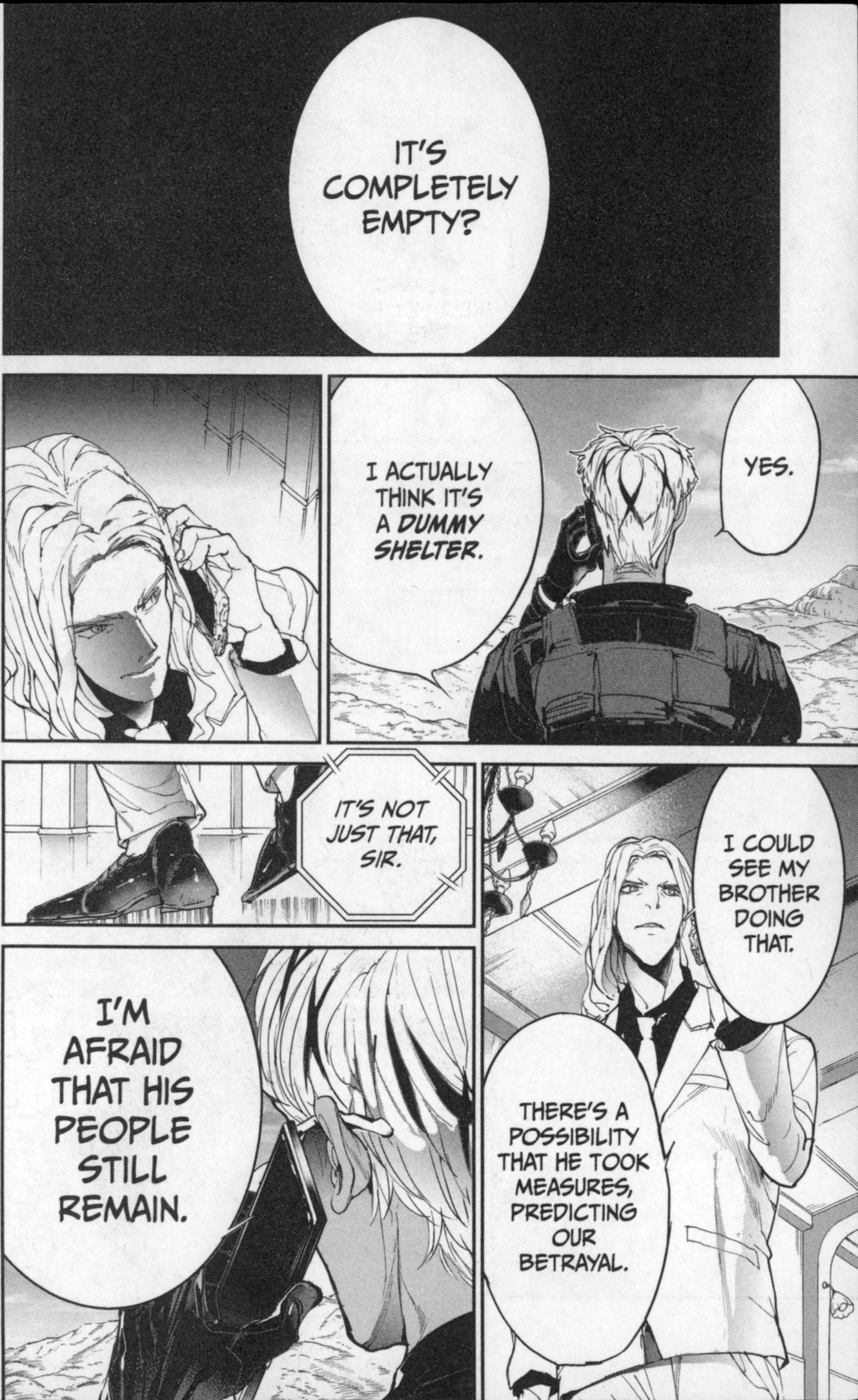
IT'S COMPLETELY EMPTY?
YES.
I ACTUALLY THINK IT'S A *DUMMY SHELTER*.
I COULD SEE MY BROTHER DOING THAT.
THERE'S A POSSIBILITY THAT HE TOOK MEASURES, PREDICTING OUR BETRAYAL.
IT'S NOT JUST THAT, SIR.
I'M AFRAID THAT HIS PEOPLE STILL REMAIN.

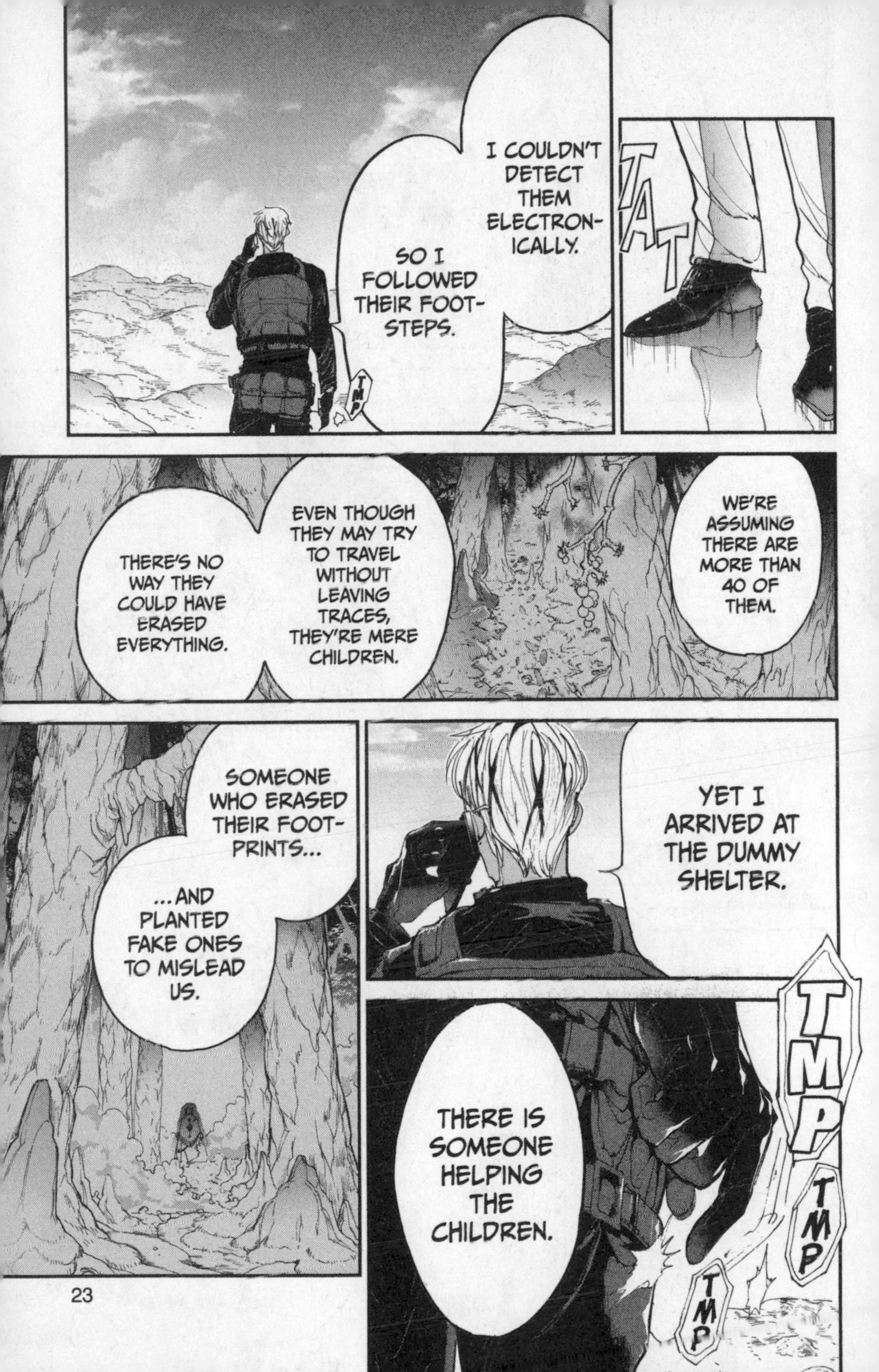
TAT
I COULDN'T DETECT THEM ELECTRONICALLY.
SO I FOLLOWED THEIR FOOTSTEPS.
TMP
WE'RE ASSUMING THERE ARE MORE THAN 40 OF THEM.
EVEN THOUGH THEY MAY TRY TO TRAVEL WITHOUT LEAVING TRACES, THEY'RE MERE CHILDREN.
THERE'S NO WAY THEY COULD HAVE ERASED EVERYTHING.
YET I ARRIVED AT THE DUMMY SHELTER.
THERE IS SOMEONE HELPING THE CHILDREN.
TMP
TMP
TMP
SOMEONE WHO ERASED THEIR FOOTPRINTS...
...AND PLANTED FAKE ONES TO MISLEAD US.

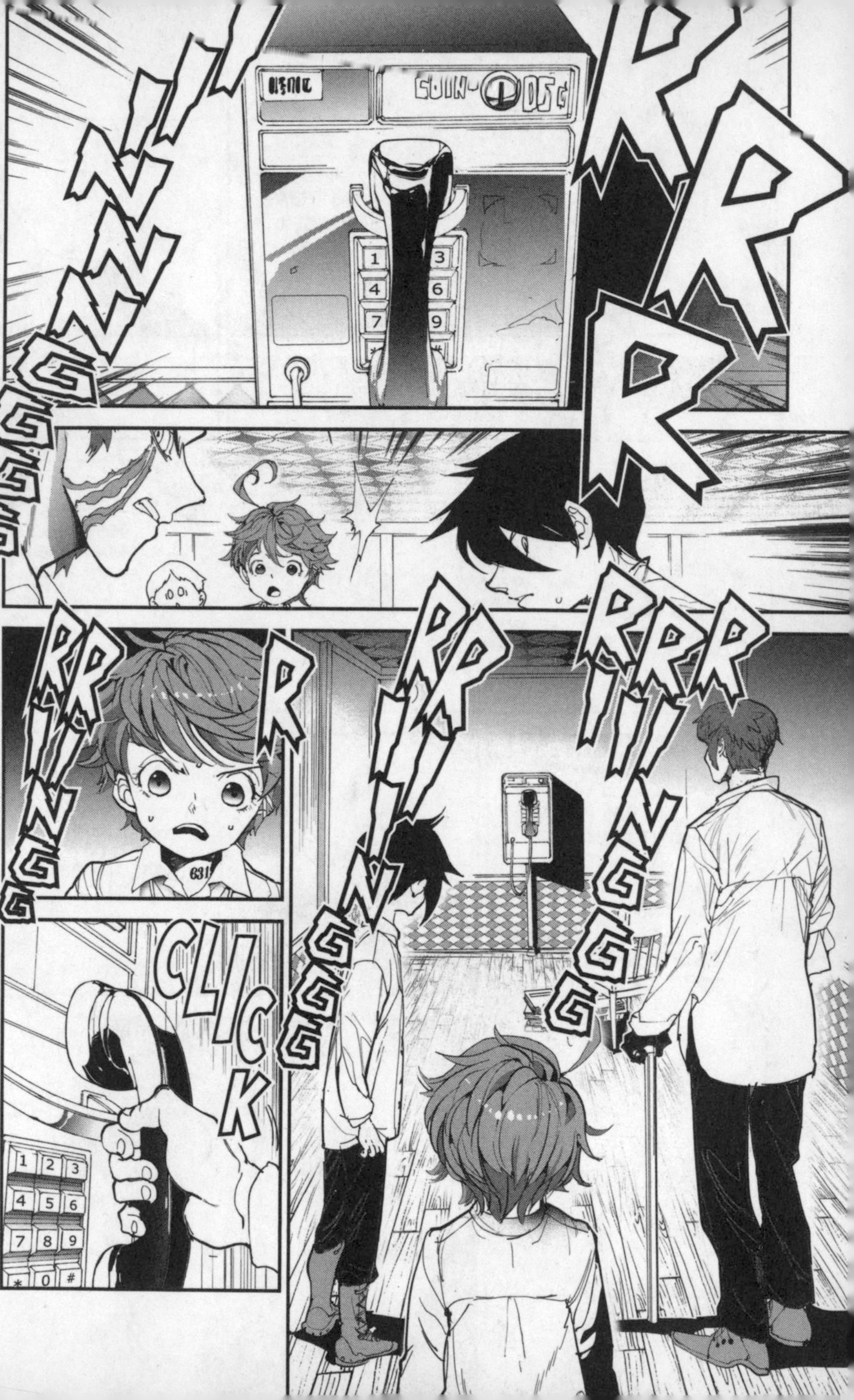
RRR
!!NNNNGGGGG
RRRIINNGGGG
RRIIINGGGG
RRIINNGG
R
CLICK

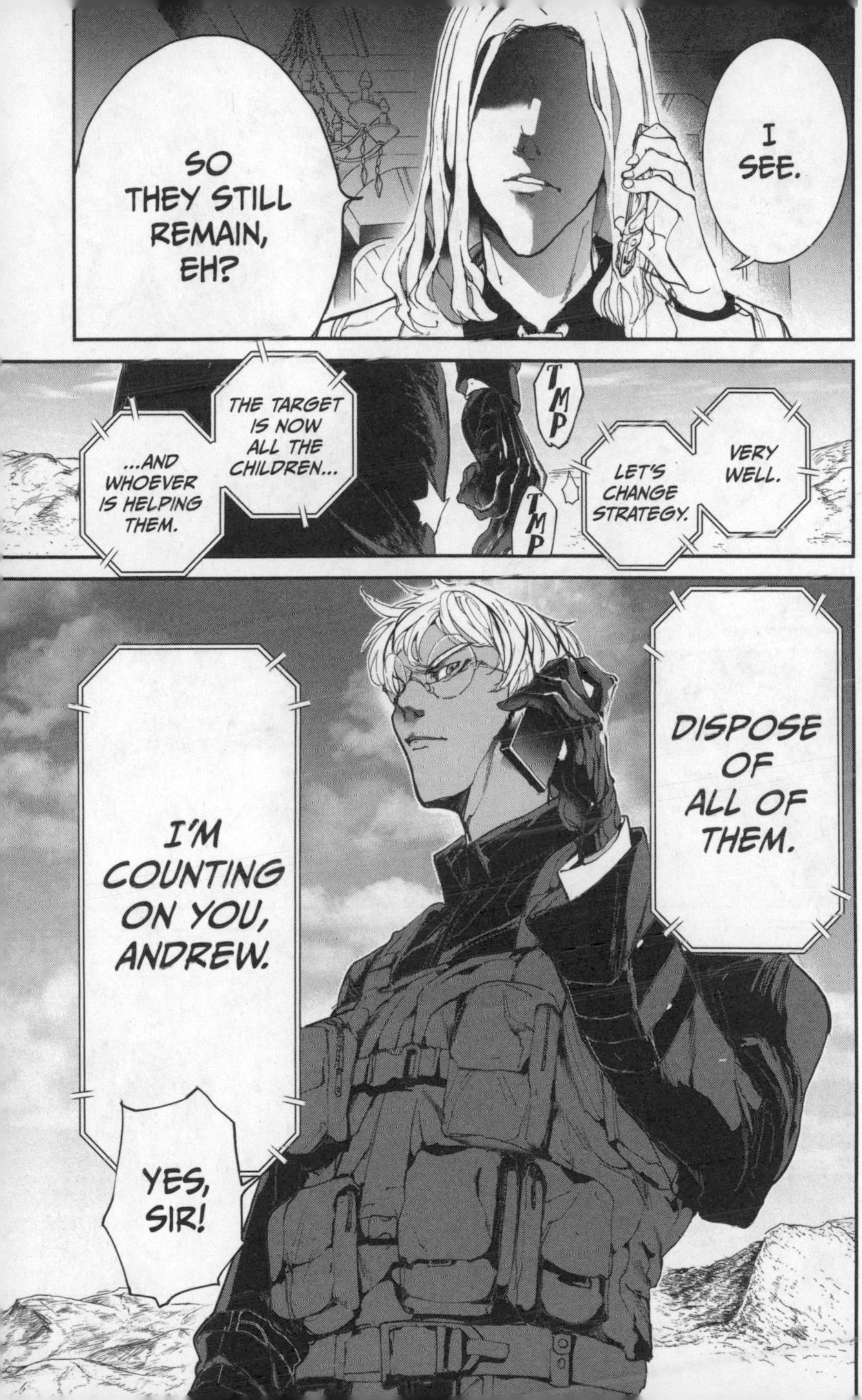
I SEE.
SO THEY STILL REMAIN, EH?
VERY WELL.
LET'S CHANGE STRATEGY.
TMP
TMP
THE TARGET IS NOW ALL THE CHILDREN...
...AND WHOEVER IS HELPING THEM.
DISPOSE OF ALL OF THEM.
I'M COUNTING ON YOU, ANDREW.
YES, SIR!

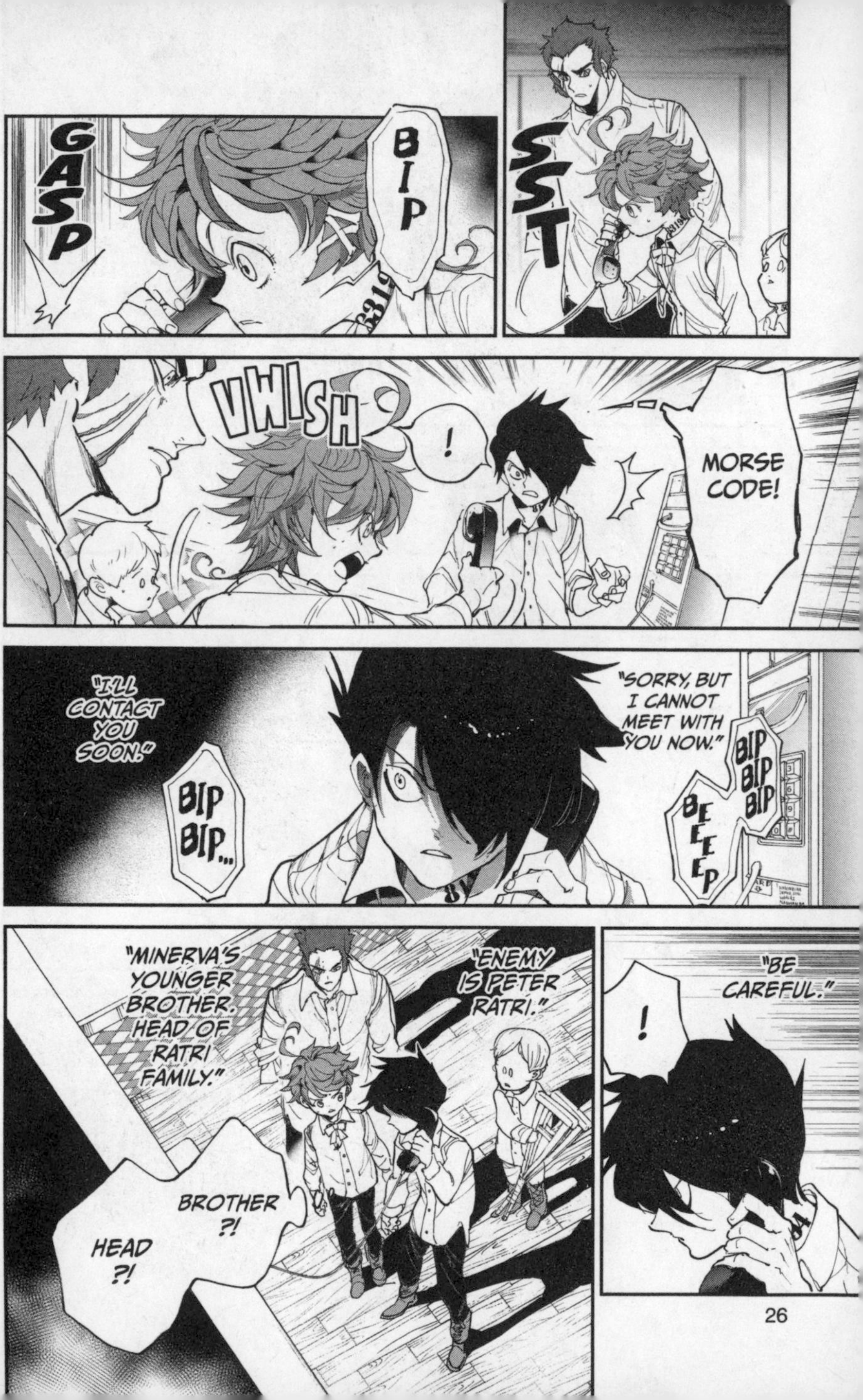
SST
BIP
GASP
MORSE CODE!
!
VWISH
"SORRY, BUT I CANNOT MEET WITH YOU NOW."
BIP BIP BIP
BEEEEP
"I'LL CONTACT YOU SOON."
BIP BIP...
"BE CAREFUL."
!
"ENEMY IS PETER RATRI."
"MINERVA'S YOUNGER BROTHER. HEAD OF RATRI FAMILY."
BROTHER ?!
HEAD ?!

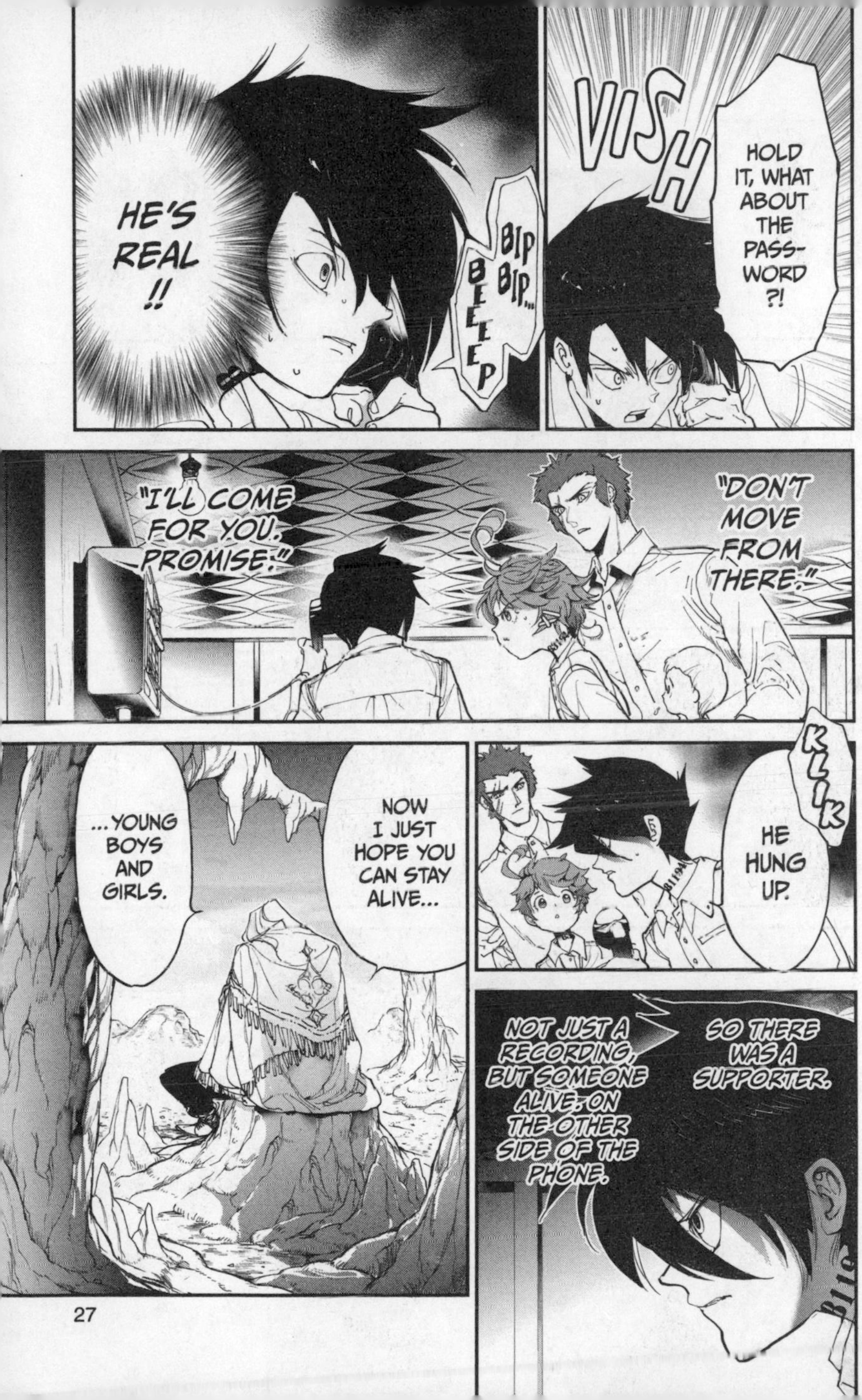
VISH
HOLD IT, WHAT ABOUT THE PASS-WORD ?!
BIP BIP...
BEEEEP
HE'S REAL !!
"DON'T MOVE FROM THERE."
"I'LL COME FOR YOU. PROMISE."
KLIK
HE HUNG UP.
SO THERE WAS A SUPPORTER.
NOT JUST A RECORDING, BUT SOMEONE ALIVE ON THE OTHER SIDE OF THE PHONE.
NOW I JUST HOPE YOU CAN STAY ALIVE...
...YOUNG BOYS AND GIRLS.

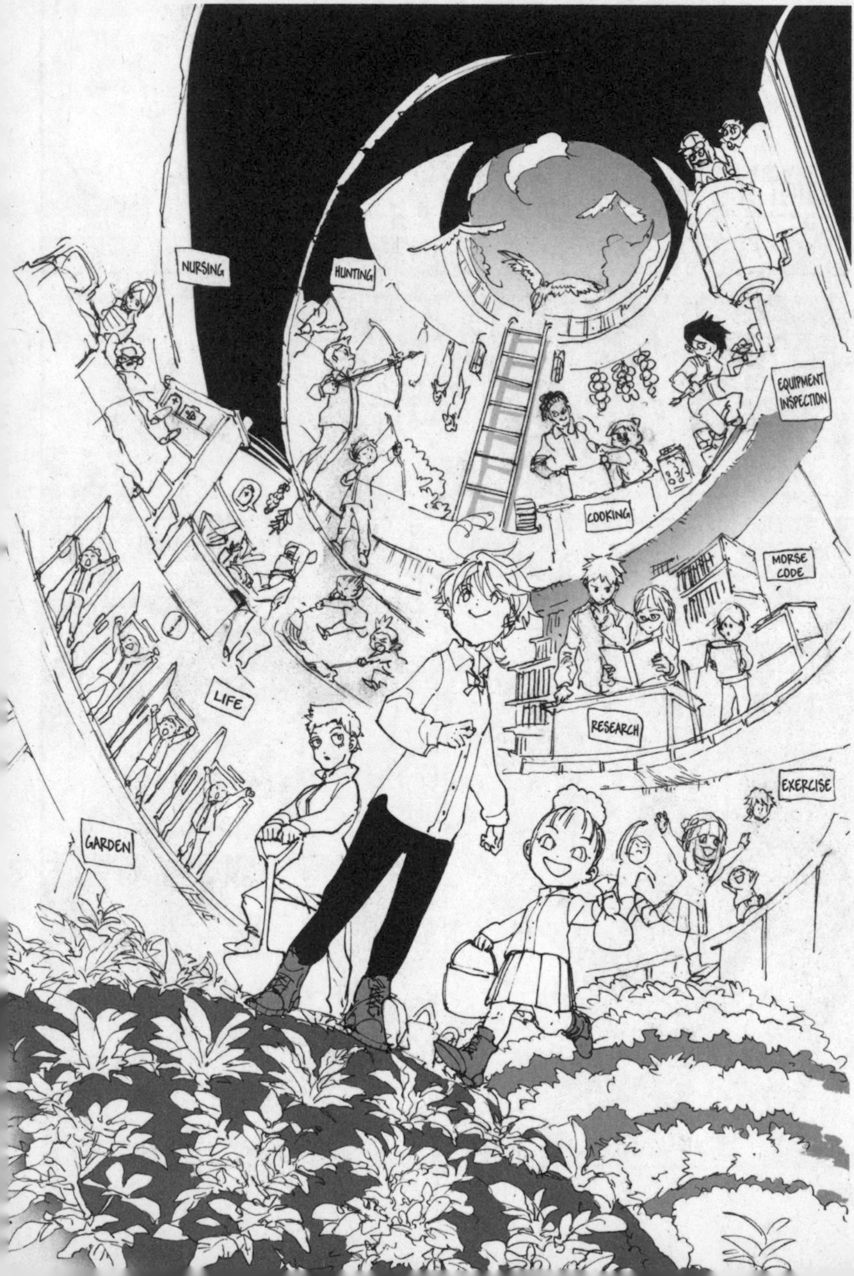
NURSING
HUNTING
EQUIPMENT INSPECTION
COOKING
MORSE CODE
LIFE
RESEARCH
EXERCISE
GARDEN

KLIK

CHAPTER 99: CUVITIDALA

SO THERE WAS...

...A SUP-PORTER.

WAS IT REALLY A **SUPPORTER?**

ON THE OTHER SIDE OF THE PHONE.

NOT JUST A RECORD-ING, BUT SOMEONE ALIVE.

YEAH.

WAS HE REAL?

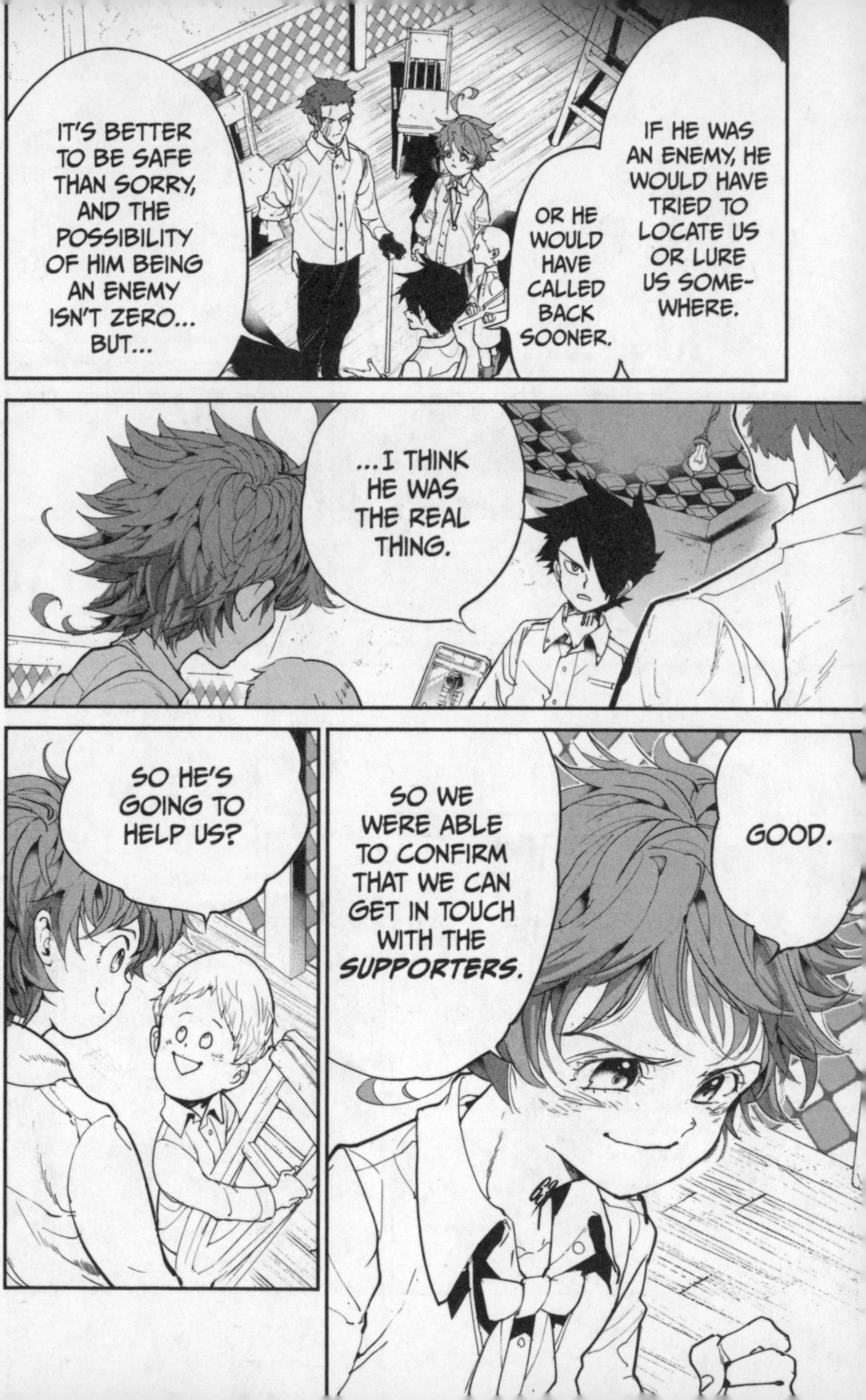
IF HE WAS AN ENEMY, HE WOULD HAVE TRIED TO LOCATE US OR LURE US SOMEWHERE.
OR HE WOULD HAVE CALLED BACK SOONER.
IT'S BETTER TO BE SAFE THAN SORRY, AND THE POSSIBILITY OF HIM BEING AN ENEMY ISN'T ZERO... BUT...
...I THINK HE WAS THE REAL THING.
GOOD.
SO WE WERE ABLE TO CONFIRM THAT WE CAN GET IN TOUCH WITH THE *SUPPORTERS*.
SO HE'S GOING TO HELP US?

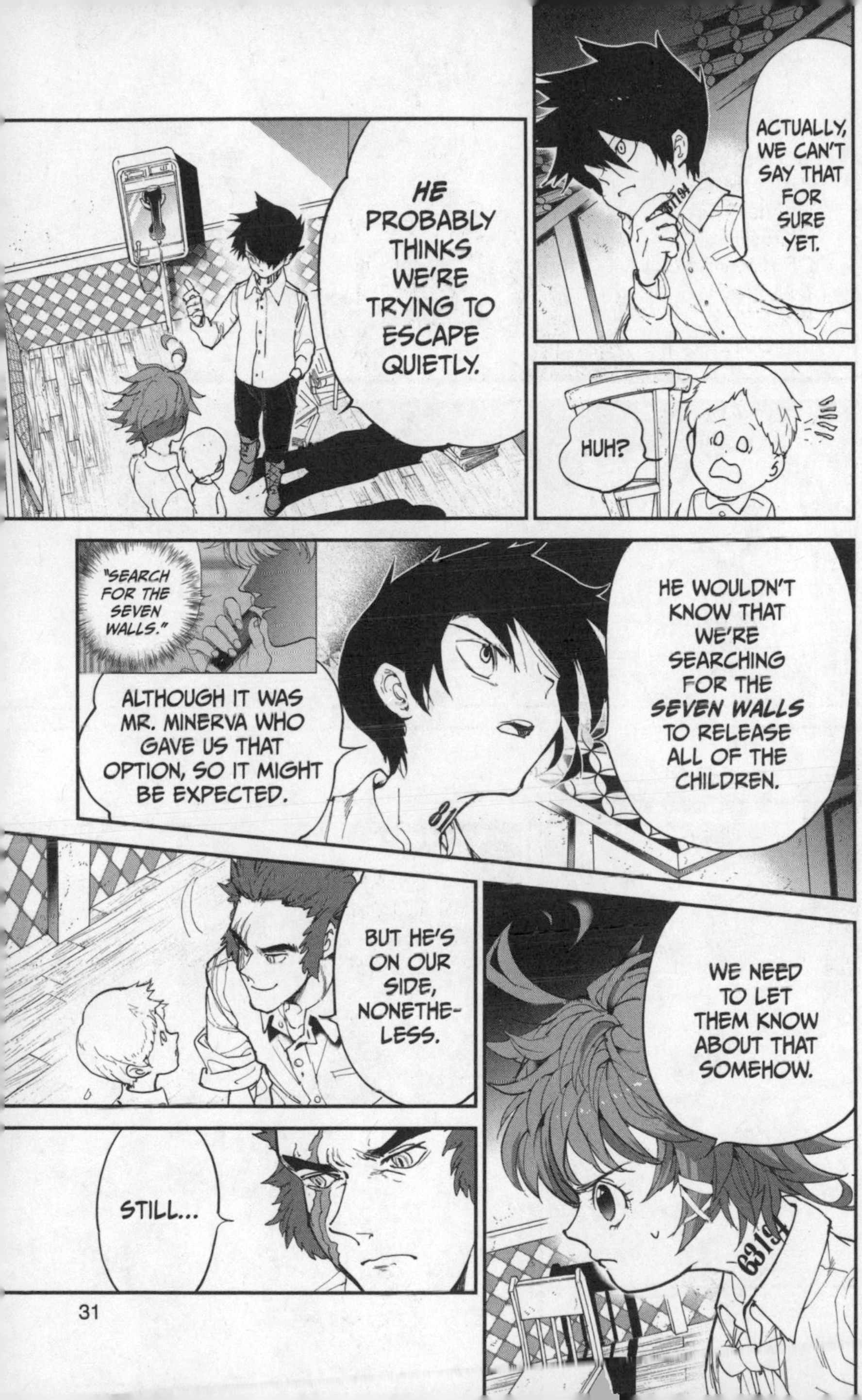
ACTUALLY, WE CAN'T SAY THAT FOR SURE YET.
HUH?
HE PROBABLY THINKS WE'RE TRYING TO ESCAPE QUIETLY.
HE WOULDN'T KNOW THAT WE'RE SEARCHING FOR THE *SEVEN WALLS* TO RELEASE ALL OF THE CHILDREN.
"SEARCH FOR THE SEVEN WALLS."
ALTHOUGH IT WAS MR. MINERVA WHO GAVE US THAT OPTION, SO IT MIGHT BE EXPECTED.
WE NEED TO LET THEM KNOW ABOUT THAT SOMEHOW.
BUT HE'S ON OUR SIDE, NONETHE-LESS.
STILL...

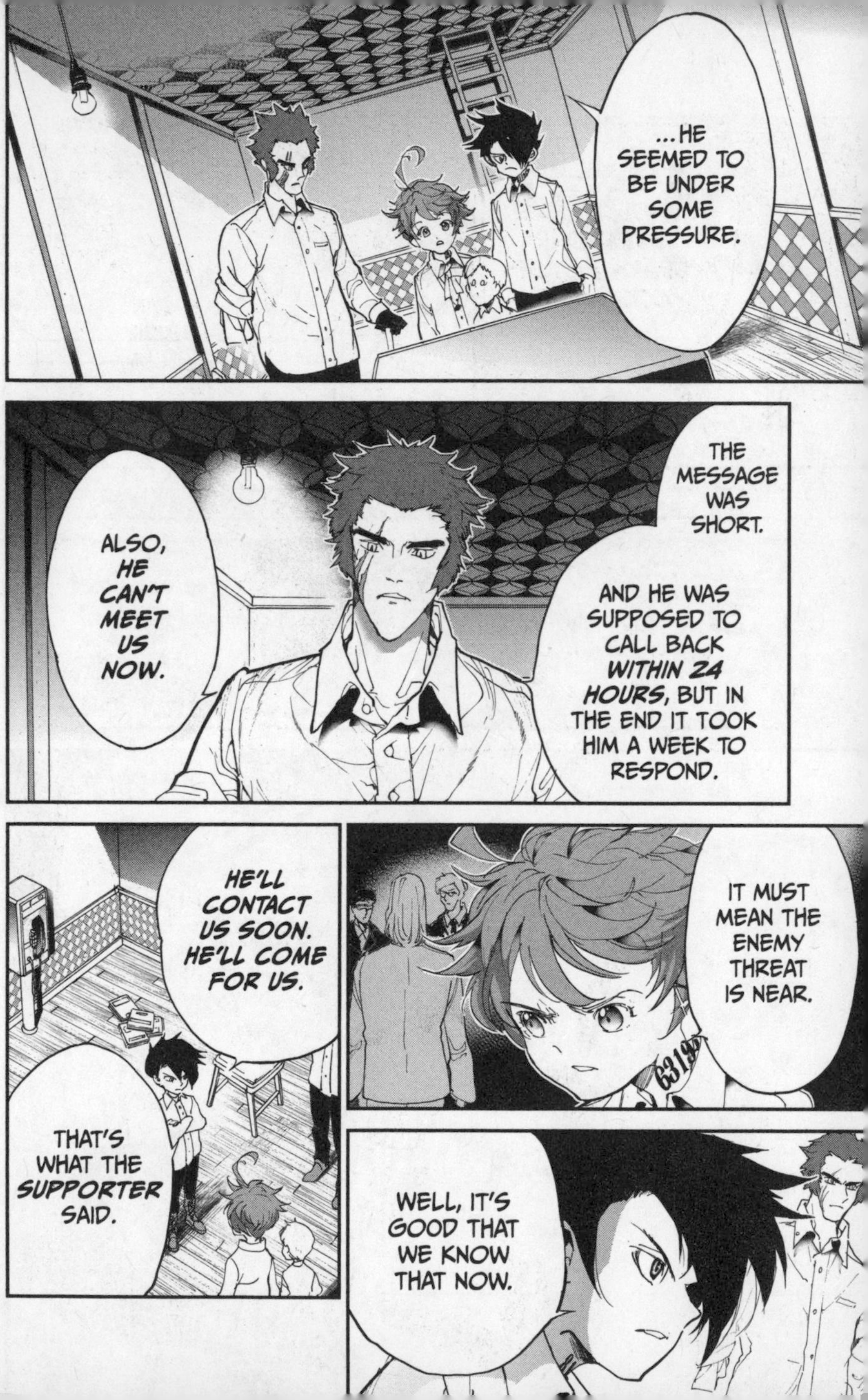
...HE SEEMED TO BE UNDER SOME PRESSURE.
THE MESSAGE WAS SHORT.
AND HE WAS SUPPOSED TO CALL BACK WITHIN 24 HOURS, BUT IN THE END IT TOOK HIM A WEEK TO RESPOND.
ALSO, HE CAN'T MEET US NOW.
IT MUST MEAN THE ENEMY THREAT IS NEAR.
WELL, IT'S GOOD THAT WE KNOW THAT NOW.
HE'LL CONTACT US SOON. HE'LL COME FOR US.
THAT'S WHAT THE SUPPORTER SAID.

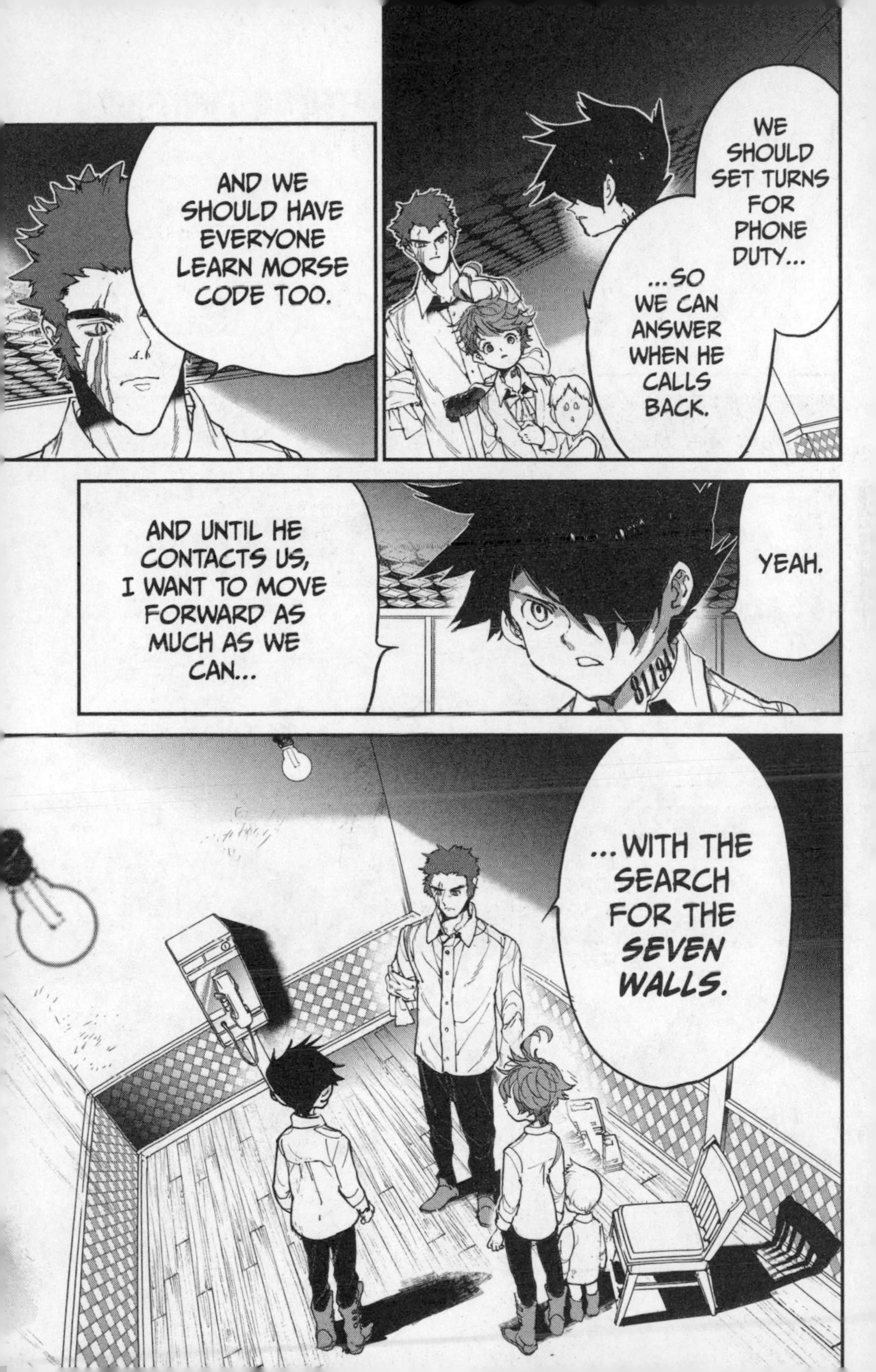
WE SHOULD SET TURNS FOR PHONE DUTY...
...SO WE CAN ANSWER WHEN HE CALLS BACK.
AND WE SHOULD HAVE EVERYONE LEARN MORSE CODE TOO.
YEAH.
AND UNTIL HE CONTACTS US, I WANT TO MOVE FORWARD AS MUCH AS WE CAN...
...WITH THE SEARCH FOR THE *SEVEN WALLS*.

CHAPTER 99: CUVITIDALA

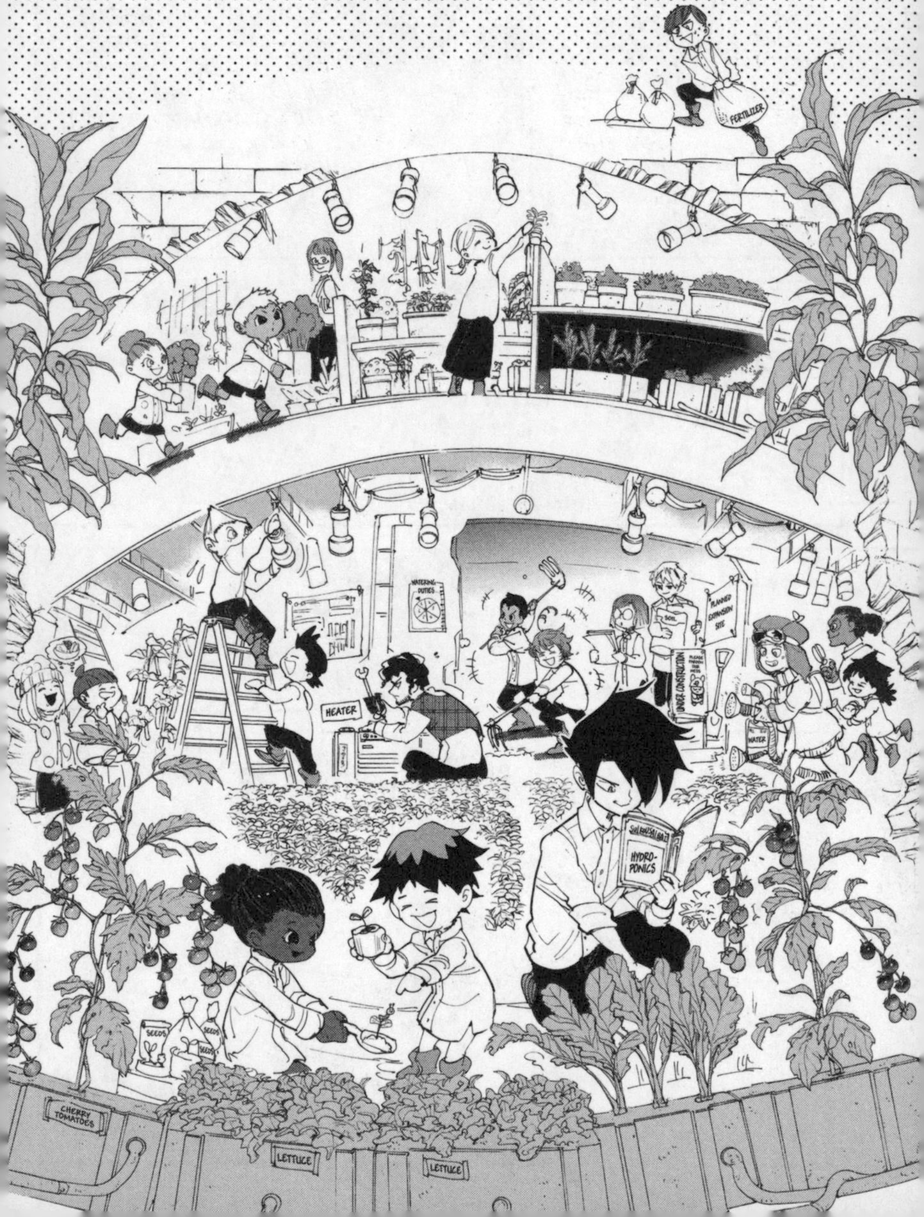
FERTILIZER
WATERING DUTIES
PLANNED EXPANSION SITE
SOIL
UNDER CONSTRUCTION
HEATER
WATER
HYDRO-PONICS
SEEDS
SEEDS
SEEDS
CHERRY TOMATOES
LETTUCE
LETTUCE

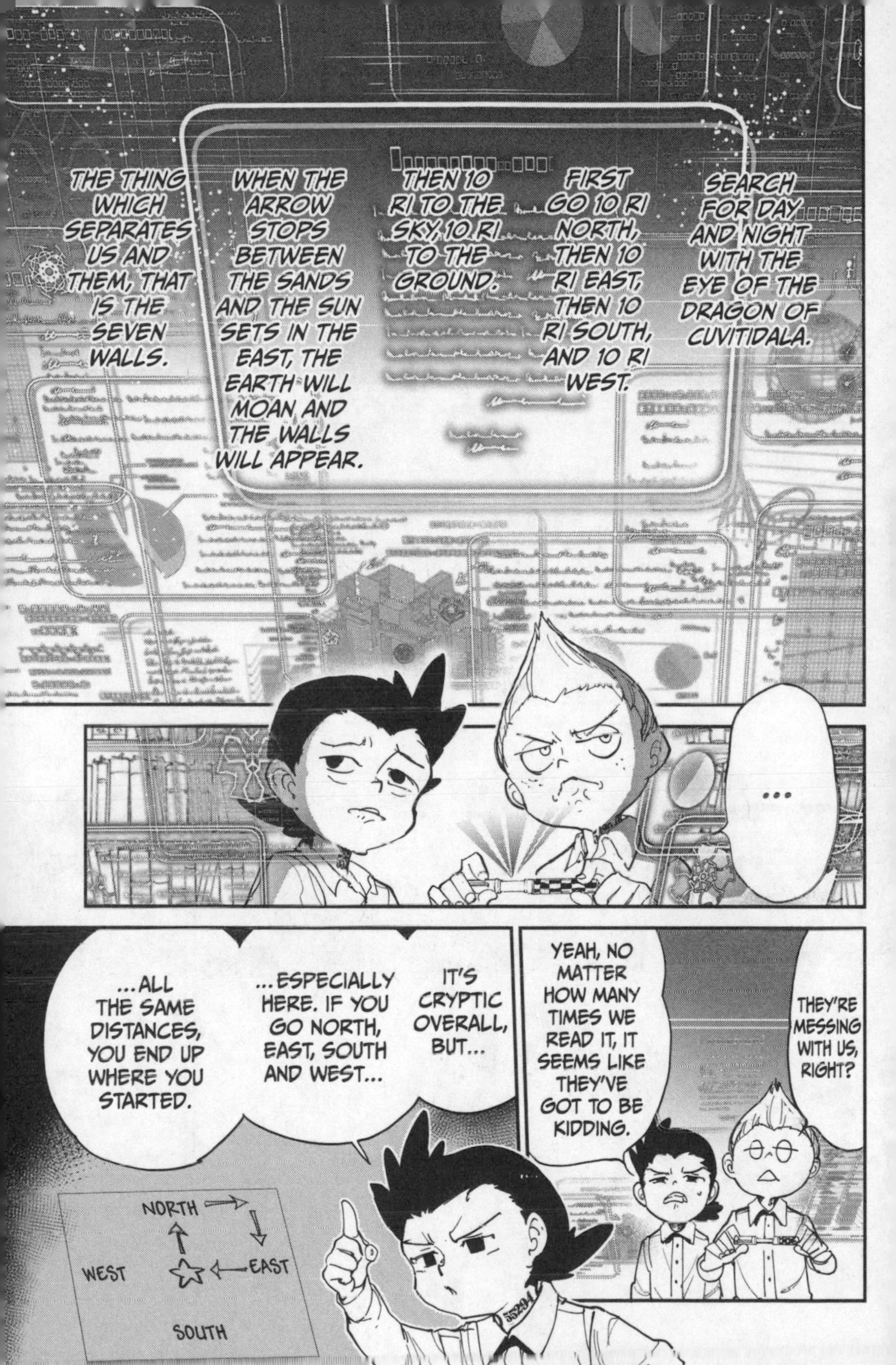
SEARCH FOR DAY AND NIGHT WITH THE EYE OF THE DRAGON OF CUVITIDALA.
FIRST GO 10 RI NORTH, THEN 10 RI EAST, THEN 10 RI SOUTH, AND 10 RI WEST.
THEN 10 RI TO THE SKY, 10 RI TO THE GROUND.
WHEN THE ARROW STOPS BETWEEN THE SANDS AND THE SUN SETS IN THE EAST, THE EARTH WILL MOAN AND THE WALLS WILL APPEAR.
THE THING WHICH SEPARATES US AND THEM, THAT IS THE SEVEN WALLS.
...
THEY'RE MESSING WITH US, RIGHT?
YEAH, NO MATTER HOW MANY TIMES WE READ IT, IT SEEMS LIKE THEY'VE GOT TO BE KIDDING.
IT'S CRYPTIC OVERALL, BUT...
...ESPECIALLY HERE. IF YOU GO NORTH, EAST, SOUTH AND WEST...
...ALL THE SAME DISTANCES, YOU END UP WHERE YOU STARTED.
NORTH
EAST
WEST
SOUTH

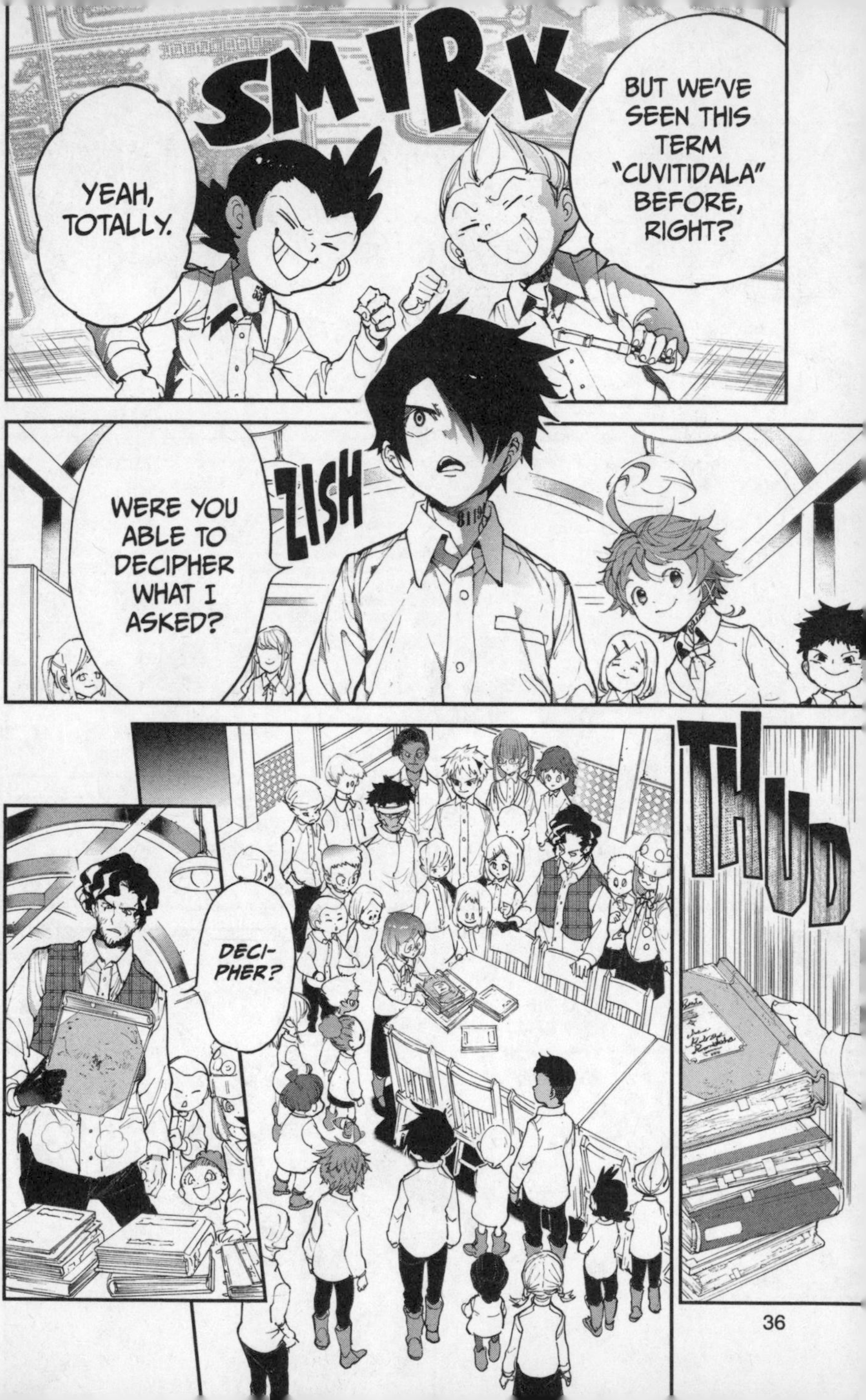
SMIRK
BUT WE'VE SEEN THIS TERM "CUVITIDALA" BEFORE, RIGHT?
YEAH, TOTALLY.
ZISH
WERE YOU ABLE TO DECIPHER WHAT I ASKED?
THUD
DECI-PHER?

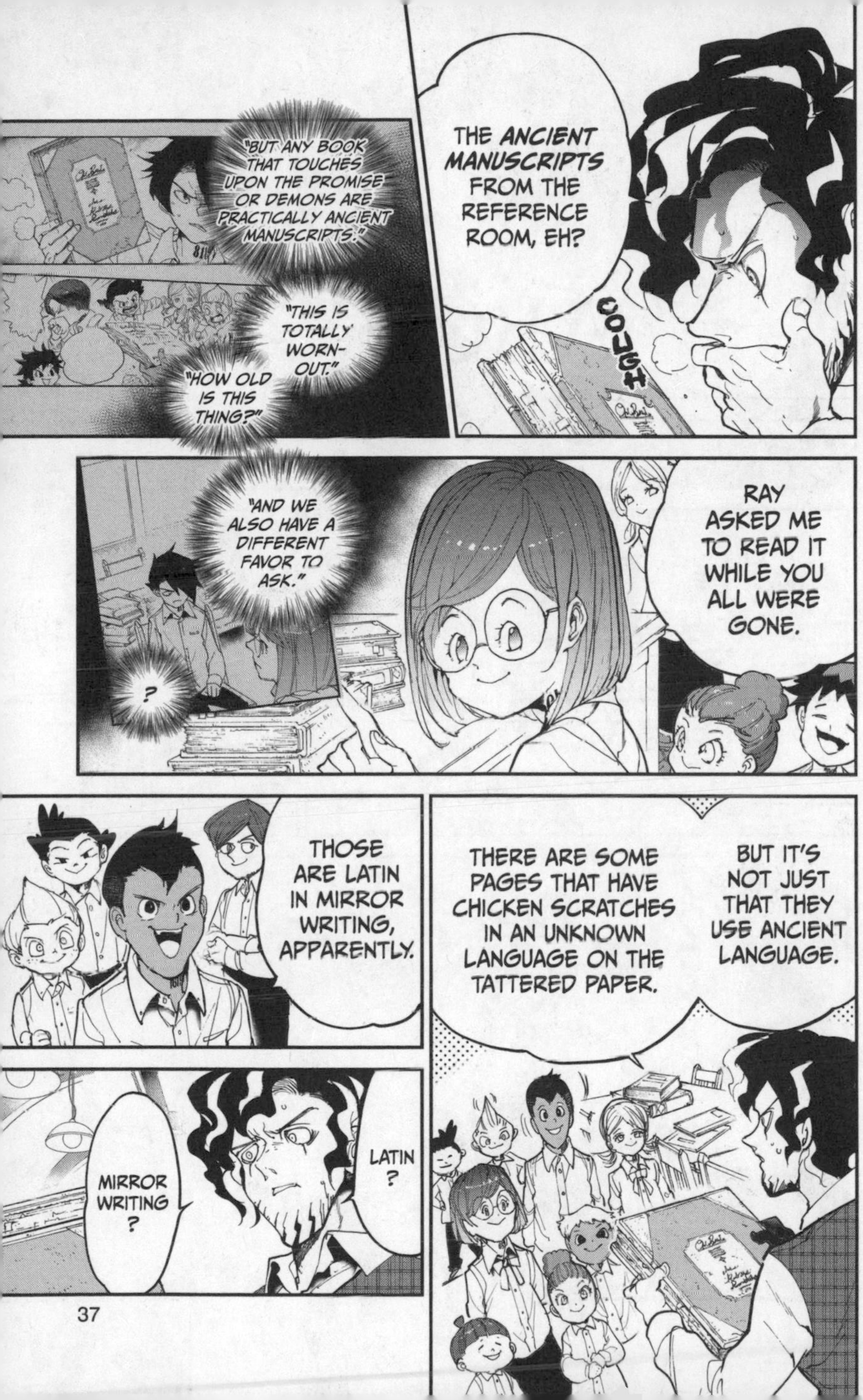
THE *ANCIENT MANUSCRIPTS* FROM THE REFERENCE ROOM, EH?
COUGH
"BUT ANY BOOK THAT TOUCHES UPON THE PROMISE OR DEMONS ARE PRACTICALLY ANCIENT MANUSCRIPTS."
"THIS IS TOTALLY WORN-OUT."
"HOW OLD IS THIS THING?"
RAY ASKED ME TO READ IT WHILE YOU ALL WERE GONE.
"AND WE ALSO HAVE A DIFFERENT FAVOR TO ASK."
?
BUT IT'S NOT JUST THAT THEY USE ANCIENT LANGUAGE.
THERE ARE SOME PAGES THAT HAVE CHICKEN SCRATCHES IN AN UNKNOWN LANGUAGE ON THE TATTERED PAPER.
THOSE ARE LATIN IN MIRROR WRITING, APPARENTLY.
LATIN?
MIRROR WRITING?

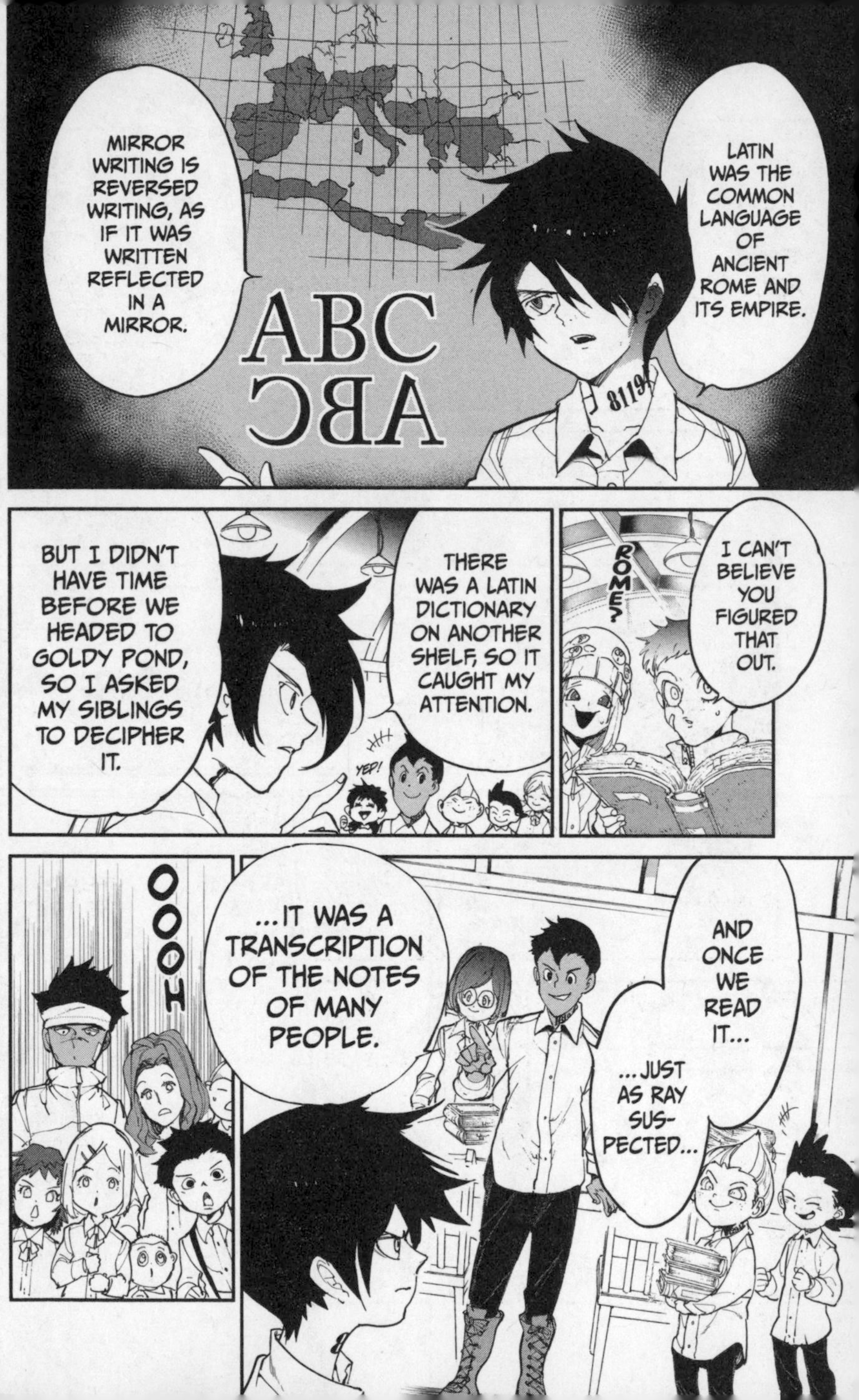
LATIN WAS THE COMMON LANGUAGE OF ANCIENT ROME AND ITS EMPIRE.
MIRROR WRITING IS REVERSED WRITING, AS IF IT WAS WRITTEN REFLECTED IN A MIRROR.
ABC
8119
ROME?
I CAN'T BELIEVE YOU FIGURED THAT OUT.
THERE WAS A LATIN DICTIONARY ON ANOTHER SHELF, SO IT CAUGHT MY ATTENTION.
BUT I DIDN'T HAVE TIME BEFORE WE HEADED TO GOLDY POND, SO I ASKED MY SIBLINGS TO DECIPHER IT.
YEP!
AND ONCE WE READ IT...
...JUST AS RAY SUS-PECTED...
...IT WAS A TRANSCRIPTION OF THE NOTES OF MANY PEOPLE.
OOOH

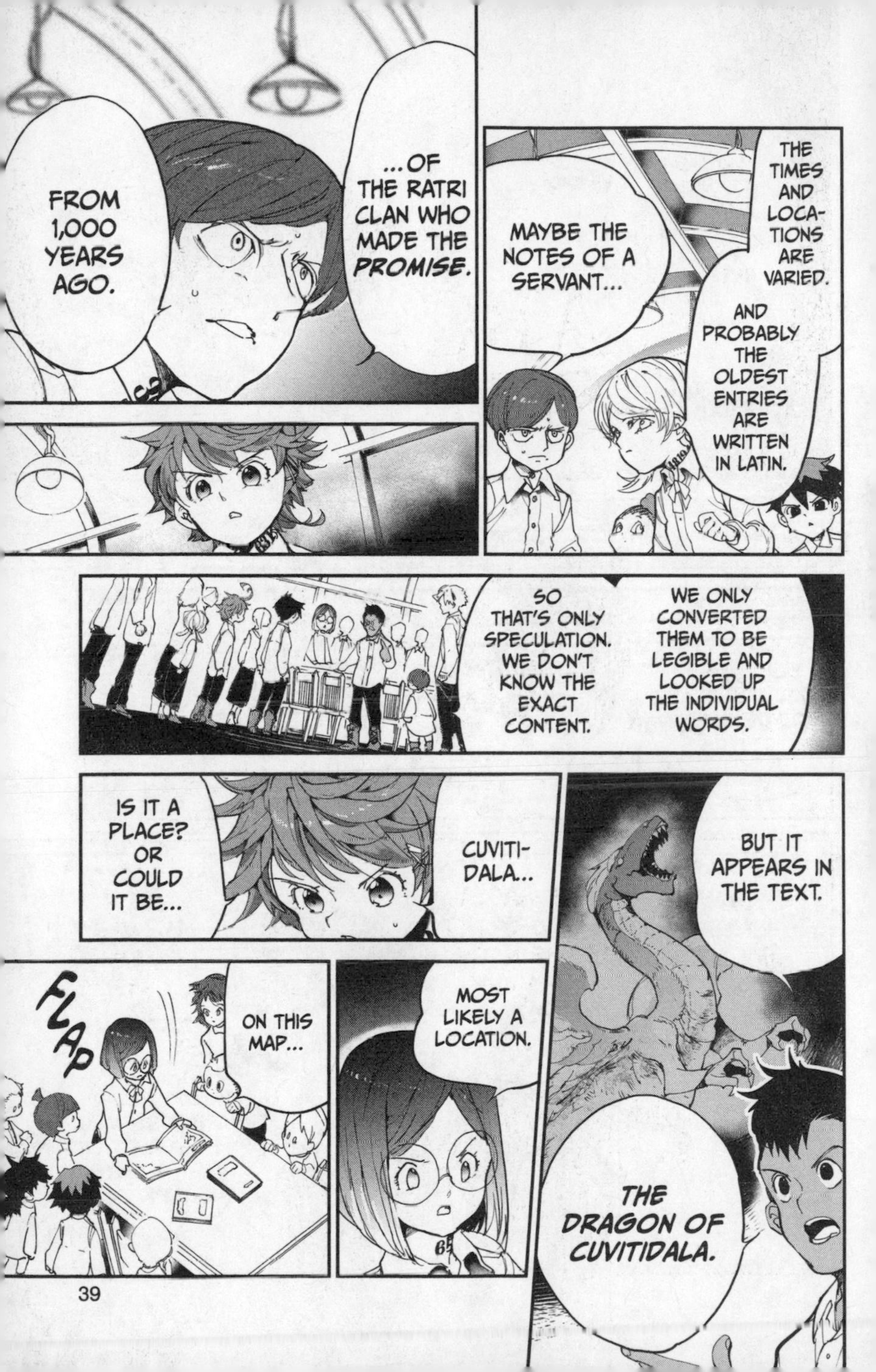
THE TIMES AND LOCATIONS ARE VARIED.
AND PROBABLY THE OLDEST ENTRIES ARE WRITTEN IN LATIN.
MAYBE THE NOTES OF A SERVANT...
...OF THE RATRI CLAN WHO MADE THE *PROMISE*.
FROM 1,000 YEARS AGO.
WE ONLY CONVERTED THEM TO BE LEGIBLE AND LOOKED UP THE INDIVIDUAL WORDS.
SO THAT'S ONLY SPECULATION. WE DON'T KNOW THE EXACT CONTENT.
BUT IT APPEARS IN THE TEXT.
THE DRAGON OF CUVITIDALA.
CUVITIDALA...
IS IT A PLACE? OR COULD IT BE...
MOST LIKELY A LOCATION.
ON THIS MAP...
FLAP

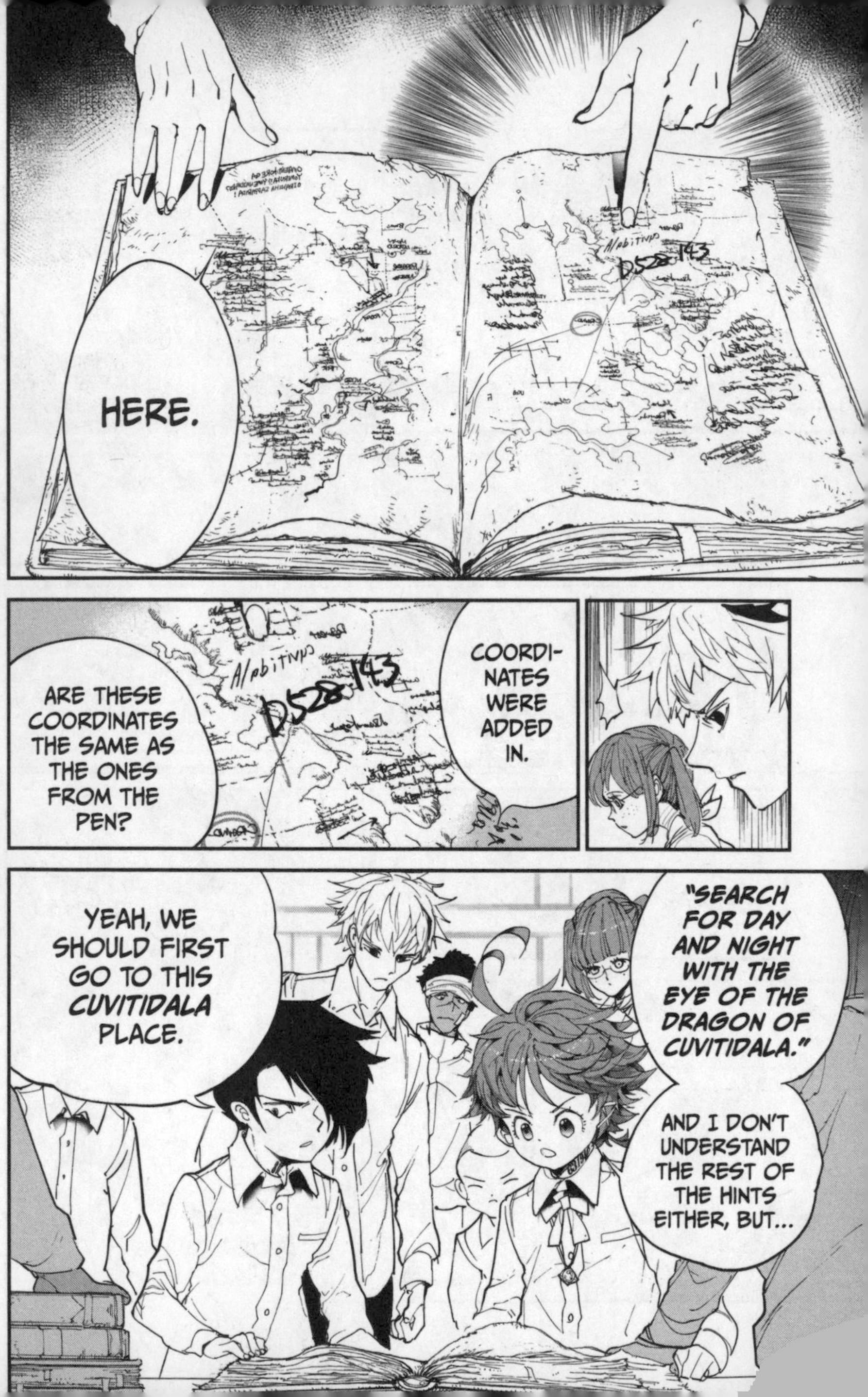
HERE.
D528.143
COORDINATES WERE ADDED IN.
ARE THESE COORDINATES THE SAME AS THE ONES FROM THE PEN?
"SEARCH FOR DAY AND NIGHT WITH THE EYE OF THE DRAGON OF CUVITIDALA."
AND I DON'T UNDERSTAND THE REST OF THE HINTS EITHER, BUT...
YEAH, WE SHOULD FIRST GO TO THIS CUVITIDALA PLACE.

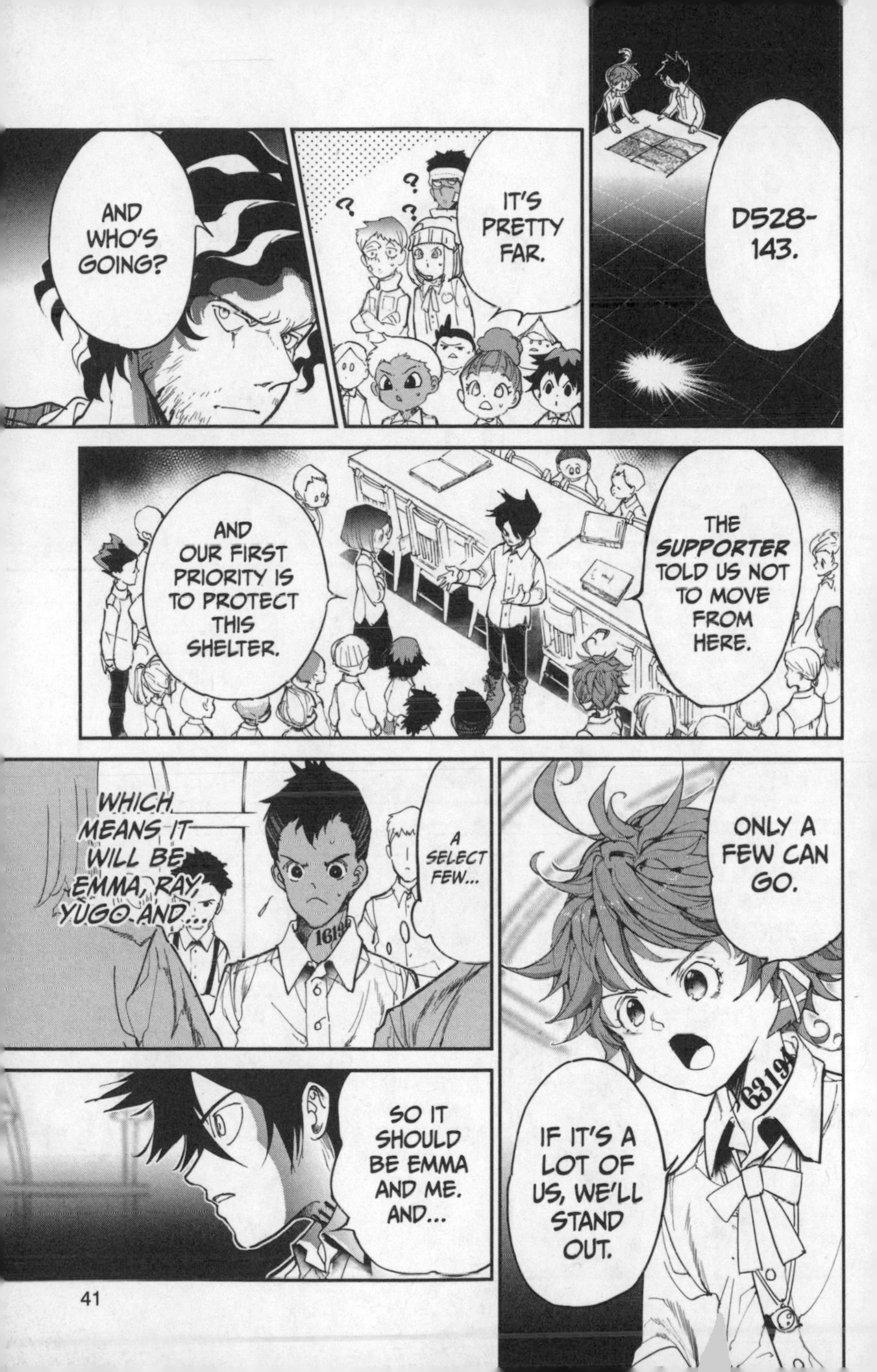
D528-143.
IT'S PRETTY FAR.
AND WHO'S GOING?
THE SUPPORTER TOLD US NOT TO MOVE FROM HERE.
AND OUR FIRST PRIORITY IS TO PROTECT THIS SHELTER.
ONLY A FEW CAN GO.
IF IT'S A LOT OF US, WE'LL STAND OUT.
A SELECT FEW...
WHICH MEANS IT WILL BE EMMA, RAY, YUGO AND...
SO IT SHOULD BE EMMA AND ME. AND...

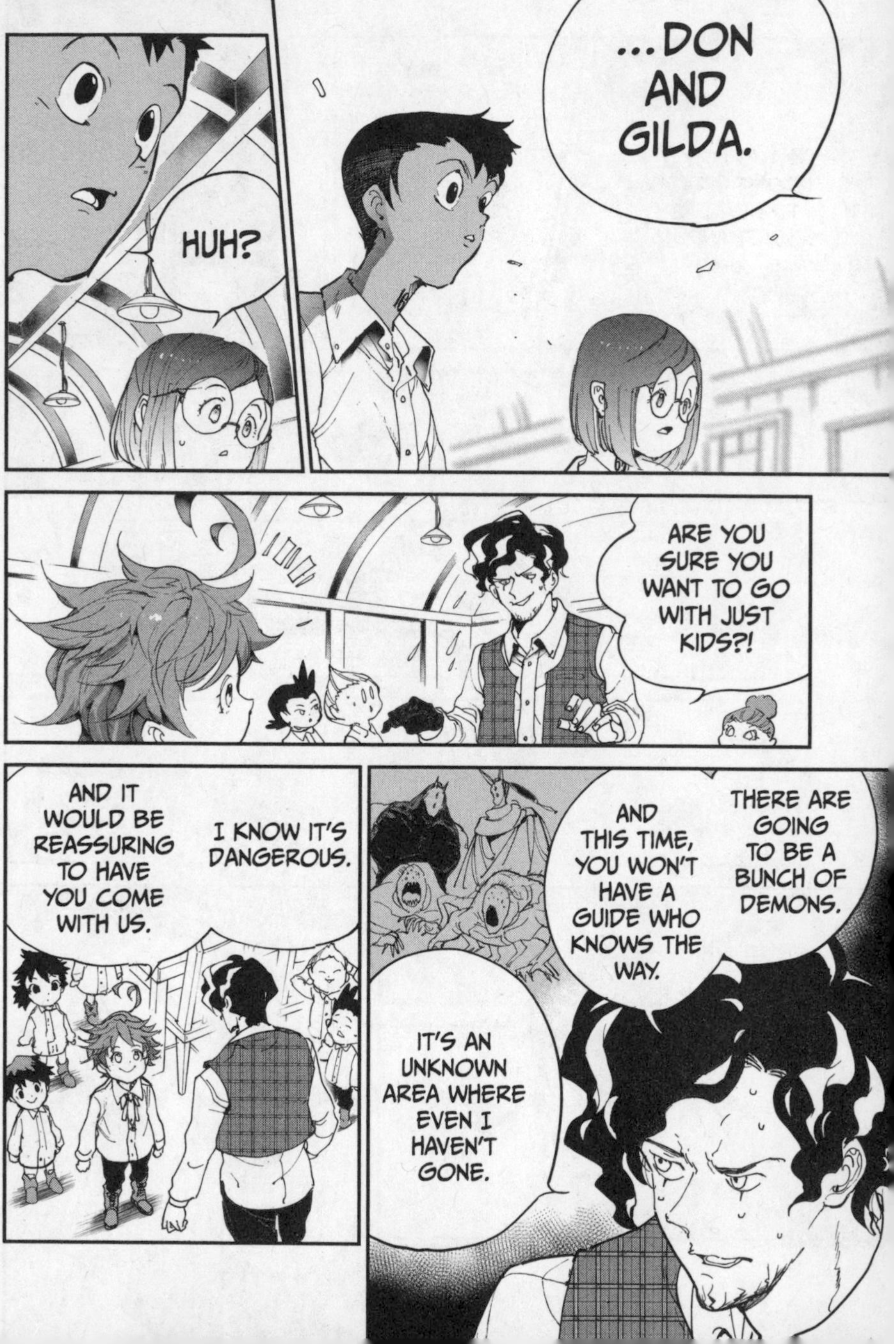
...DON AND GILDA.
HUH?
ARE YOU SURE YOU WANT TO GO WITH JUST KIDS?!
THERE ARE GOING TO BE A BUNCH OF DEMONS.
AND THIS TIME, YOU WON'T HAVE A GUIDE WHO KNOWS THE WAY.
IT'S AN UNKNOWN AREA WHERE EVEN I HAVEN'T GONE.
I KNOW IT'S DANGEROUS.
AND IT WOULD BE REASSURING TO HAVE YOU COME WITH US.

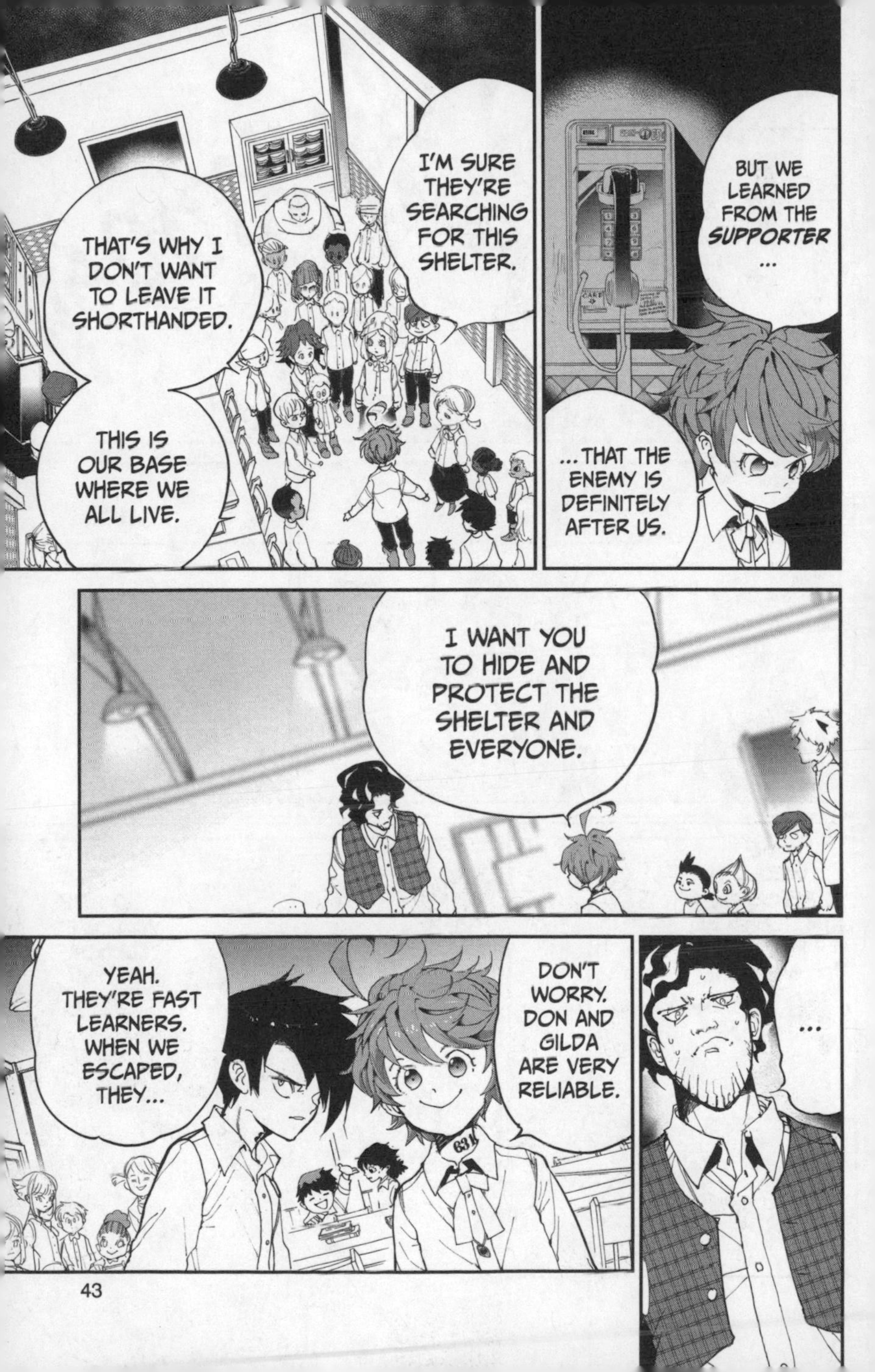
BUT WE LEARNED FROM THE *SUPPORTER* ...
...THAT THE ENEMY IS DEFINITELY AFTER US.
I'M SURE THEY'RE SEARCHING FOR THIS SHELTER.
THAT'S WHY I DON'T WANT TO LEAVE IT SHORTHANDED.
THIS IS OUR BASE WHERE WE ALL LIVE.
I WANT YOU TO HIDE AND PROTECT THE SHELTER AND EVERYONE.
...
DON'T WORRY. DON AND GILDA ARE VERY RELIABLE.
YEAH. THEY'RE FAST LEARNERS. WHEN WE ESCAPED, THEY...

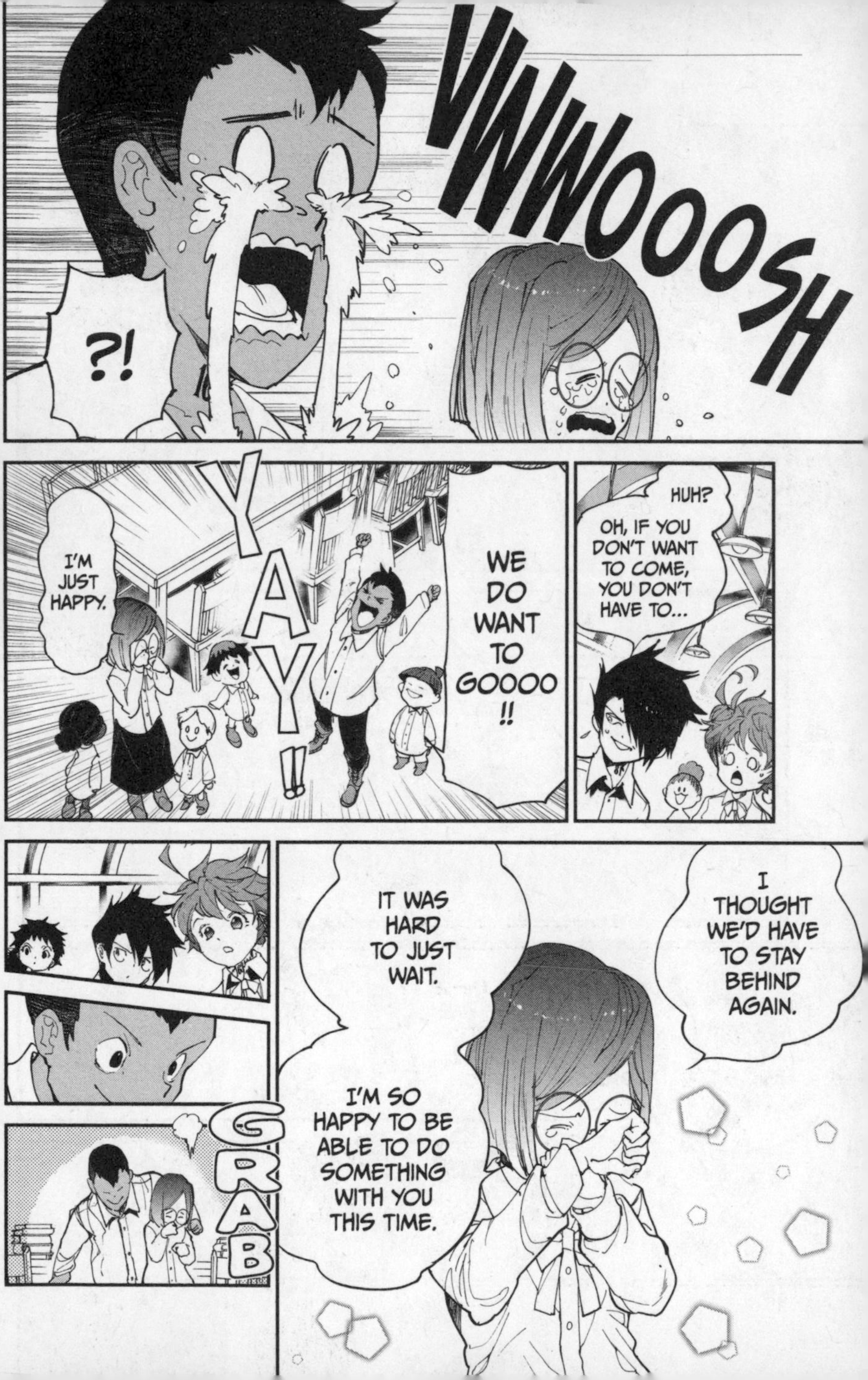
VWOOOSH
?!
HUH?
OH, IF YOU DON'T WANT TO COME, YOU DON'T HAVE TO...
WE DO WANT TO GOOOO!!
YAY!!
I'M JUST HAPPY.
I THOUGHT WE'D HAVE TO STAY BEHIND AGAIN.
IT WAS HARD TO JUST WAIT.
I'M SO HAPPY TO BE ABLE TO DO SOMETHING WITH YOU THIS TIME.
GRAB

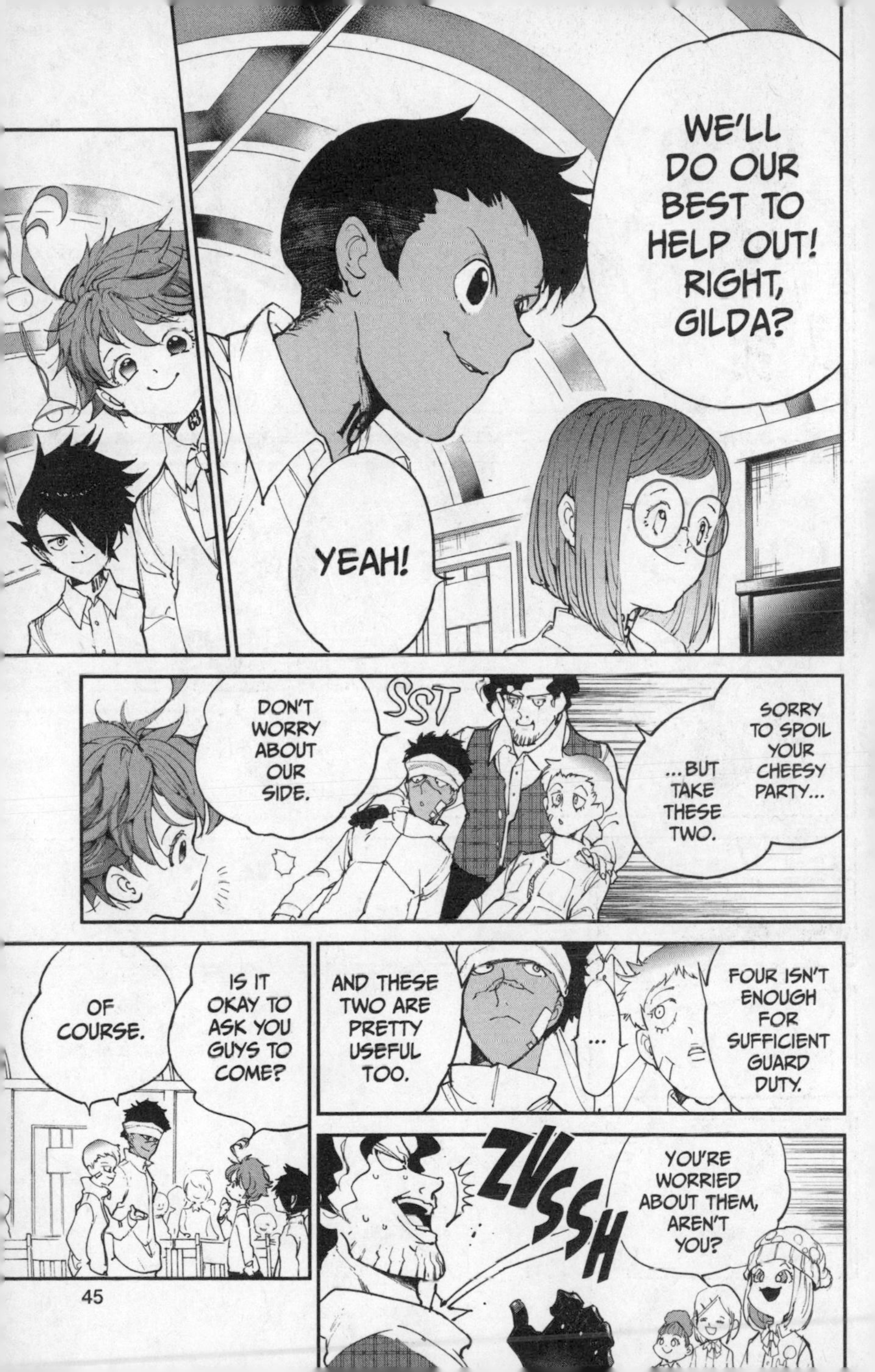
WE'LL DO OUR BEST TO HELP OUT! RIGHT, GILDA?
YEAH!
SORRY TO SPOIL YOUR CHEESY PARTY...
...BUT TAKE THESE TWO.
SST
DON'T WORRY ABOUT OUR SIDE.
FOUR ISN'T ENOUGH FOR SUFFICIENT GUARD DUTY.
...
AND THESE TWO ARE PRETTY USEFUL TOO.
YOU'RE WORRIED ABOUT THEM, AREN'T YOU?
ZVSSH
IS IT OKAY TO ASK YOU GUYS TO COME?
OF COURSE.

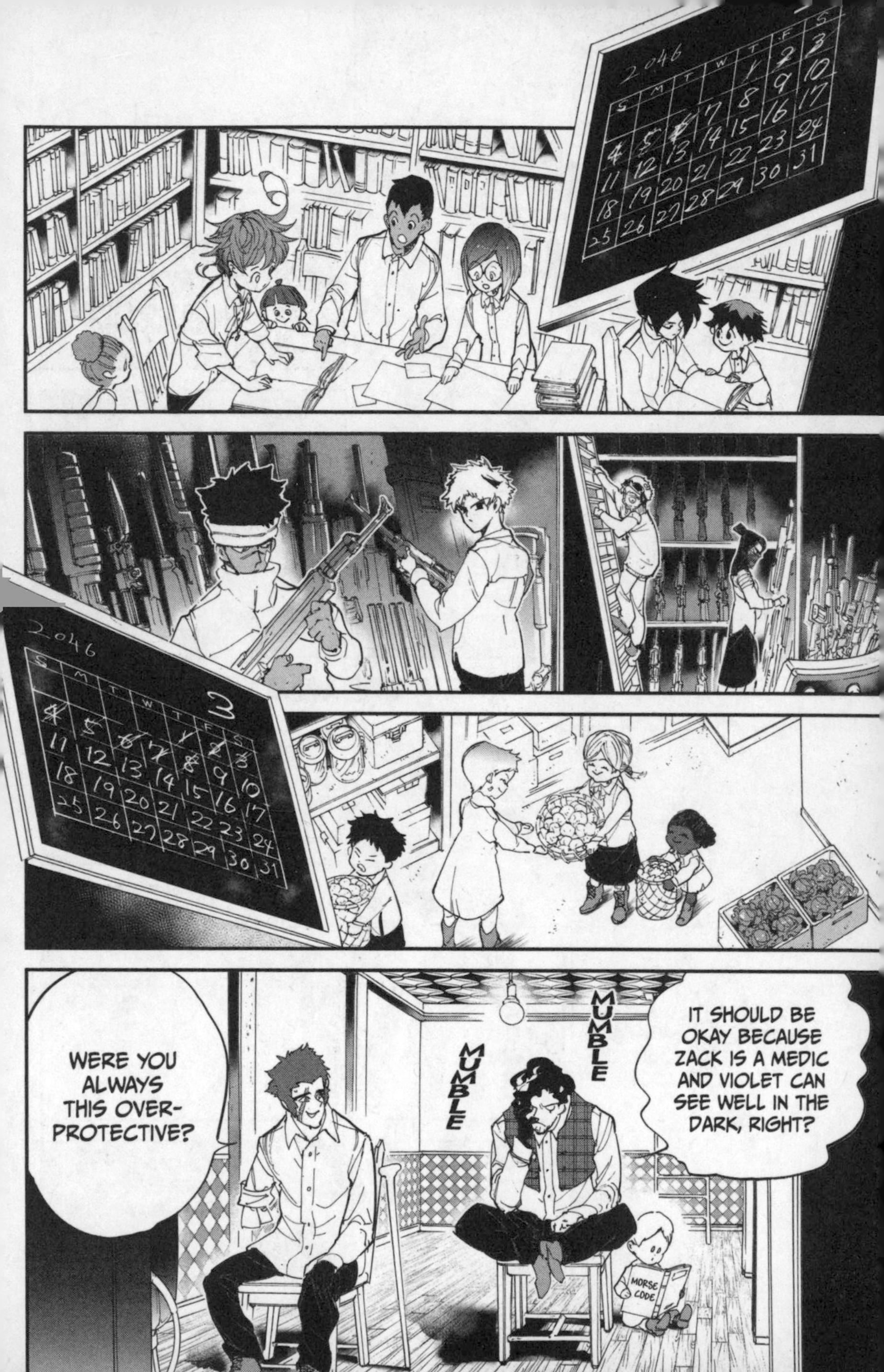
2046
2046
IT SHOULD BE OKAY BECAUSE ZACK IS A MEDIC AND VIOLET CAN SEE WELL IN THE DARK, RIGHT?
MUMBLE
MUMBLE
WERE YOU ALWAYS THIS OVER-PROTECTIVE?
MORSE CODE

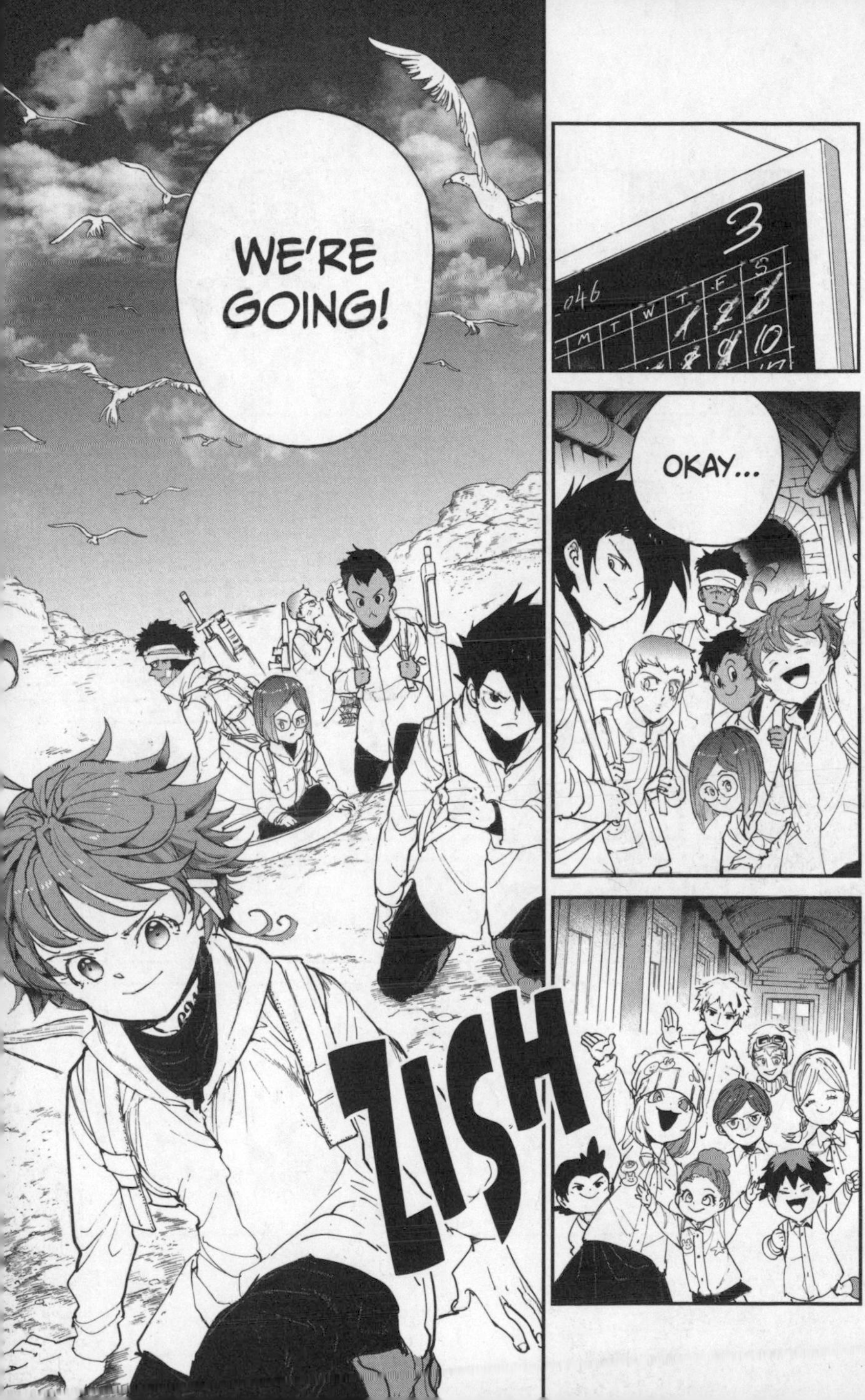
OKAY...
WE'RE GOING!
ZISH

DECEMBER 2046

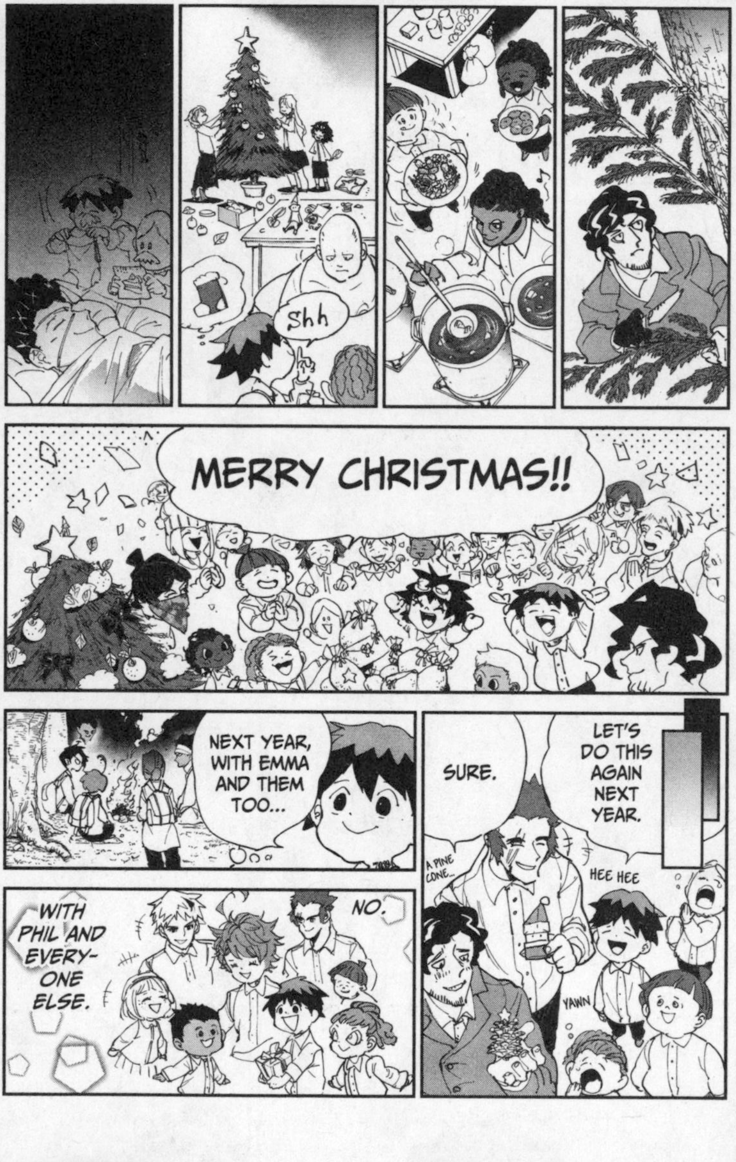
Shh
MERRY CHRISTMAS!!
LET'S DO THIS AGAIN NEXT YEAR.
SURE.
A PINE CONE...
HEE HEE
YAWN
NEXT YEAR, WITH EMMA AND THEM TOO...
WITH PHIL AND EVERY-ONE ELSE.
NO.

SIDE STORY 9 FIN

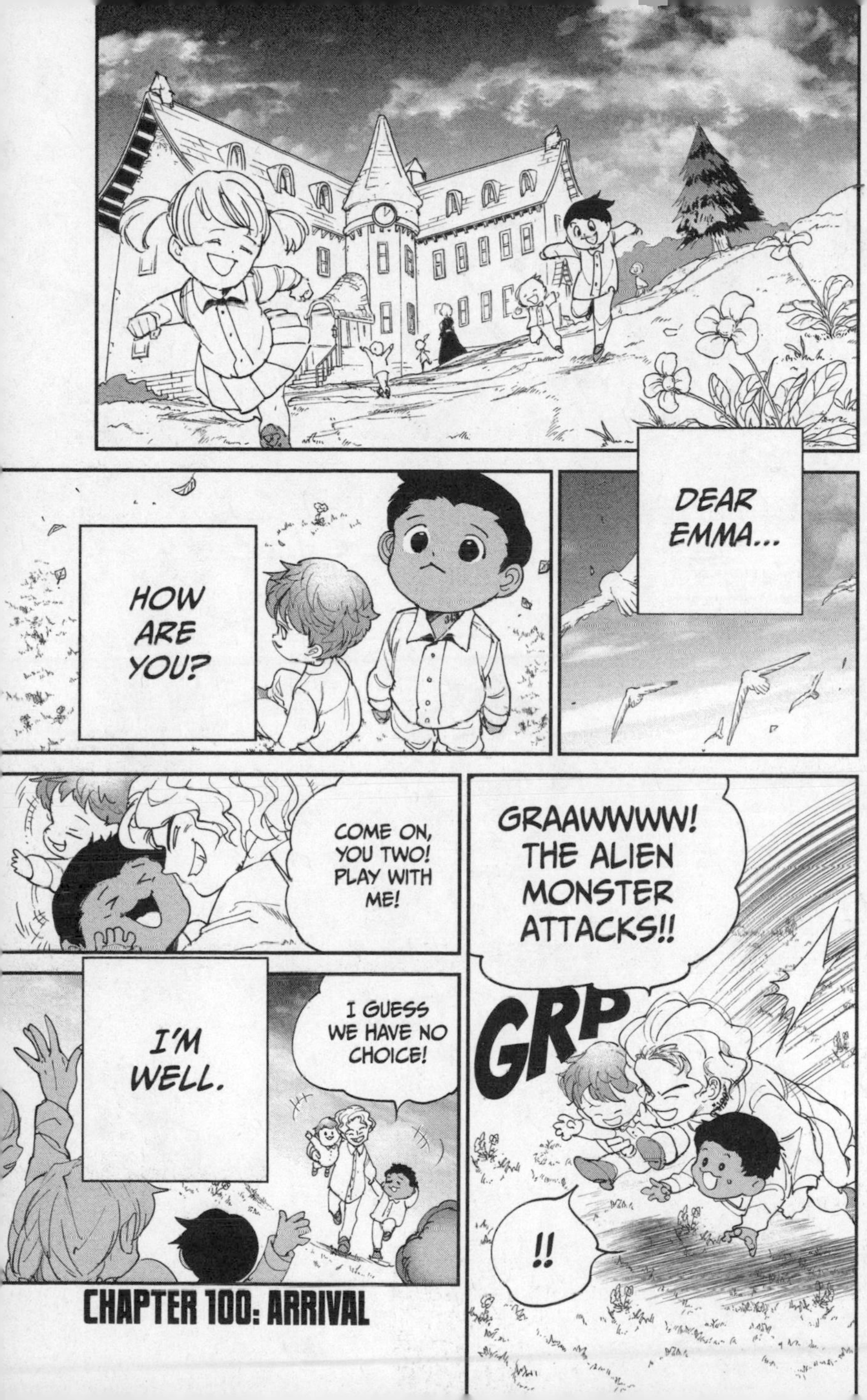
DEAR EMMA...
HOW ARE YOU?
GRAAWWWW! THE ALIEN MONSTER ATTACKS!!
GRP
!!
COME ON, YOU TWO! PLAY WITH ME!
I GUESS WE HAVE NO CHOICE!
I'M WELL.

CHAPTER 100: ARRIVAL

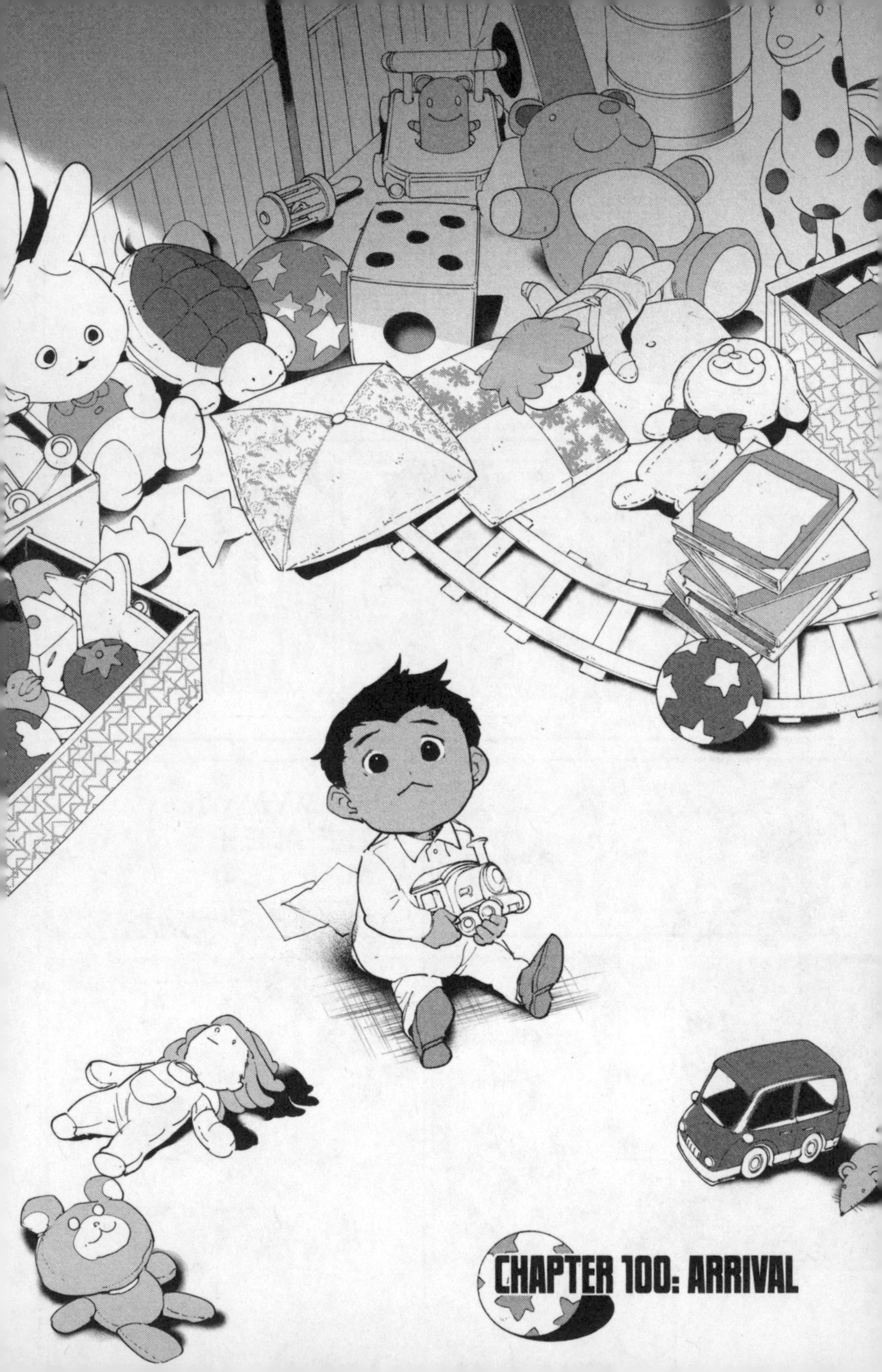
CHAPTER 100: ARRIVAL

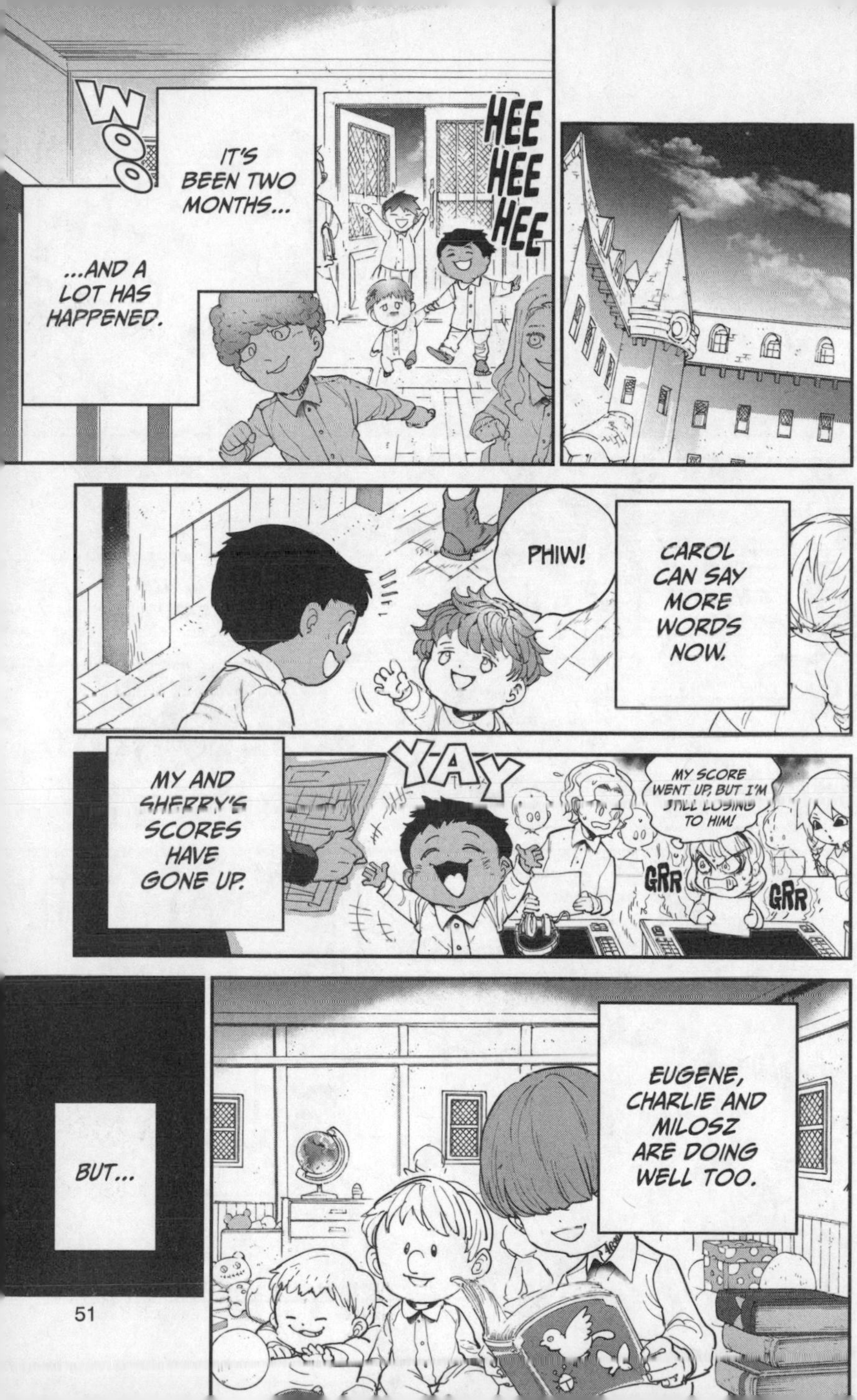
HEE HEE HEE
IT'S BEEN TWO MONTHS...
WOO
...AND A LOT HAS HAPPENED.
CAROL CAN SAY MORE WORDS NOW.
PHIW!
MY SCORE WENT UP, BUT I'M STILL LOSING TO HIM!
GRR
GRR
YAY
MY AND SHERRY'S SCORES HAVE GONE UP.
EUGENE, CHARLIE AND MILOSZ ARE DOING WELL TOO.
BUT...

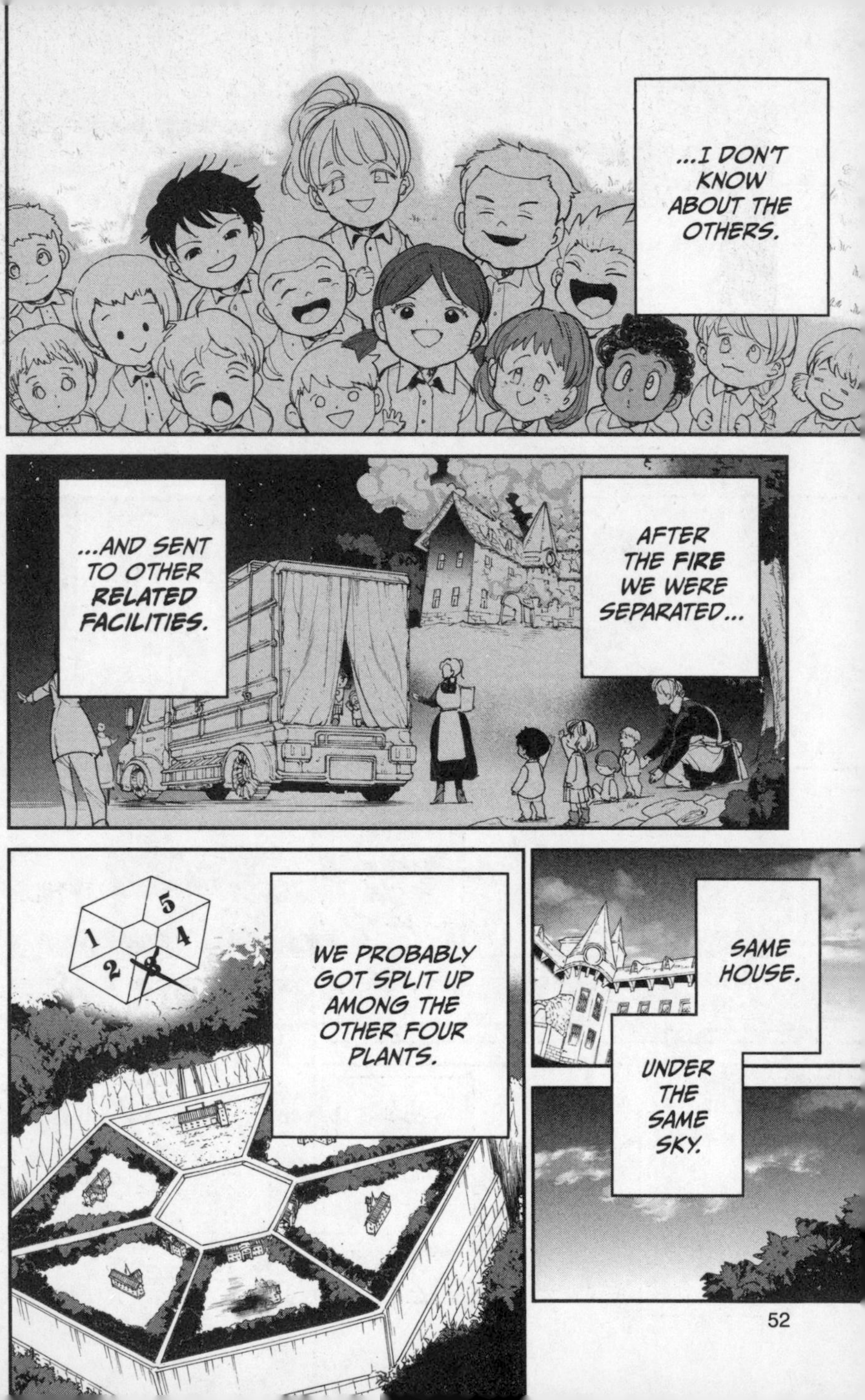
...I DON'T KNOW ABOUT THE OTHERS.
AFTER THE FIRE WE WERE SEPARATED...
...AND SENT TO OTHER RELATED FACILITIES.
SAME HOUSE.
UNDER THE SAME SKY.
WE PROBABLY GOT SPLIT UP AMONG THE OTHER FOUR PLANTS.
5
4
1
2
3

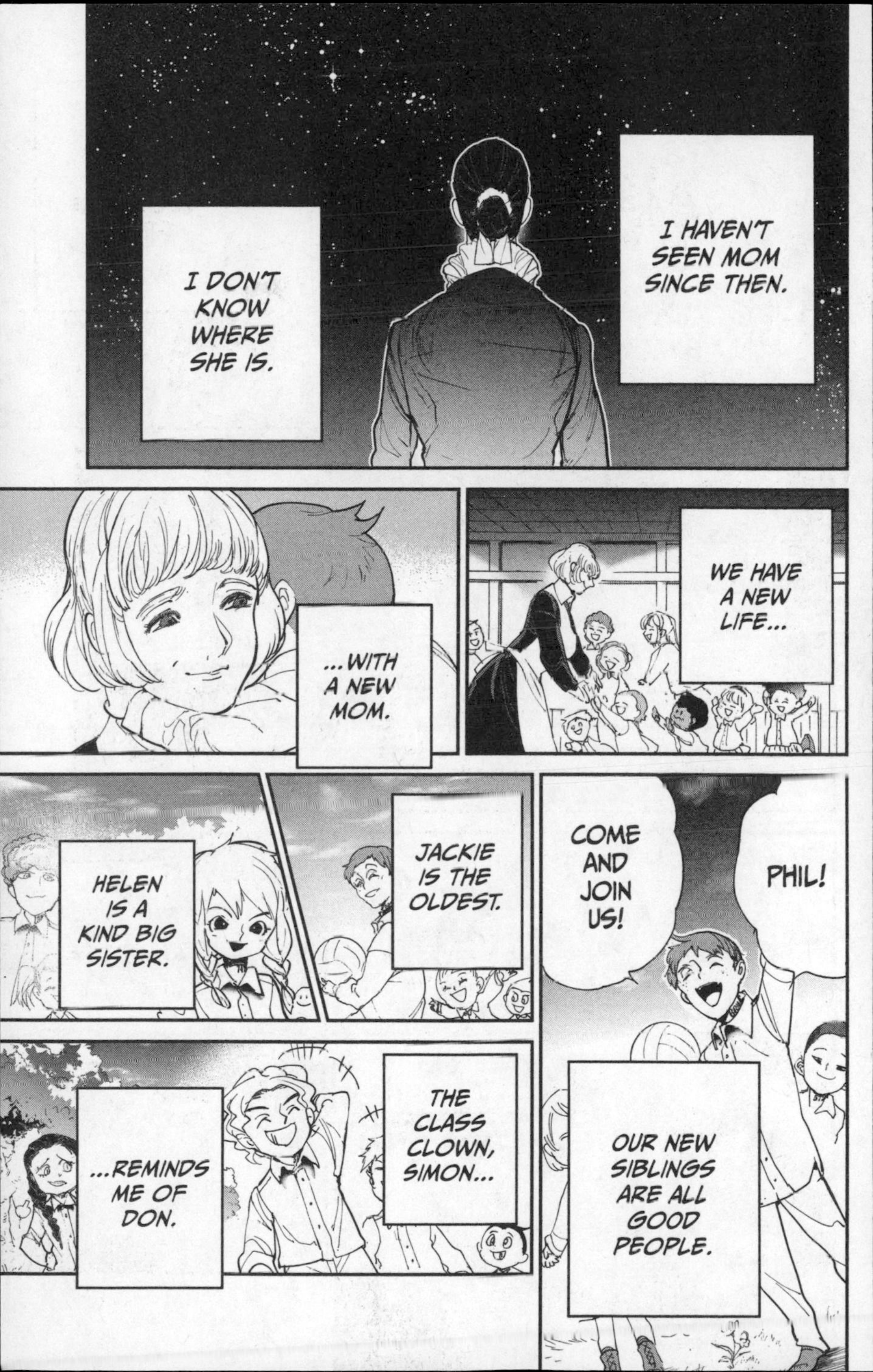
I HAVEN'T SEEN MOM SINCE THEN.
I DON'T KNOW WHERE SHE IS.
WE HAVE A NEW LIFE...
...WITH A NEW MOM.
PHIL!
COME AND JOIN US!
OUR NEW SIBLINGS ARE ALL GOOD PEOPLE.
JACKIE IS THE OLDEST.
HELEN IS A KIND BIG SISTER.
THE CLASS CLOWN, SIMON...
...REMINDS ME OF DON.

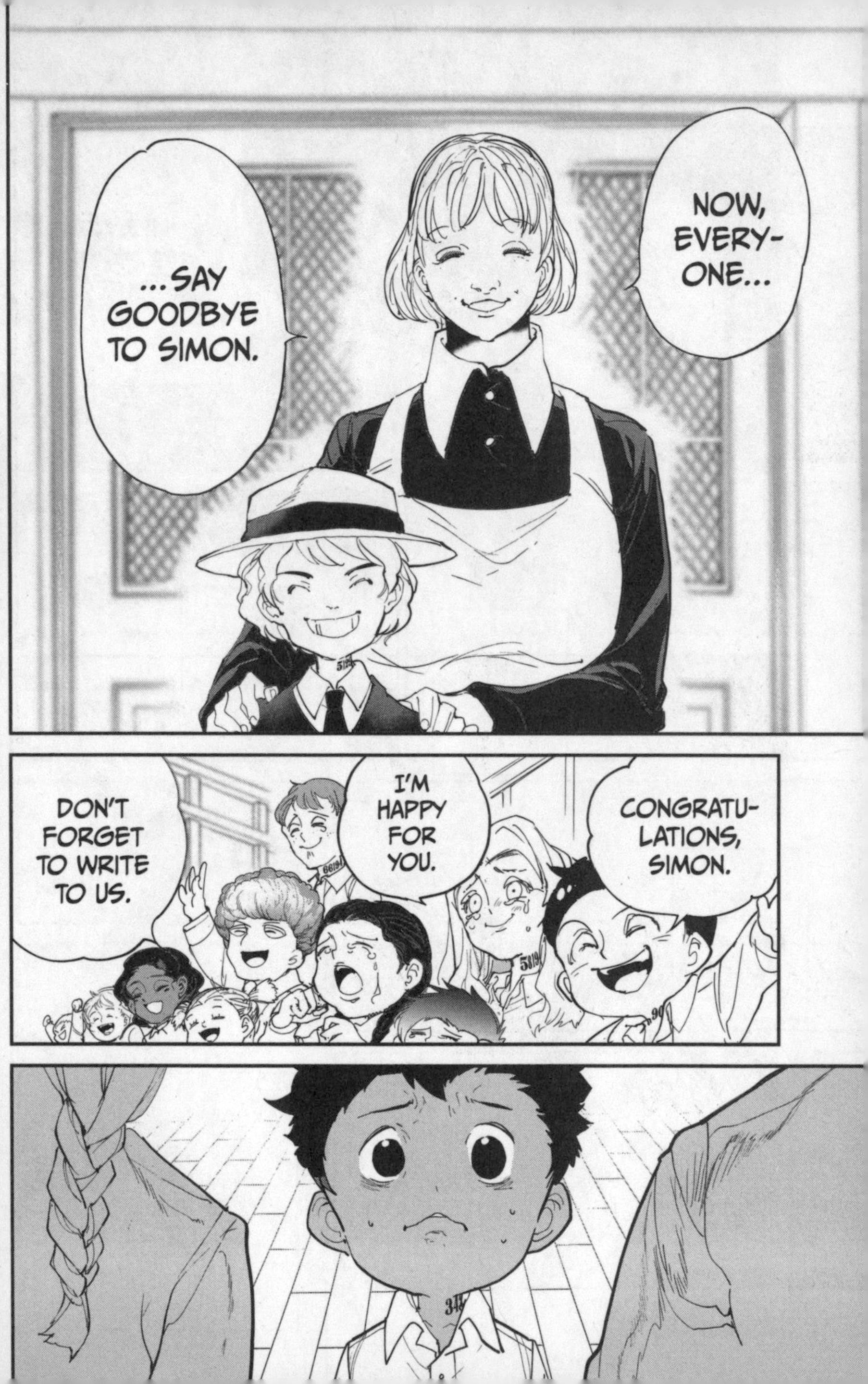
NOW, EVERY-ONE...
...SAY GOODBYE TO SIMON.
CONGRATU-LATIONS, SIMON.
I'M HAPPY FOR YOU.
DON'T FORGET TO WRITE TO US.

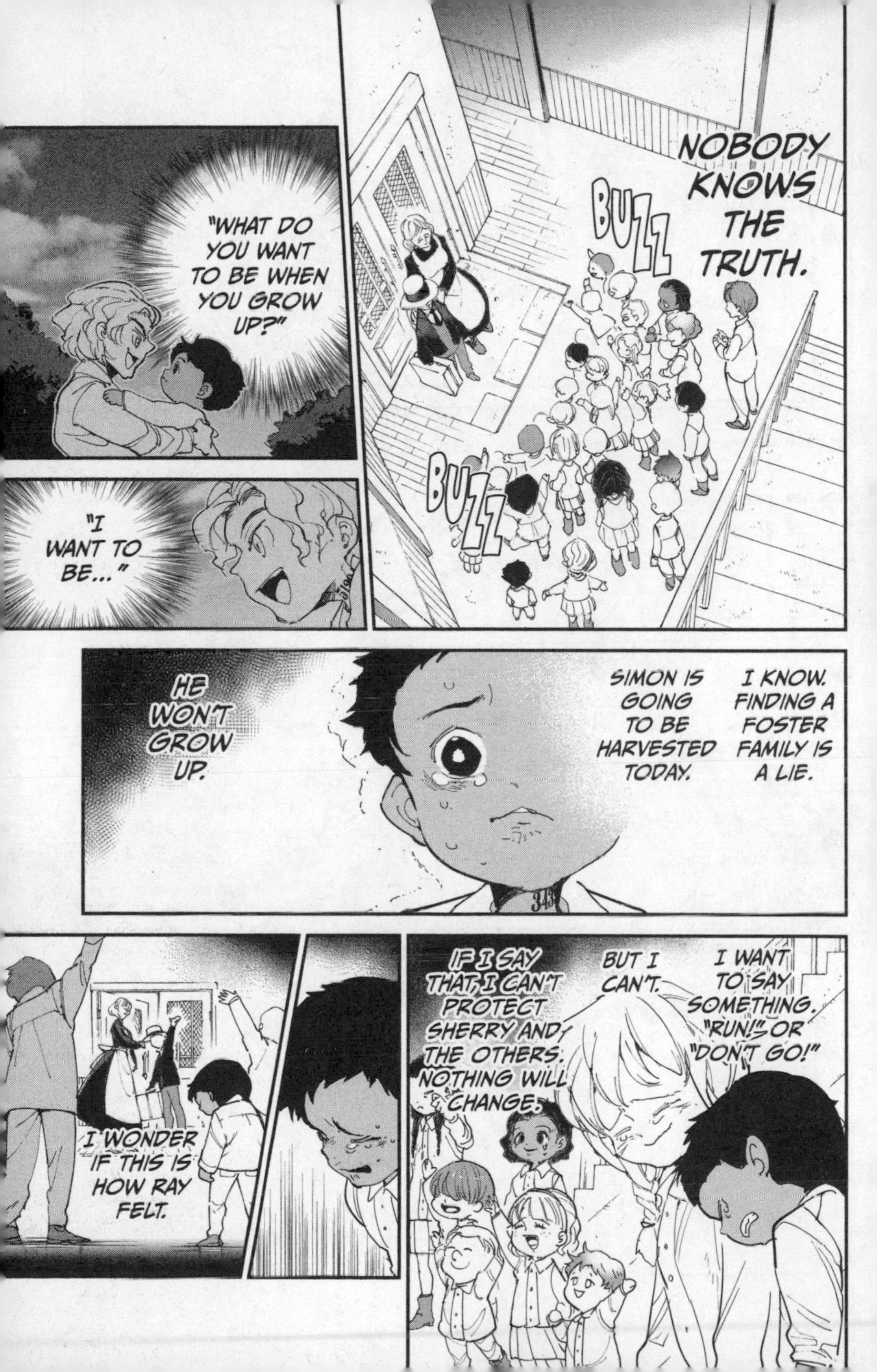
NOBODY KNOWS THE TRUTH.
BUZZ
BUZZ
"WHAT DO YOU WANT TO BE WHEN YOU GROW UP?"
"I WANT TO BE..."
I KNOW. FINDING A FOSTER FAMILY IS A LIE.
SIMON IS GOING TO BE HARVESTED TODAY.
HE WON'T GROW UP.
I WANT TO SAY SOMETHING. "RUN!" OR "DON'T GO!"
BUT I CAN'T.
IF I SAY THAT, I CAN'T PROTECT SHERRY AND THE OTHERS. NOTHING WILL CHANGE.
I WONDER IF THIS IS HOW RAY FELT.

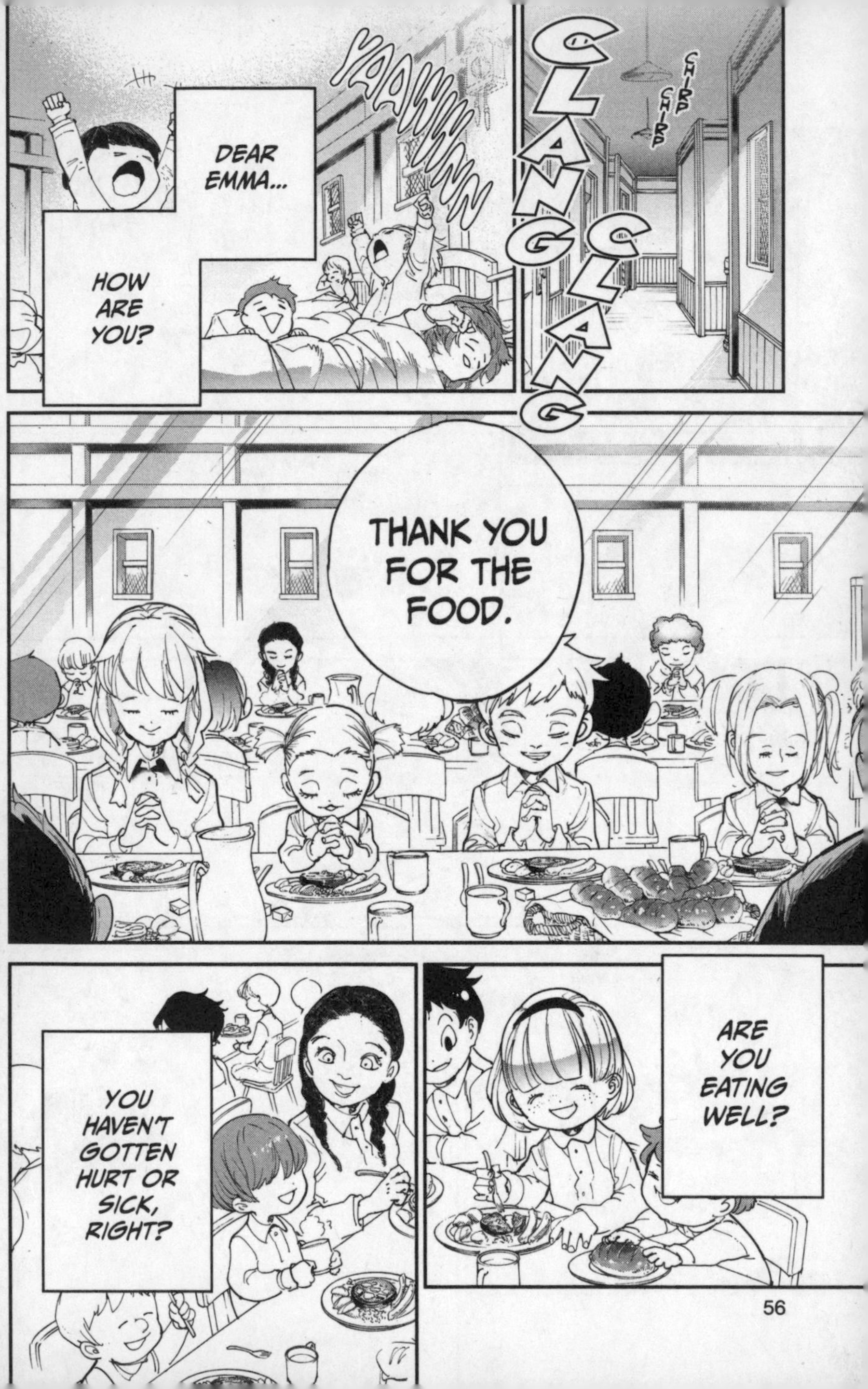
CLANG
CLANG
CHIRP
CHIRP
DEAR EMMA...
HOW ARE YOU?
THANK YOU FOR THE FOOD.
ARE YOU EATING WELL?
YOU HAVEN'T GOTTEN HURT OR SICK, RIGHT?

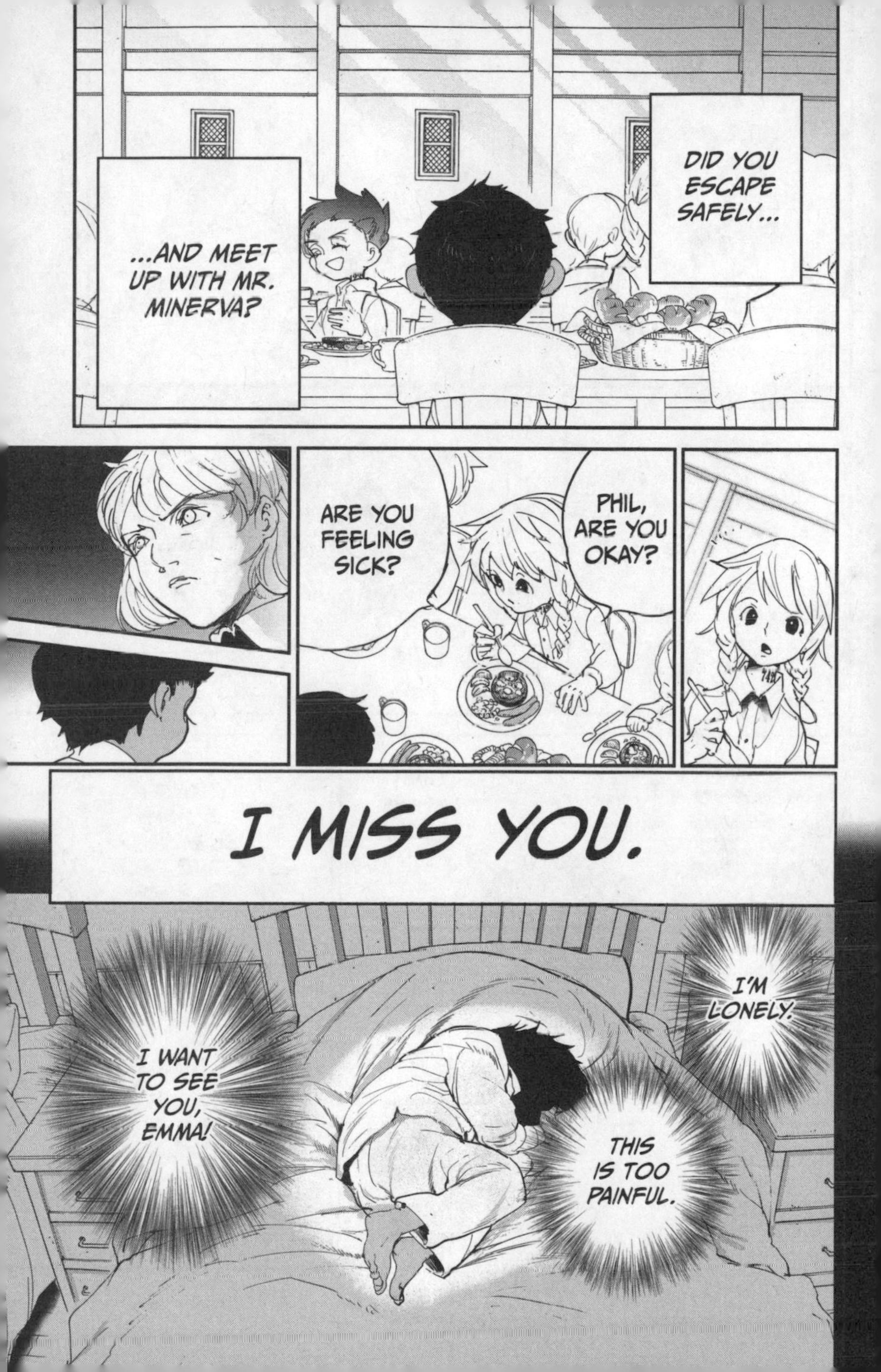
DID YOU ESCAPE SAFELY...
...AND MEET UP WITH MR. MINERVA?
PHIL, ARE YOU OKAY?
ARE YOU FEELING SICK?
I MISS YOU.
I'M LONELY.
THIS IS TOO PAINFUL.
I WANT TO SEE YOU, EMMA!

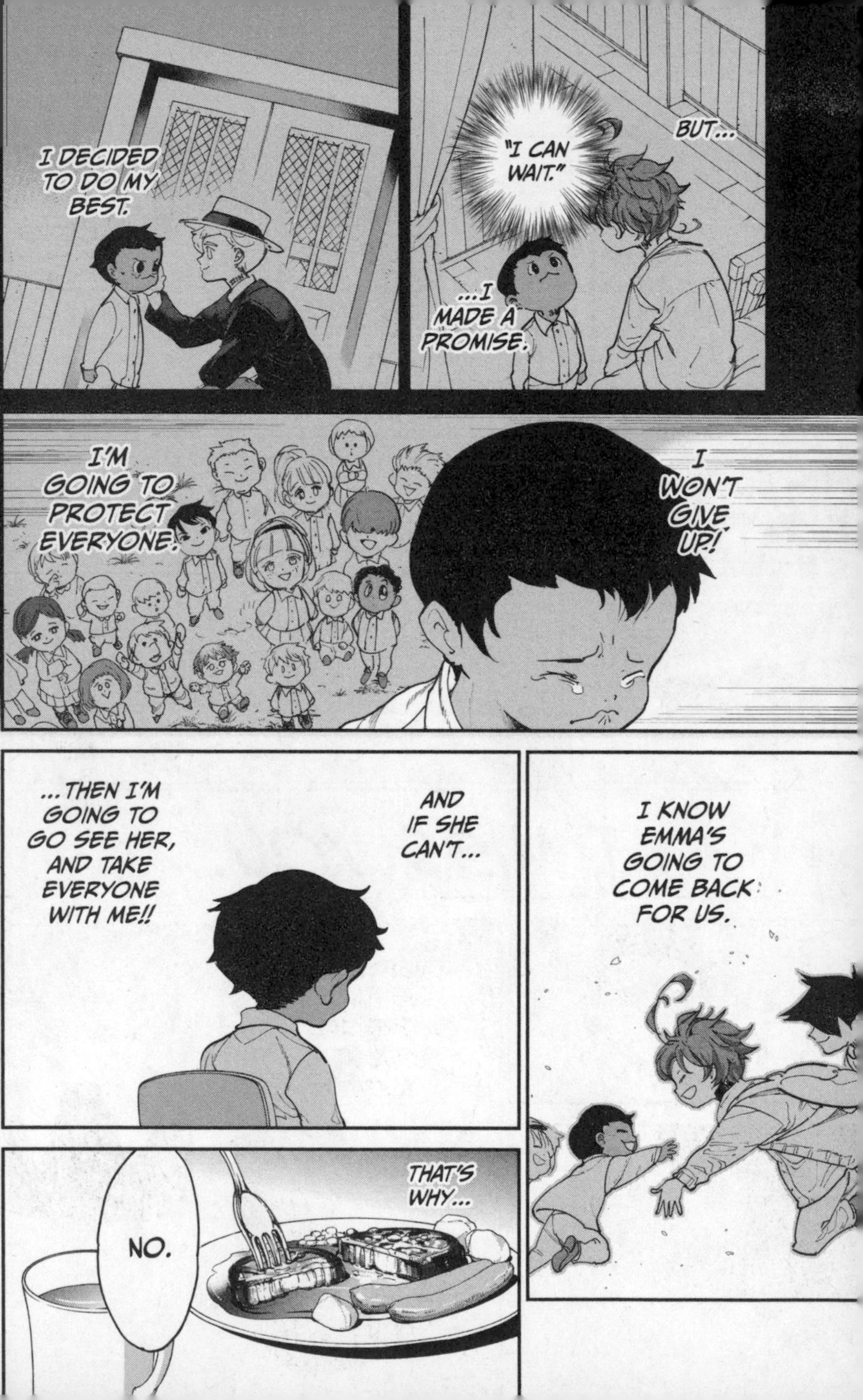
BUT...
"I CAN WAIT."
...I MADE A PROMISE.
I DECIDED TO DO MY BEST.
I WON'T GIVE UP!
I'M GOING TO PROTECT EVERYONE.
I KNOW EMMA'S GOING TO COME BACK FOR US.
AND IF SHE CAN'T...
...THEN I'M GOING TO GO SEE HER, AND TAKE EVERYONE WITH ME!!
THAT'S WHY...
NO.

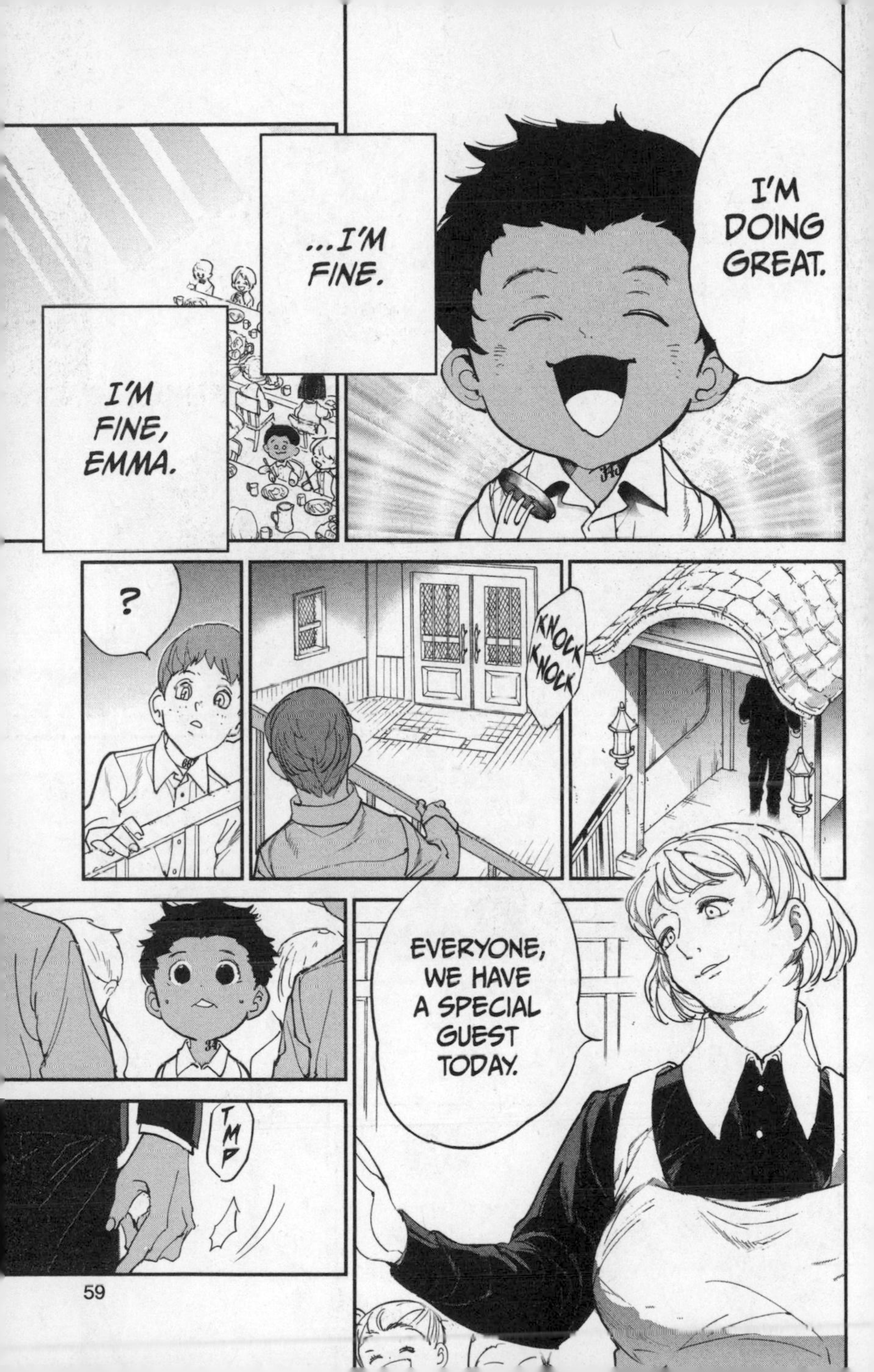
I'M DOING GREAT.
...I'M FINE.
I'M FINE, EMMA.
KNOCK KNOCK
?
EVERYONE, WE HAVE A SPECIAL GUEST TODAY.
TMP

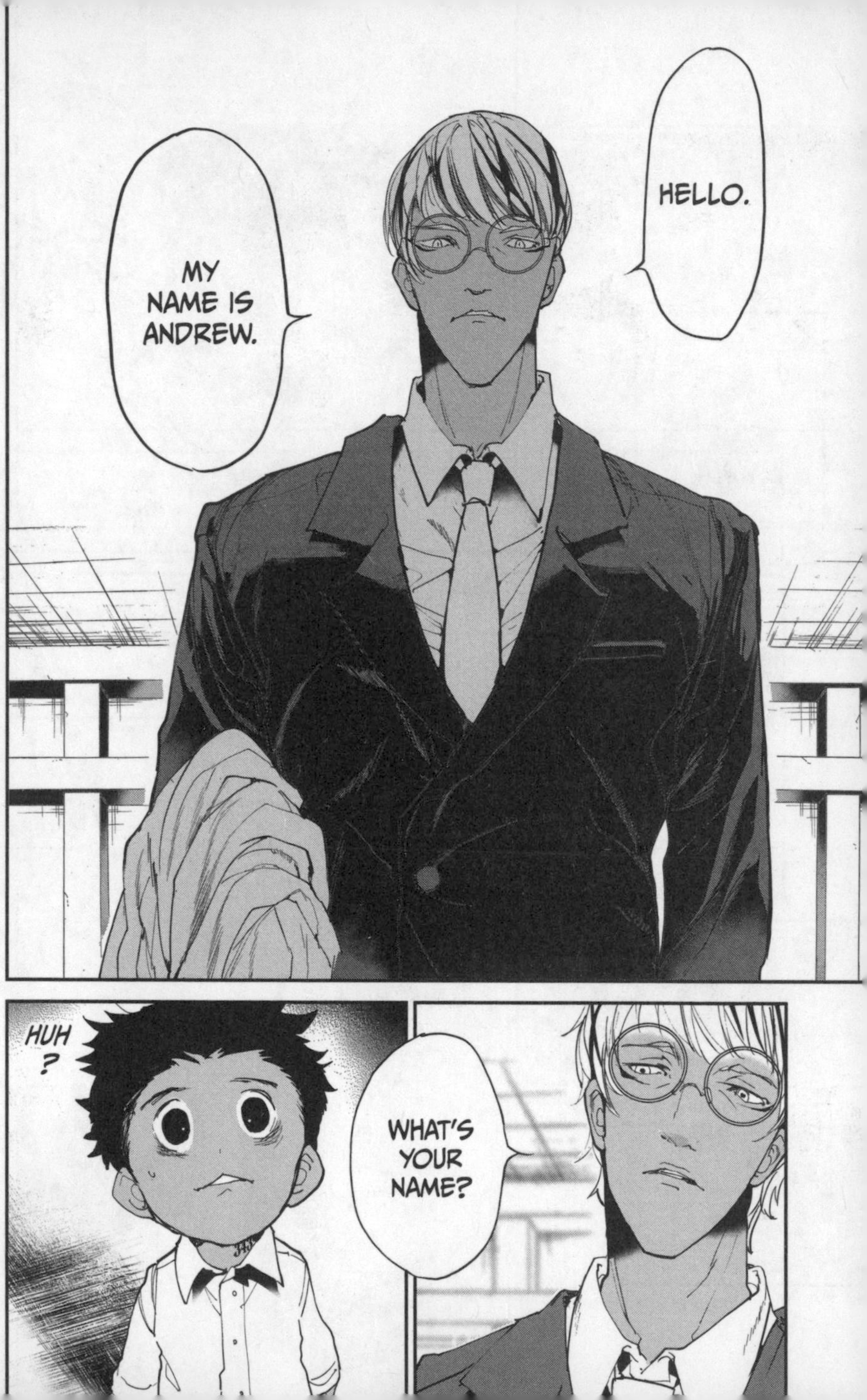
HELLO.
MY NAME IS ANDREW.
WHAT'S YOUR NAME?
HUH?

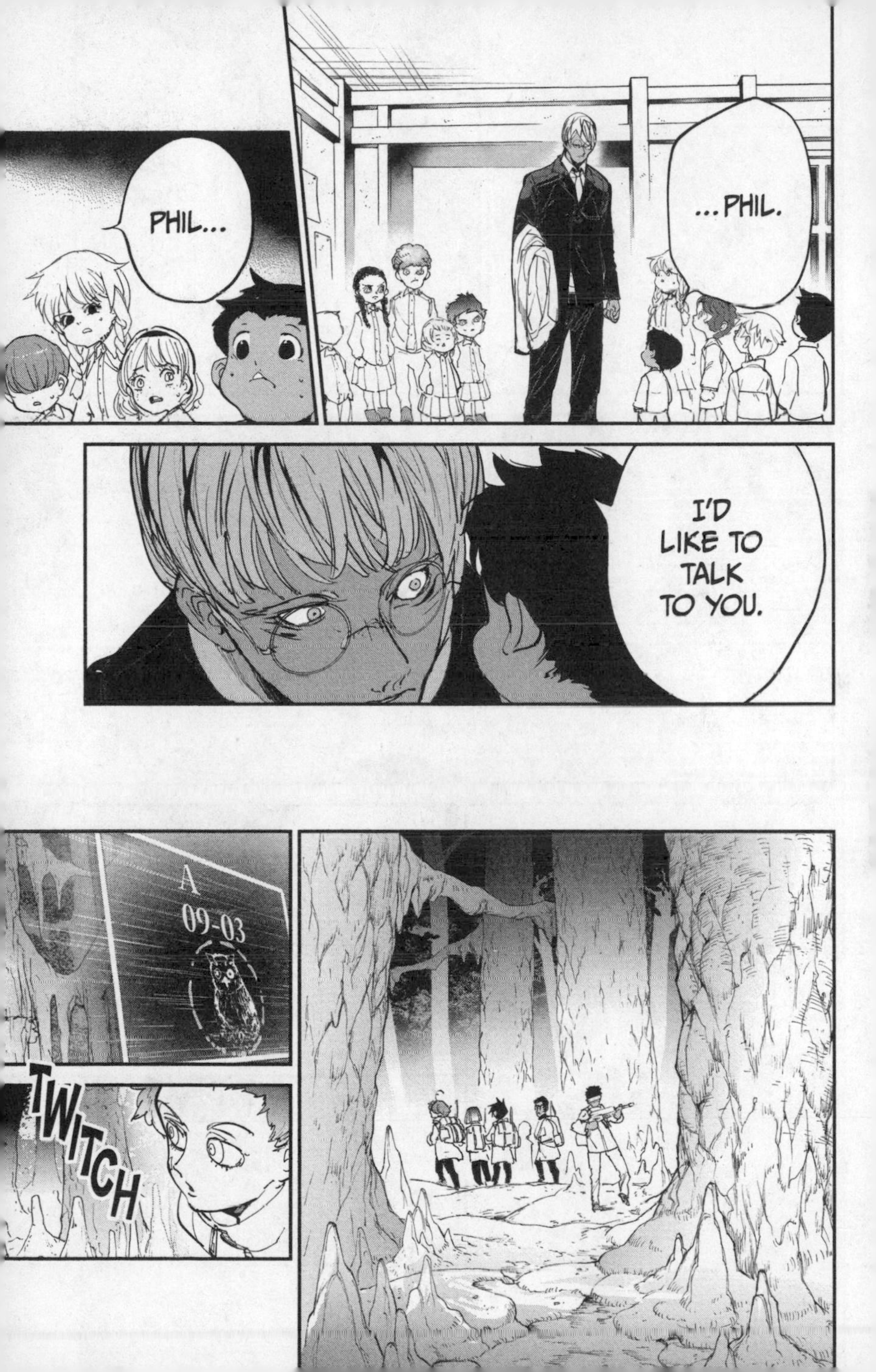
...PHIL.
PHIL...
I'D LIKE TO TALK TO YOU.
A
09-03
TWITCH

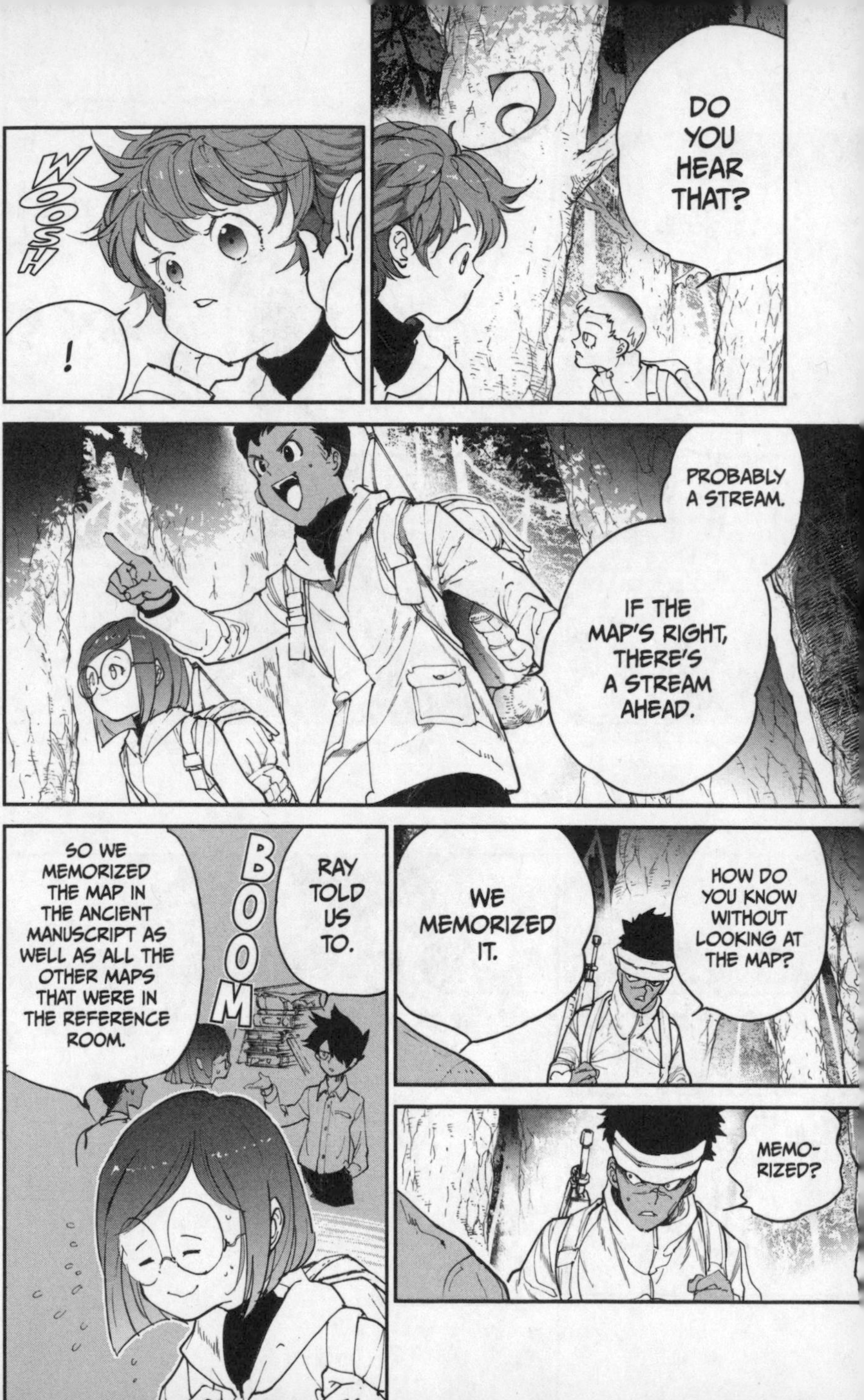
DO YOU HEAR THAT?
WOOSH
!
PROBABLY A STREAM.
IF THE MAP'S RIGHT, THERE'S A STREAM AHEAD.
HOW DO YOU KNOW WITHOUT LOOKING AT THE MAP?
WE MEMORIZED IT.
MEMO-RIZED?
RAY TOLD US TO.
BOOM
SO WE MEMORIZED THE MAP IN THE ANCIENT MANUSCRIPT AS WELL AS ALL THE OTHER MAPS THAT WERE IN THE REFERENCE ROOM.

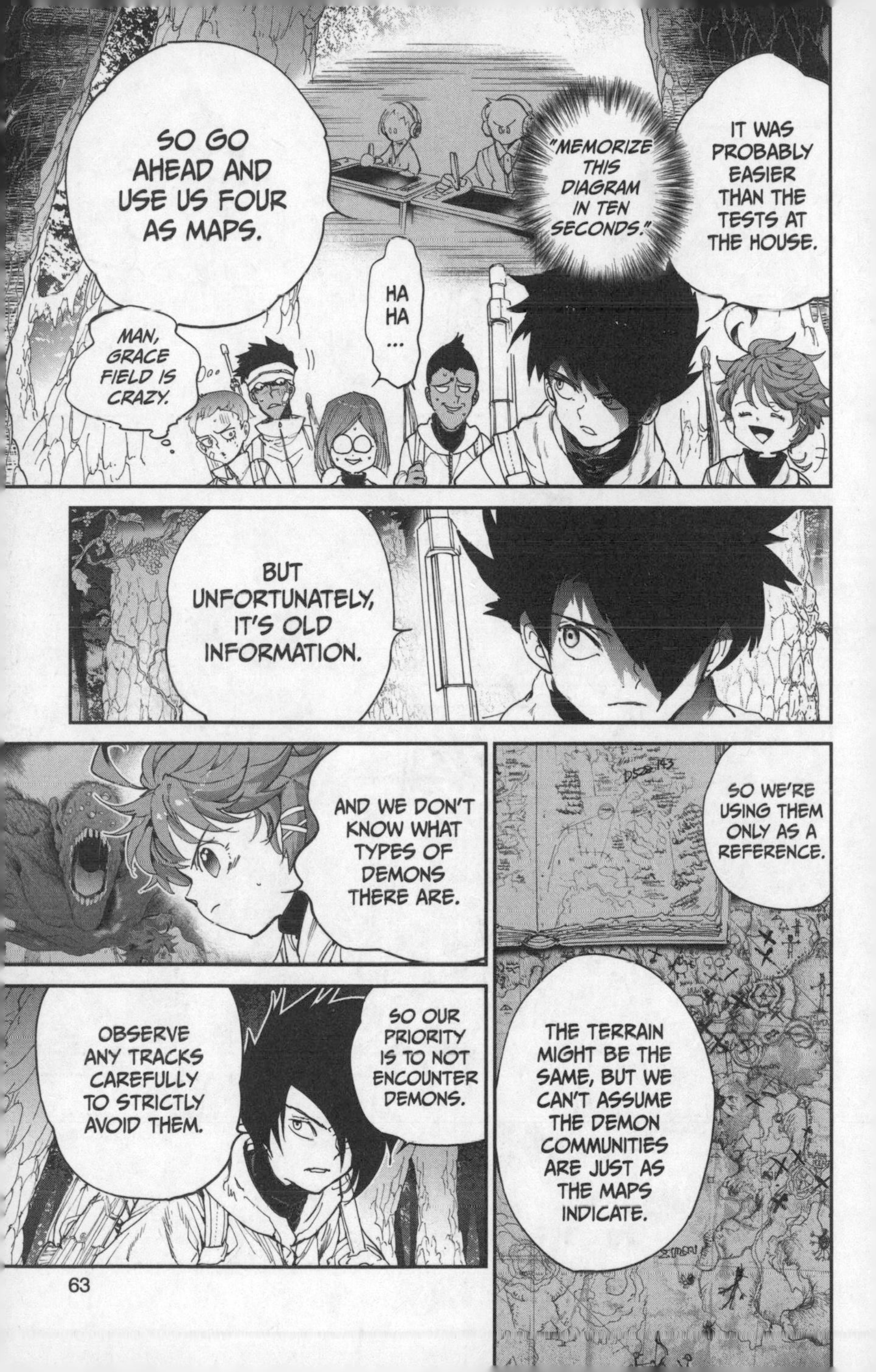
IT WAS PROBABLY EASIER THAN THE TESTS AT THE HOUSE.
"MEMORIZE THIS DIAGRAM IN TEN SECONDS."
SO GO AHEAD AND USE US FOUR AS MAPS.
HA HA ...
MAN, GRACE FIELD IS CRAZY.
BUT UNFORTUNATELY, IT'S OLD INFORMATION.
SO WE'RE USING THEM ONLY AS A REFERENCE.
THE TERRAIN MIGHT BE THE SAME, BUT WE CAN'T ASSUME THE DEMON COMMUNITIES ARE JUST AS THE MAPS INDICATE.
AND WE DON'T KNOW WHAT TYPES OF DEMONS THERE ARE.
SO OUR PRIORITY IS TO NOT ENCOUNTER DEMONS.
OBSERVE ANY TRACKS CAREFULLY TO STRICTLY AVOID THEM.

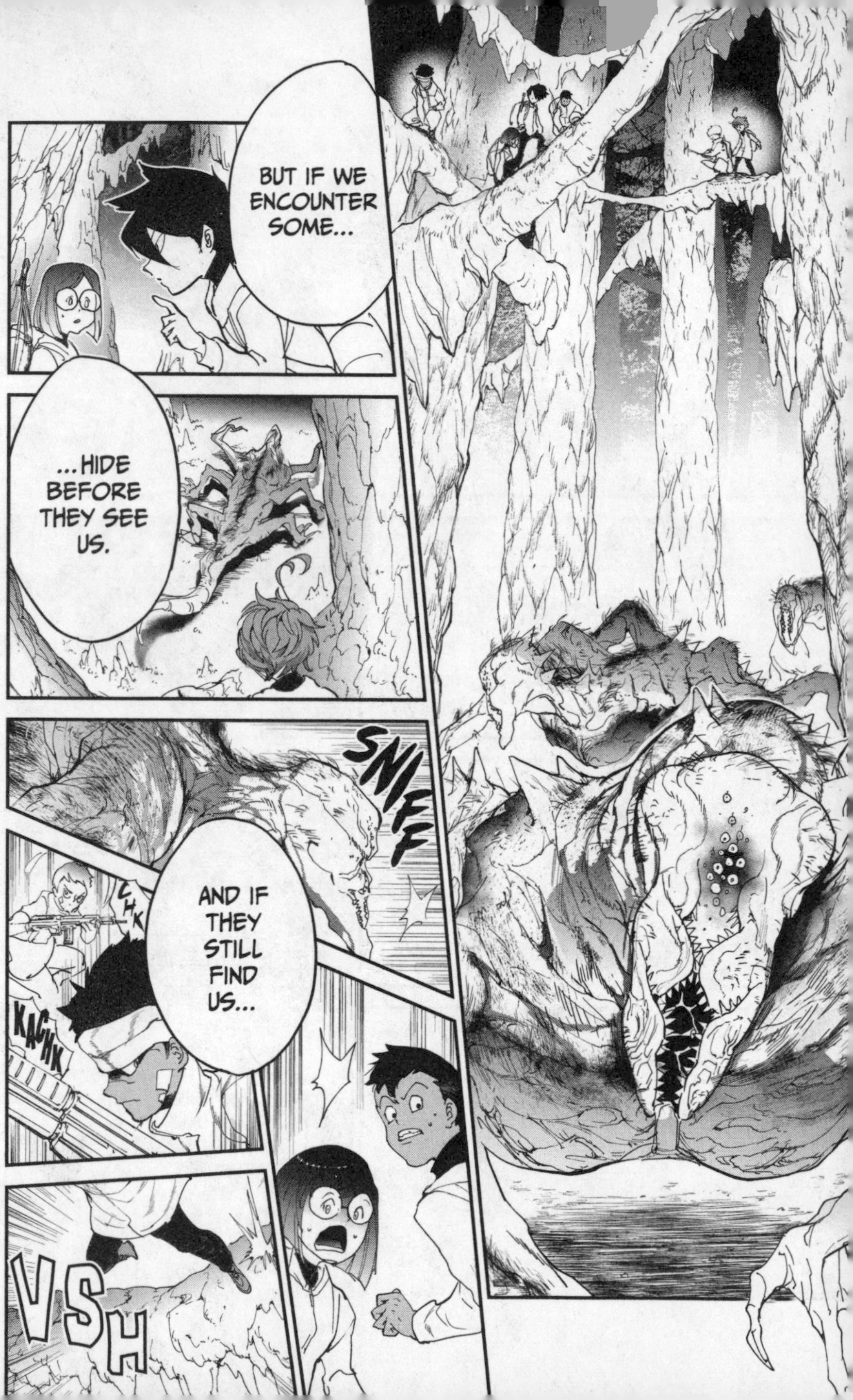
BUT IF WE ENCOUNTER SOME...
...HIDE BEFORE THEY SEE US.
SNIFF
CHK
AND IF THEY STILL FIND US...
KACHK
VSH

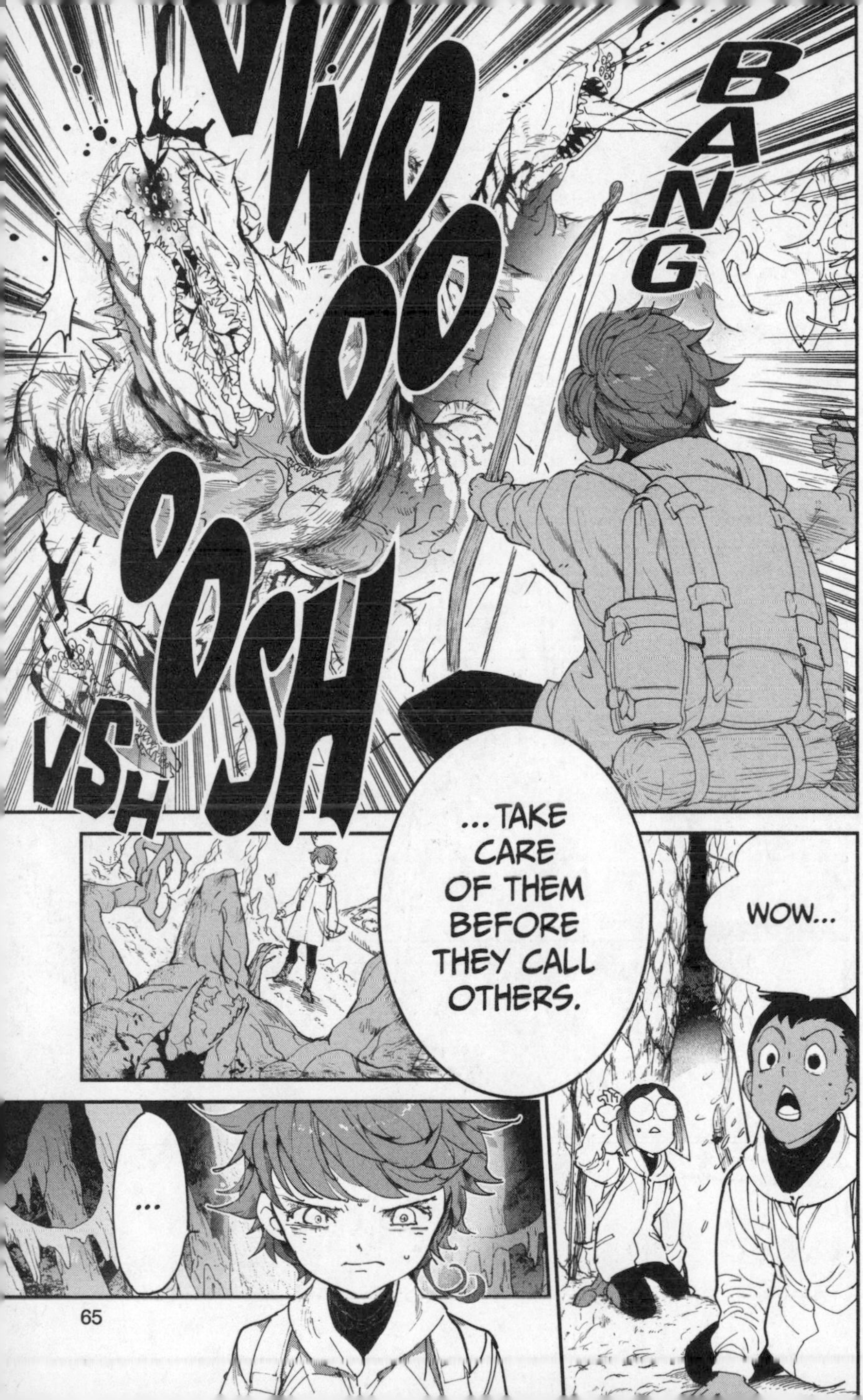
BANG
VWOOOOOOSH
VSH
WOW...
...TAKE CARE OF THEM BEFORE THEY CALL OTHERS.
...

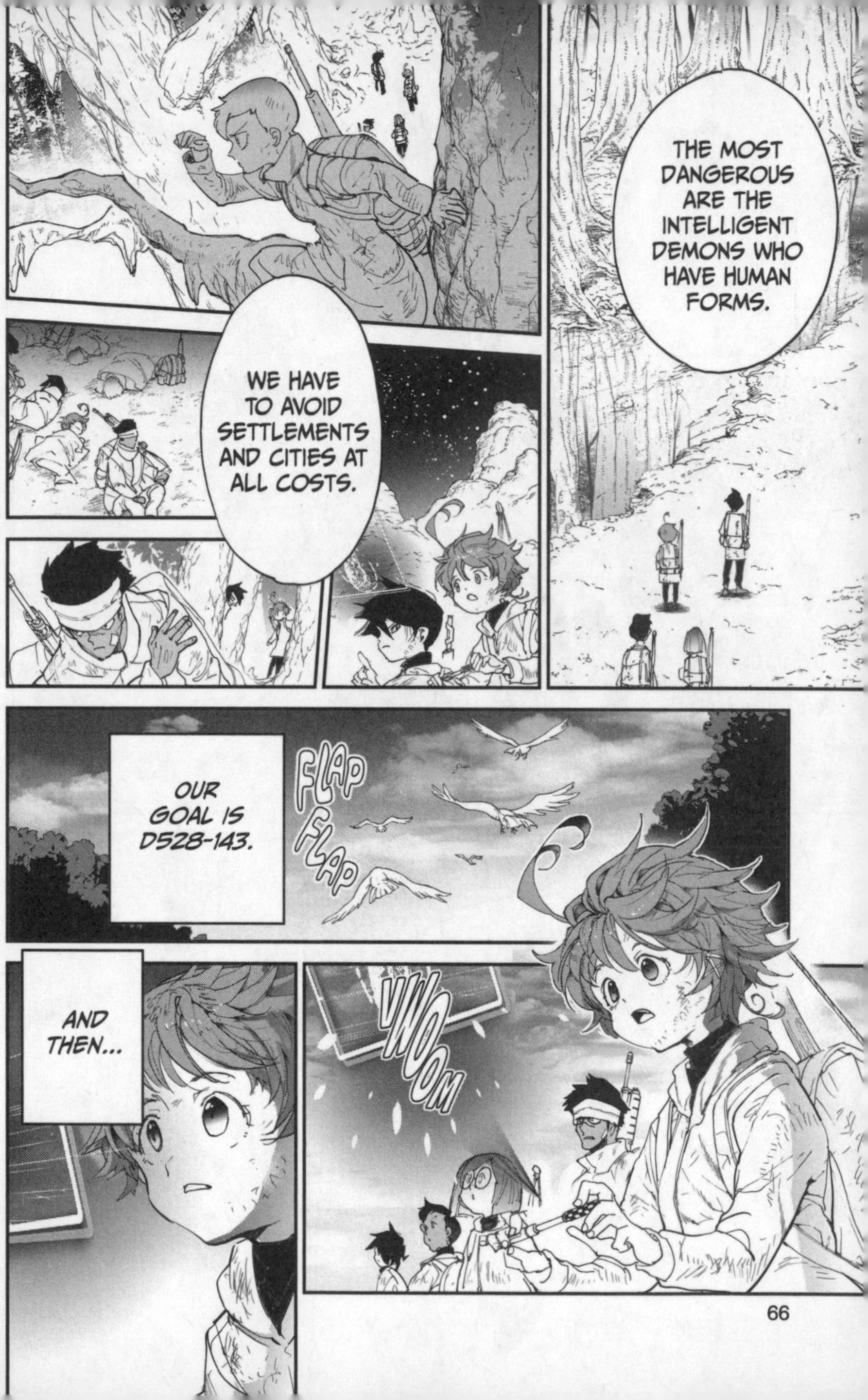
THE MOST DANGEROUS ARE THE INTELLIGENT DEMONS WHO HAVE HUMAN FORMS.
WE HAVE TO AVOID SETTLEMENTS AND CITIES AT ALL COSTS.
OUR GOAL IS D528-143.
FLAP
FLAP
FLAP
VWOOM
AND THEN...

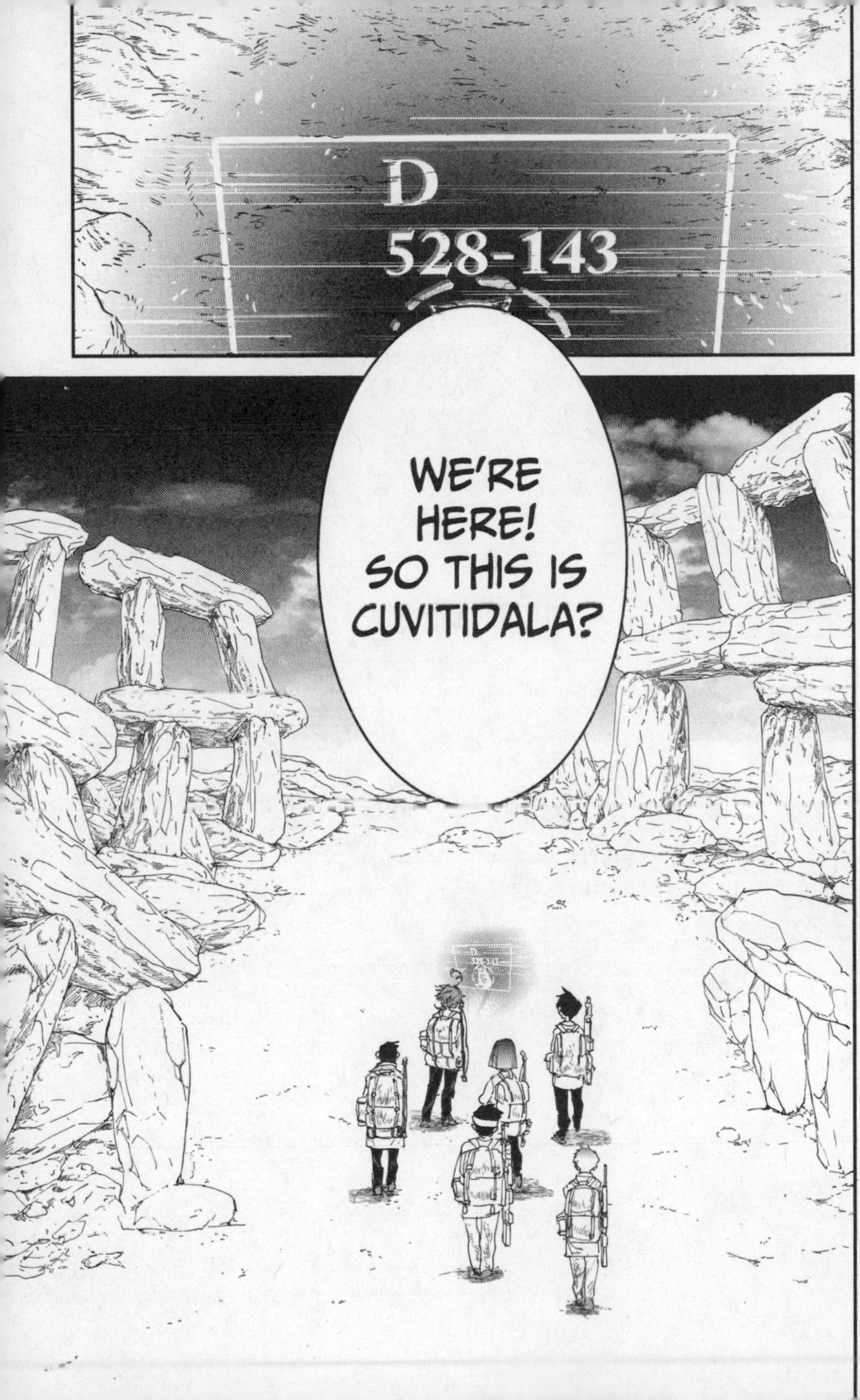
D
528-143
WE'RE HERE! SO THIS IS CUVITIDALA?

GOT YELLED AT

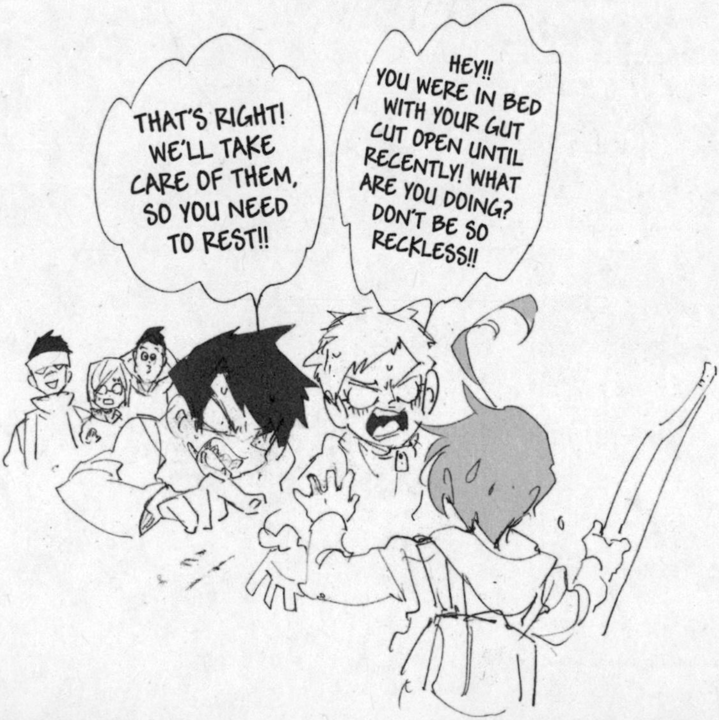
HEY!! YOU WERE IN BED WITH YOUR GUT CUT OPEN UNTIL RECENTLY! WHAT ARE YOU DOING? DON'T BE SO RECKLESS!!
THAT'S RIGHT! WE'LL TAKE CARE OF THEM, SO YOU NEED TO REST!!

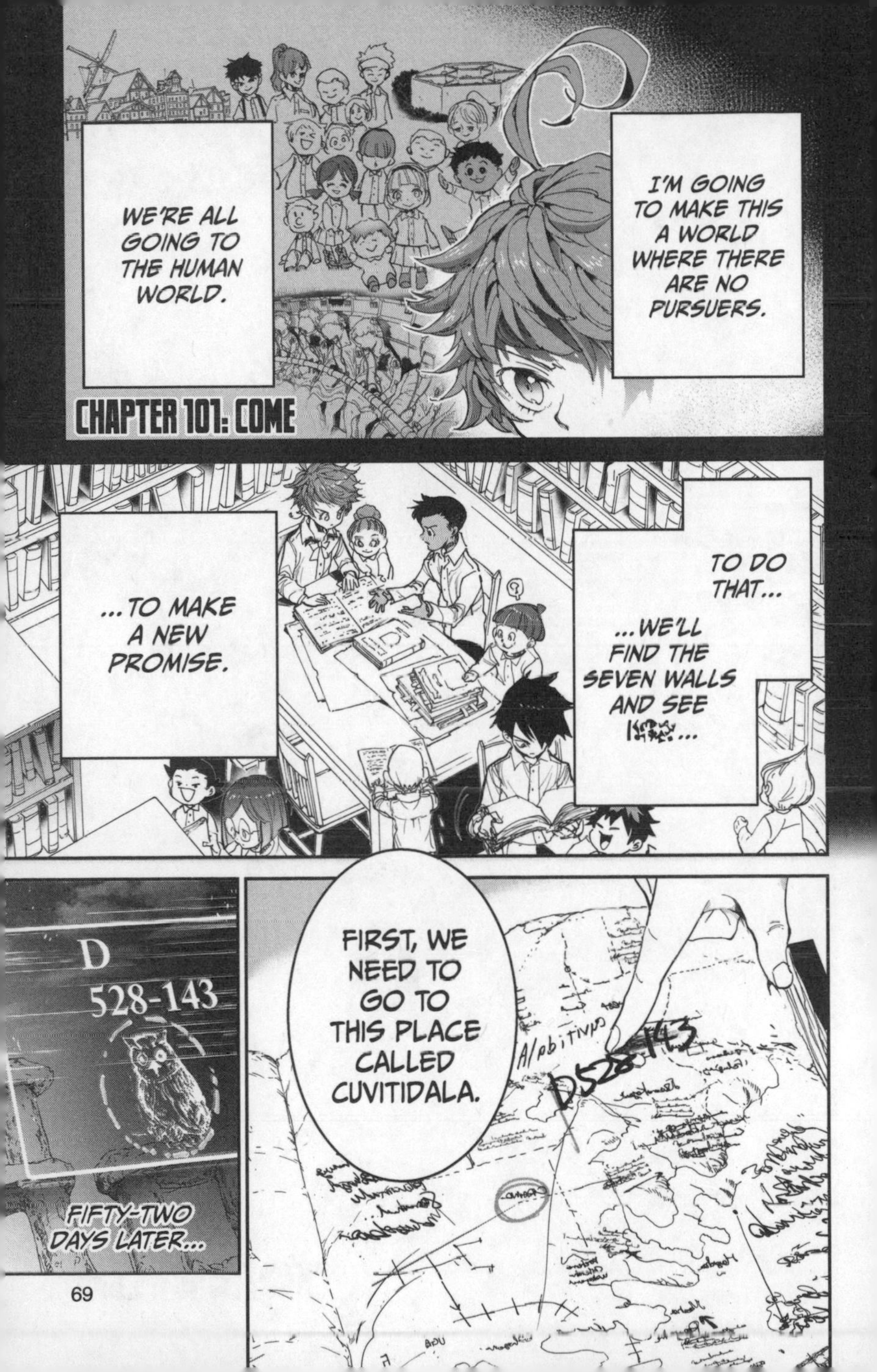
I'M GOING TO MAKE THIS A WORLD WHERE THERE ARE NO PURSUERS.
WE'RE ALL GOING TO THE HUMAN WORLD.
CHAPTER 101: COME
TO DO THAT...
...WE'LL FIND THE SEVEN WALLS AND SEE
...TO MAKE A NEW PROMISE.
FIRST, WE NEED TO GO TO THIS PLACE CALLED CUVITIDALA.
D528-143
D
528-143
FIFTY-TWO DAYS LATER...

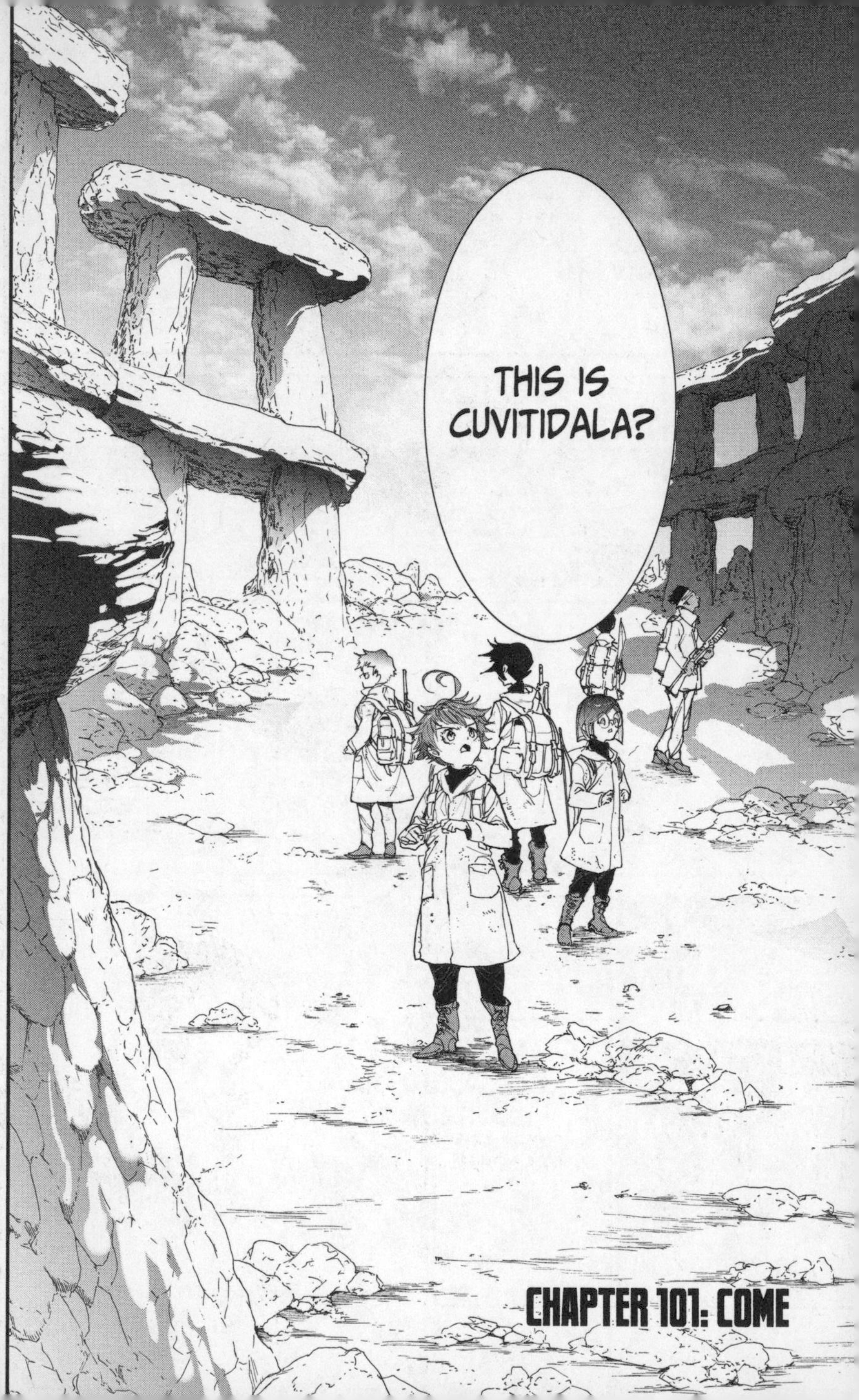
THIS IS CUVITIDALA?
CHAPTER 101: COME

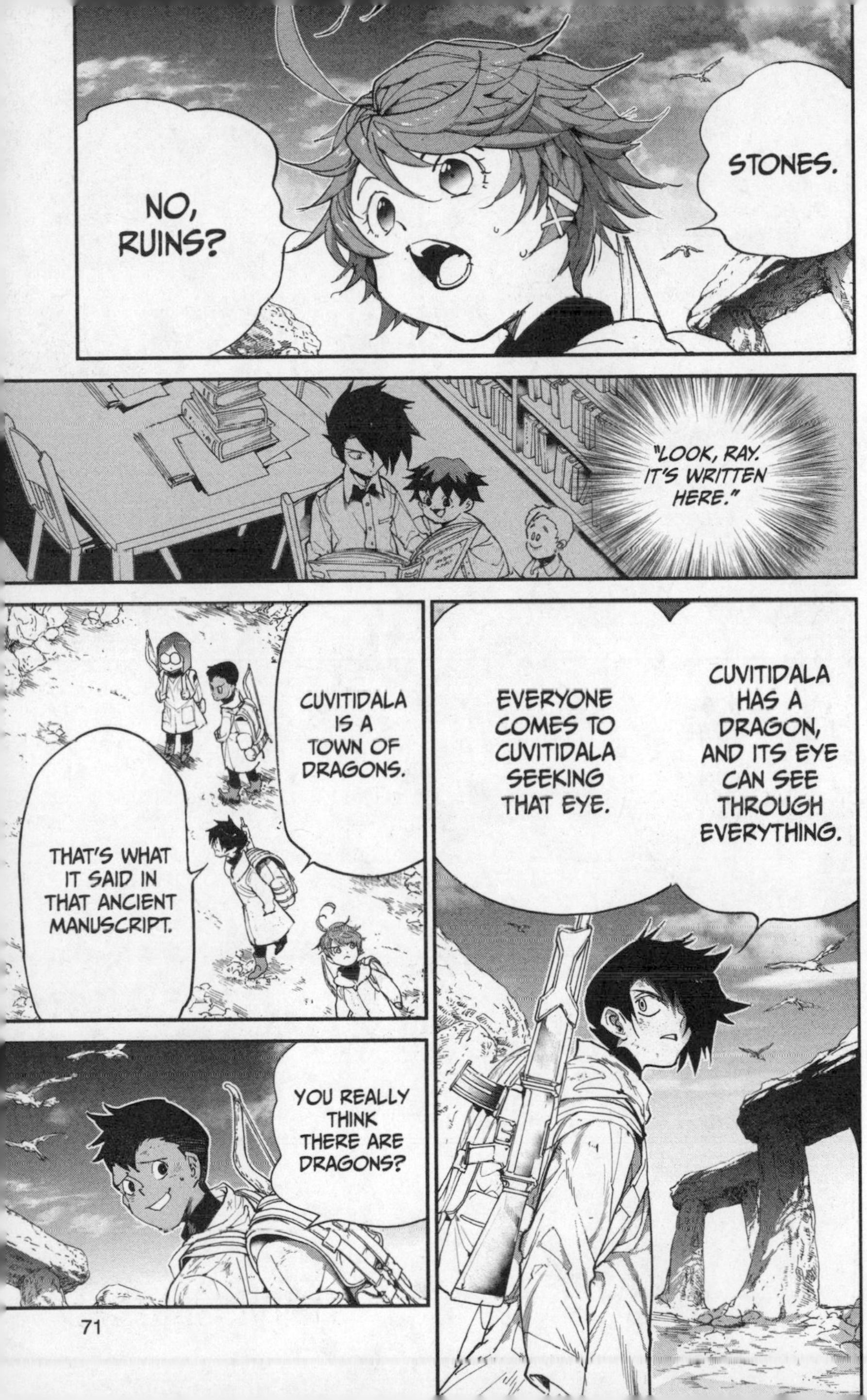
STONES.
NO, RUINS?
"LOOK, RAY. IT'S WRITTEN HERE."
CUVITIDALA HAS A DRAGON, AND ITS EYE CAN SEE THROUGH EVERYTHING.
EVERYONE COMES TO CUVITIDALA SEEKING THAT EYE.
CUVITIDALA IS A TOWN OF DRAGONS.
THAT'S WHAT IT SAID IN THAT ANCIENT MANUSCRIPT.
YOU REALLY THINK THERE ARE DRAGONS?

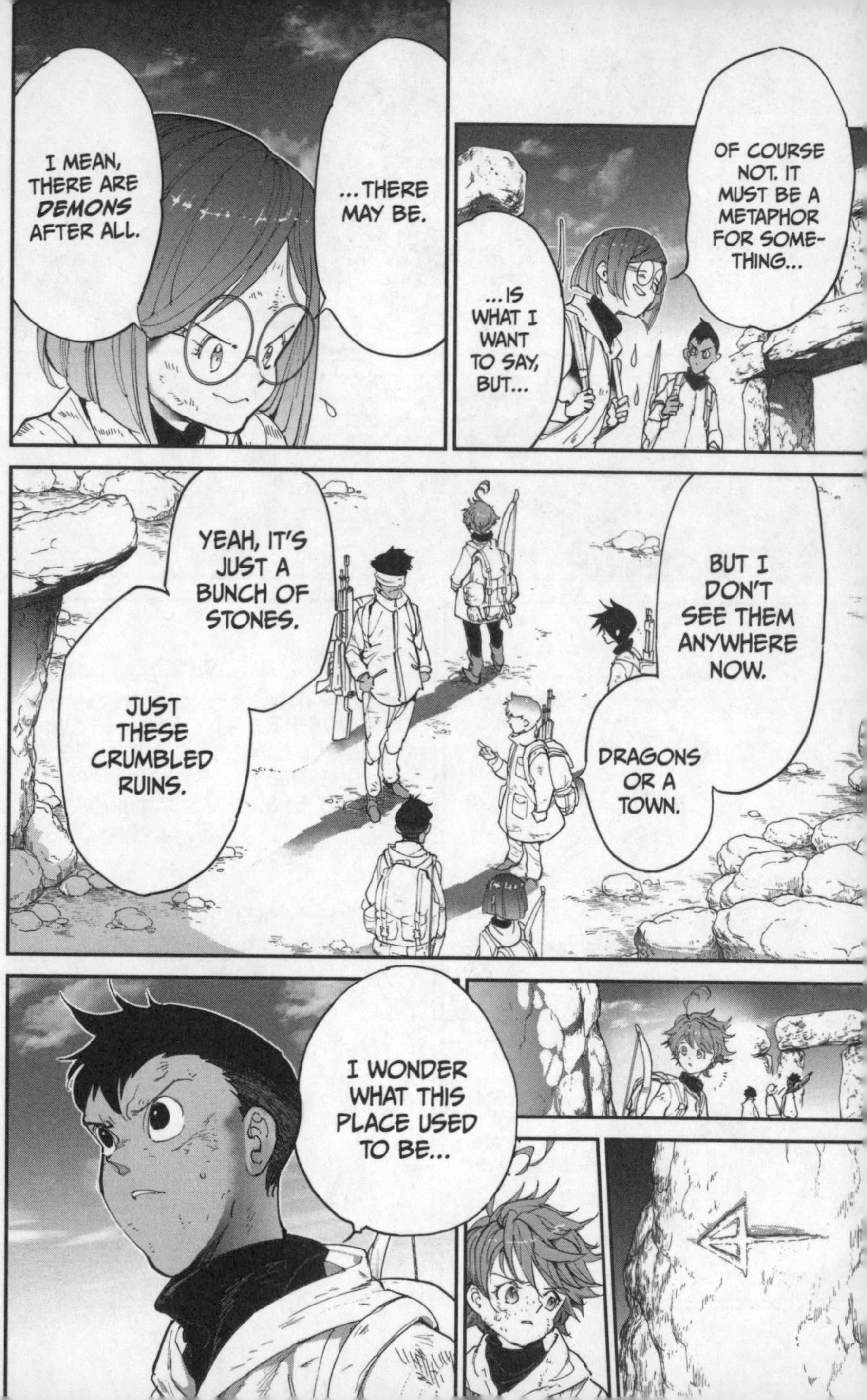
OF COURSE NOT. IT MUST BE A METAPHOR FOR SOME-THING...
...IS WHAT I WANT TO SAY, BUT...
...THERE MAY BE.
I MEAN, THERE ARE *DEMONS* AFTER ALL.
BUT I DON'T SEE THEM ANYWHERE NOW.
DRAGONS OR A TOWN.
YEAH, IT'S JUST A BUNCH OF STONES.
JUST THESE CRUMBLED RUINS.
I WONDER WHAT THIS PLACE USED TO BE...

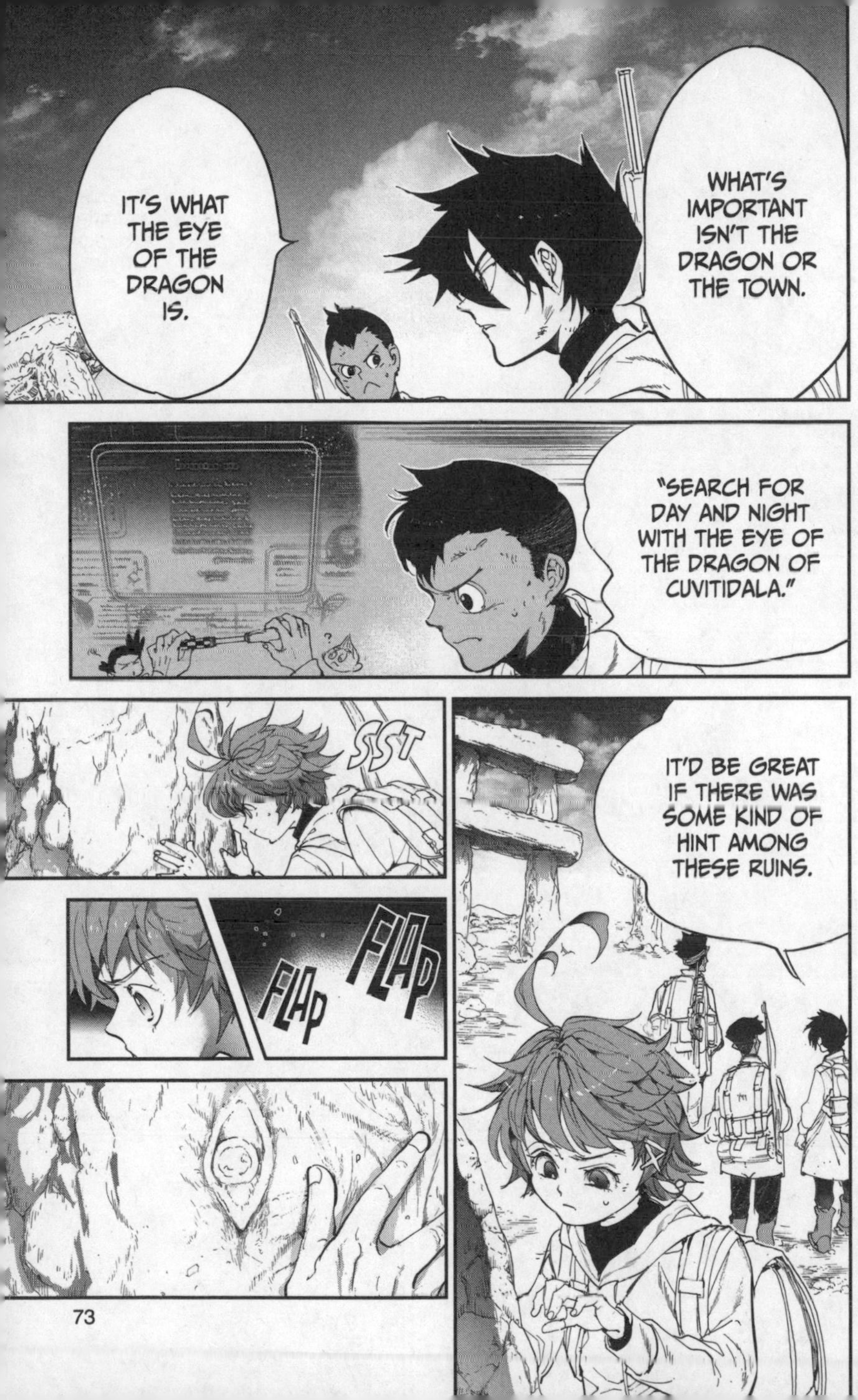
WHAT'S IMPORTANT ISN'T THE DRAGON OR THE TOWN.
IT'S WHAT THE EYE OF THE DRAGON IS.
"SEARCH FOR DAY AND NIGHT WITH THE EYE OF THE DRAGON OF CUVITIDALA."
IT'D BE GREAT IF THERE WAS SOME KIND OF HINT AMONG THESE RUINS.
SST
FLAP
FLAP

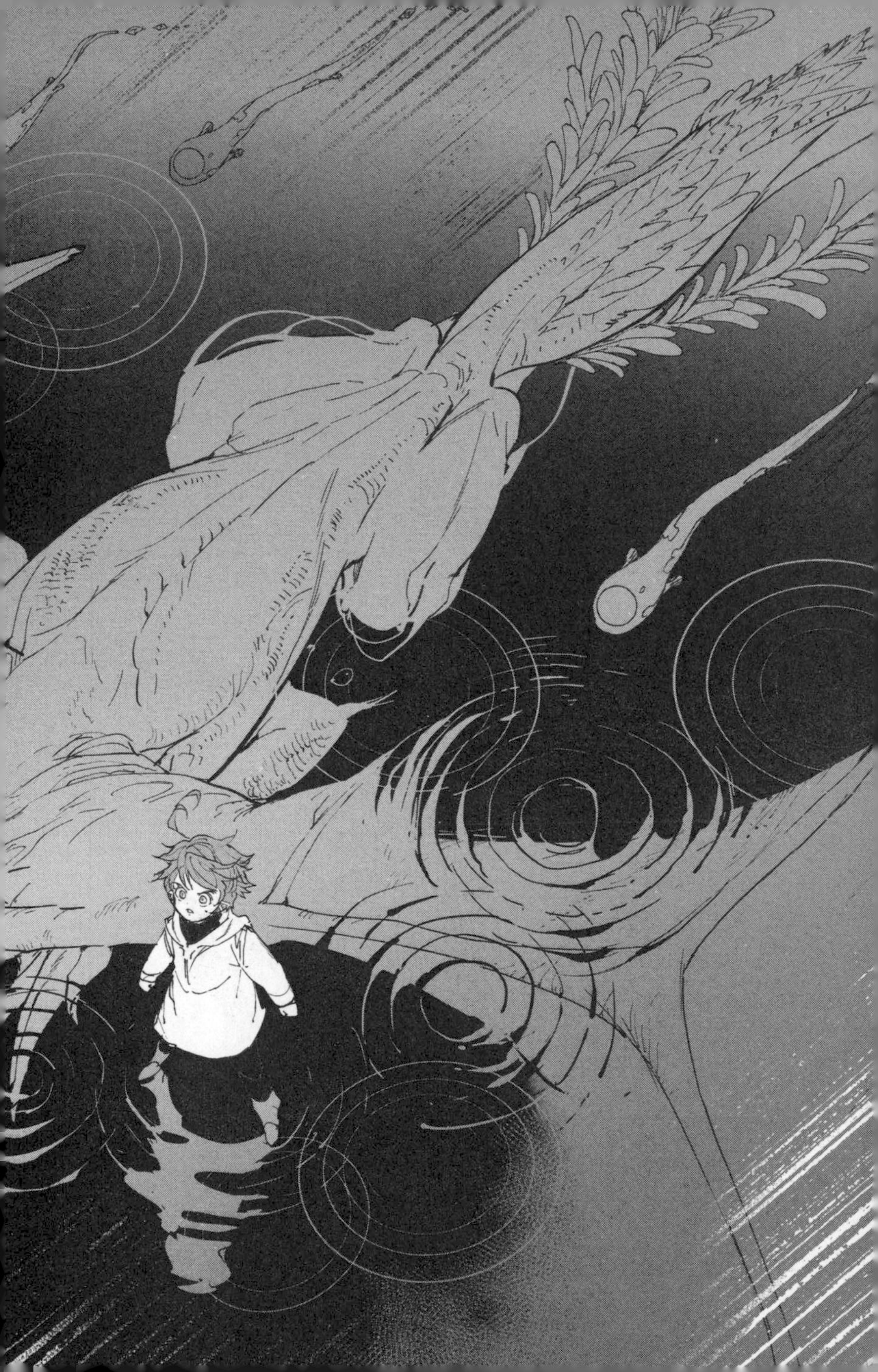

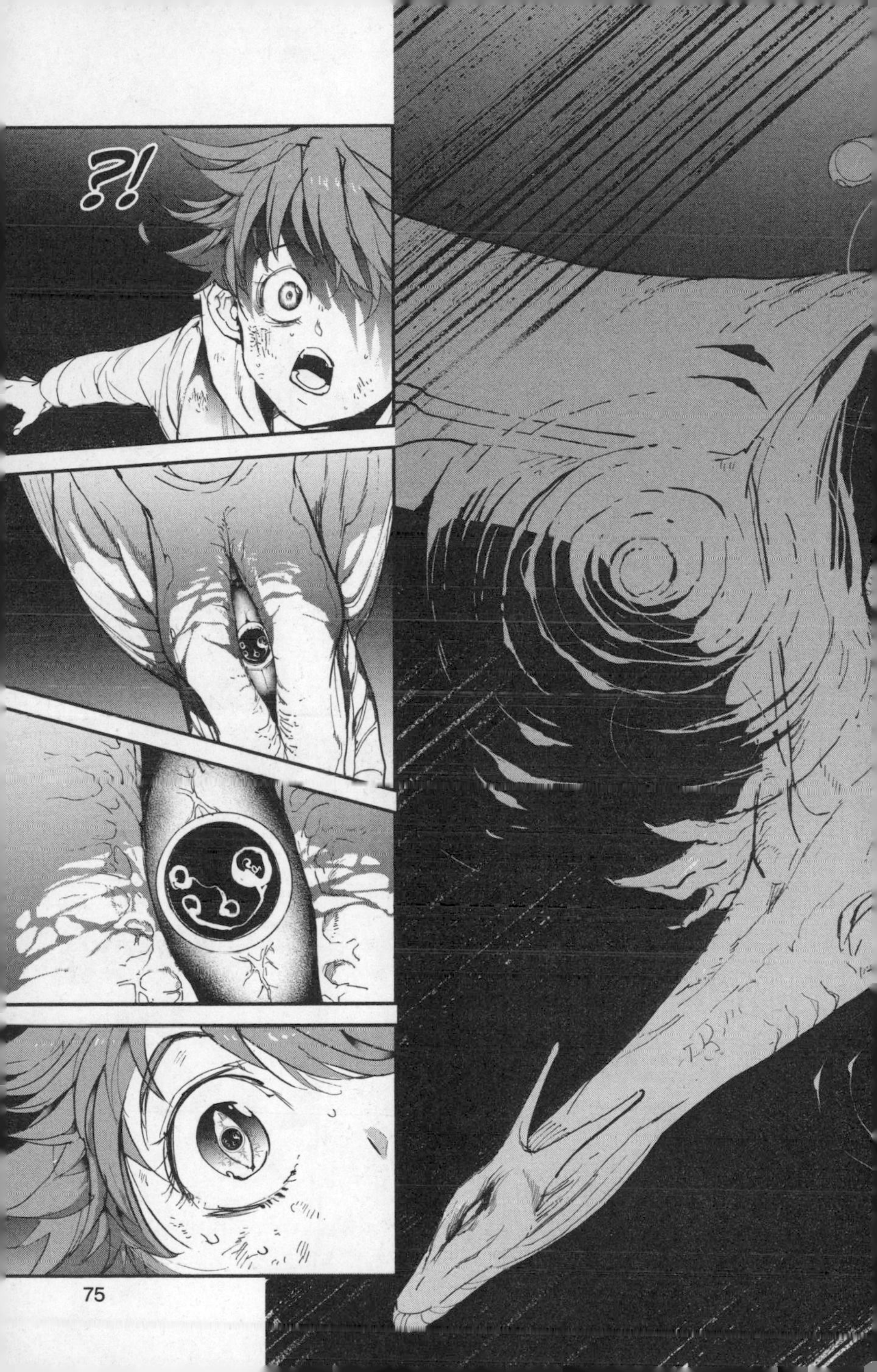
?!

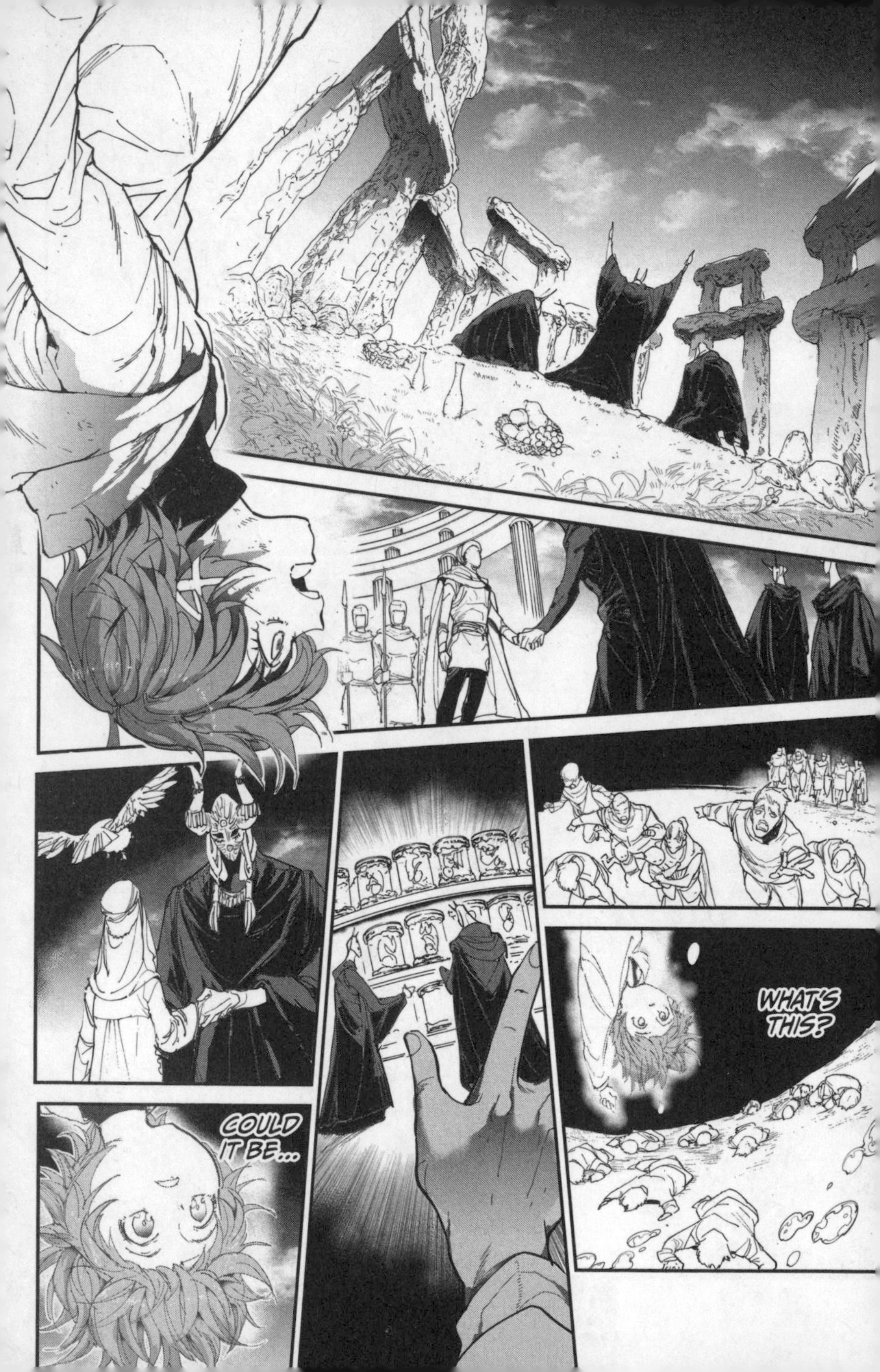
WHAT'S THIS?
COULD IT BE...

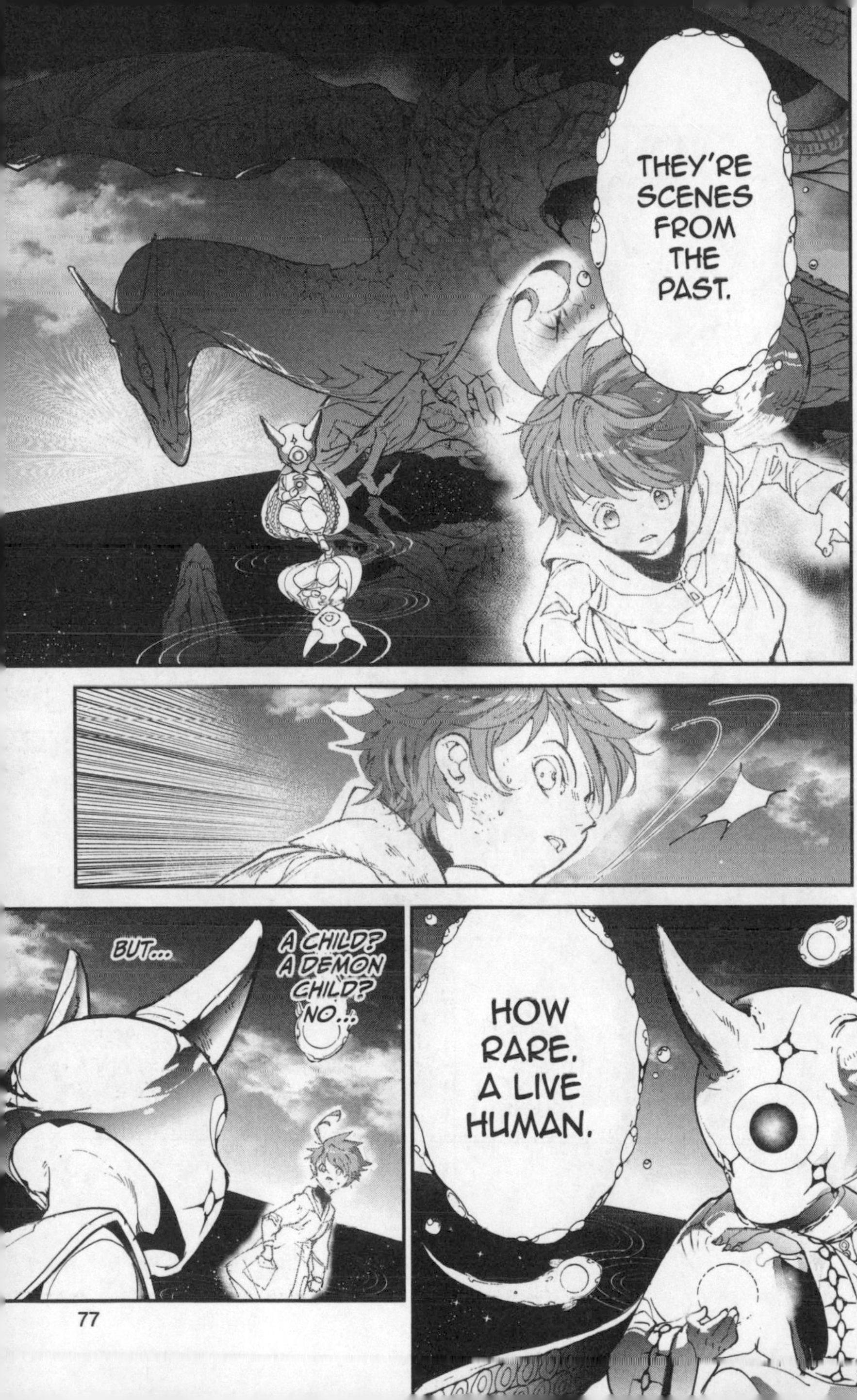
THEY'RE SCENES FROM THE PAST.
HOW RARE. A LIVE HUMAN.
A CHILD? A DEMON CHILD? NO...
BUT...

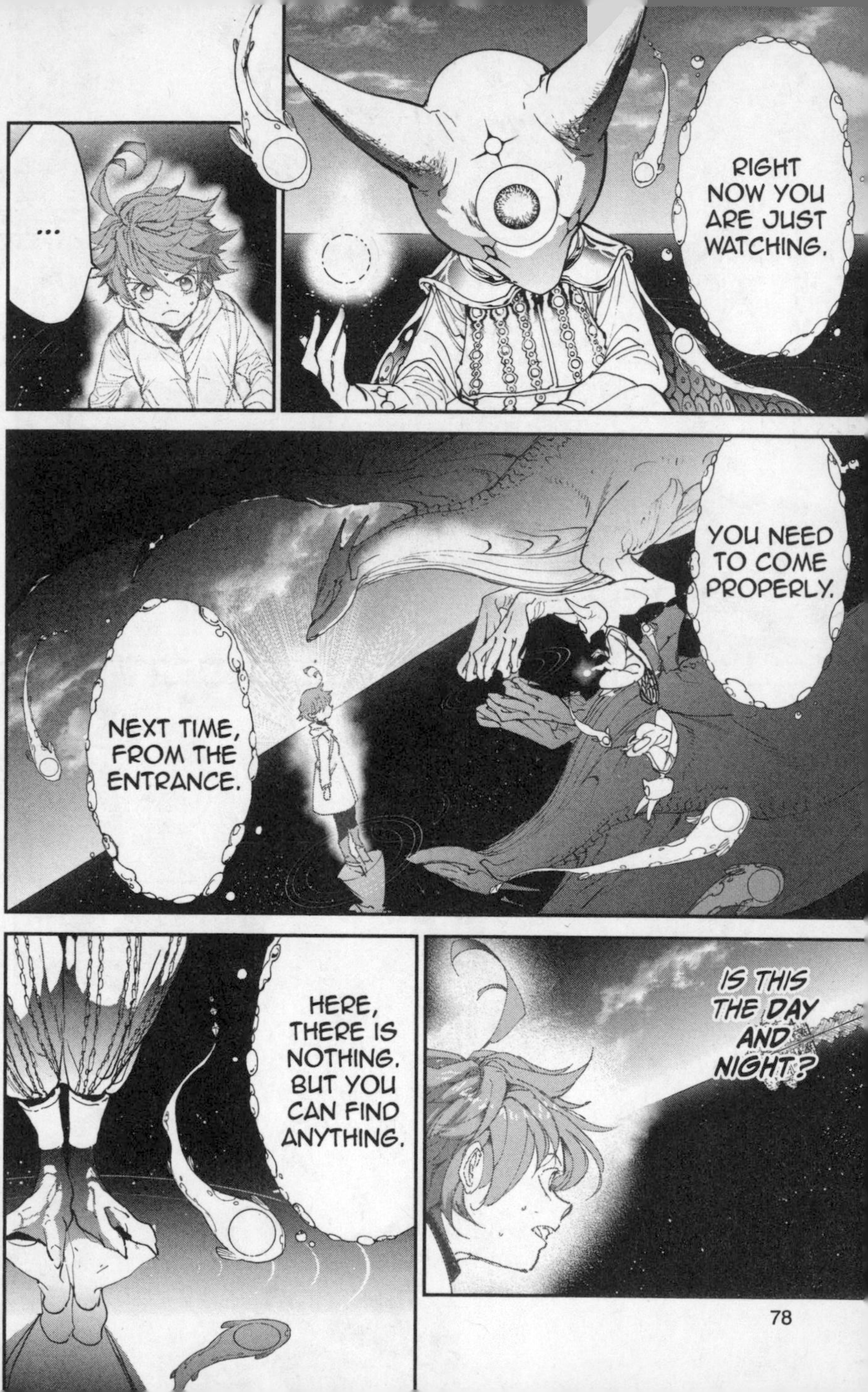
RIGHT NOW YOU ARE JUST WATCHING.
...
YOU NEED TO COME PROPERLY.
NEXT TIME, FROM THE ENTRANCE.
IS THIS THE DAY AND NIGHT?
HERE, THERE IS NOTHING. BUT YOU CAN FIND ANYTHING.

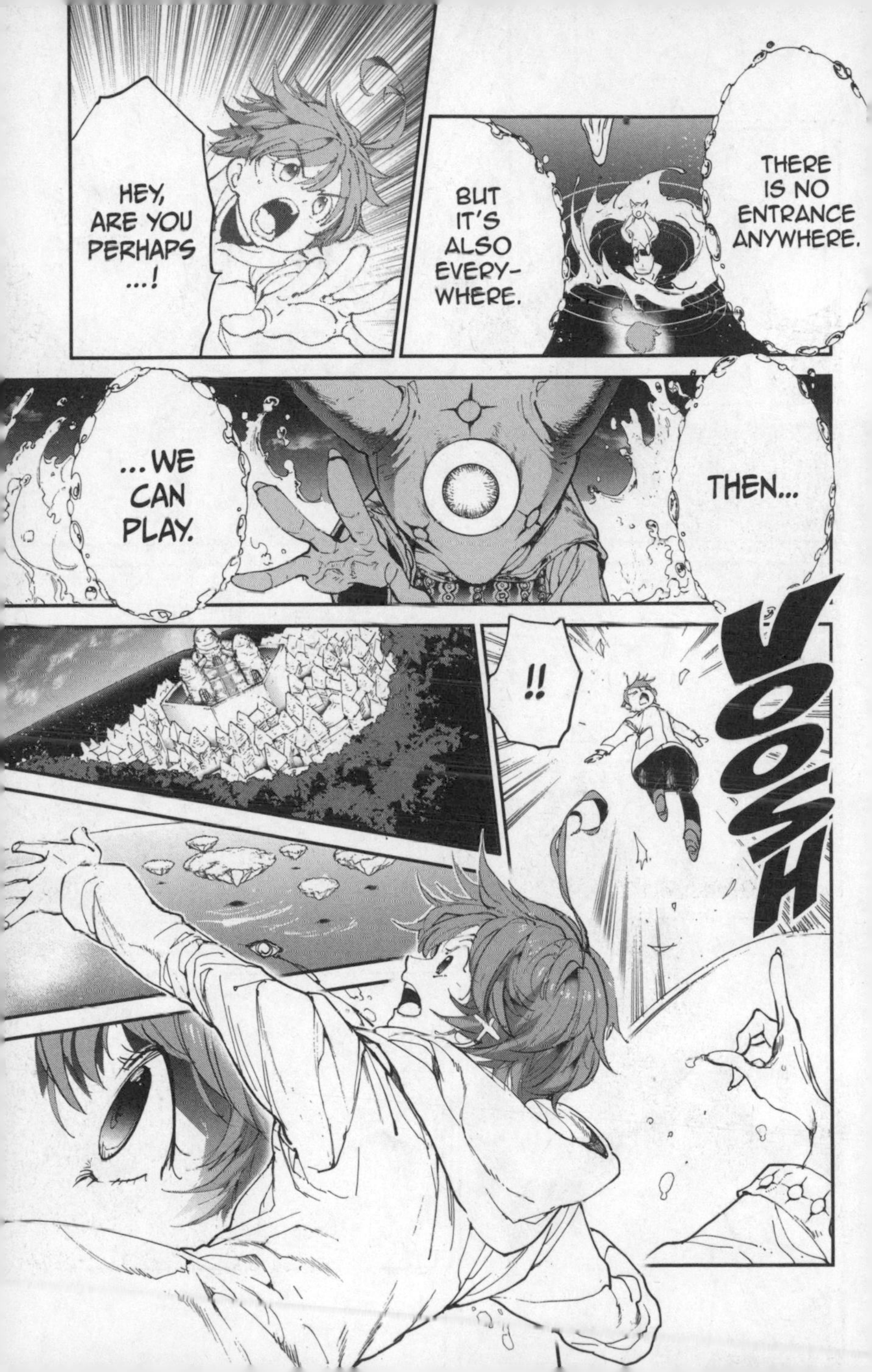
THERE IS NO ENTRANCE ANYWHERE.
BUT IT'S ALSO EVERY-WHERE.
HEY, ARE YOU PERHAPS ...!
THEN...
...WE CAN PLAY.
VOOSH
!!

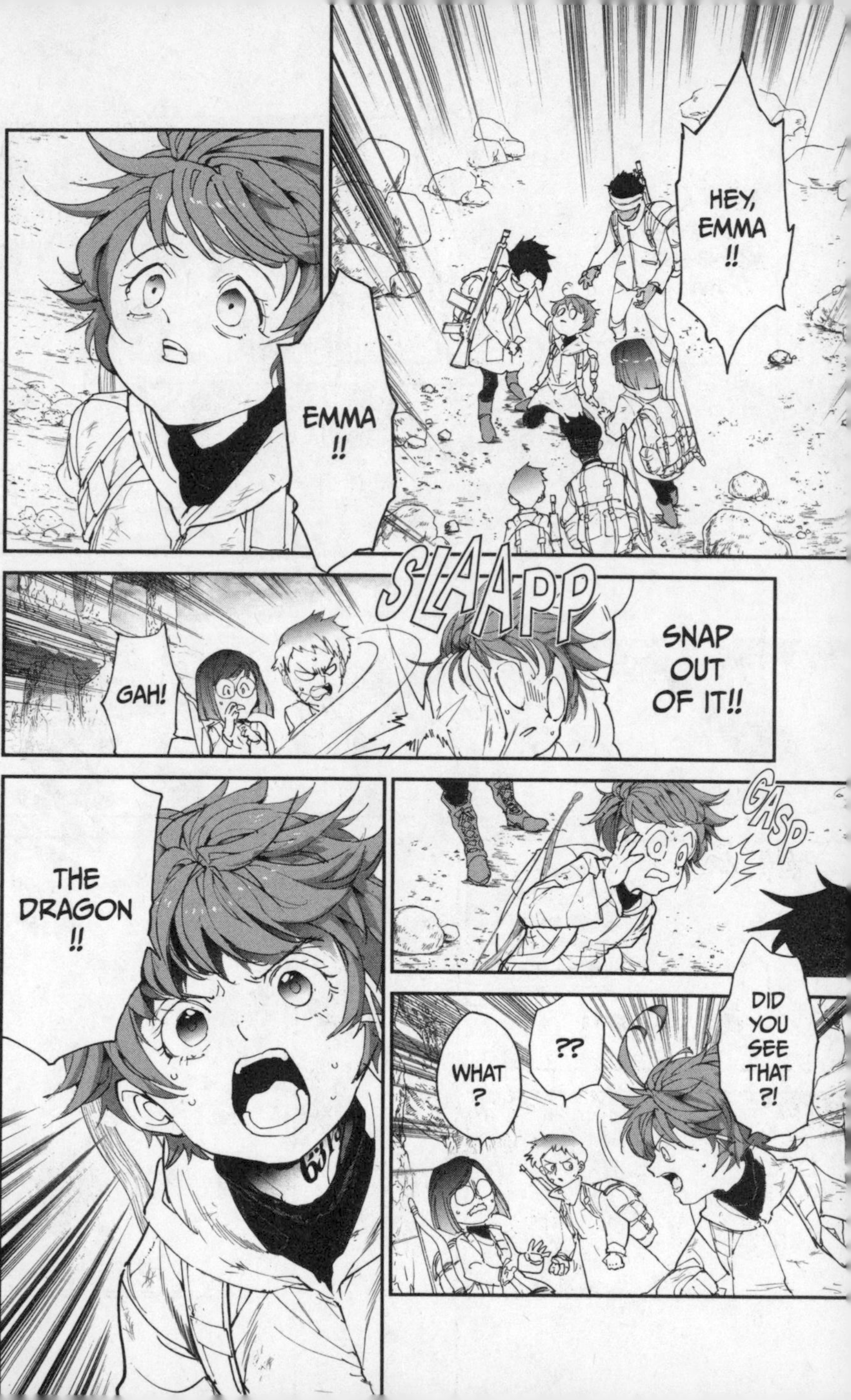
HEY, EMMA !!
EMMA !!
SLAAPP
SNAP OUT OF IT!!
GAH!
GASP
DID YOU SEE THAT ?!
??
WHAT ?
THE DRAGON !!

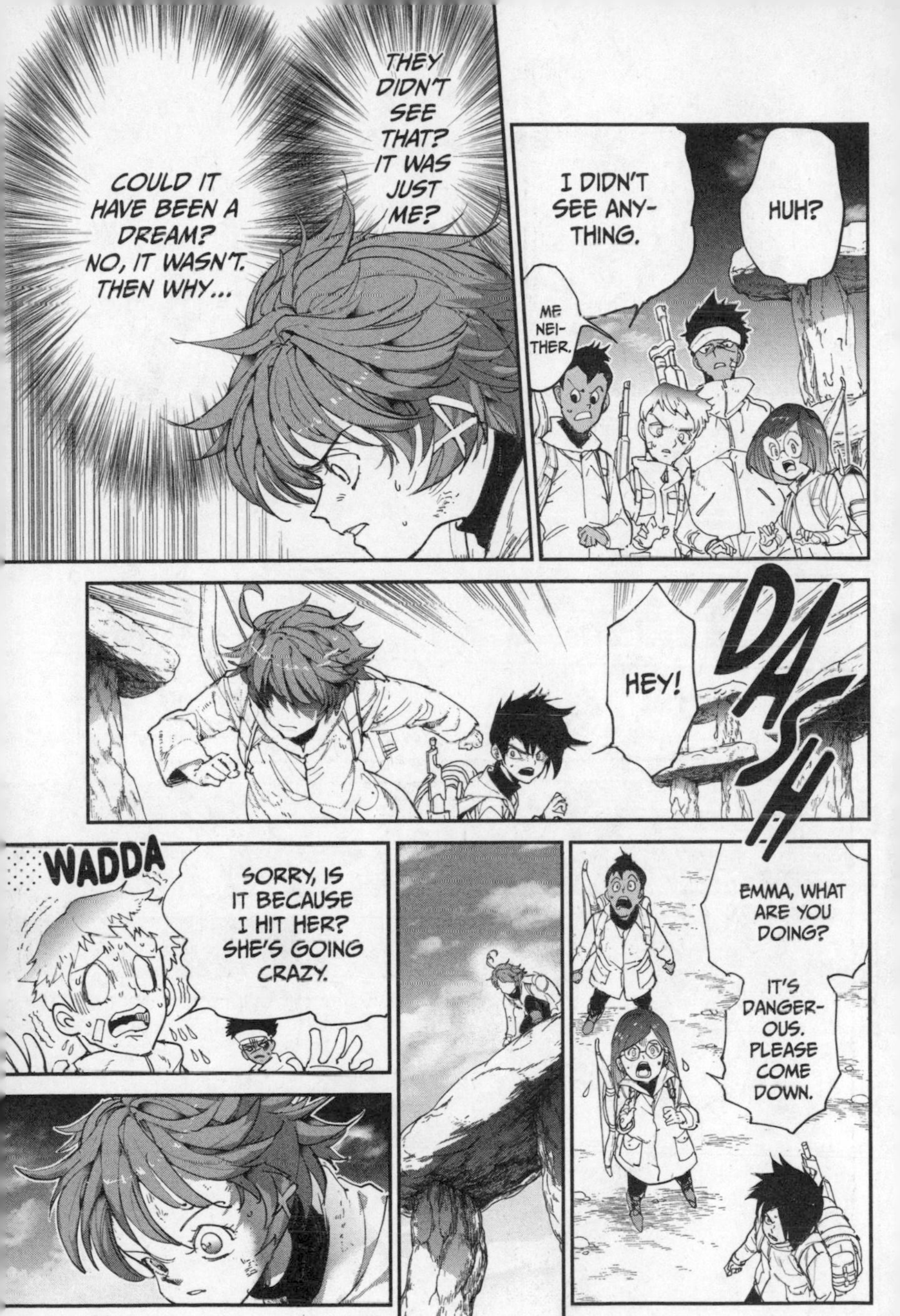
HUH?
I DIDN'T SEE ANY-THING.
ME NEI-THER.
THEY DIDN'T SEE THAT? IT WAS JUST ME?
COULD IT HAVE BEEN A DREAM? NO, IT WASN'T. THEN WHY...
DASH
HEY!
EMMA, WHAT ARE YOU DOING?
IT'S DANGER-OUS. PLEASE COME DOWN.
WADDA
SORRY, IS IT BECAUSE I HIT HER? SHE'S GOING CRAZY.

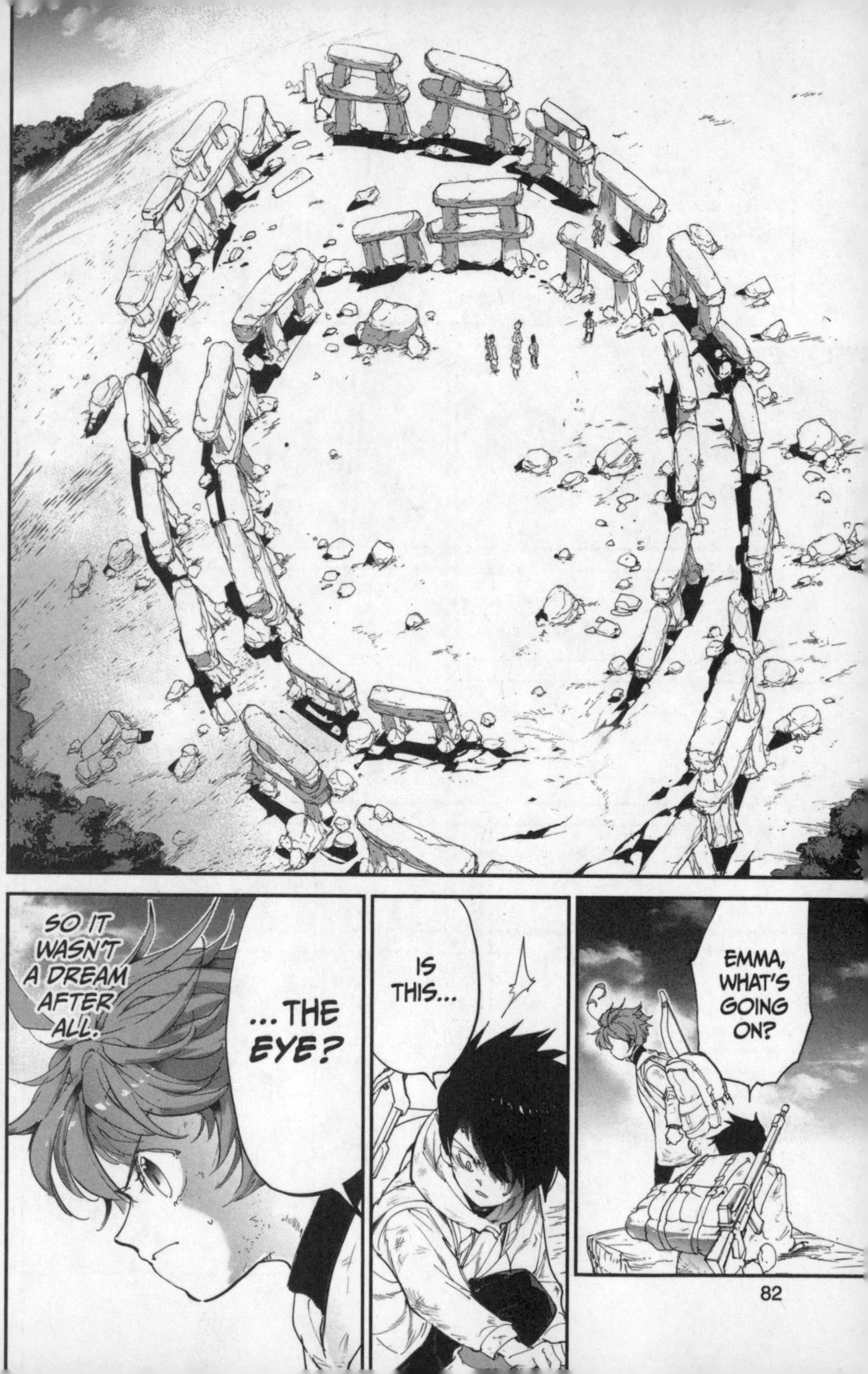
EMMA, WHAT'S GOING ON?
IS THIS...
...THE EYE?
SO IT WASN'T A DREAM AFTER ALL.

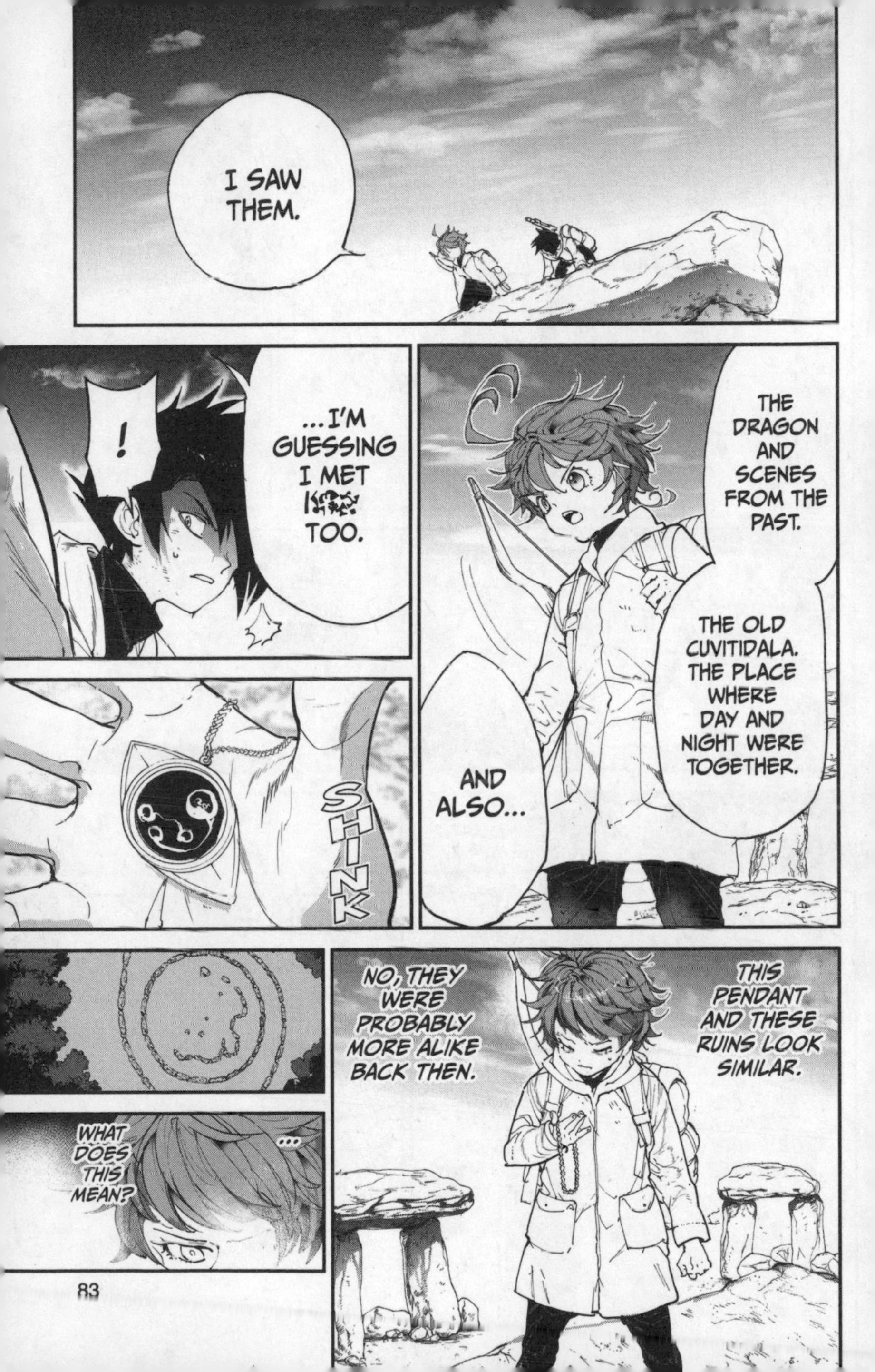
I SAW THEM.
THE DRAGON AND SCENES FROM THE PAST.
THE OLD CUVITIDALA. THE PLACE WHERE DAY AND NIGHT WERE TOGETHER.
AND ALSO...
...I'M GUESSING I MET TOO.
!
SHINK
THIS PENDANT AND THESE RUINS LOOK SIMILAR.
NO, THEY WERE PROBABLY MORE ALIKE BACK THEN.
...
WHAT DOES THIS MEAN?

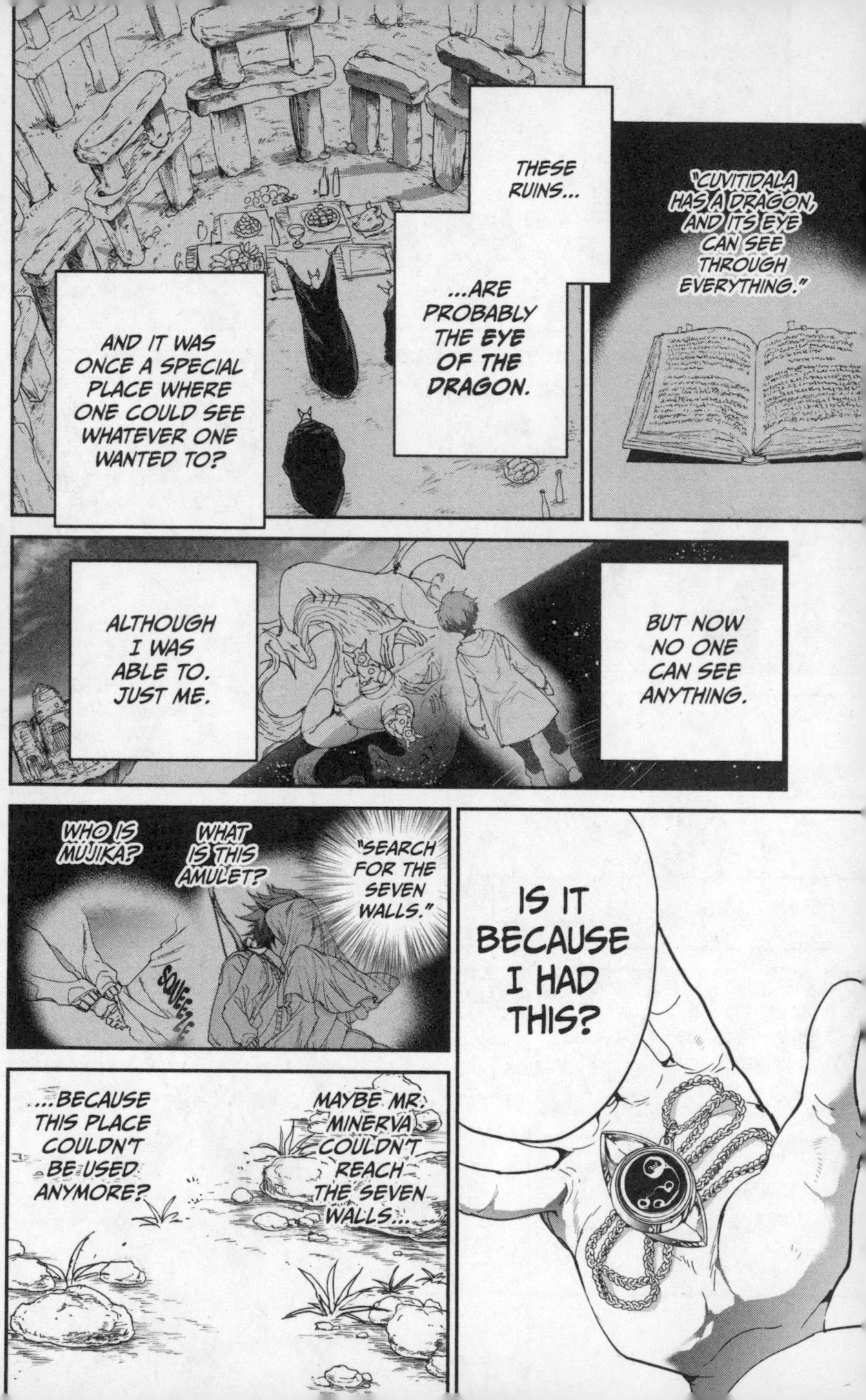
"CUVITIDALA HAS A DRAGON, AND ITS EYE CAN SEE THROUGH EVERYTHING."
THESE RUINS...
...ARE PROBABLY THE EYE OF THE DRAGON.
AND IT WAS ONCE A SPECIAL PLACE WHERE ONE COULD SEE WHATEVER ONE WANTED TO?
BUT NOW NO ONE CAN SEE ANYTHING.
ALTHOUGH I WAS ABLE TO. JUST ME.
IS IT BECAUSE I HAD THIS?
"SEARCH FOR THE SEVEN WALLS."
WHAT IS THIS AMULET?
WHO IS MUJIKA?
SQUEEZE
MAYBE MR. MINERVA COULDN'T REACH THE SEVEN WALLS...
...BECAUSE THIS PLACE COULDN'T BE USED ANYMORE?

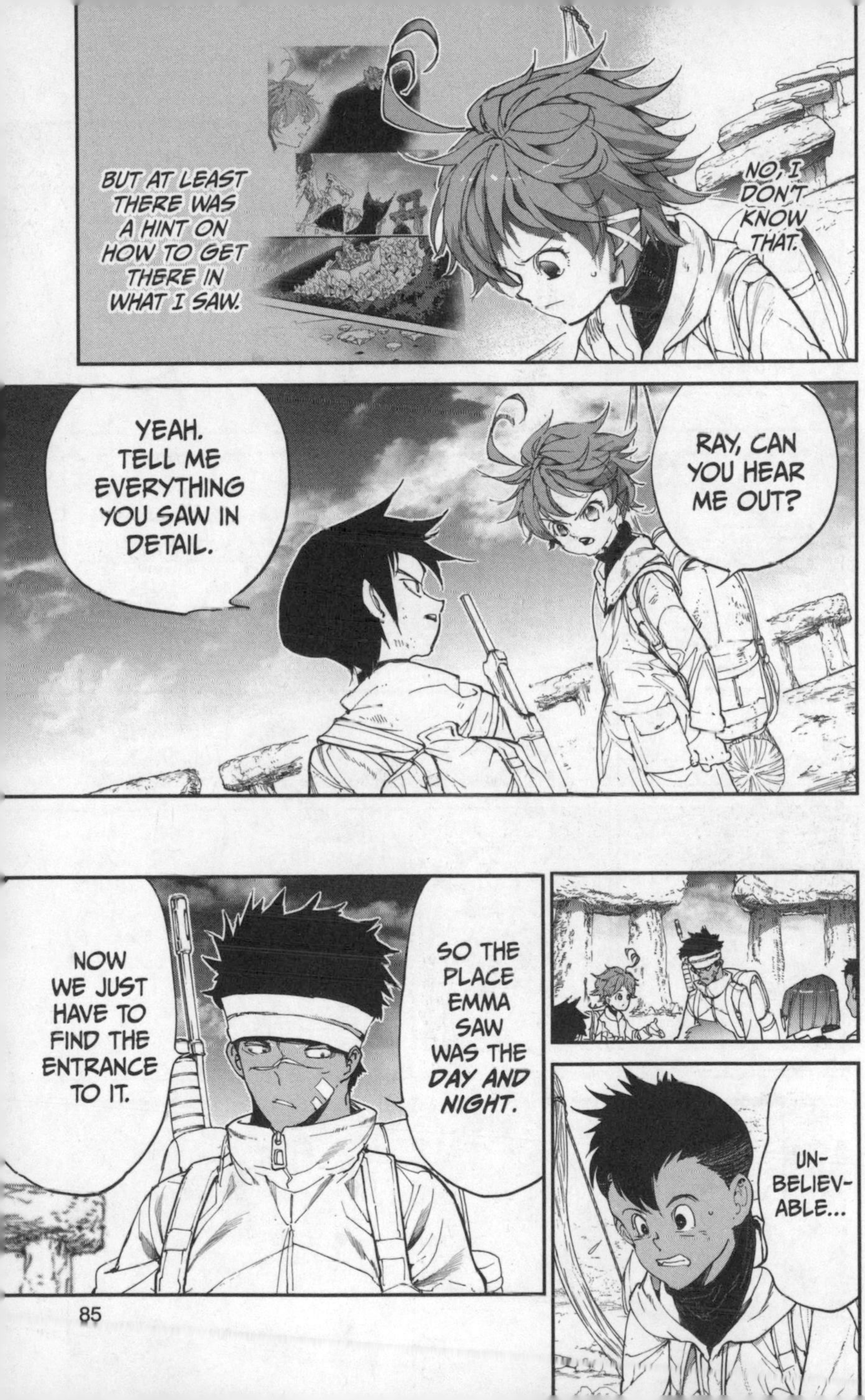
NO, I DON'T KNOW THAT.
BUT AT LEAST THERE WAS A HINT ON HOW TO GET THERE IN WHAT I SAW.
RAY, CAN YOU HEAR ME OUT?
YEAH. TELL ME EVERYTHING YOU SAW IN DETAIL.
UN-BELIEVABLE...
SO THE PLACE EMMA SAW WAS THE *DAY AND NIGHT*.
NOW WE JUST HAVE TO FIND THE ENTRANCE TO IT.

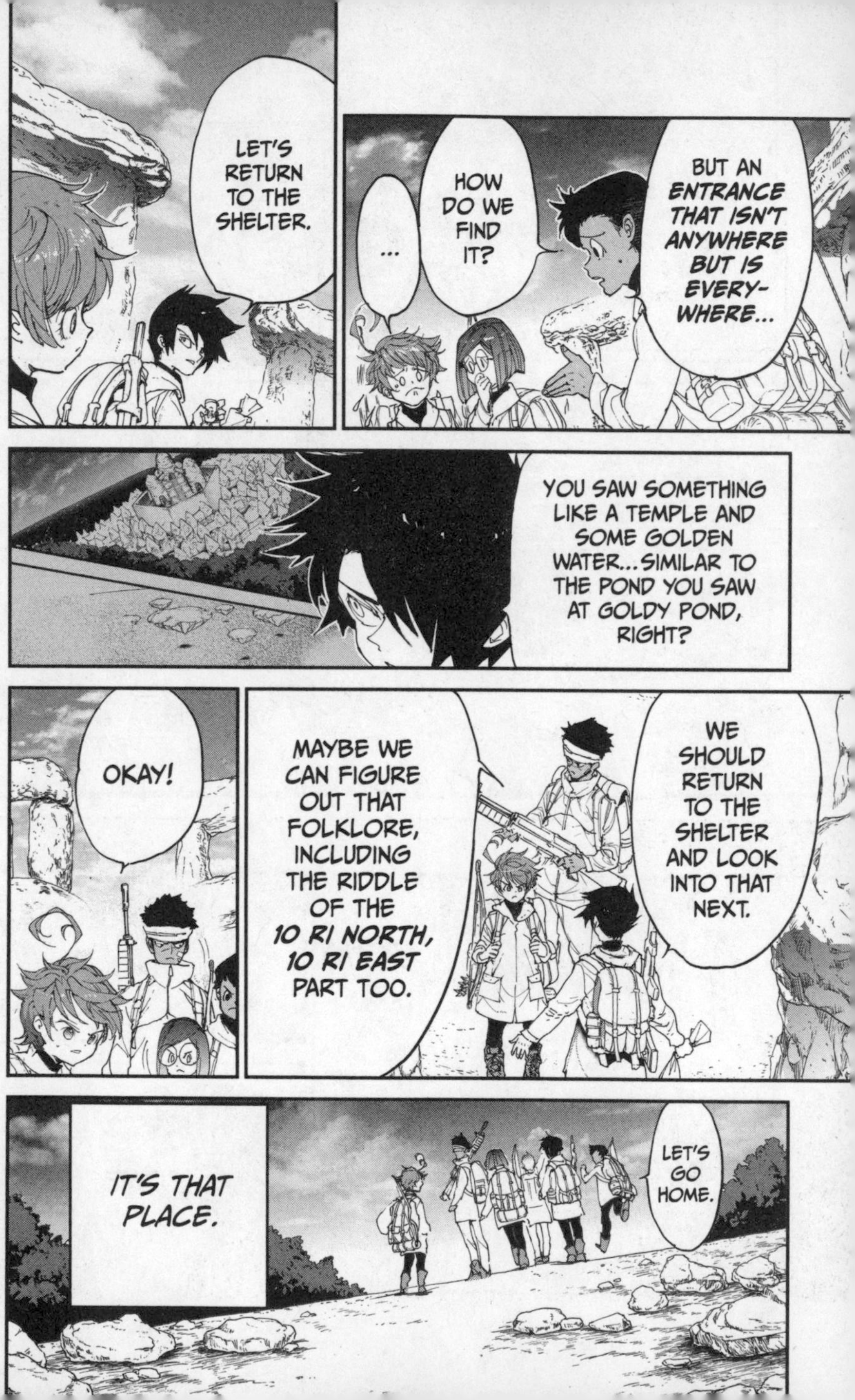
BUT AN ENTRANCE THAT ISN'T ANYWHERE BUT IS EVERYWHERE...
HOW DO WE FIND IT?
...
LET'S RETURN TO THE SHELTER.
YOU SAW SOMETHING LIKE A TEMPLE AND SOME GOLDEN WATER...SIMILAR TO THE POND YOU SAW AT GOLDY POND, RIGHT?
WE SHOULD RETURN TO THE SHELTER AND LOOK INTO THAT NEXT.
MAYBE WE CAN FIGURE OUT THAT FOLKLORE, INCLUDING THE RIDDLE OF THE 10 RI NORTH, 10 RI EAST PART TOO.
OKAY!
LET'S GO HOME.
IT'S THAT PLACE.

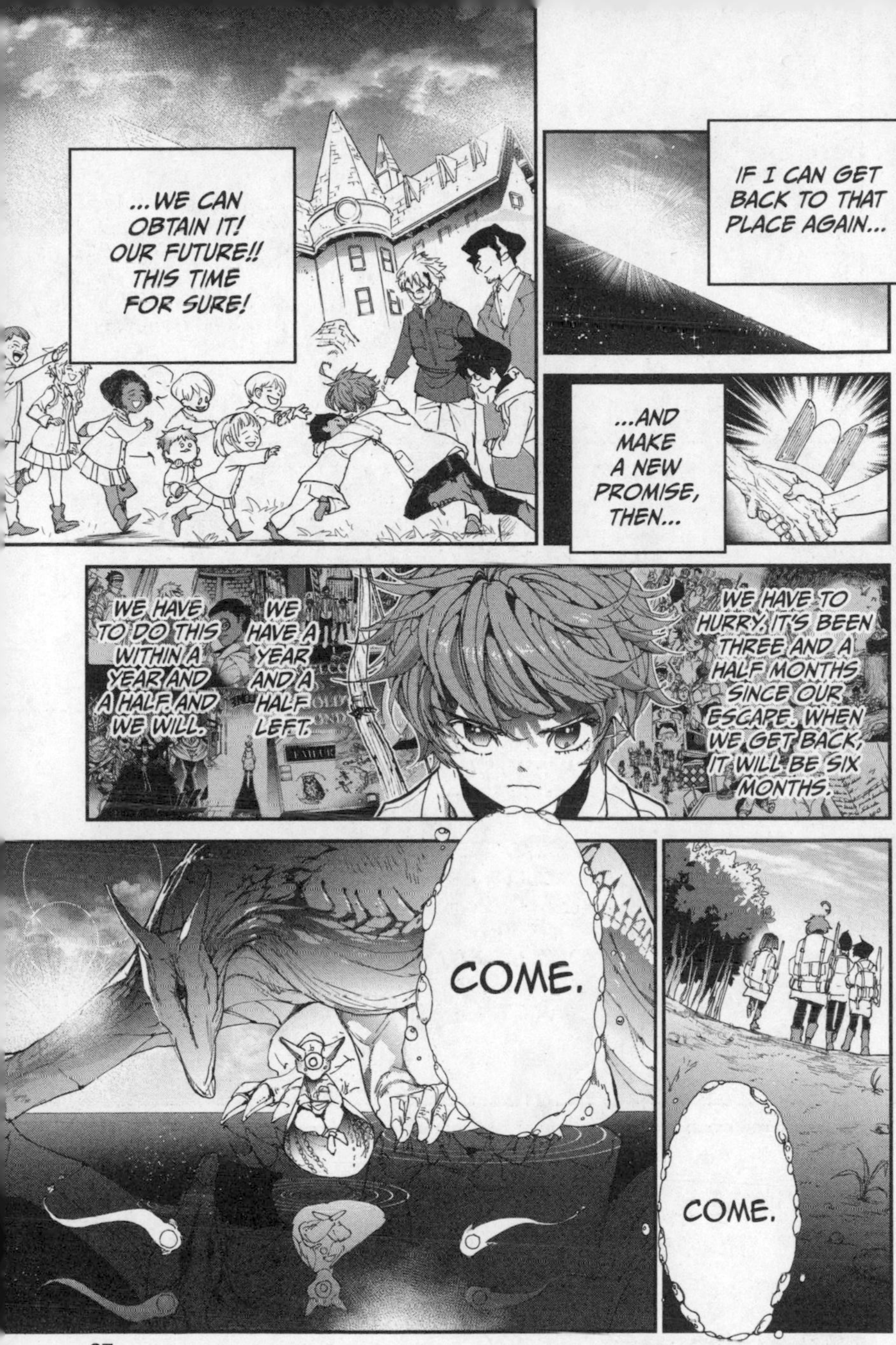
IF I CAN GET BACK TO THAT PLACE AGAIN...
...AND MAKE A NEW PROMISE, THEN...
...WE CAN OBTAIN IT! OUR FUTURE!! THIS TIME FOR SURE!
WE HAVE TO HURRY. IT'S BEEN THREE AND A HALF MONTHS SINCE OUR ESCAPE. WHEN WE GET BACK, IT WILL BE SIX MONTHS.
WE HAVE A YEAR AND A HALF LEFT.
WE HAVE TO DO THIS WITHIN A YEAR AND A HALF AND WE WILL.
COME.
COME.

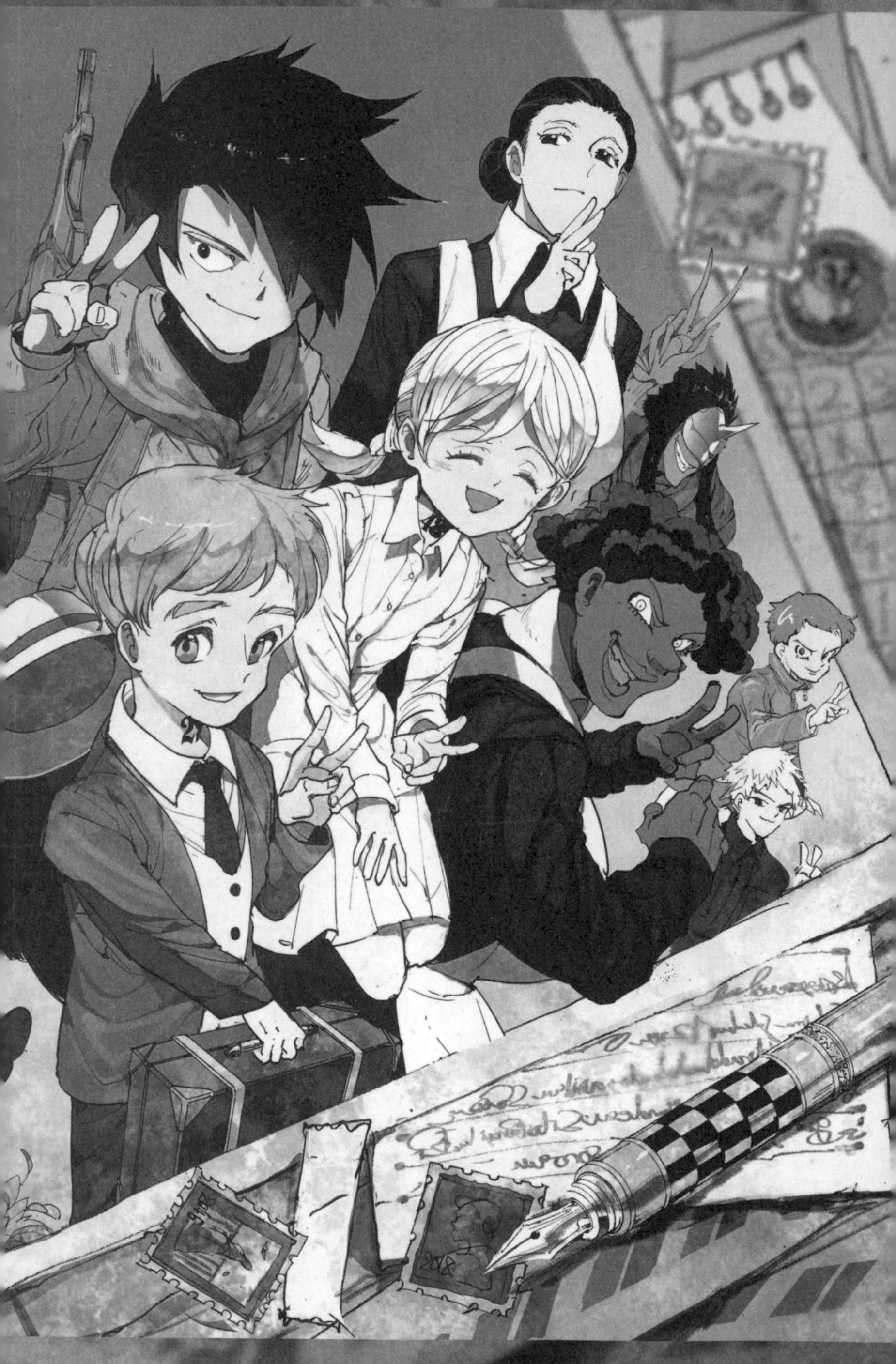

CHAPTER 102: FOUND IT

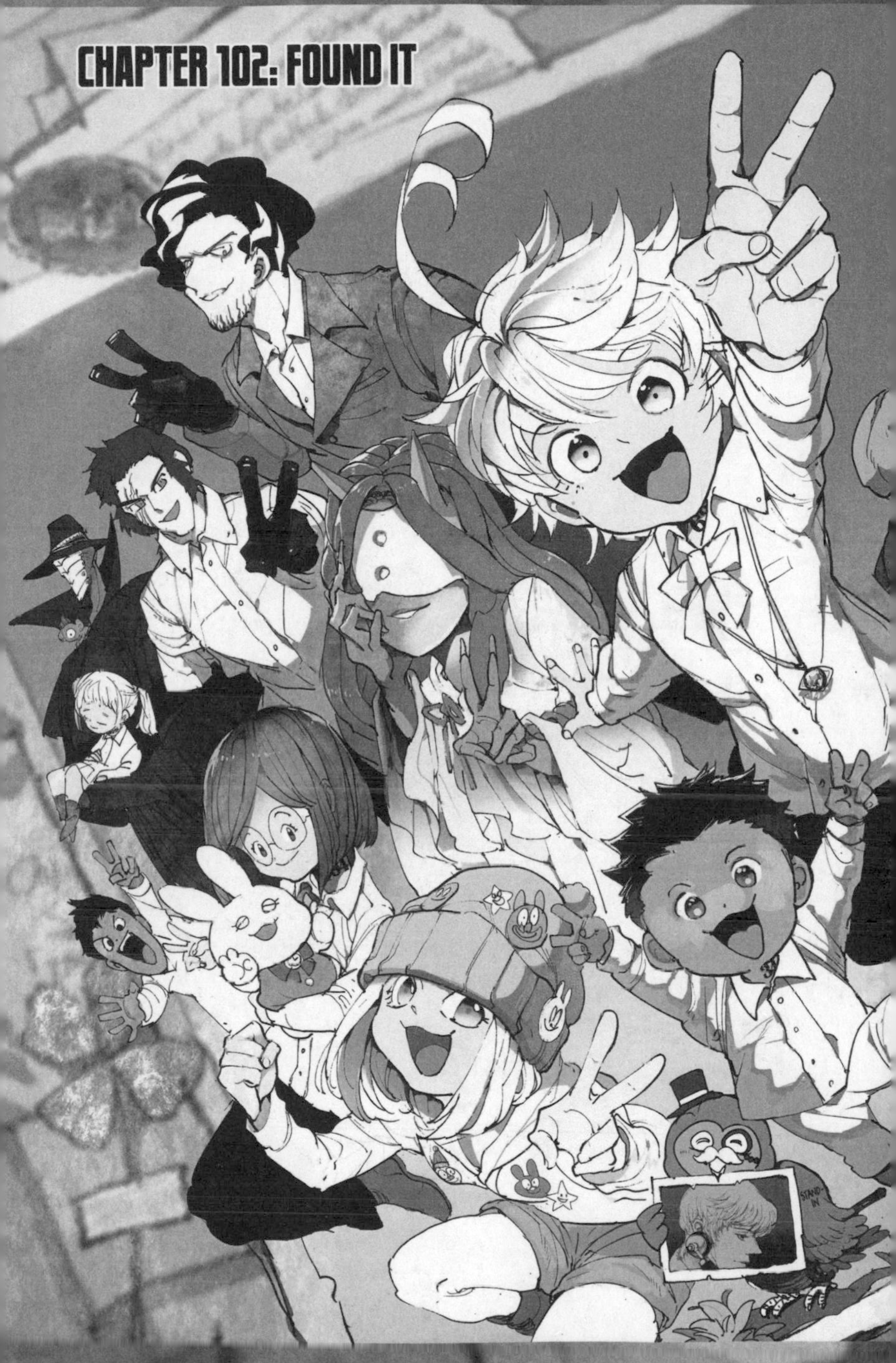
STAND-IN

THE PROMISED NEVERLAND SIDE SCENE 018

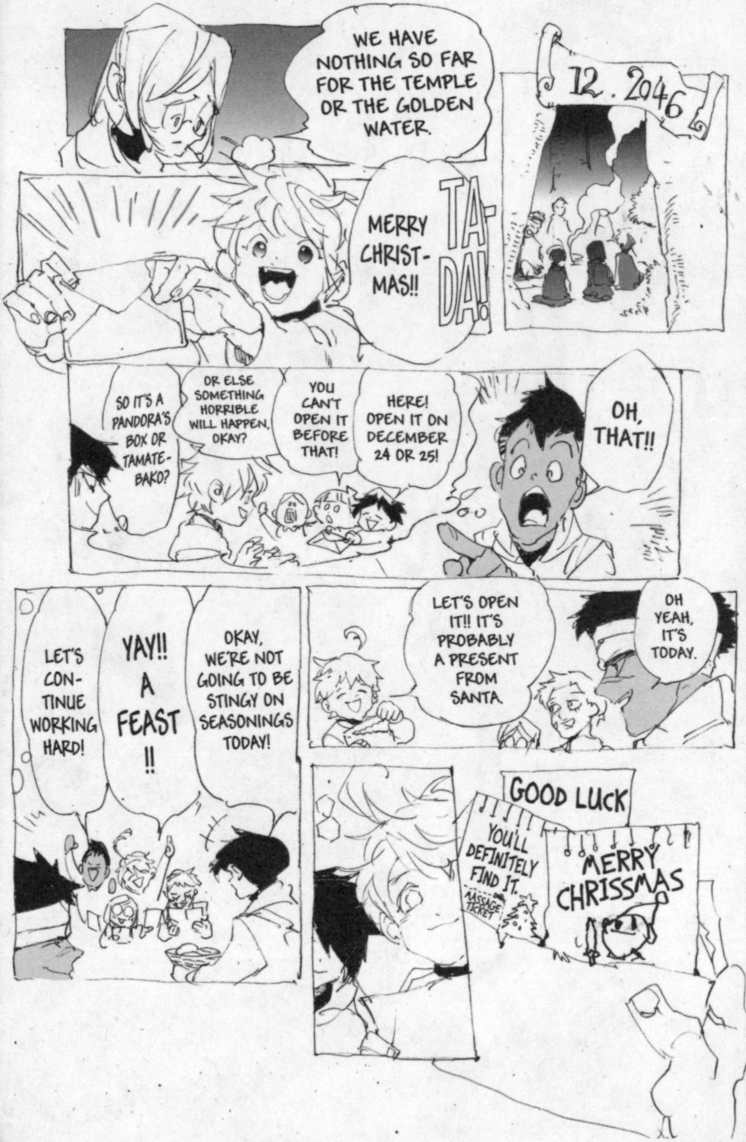
12.2046
WE HAVE NOTHING SO FAR FOR THE TEMPLE OR THE GOLDEN WATER.
TA-DA!
MERRY CHRIST-MAS!!
OH, THAT!!
HERE! OPEN IT ON DECEMBER 24 OR 25!
YOU CAN'T OPEN IT BEFORE THAT!
OR ELSE SOMETHING HORRIBLE WILL HAPPEN, OKAY?
SO IT'S A PANDORA'S BOX OR TAMATE-BAKO?
OH YEAH, IT'S TODAY.
LET'S OPEN IT!! IT'S PROBABLY A PRESENT FROM SANTA.
GOOD LUCK
YOU'LL DEFINITELY FIND IT.
MASSAGE TICKET
MERRY CHRISSMAS
OKAY, WE'RE NOT GOING TO BE STINGY ON SEASONINGS TODAY!
YAY!! A FEAST!!
LET'S CON-TINUE WORKING HARD!

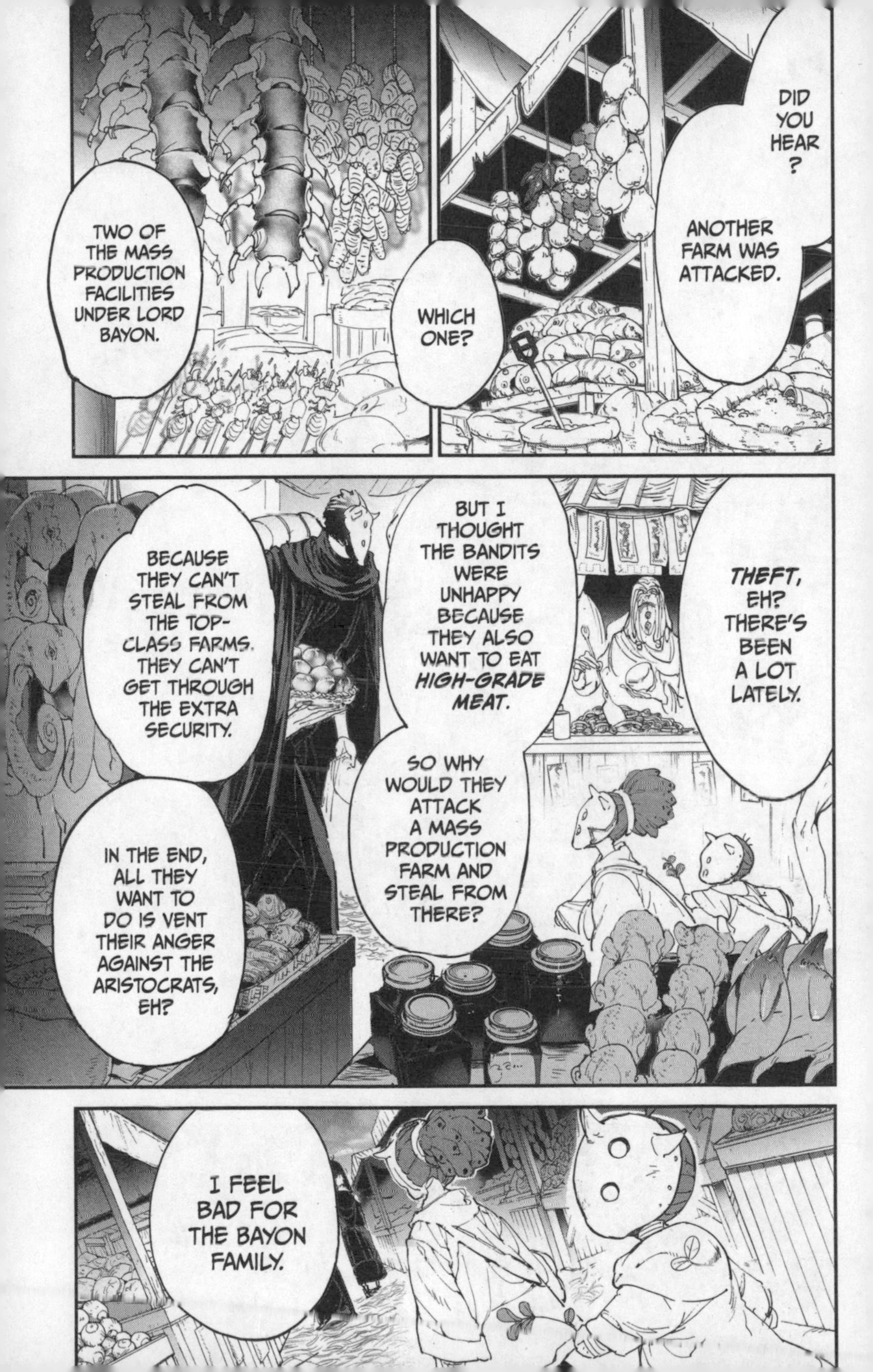

DID YOU HEAR?
ANOTHER FARM WAS ATTACKED.
WHICH ONE?
TWO OF THE MASS PRODUCTION FACILITIES UNDER LORD BAYON.
THEFT, EH? THERE'S BEEN A LOT LATELY.
BUT I THOUGHT THE BANDITS WERE UNHAPPY BECAUSE THEY ALSO WANT TO EAT *HIGH-GRADE MEAT*.
SO WHY WOULD THEY ATTACK A MASS PRODUCTION FARM AND STEAL FROM THERE?
BECAUSE THEY CAN'T STEAL FROM THE TOP-CLASS FARMS. THEY CAN'T GET THROUGH THE EXTRA SECURITY.
IN THE END, ALL THEY WANT TO DO IS VENT THEIR ANGER AGAINST THE ARISTOCRATS, EH?
I FEEL BAD FOR THE BAYON FAMILY.

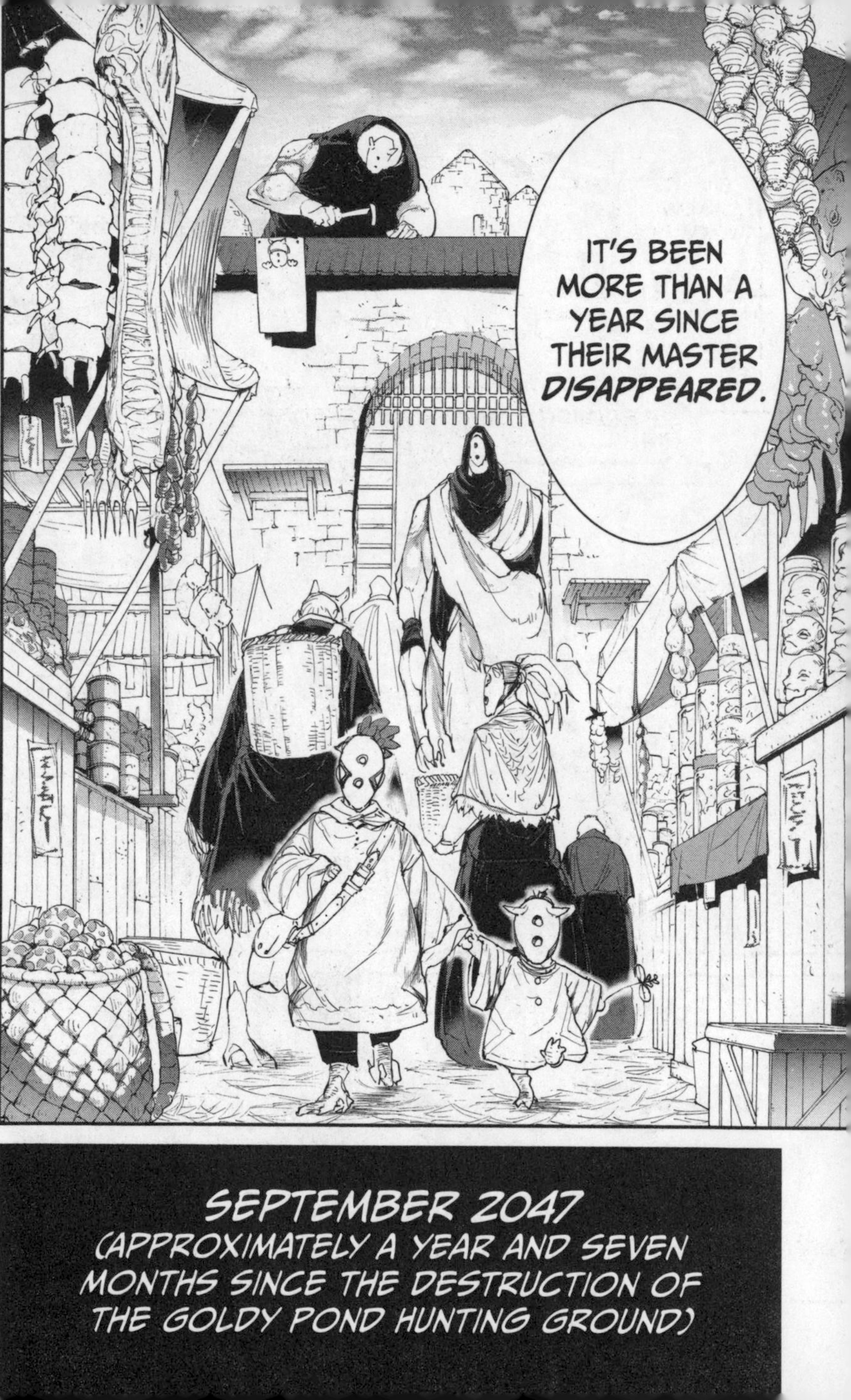
IT'S BEEN MORE THAN A YEAR SINCE THEIR MASTER DISAPPEARED.
SEPTEMBER 2047
(APPROXIMATELY A YEAR AND SEVEN MONTHS SINCE THE DESTRUCTION OF THE GOLDY POND HUNTING GROUND)

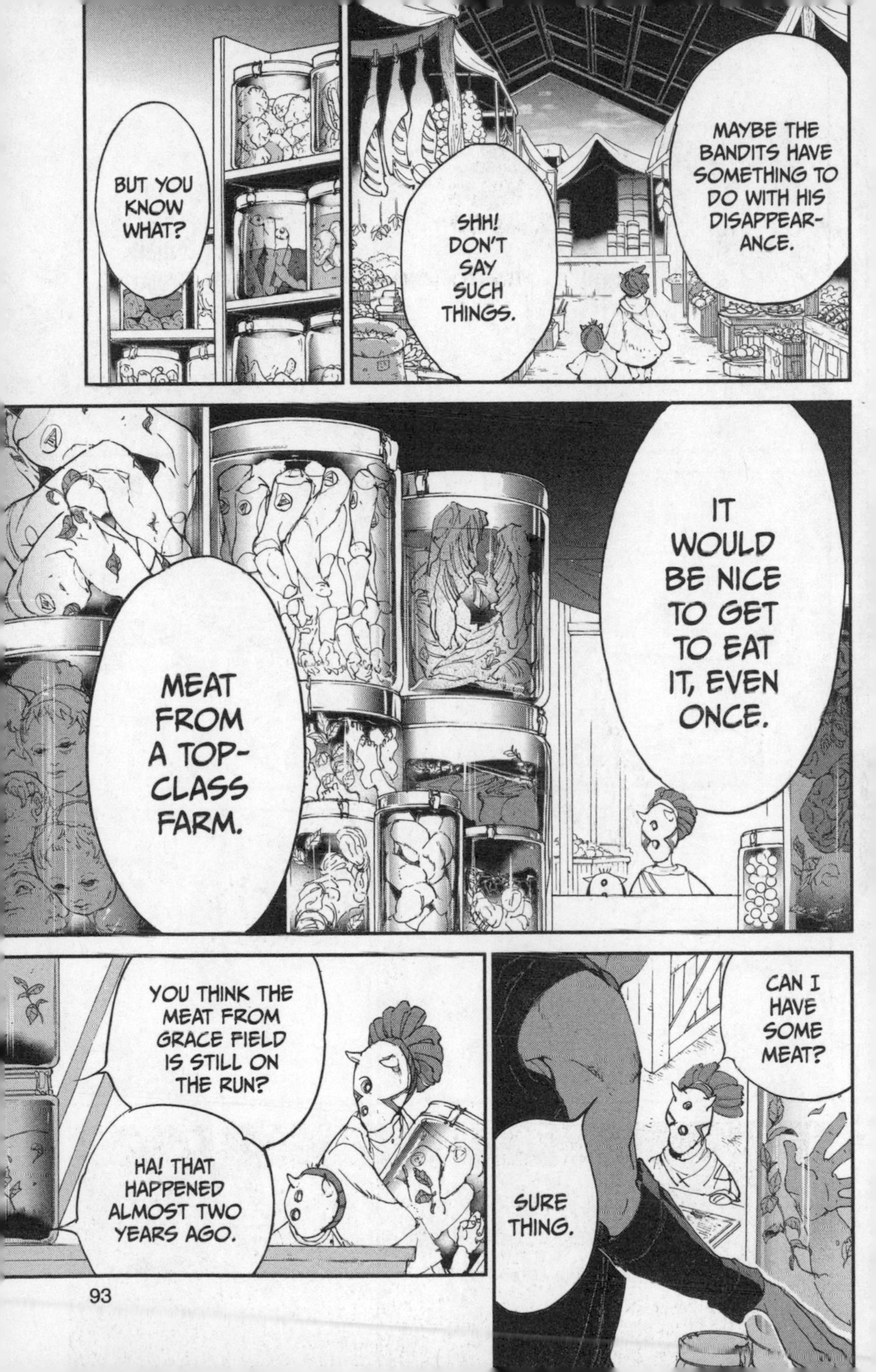
MAYBE THE BANDITS HAVE SOMETHING TO DO WITH HIS DISAPPEAR-ANCE.
SHH! DON'T SAY SUCH THINGS.
BUT YOU KNOW WHAT?
IT WOULD BE NICE TO GET TO EAT IT, EVEN ONCE.
MEAT FROM A TOP-CLASS FARM.
CAN I HAVE SOME MEAT?
SURE THING.
YOU THINK THE MEAT FROM GRACE FIELD IS STILL ON THE RUN?
HA! THAT HAPPENED ALMOST TWO YEARS AGO.

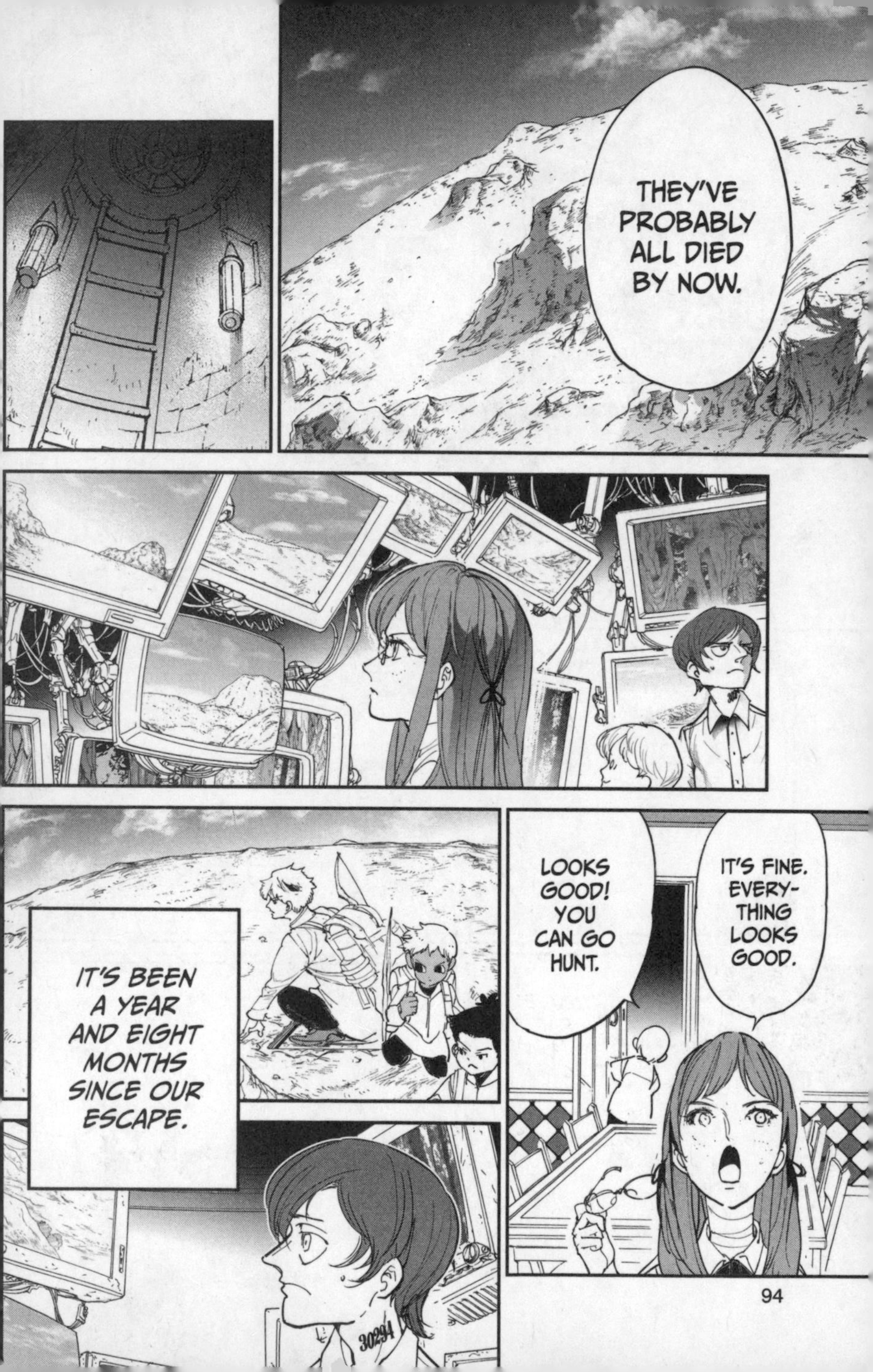
THEY'VE PROBABLY ALL DIED BY NOW.
IT'S FINE. EVERY-THING LOOKS GOOD.
LOOKS GOOD! YOU CAN GO HUNT.
IT'S BEEN A YEAR AND EIGHT MONTHS SINCE OUR ESCAPE.
30294

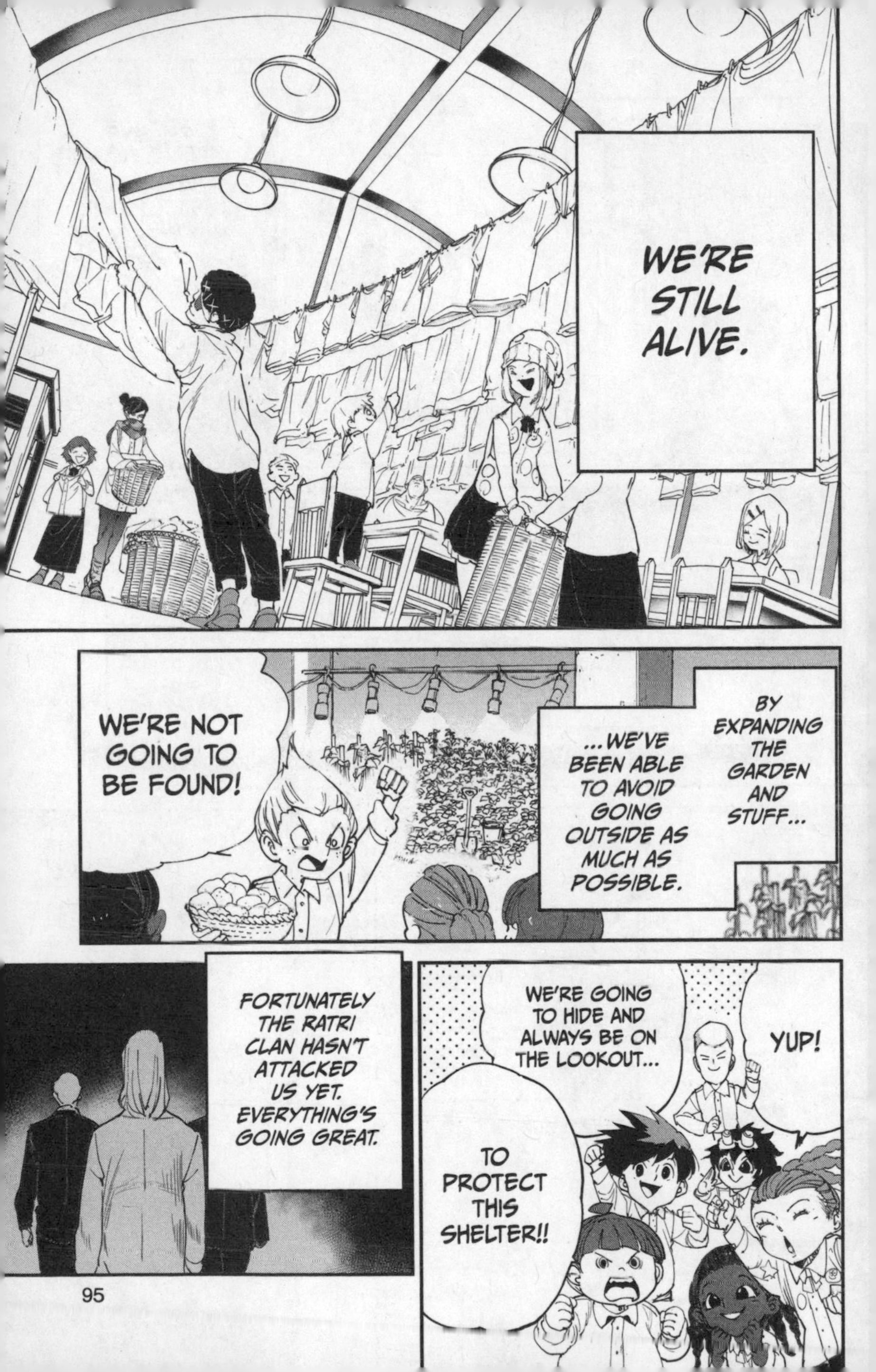
WE'RE STILL ALIVE.
BY EXPANDING THE GARDEN AND STUFF...
...WE'VE BEEN ABLE TO AVOID GOING OUTSIDE AS MUCH AS POSSIBLE.
WE'RE NOT GOING TO BE FOUND!
WE'RE GOING TO HIDE AND ALWAYS BE ON THE LOOKOUT...
YUP!
TO PROTECT THIS SHELTER!!
FORTUNATELY THE RATRI CLAN HASN'T ATTACKED US YET. EVERYTHING'S GOING GREAT.

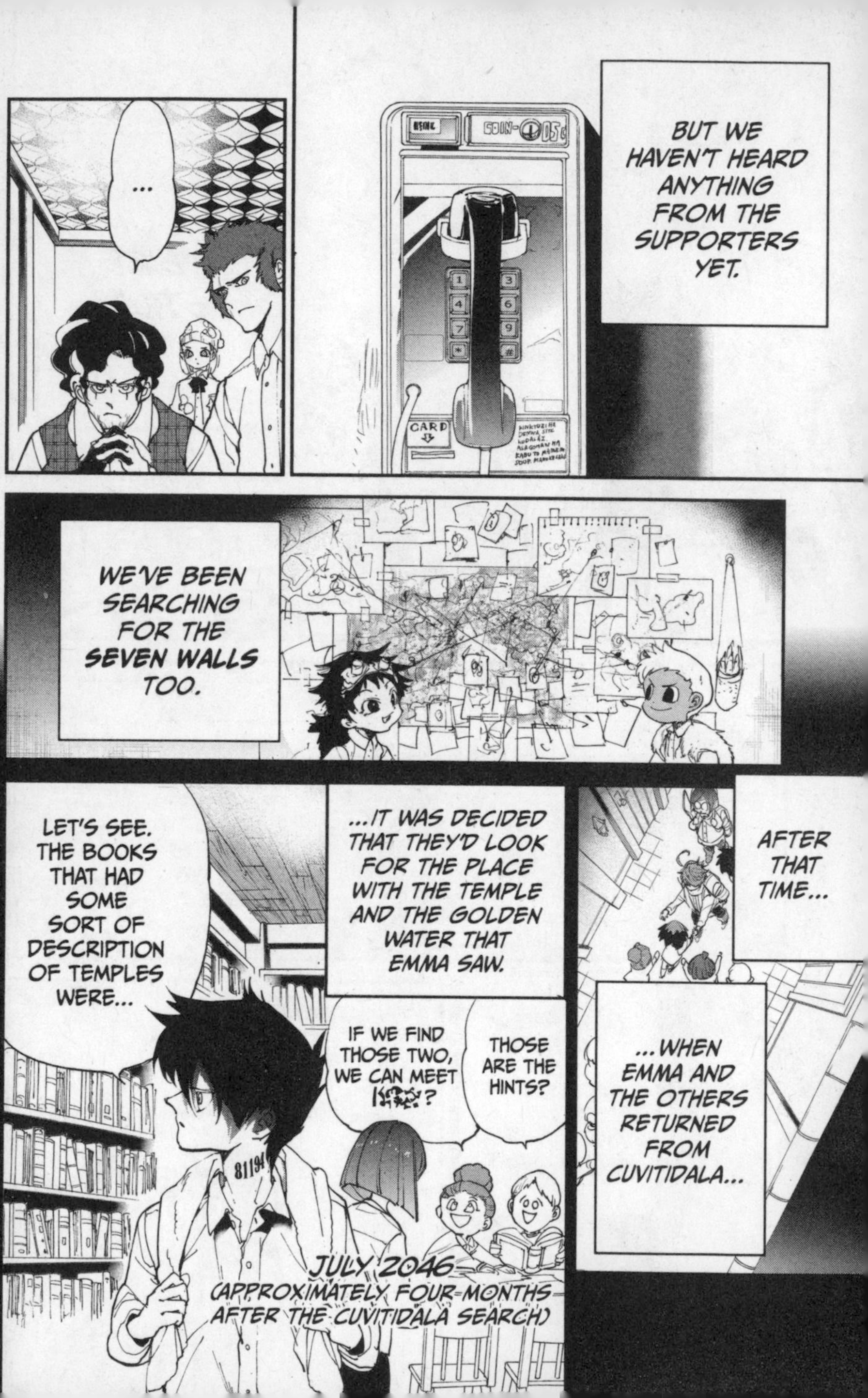
BUT WE HAVEN'T HEARD ANYTHING FROM THE SUPPORTERS YET.
...
CARD
WE'VE BEEN SEARCHING FOR THE SEVEN WALLS TOO.
AFTER THAT TIME...
...WHEN EMMA AND THE OTHERS RETURNED FROM CUVITIDALA...
...IT WAS DECIDED THAT THEY'D LOOK FOR THE PLACE WITH THE TEMPLE AND THE GOLDEN WATER THAT EMMA SAW.
THOSE ARE THE HINTS?
IF WE FIND THOSE TWO, WE CAN MEET ?
LET'S SEE. THE BOOKS THAT HAD SOME SORT OF DESCRIPTION OF TEMPLES WERE...
81194
JULY 2046
(APPROXIMATELY FOUR MONTHS AFTER THE CUVITIDALA SEARCH)

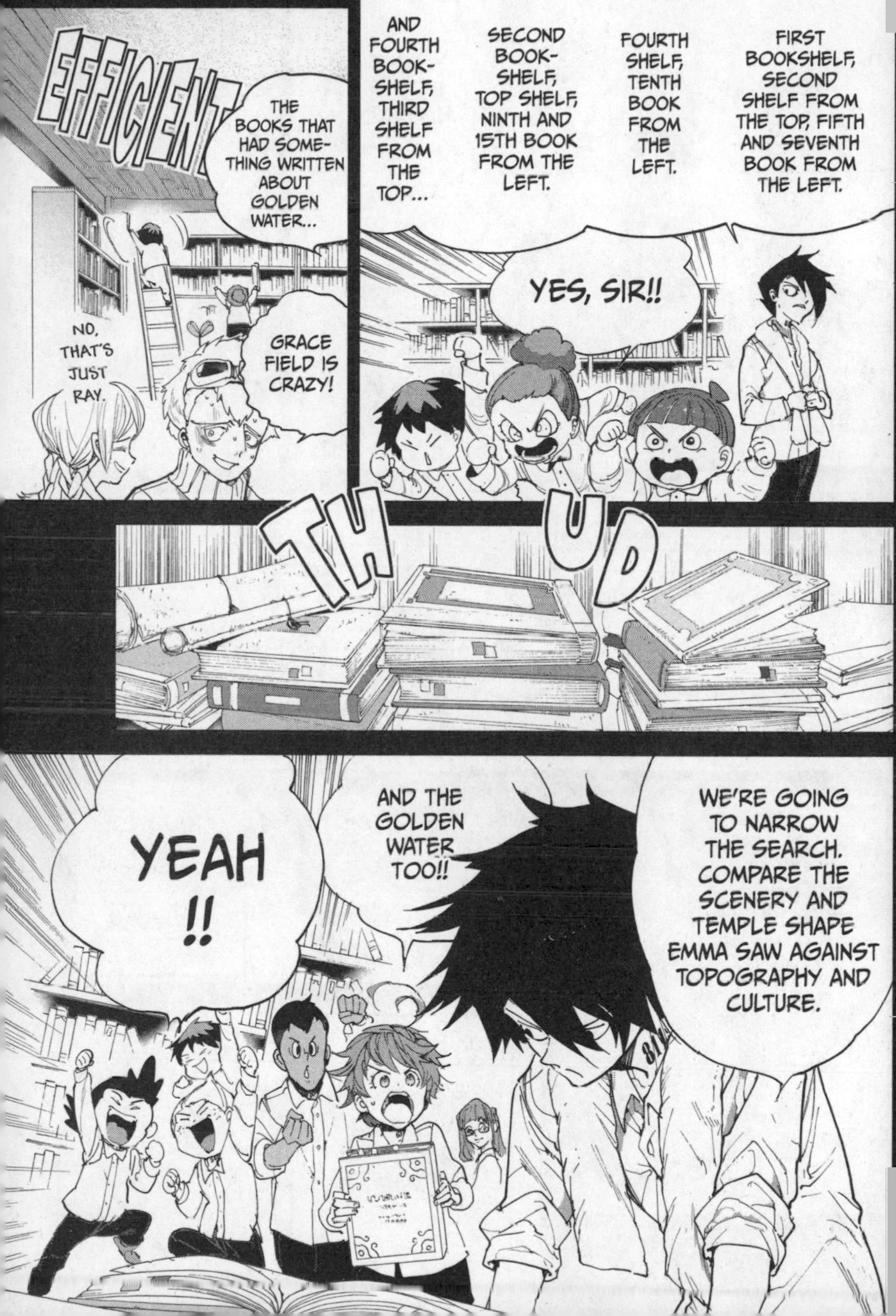
FIRST BOOKSHELF, SECOND SHELF FROM THE TOP, FIFTH AND SEVENTH BOOK FROM THE LEFT.
FOURTH SHELF, TENTH BOOK FROM THE LEFT.
SECOND BOOK-SHELF, TOP SHELF, NINTH AND 15TH BOOK FROM THE LEFT.
AND FOURTH BOOK-SHELF, THIRD SHELF FROM THE TOP...
YES, SIR!!
EFFICIENT
THE BOOKS THAT HAD SOME-THING WRITTEN ABOUT GOLDEN WATER...
GRACE FIELD IS CRAZY!
NO, THAT'S JUST RAY.
THUD
WE'RE GOING TO NARROW THE SEARCH. COMPARE THE SCENERY AND TEMPLE SHAPE EMMA SAW AGAINST TOPOGRAPHY AND CULTURE.
AND THE GOLDEN WATER TOO!!
YEAH !!

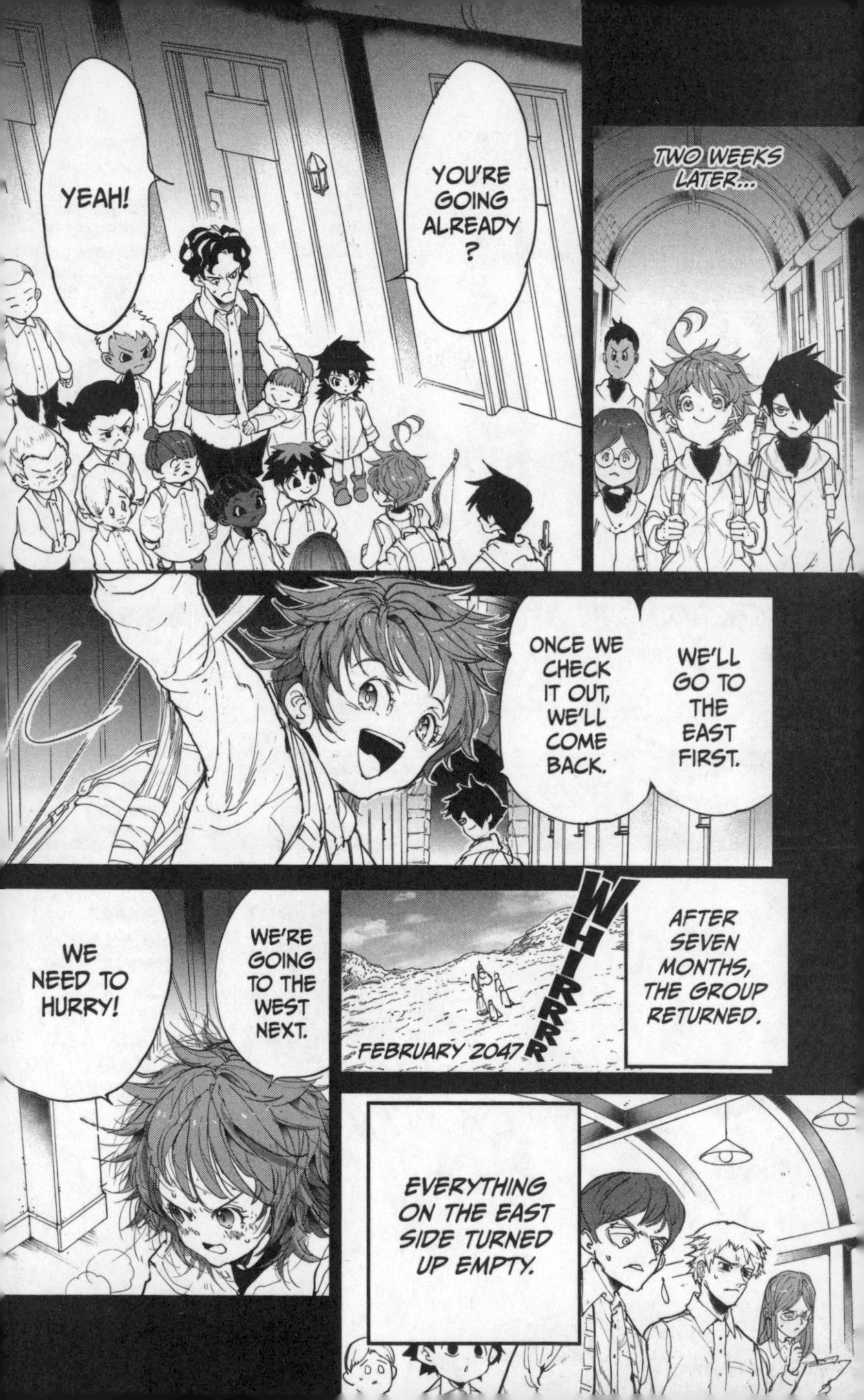
TWO WEEKS LATER...
YOU'RE GOING ALREADY?
YEAH!
WE'LL GO TO THE EAST FIRST.
ONCE WE CHECK IT OUT, WE'LL COME BACK.
AFTER SEVEN MONTHS, THE GROUP RETURNED.
WHIRRRR
FEBRUARY 2047
EVERYTHING ON THE EAST SIDE TURNED UP EMPTY.
WE'RE GOING TO THE WEST NEXT.
WE NEED TO HURRY!

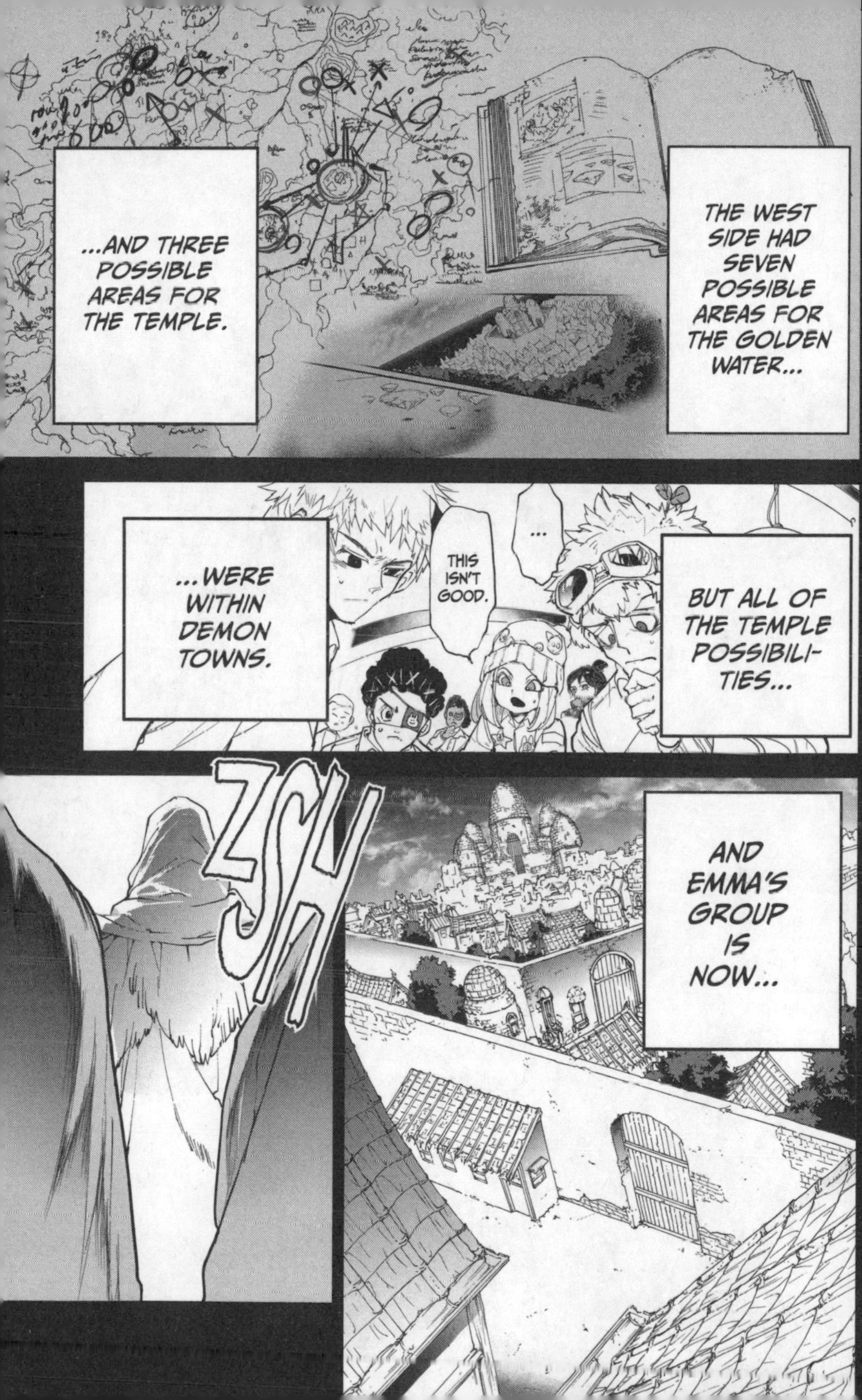
THE WEST SIDE HAD SEVEN POSSIBLE AREAS FOR THE GOLDEN WATER...
...AND THREE POSSIBLE AREAS FOR THE TEMPLE.
BUT ALL OF THE TEMPLE POSSIBILITIES...
...
THIS ISN'T GOOD.
...WERE WITHIN DEMON TOWNS.
AND EMMA'S GROUP IS NOW...
ZSH

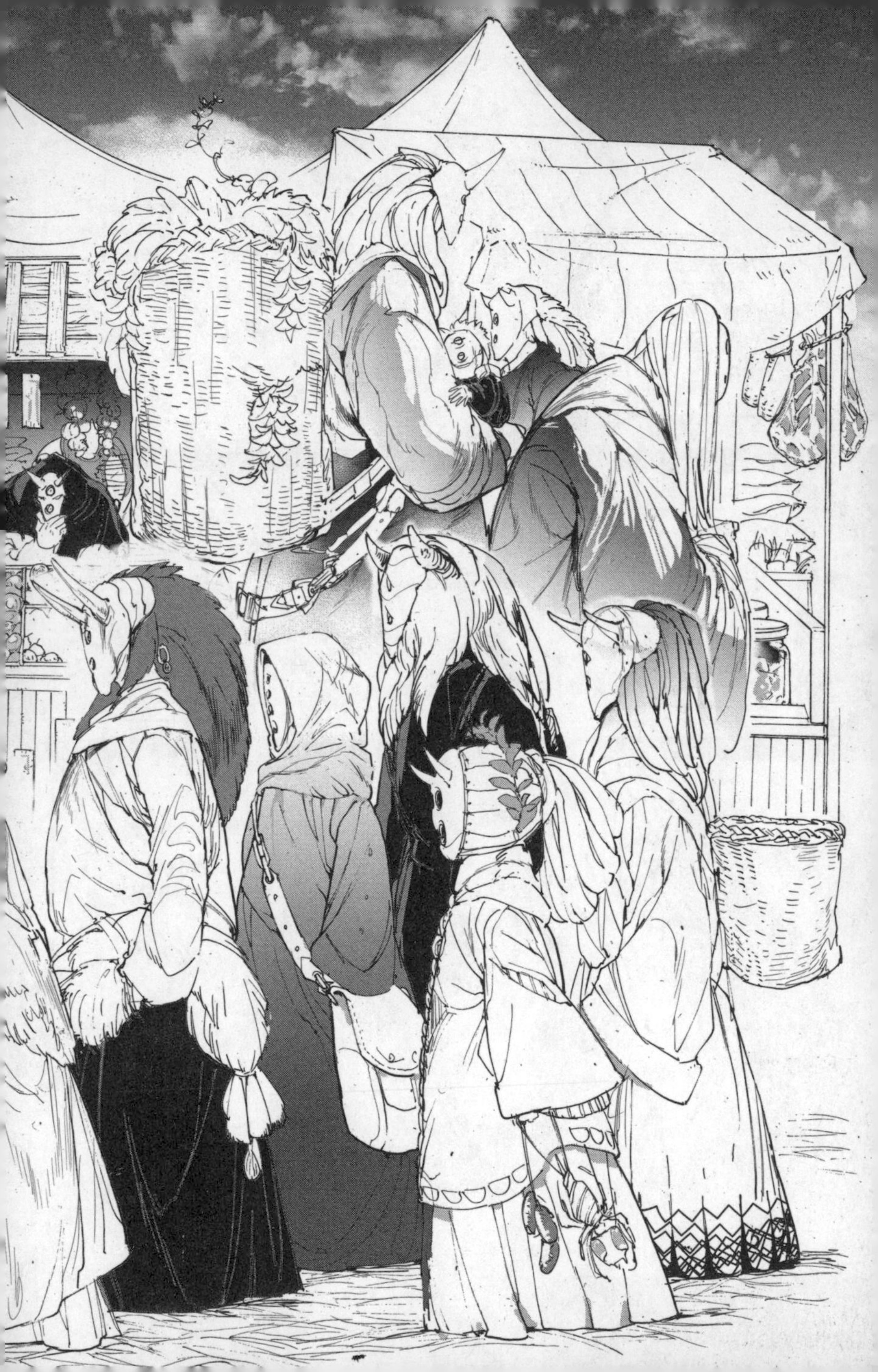

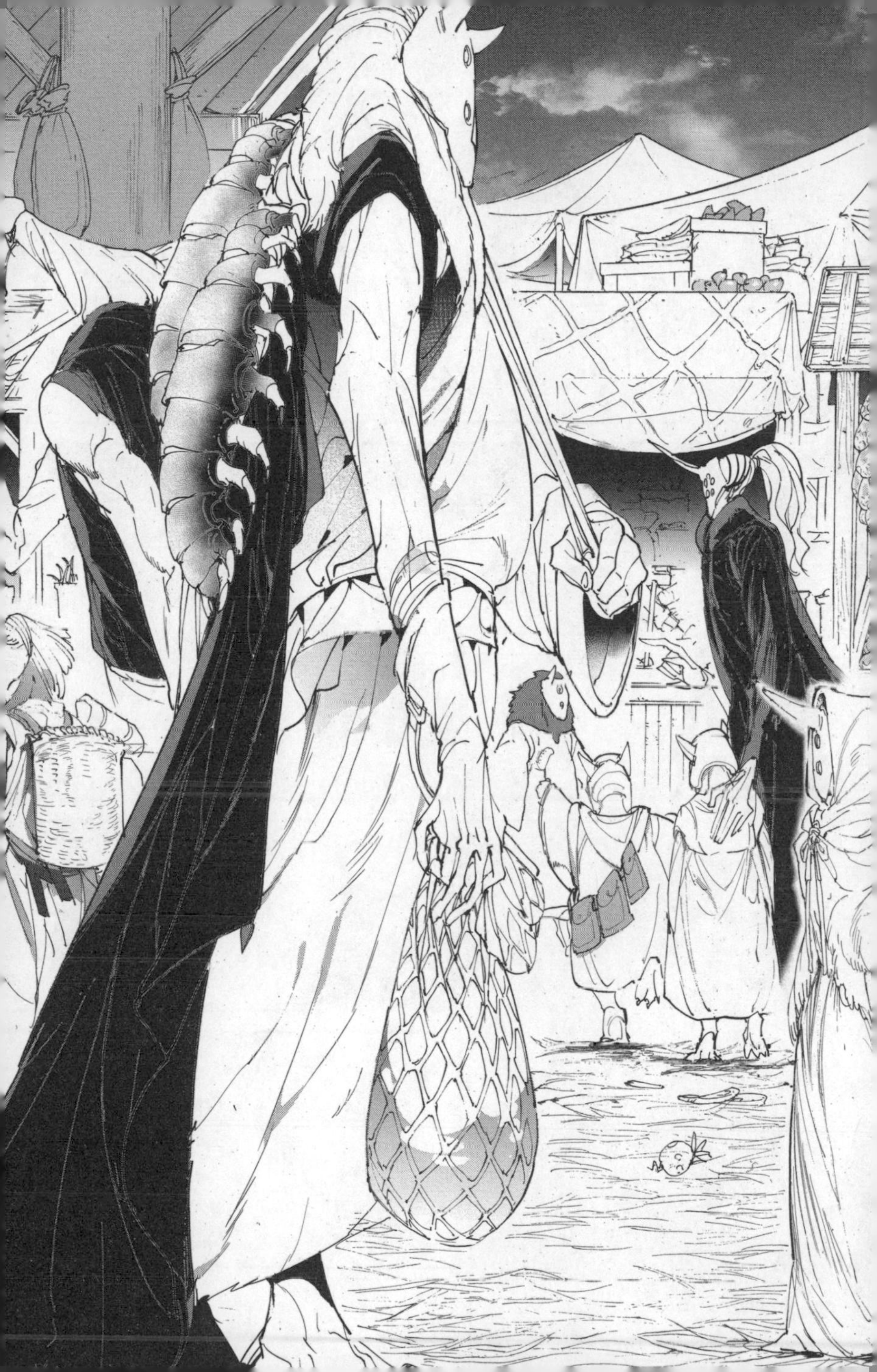

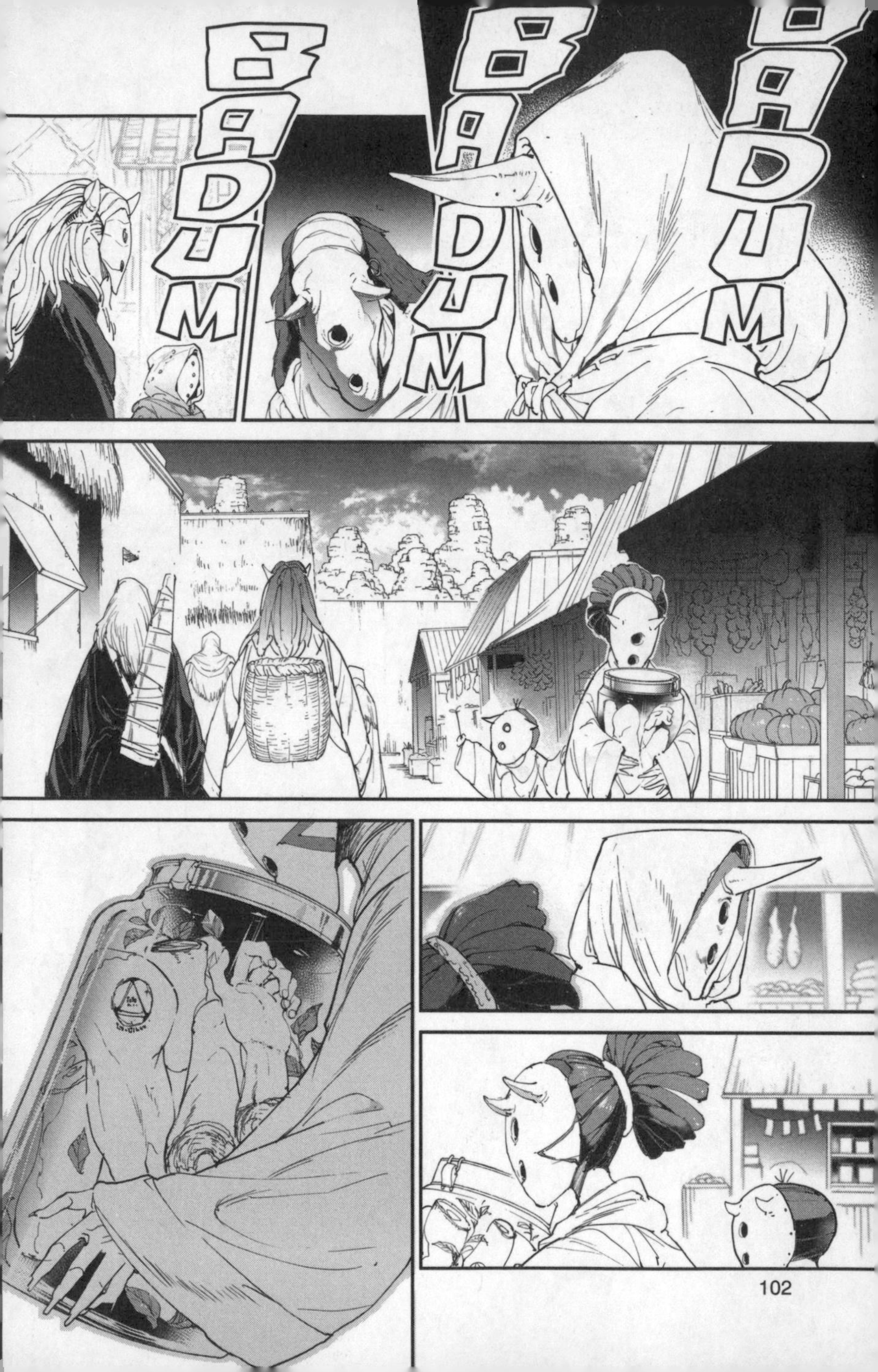
BADUM
BADUM
BADUM

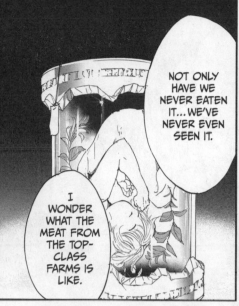

THIS MEAT IS ALSO MASS-PRODUCED.
FWSH
NOT ONLY HAVE WE NEVER EATEN IT... WE'VE NEVER EVEN SEEN IT.
I WONDER WHAT THE MEAT FROM THE TOP-CLASS FARMS IS LIKE.
IS IT THAT GOOD?
IS IT REALLY DIFFERENT?

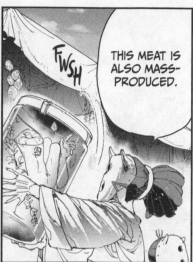

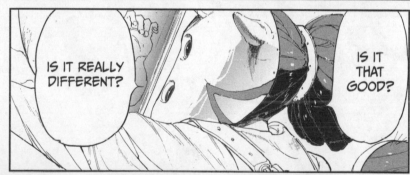

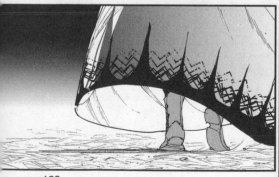

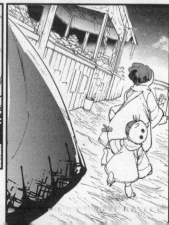

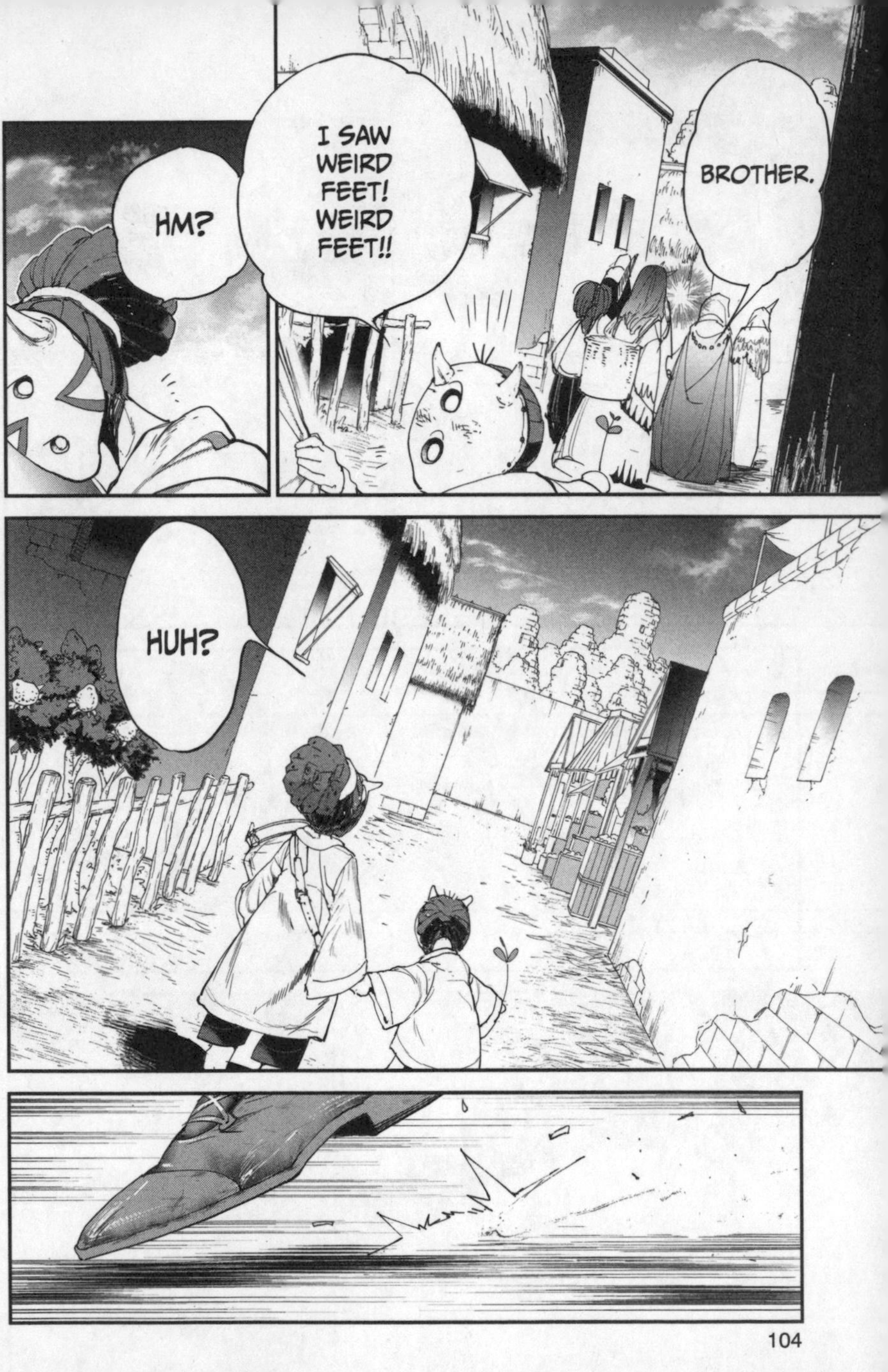
BROTHER.
I SAW WEIRD FEET! WEIRD FEET!!
HM?
HUH?

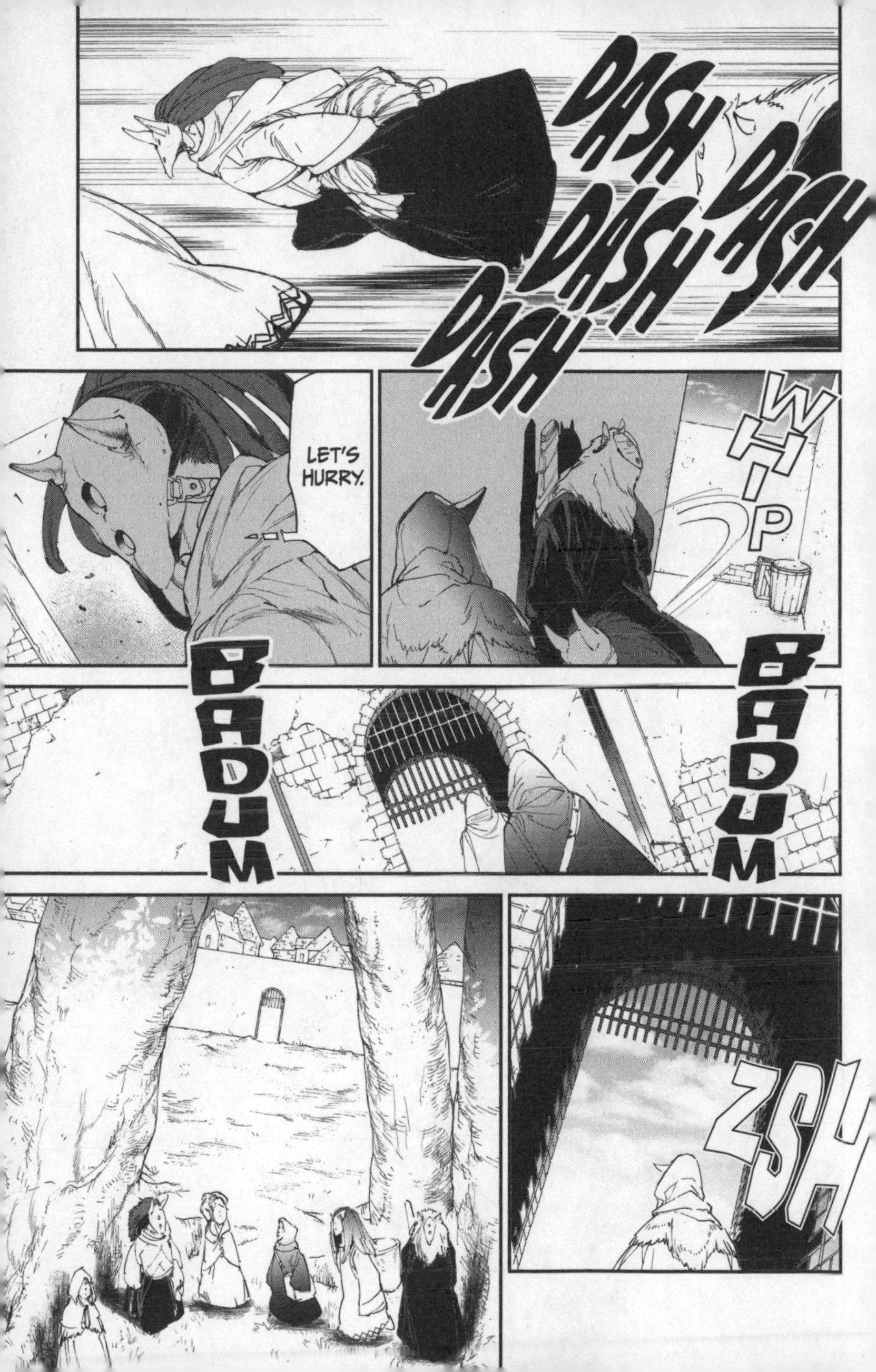
DASH
DASH
DASH
DASH
DASH
WHIP
LET'S HURRY.
BADUM
BADUM
ZSH

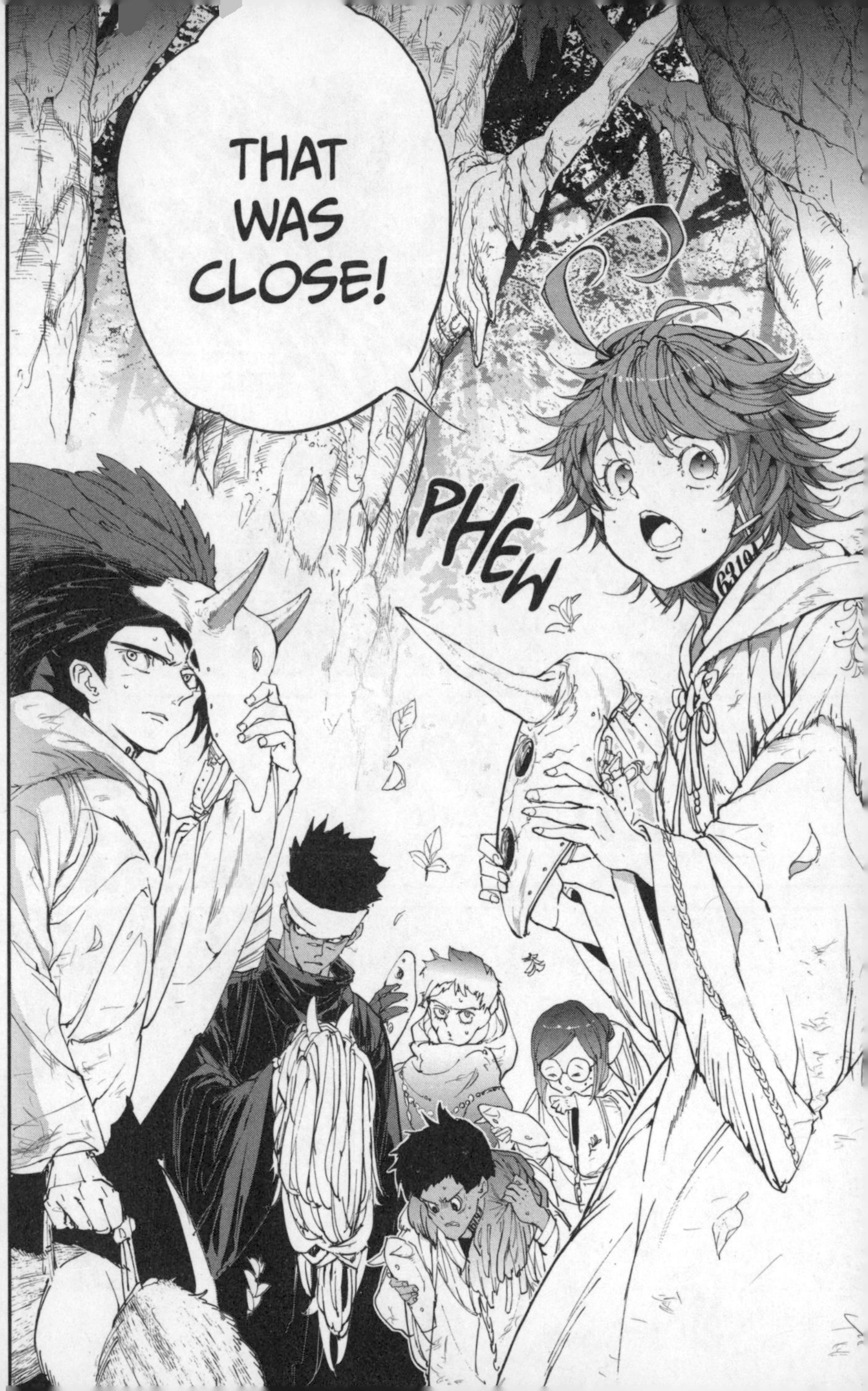
THAT WAS CLOSE!
PHEW

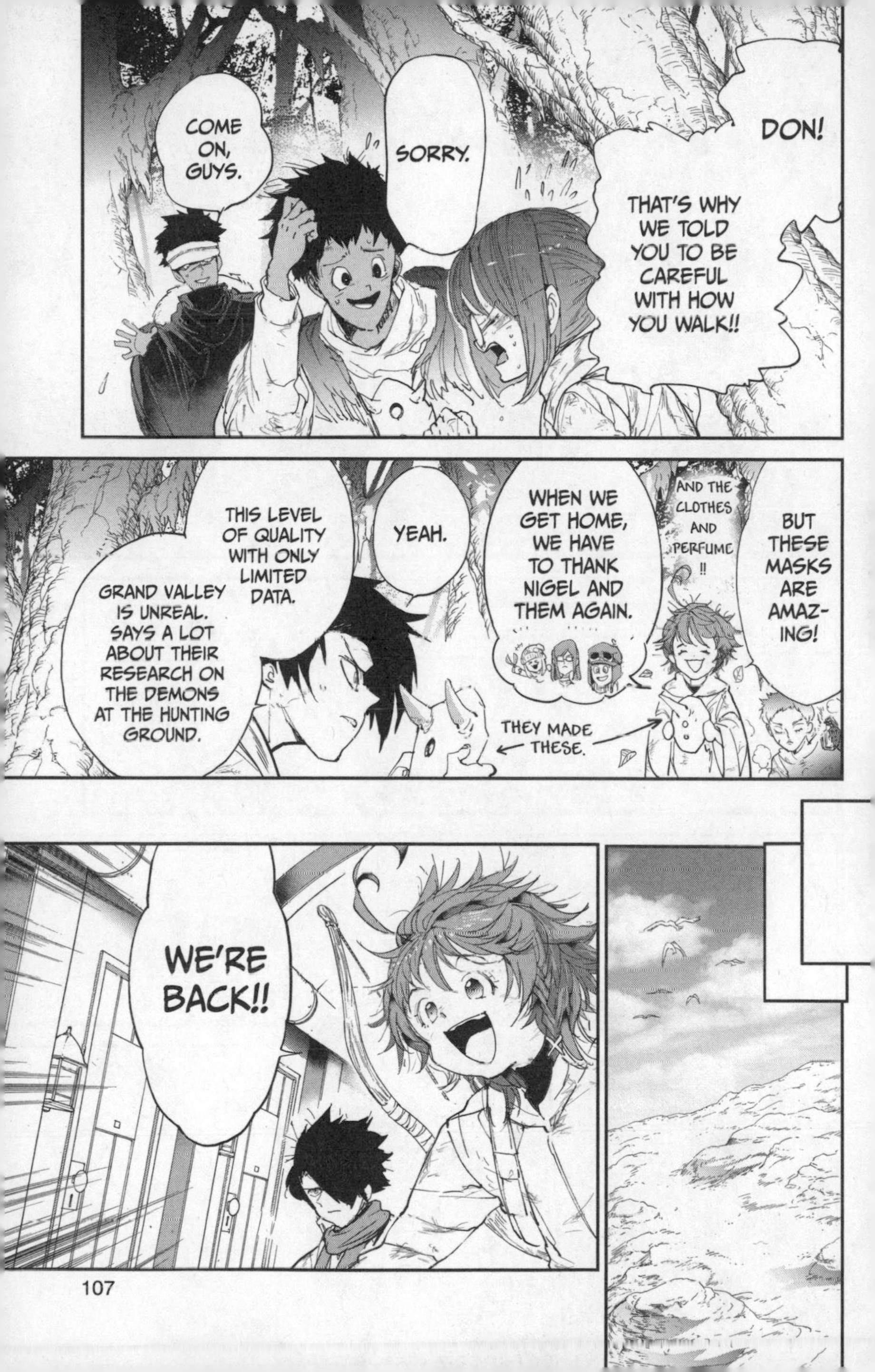
DON!
THAT'S WHY WE TOLD YOU TO BE CAREFUL WITH HOW YOU WALK!!
SORRY.
COME ON, GUYS.
BUT THESE MASKS ARE AMAZ-ING!
AND THE CLOTHES AND PERFUME!!
WHEN WE GET HOME, WE HAVE TO THANK NIGEL AND THEM AGAIN.
THEY MADE THESE.
YEAH.
THIS LEVEL OF QUALITY WITH ONLY LIMITED DATA.
GRAND VALLEY IS UNREAL. SAYS A LOT ABOUT THEIR RESEARCH ON THE DEMONS AT THE HUNTING GROUND.
WE'RE BACK!!

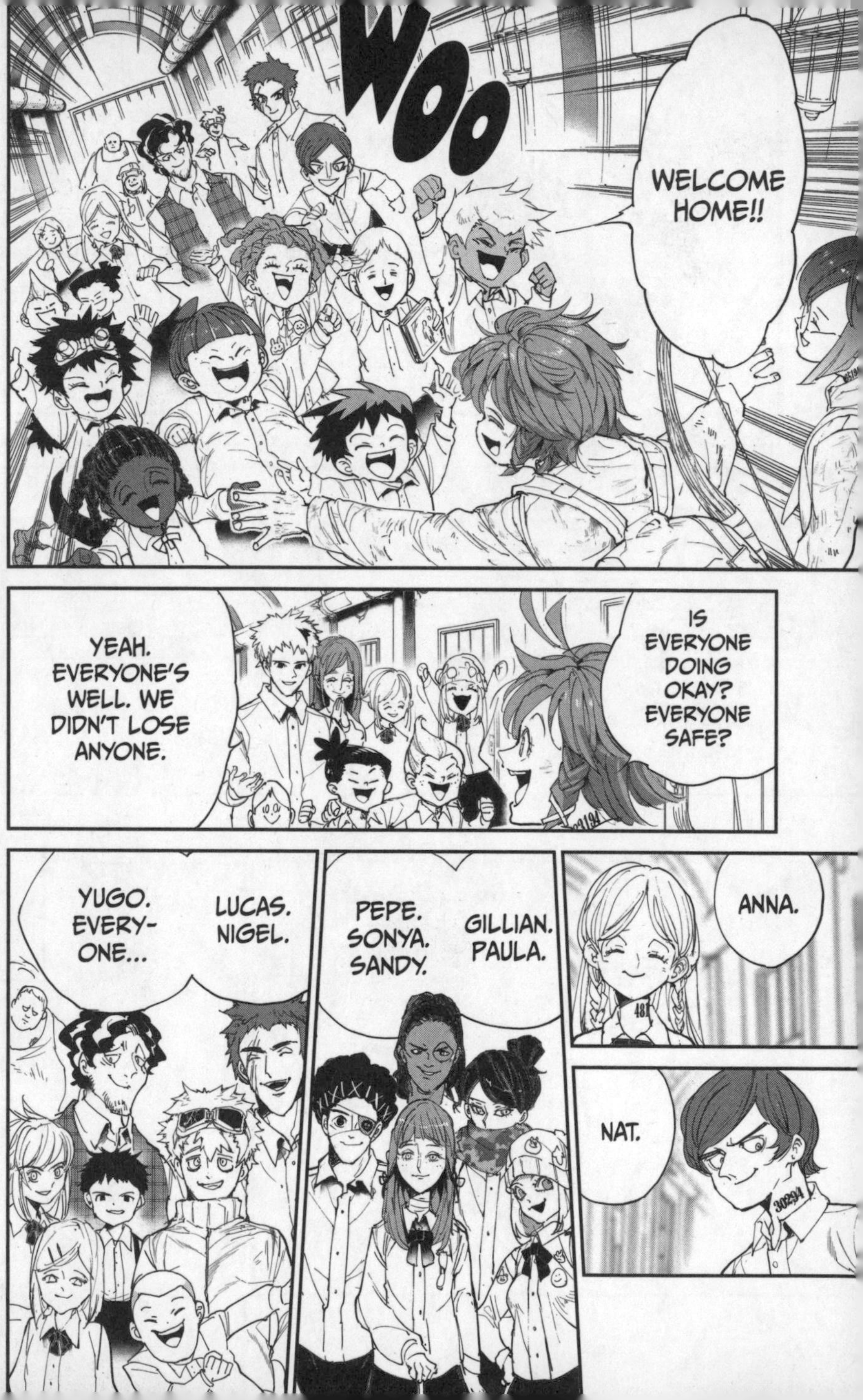
WOO
WELCOME HOME!!
IS EVERYONE DOING OKAY? EVERYONE SAFE?
YEAH. EVERYONE'S WELL. WE DIDN'T LOSE ANYONE.
ANNA.
481
NAT.
30294
GILLIAN. PAULA.
PEPE. SONYA. SANDY.
LUCAS. NIGEL.
YUGO. EVERY-ONE...

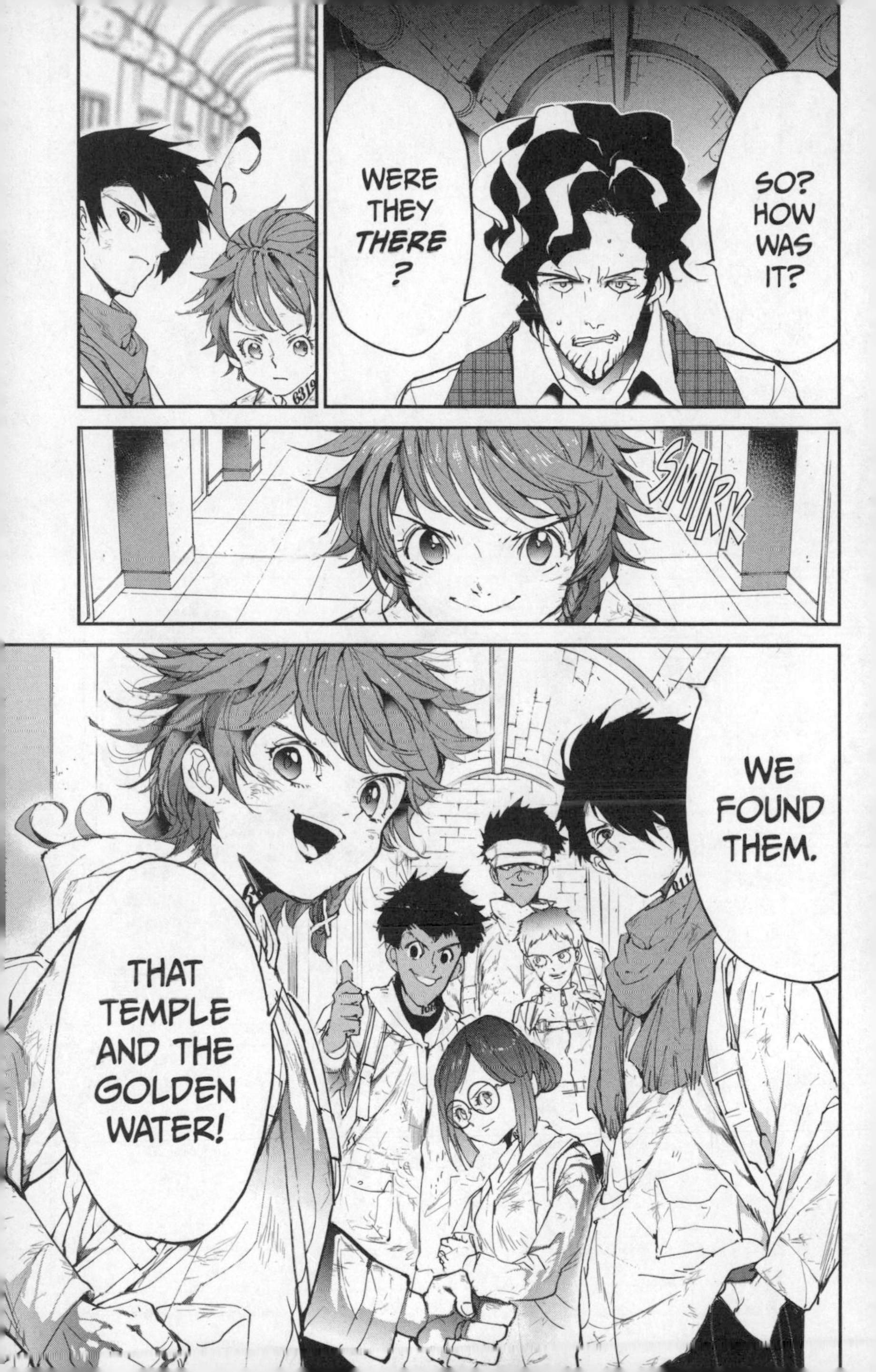
SO? HOW WAS IT?
WERE THEY *THERE*?
SMIRK
WE FOUND THEM.
THAT TEMPLE AND THE GOLDEN WATER!

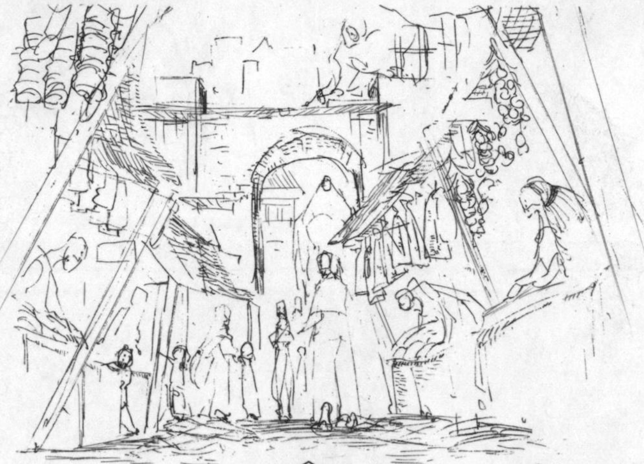

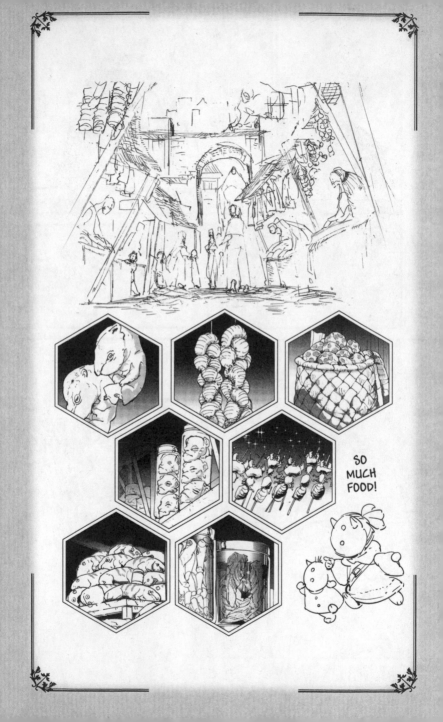

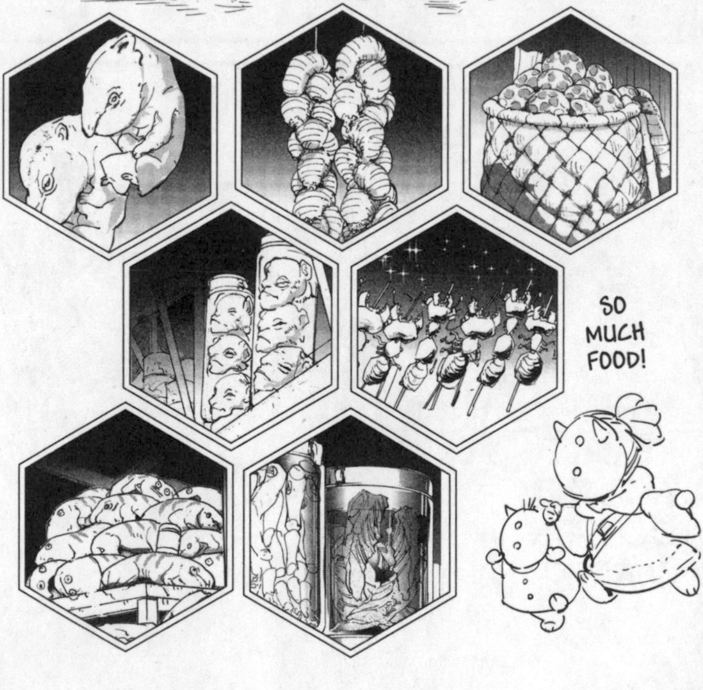
SO MUCH FOOD!

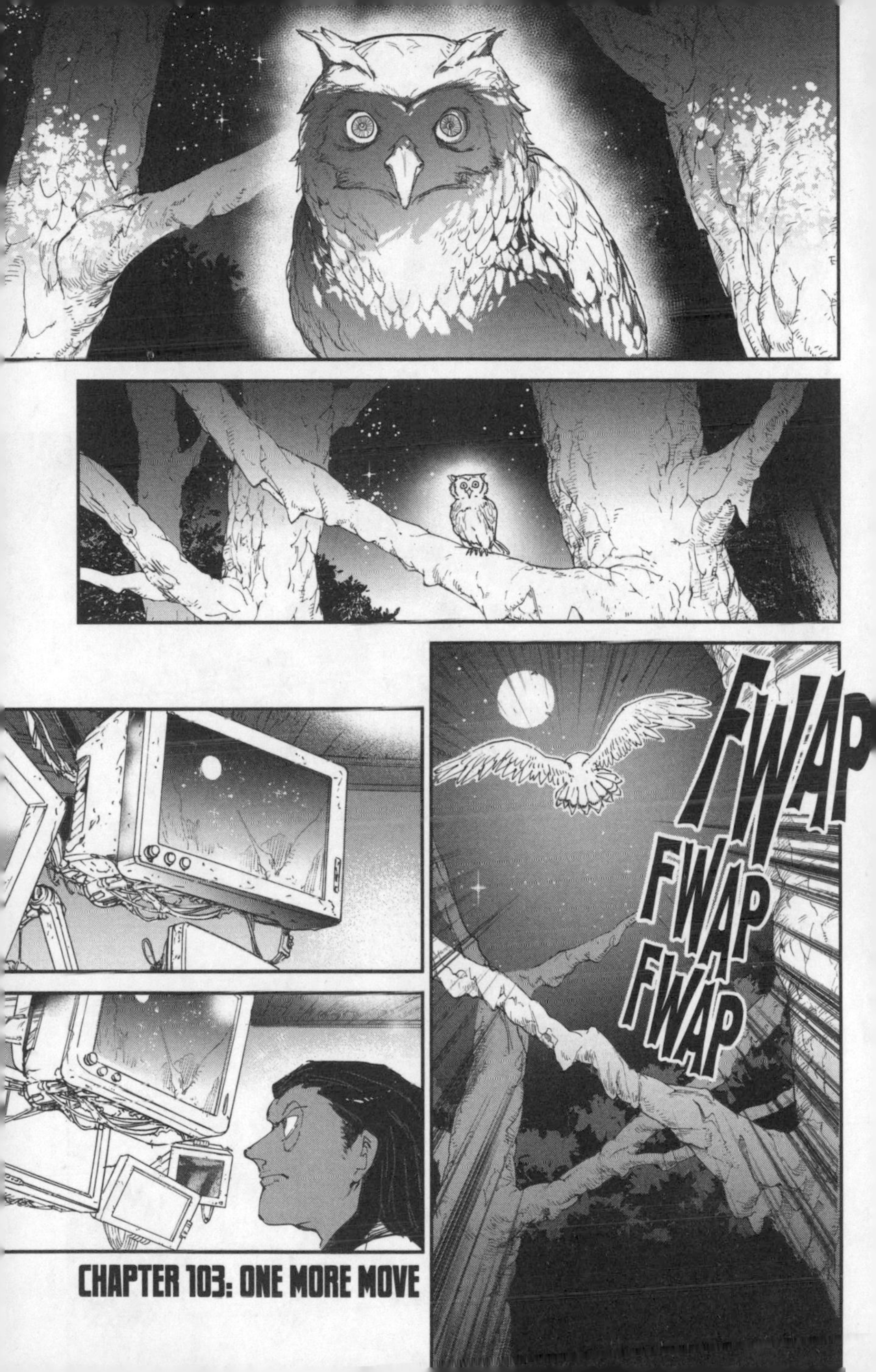
FWAP
FWAP
FWAP
CHAPTER 103: ONE MORE MOVE

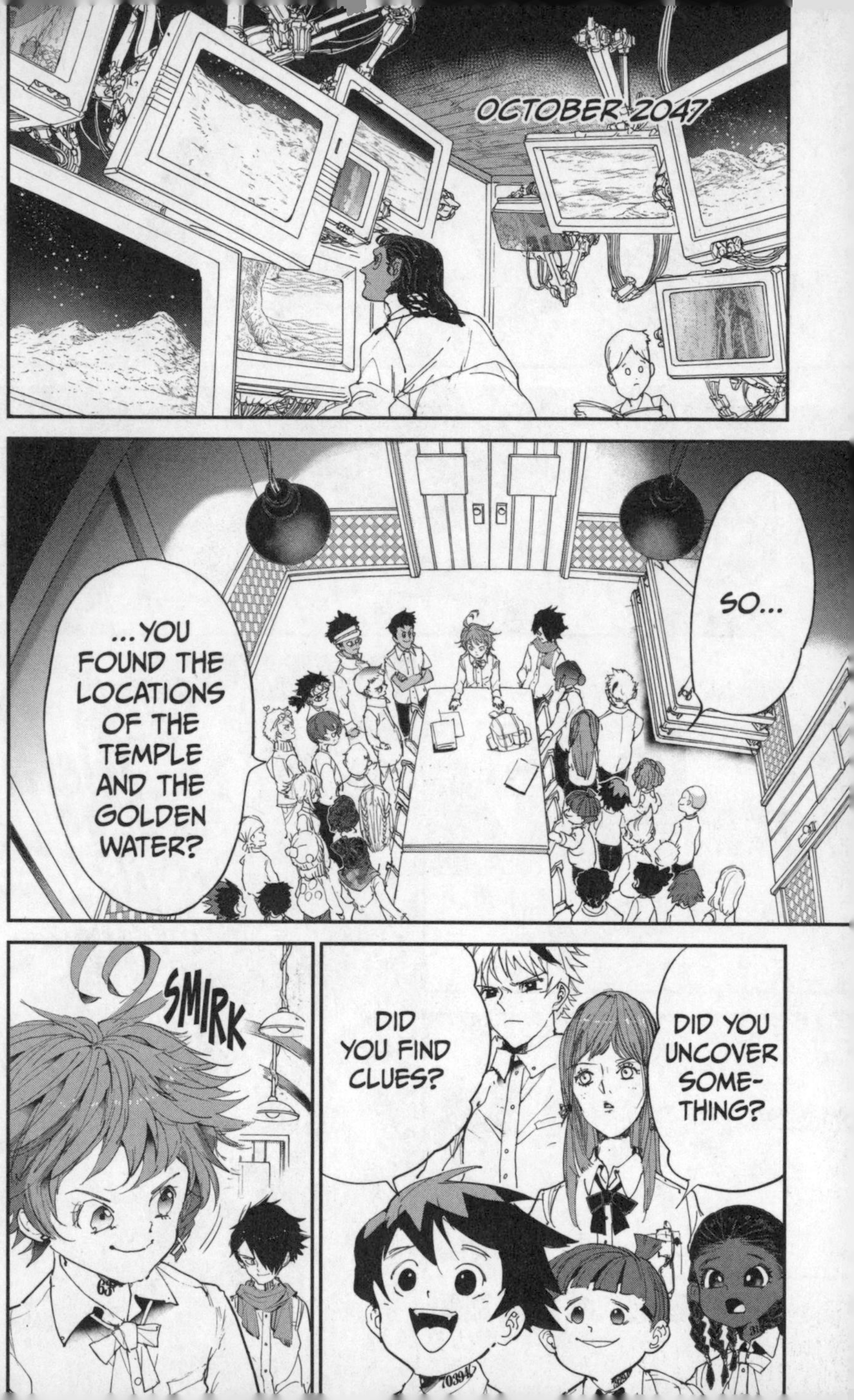
OCTOBER 2047
SO...
...YOU FOUND THE LOCATIONS OF THE TEMPLE AND THE GOLDEN WATER?
DID YOU UNCOVER SOME-THING?
DID YOU FIND CLUES?
SMIRK

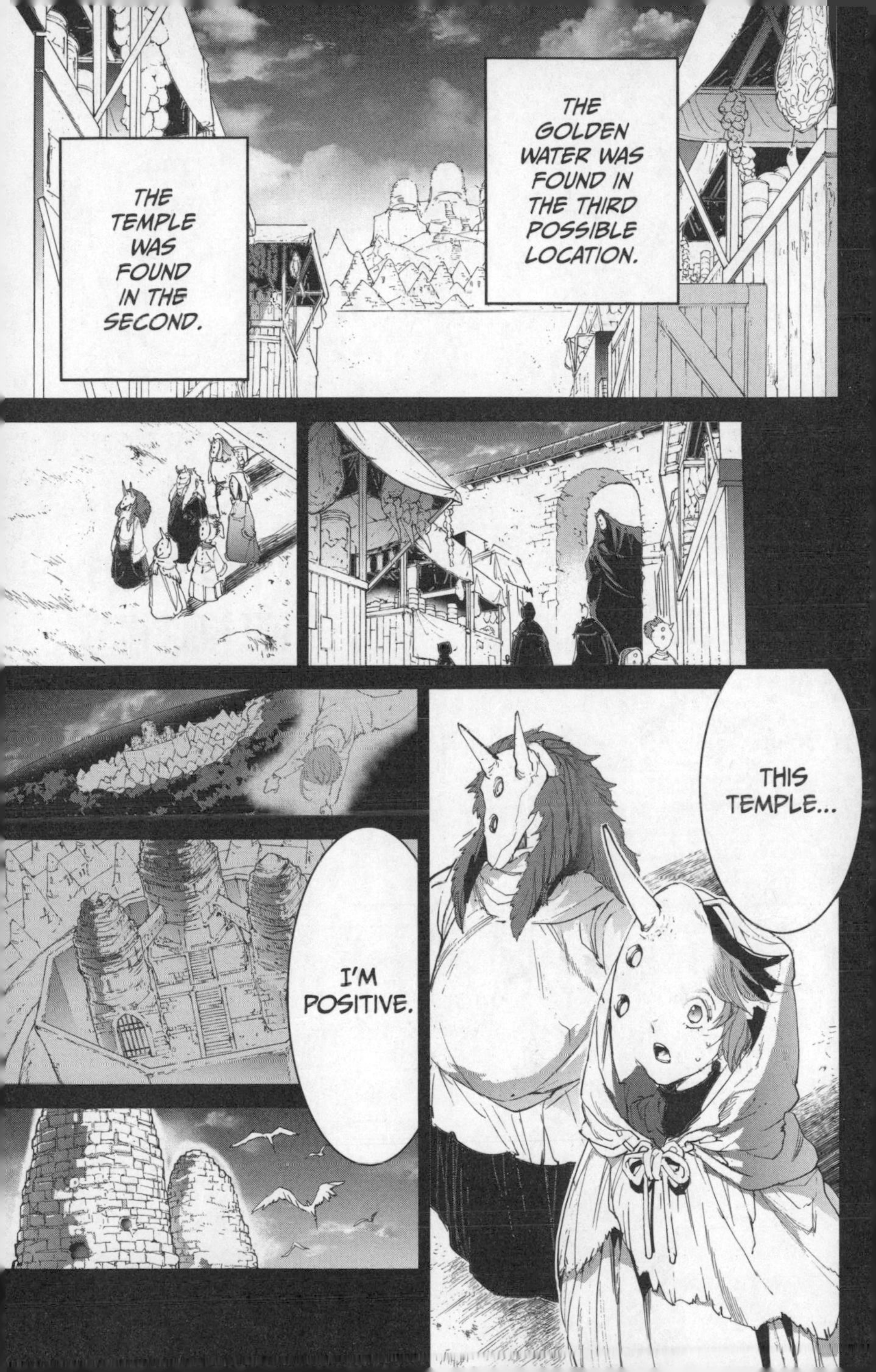
THE GOLDEN WATER WAS FOUND IN THE THIRD POSSIBLE LOCATION.
THE TEMPLE WAS FOUND IN THE SECOND.
THIS TEMPLE...
I'M POSITIVE.

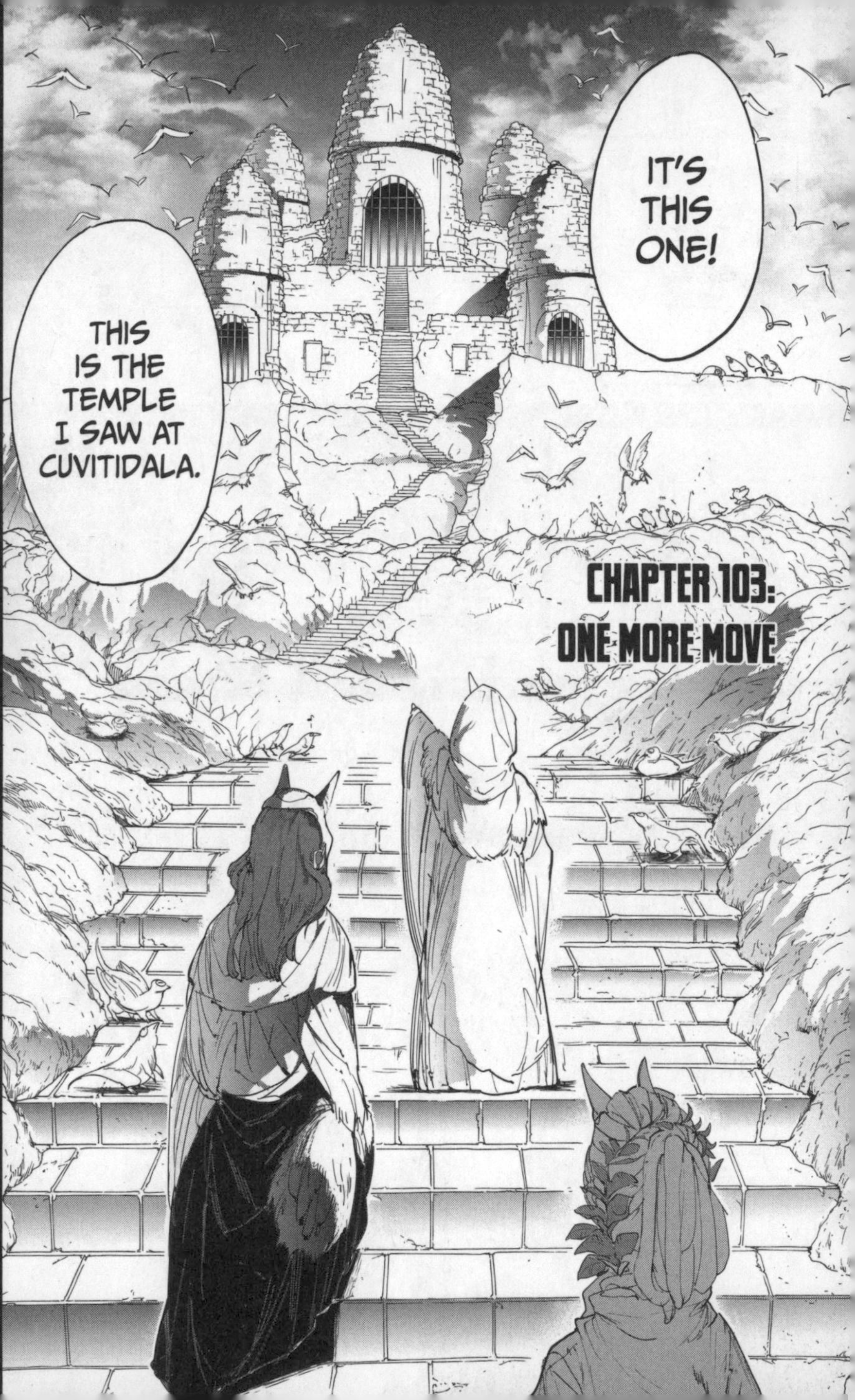
IT'S THIS ONE!
THIS IS THE TEMPLE I SAW AT CUVITIDALA.

CHAPTER 103: ONE MORE MOVE

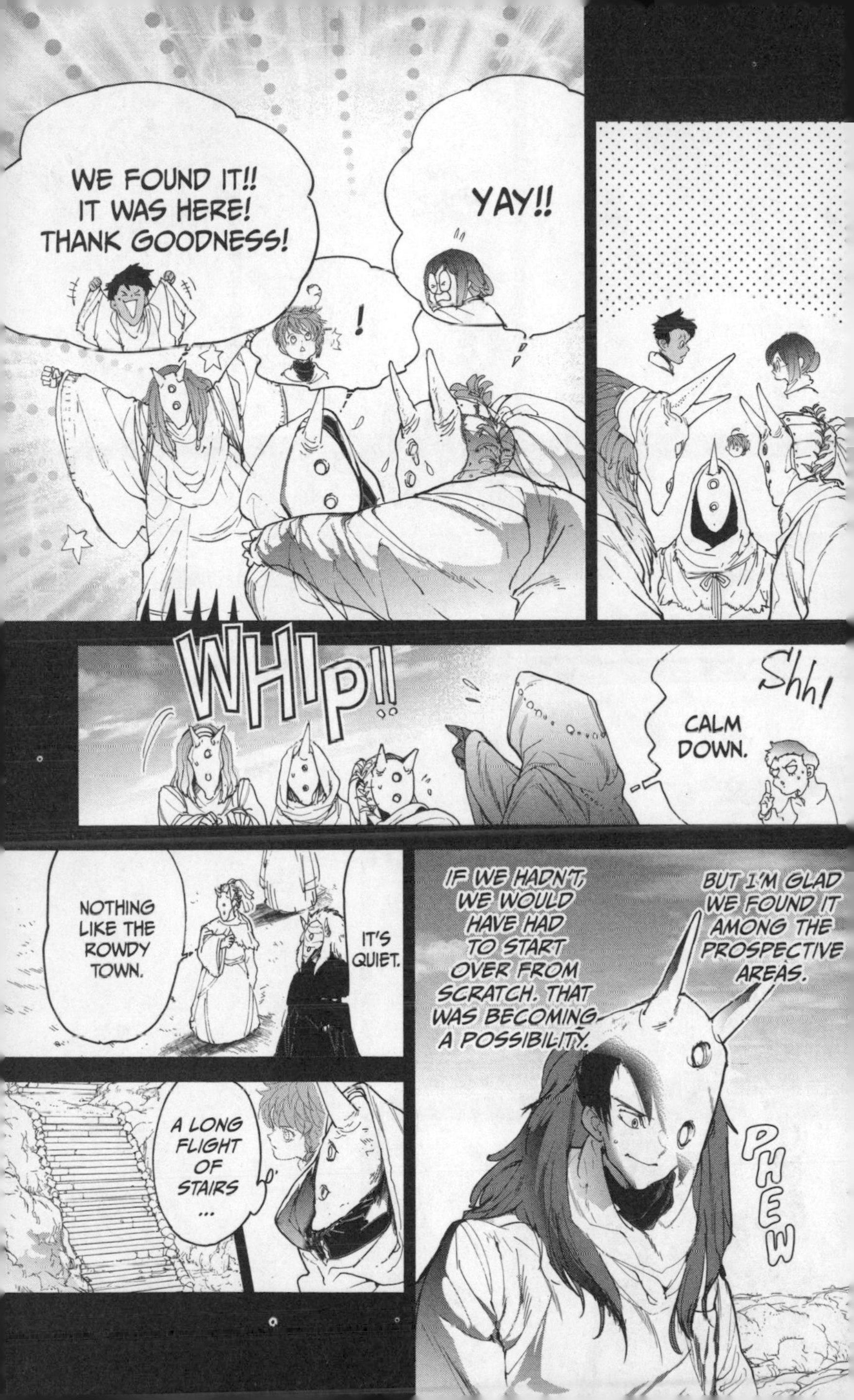

YAY!!
WE FOUND IT!! IT WAS HERE! THANK GOODNESS!
!
Shh!
CALM DOWN.
WHIP!!
BUT I'M GLAD WE FOUND IT AMONG THE PROSPECTIVE AREAS.
IF WE HADN'T, WE WOULD HAVE HAD TO START OVER FROM SCRATCH. THAT WAS BECOMING A POSSIBILITY.
PHEW
IT'S QUIET.
NOTHING LIKE THE ROWDY TOWN.
A LONG FLIGHT OF STAIRS ...

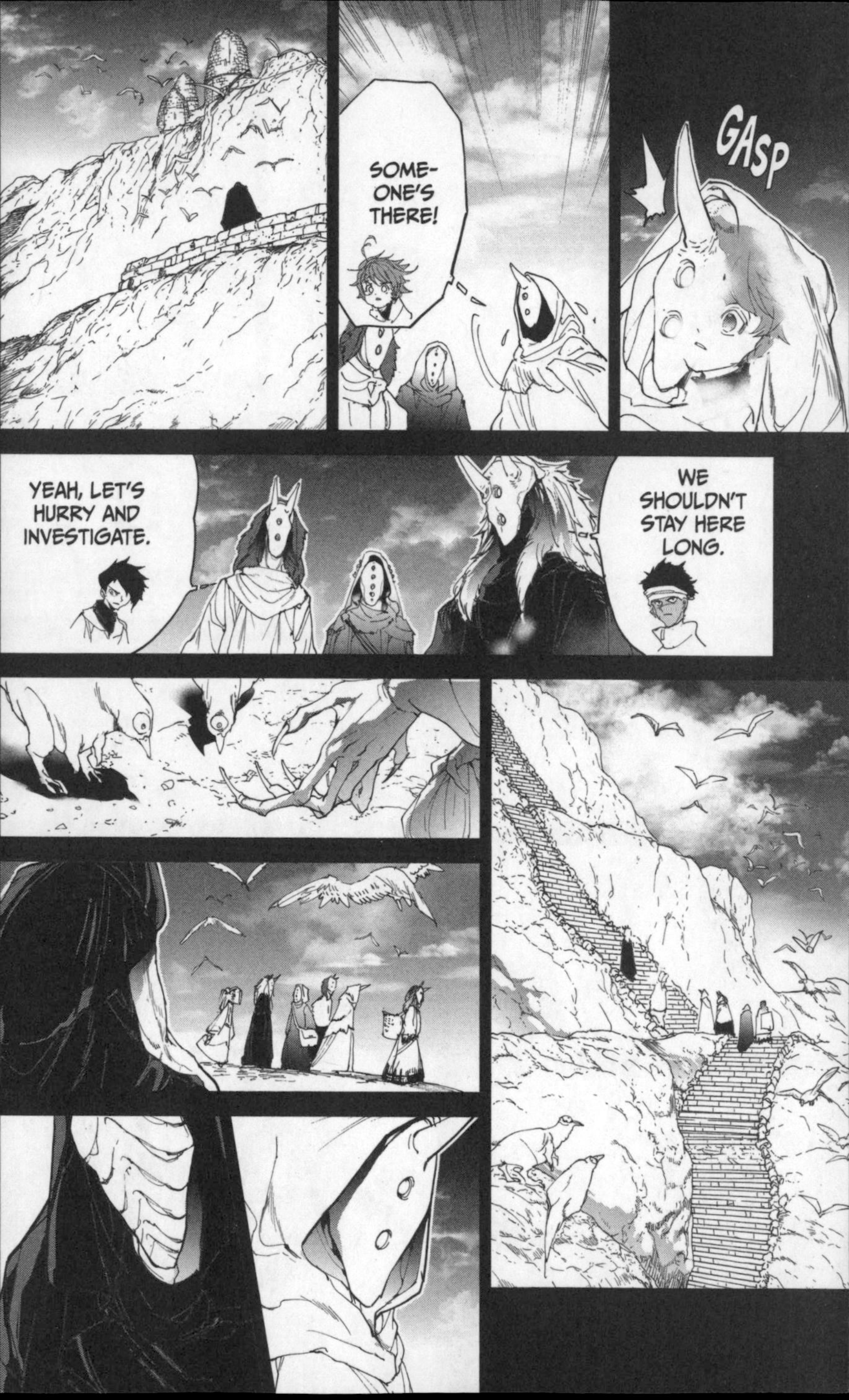
GASP
SOME-ONE'S THERE!
WE SHOULDN'T STAY HERE LONG.
YEAH, LET'S HURRY AND INVESTIGATE.

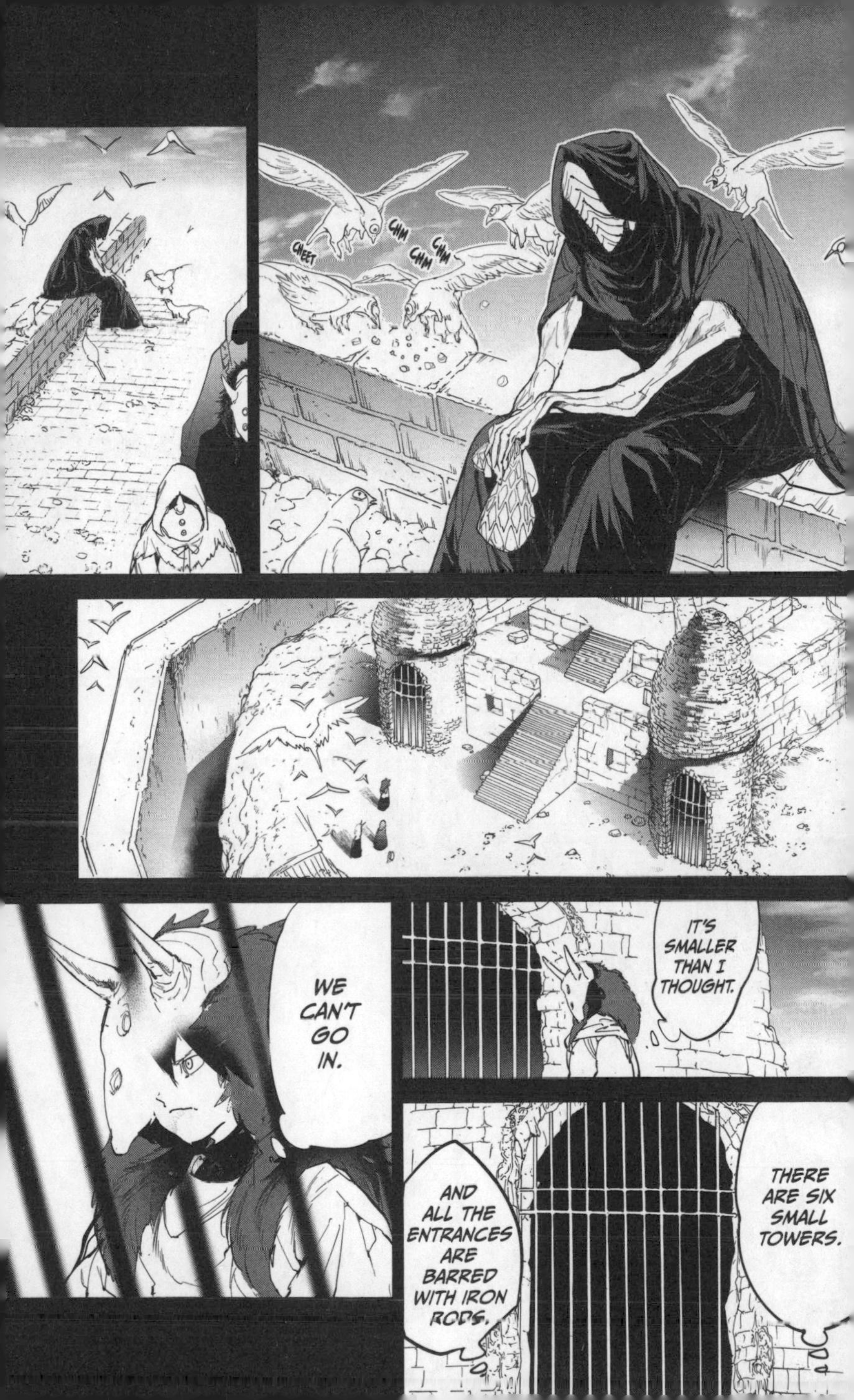
CHM
CHM
CHM
CHEET
IT'S SMALLER THAN I THOUGHT.
THERE ARE SIX SMALL TOWERS.
AND ALL THE ENTRANCES ARE BARRED WITH IRON RODS.
WE CAN'T GO IN.

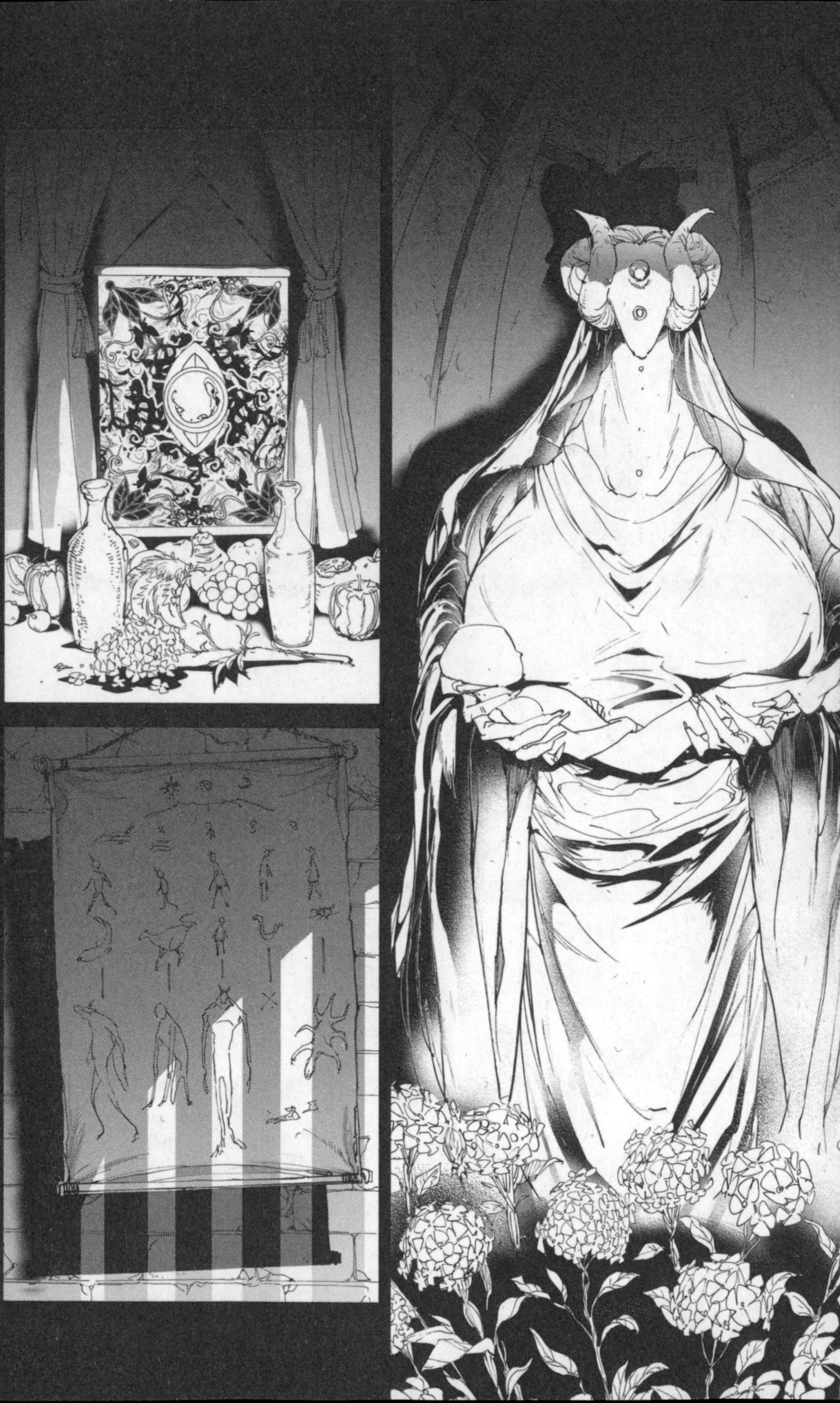

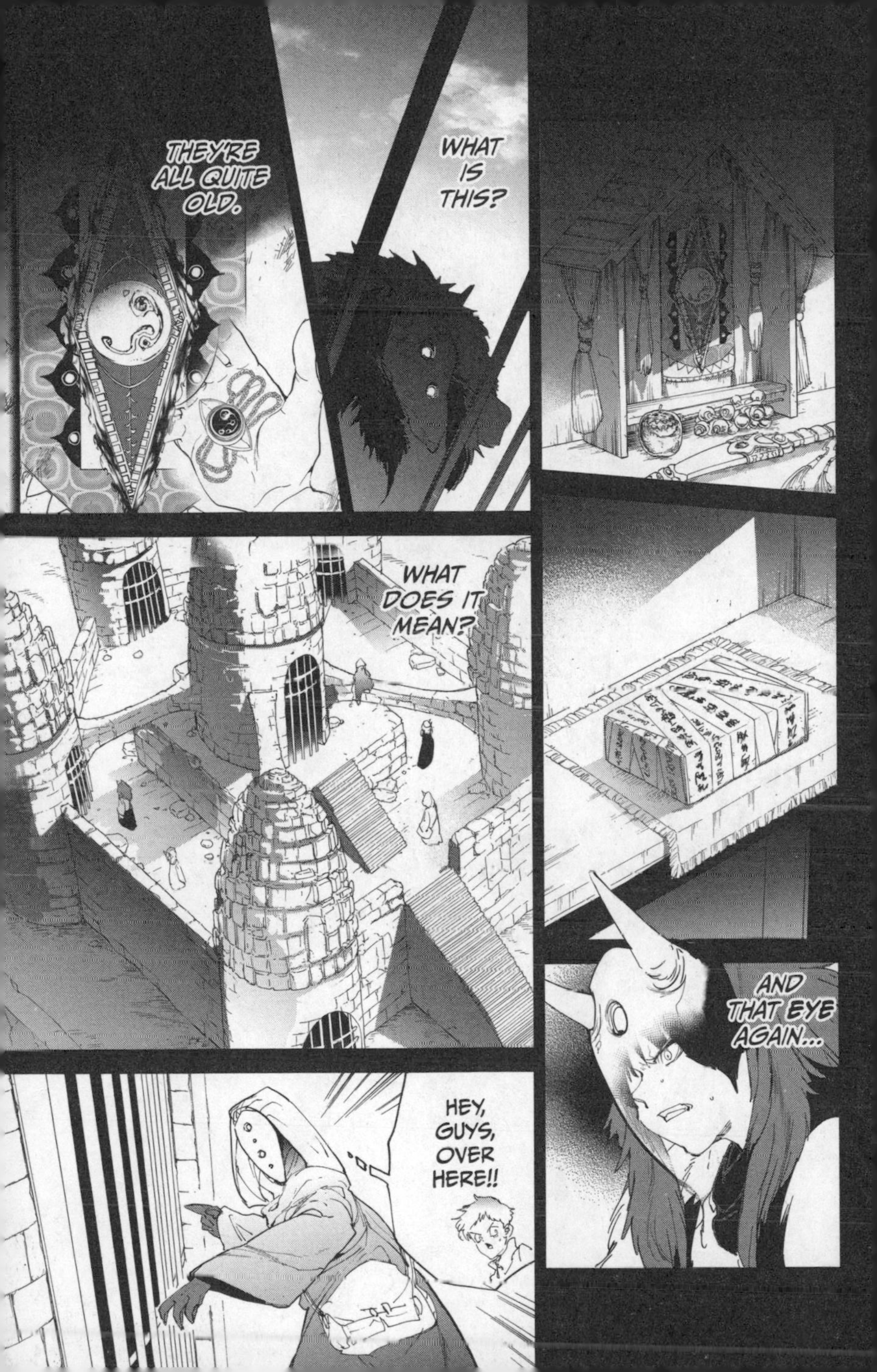
WHAT IS THIS?
THEY'RE ALL QUITE OLD.
AND THAT EYE AGAIN...
WHAT DOES IT MEAN?
HEY, GUYS, OVER HERE!!

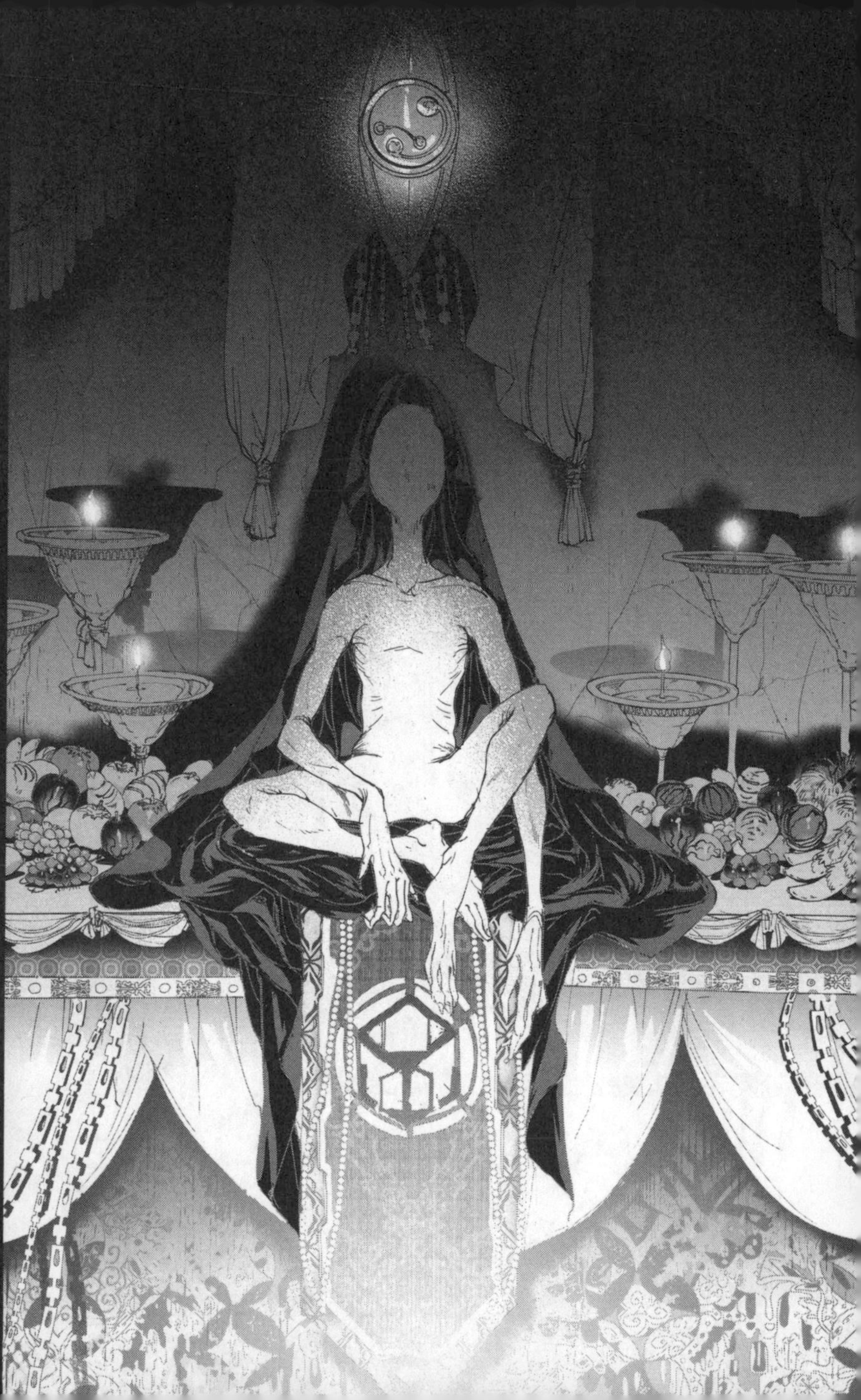

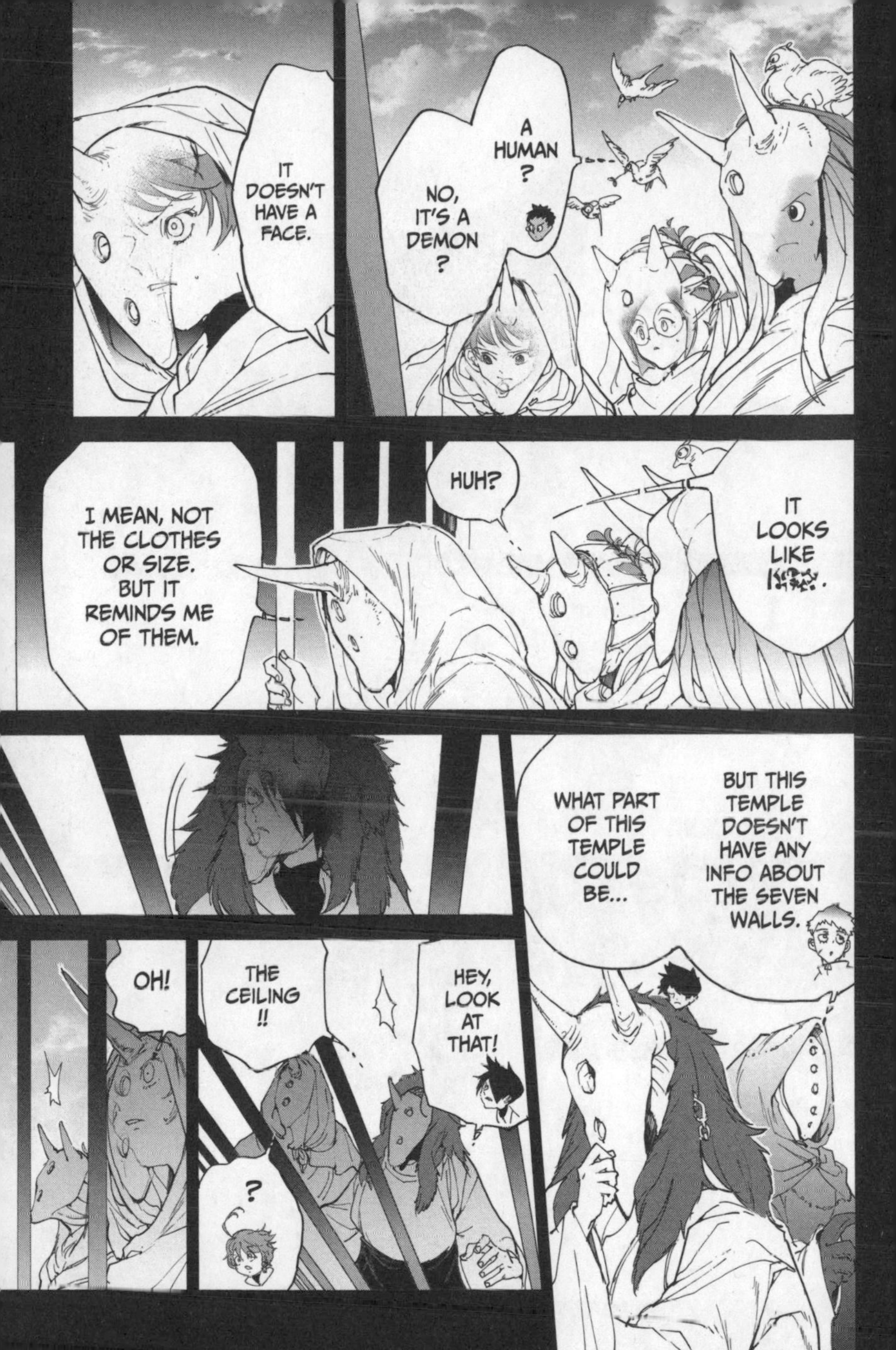
A HUMAN?
NO, IT'S A DEMON?
IT DOESN'T HAVE A FACE.
IT LOOKS LIKE
HUH?
I MEAN, NOT THE CLOTHES OR SIZE. BUT IT REMINDS ME OF THEM.
BUT THIS TEMPLE DOESN'T HAVE ANY INFO ABOUT THE SEVEN WALLS.
WHAT PART OF THIS TEMPLE COULD BE...
HEY, LOOK AT THAT!
THE CEILING!!
OH!
?

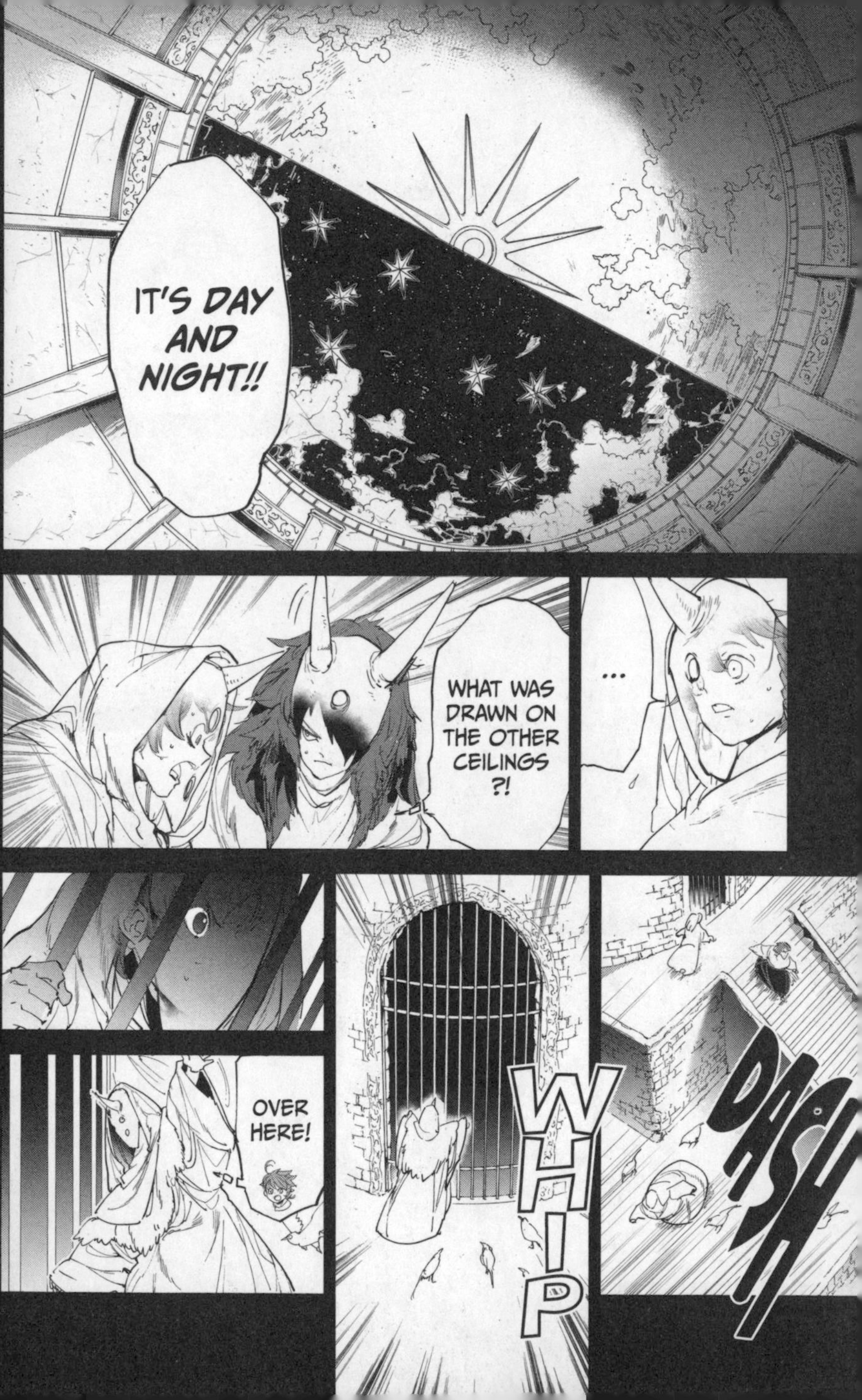
IT'S DAY AND NIGHT!!
...
WHAT WAS DRAWN ON THE OTHER CEILINGS ?!
DASH
WHIP
OVER HERE!

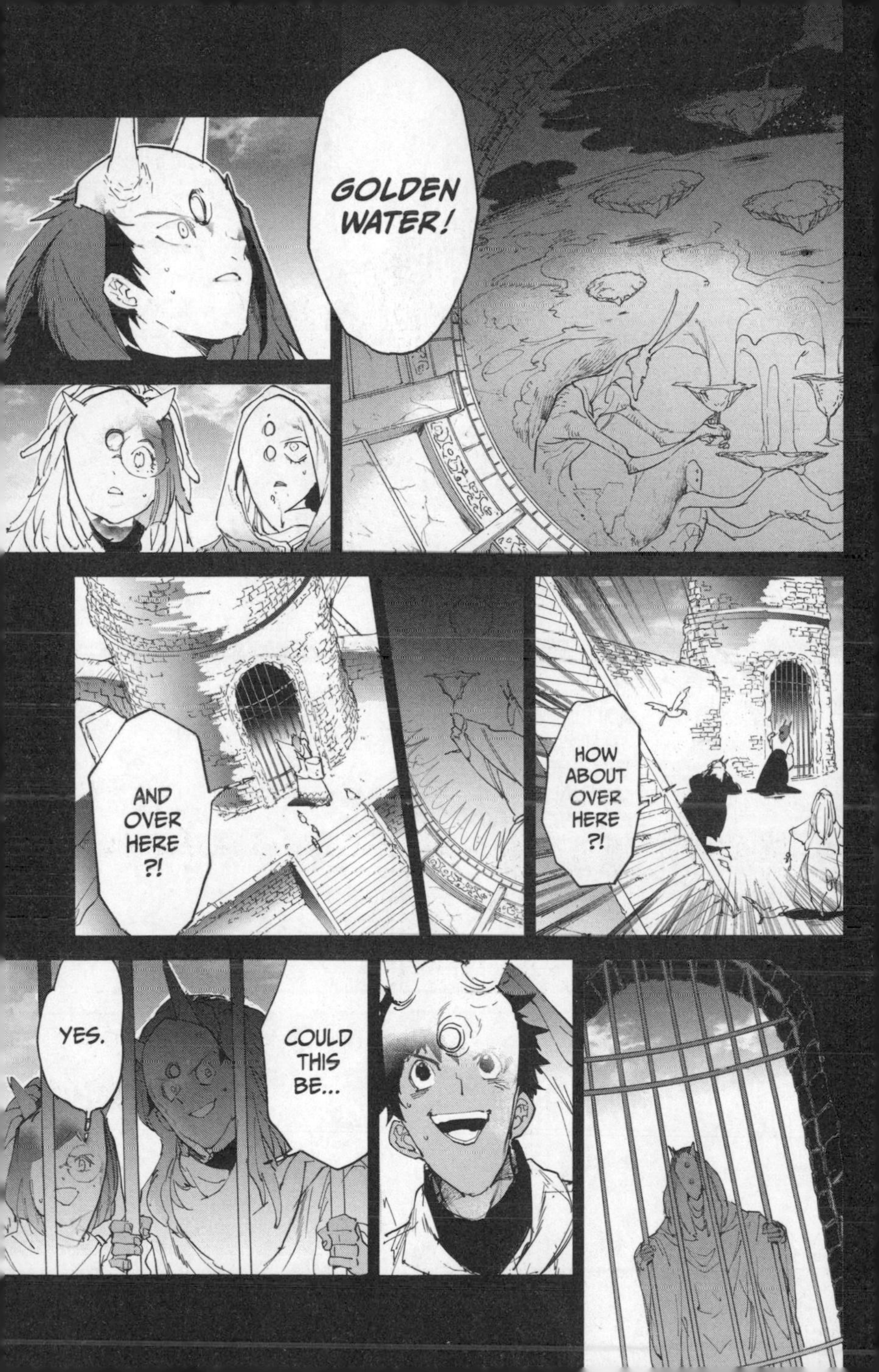
GOLDEN WATER!
HOW ABOUT OVER HERE?!
AND OVER HERE?!
COULD THIS BE...
YES.

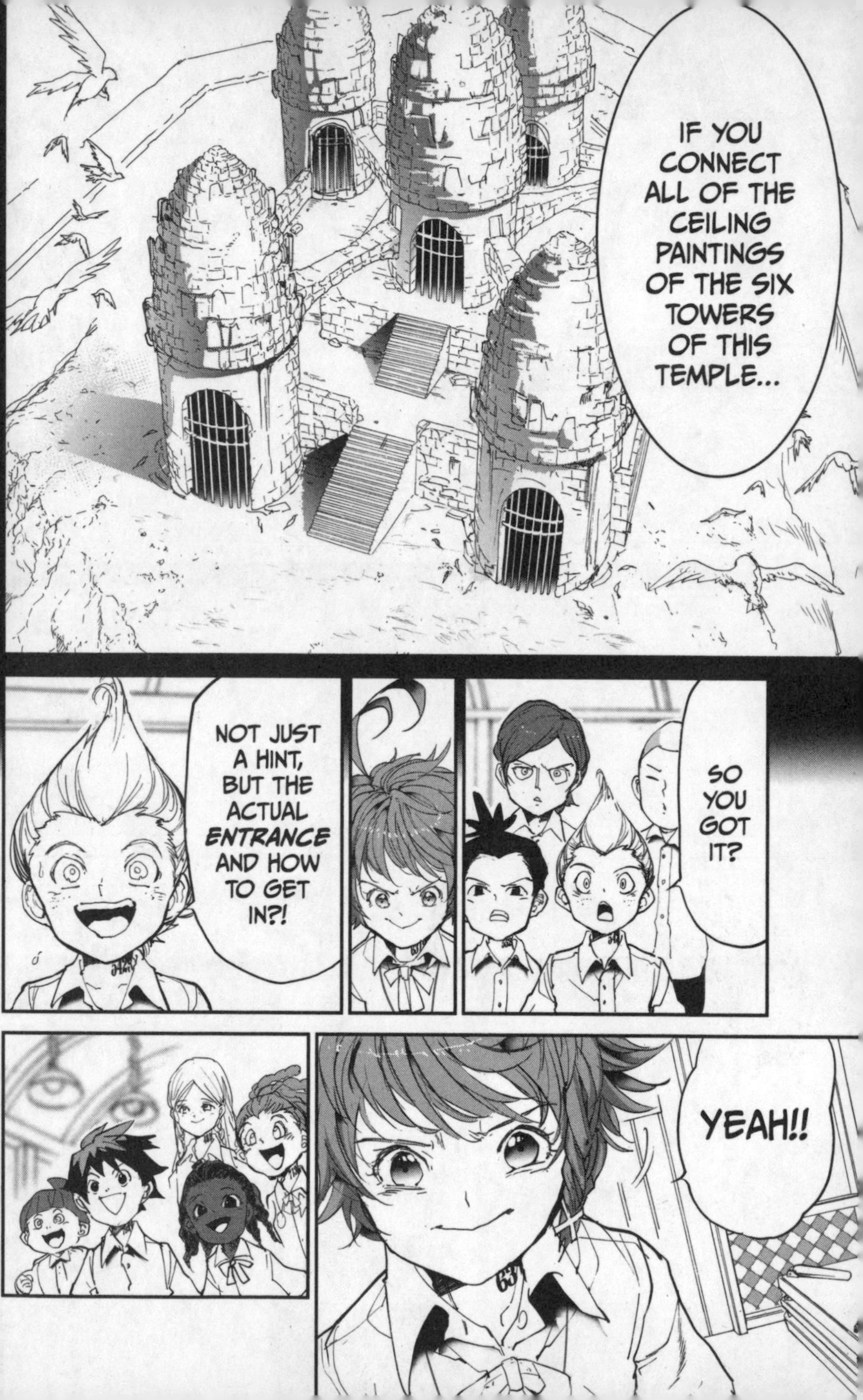
IF YOU CONNECT ALL OF THE CEILING PAINTINGS OF THE SIX TOWERS OF THIS TEMPLE...
SO YOU GOT IT?
NOT JUST A HINT, BUT THE ACTUAL *ENTRANCE* AND HOW TO GET IN?!
YEAH!!

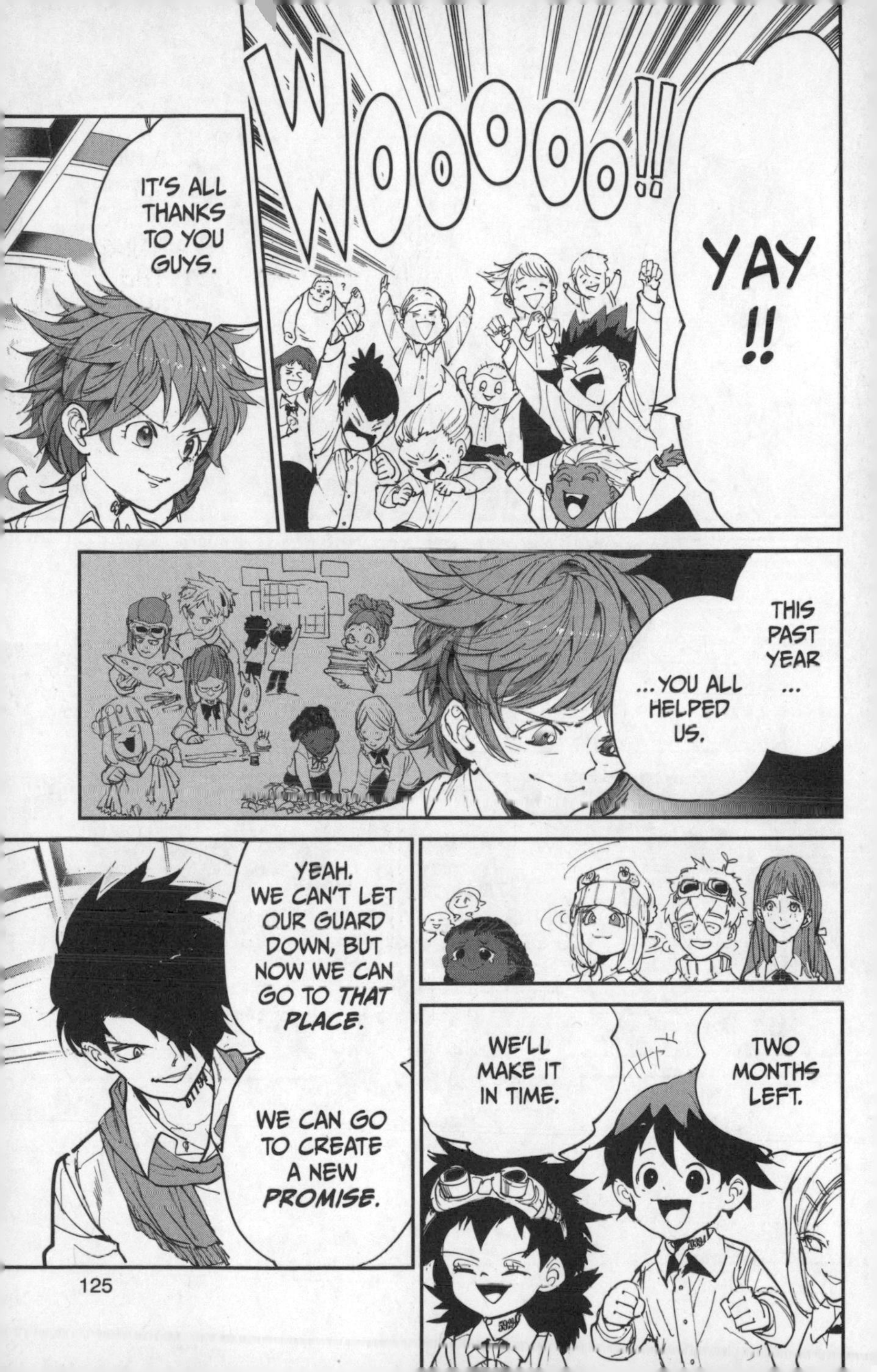
WOOOOOO!!
YAY!!
IT'S ALL THANKS TO YOU GUYS.
THIS PAST YEAR...
...YOU ALL HELPED US.
TWO MONTHS LEFT.
WE'LL MAKE IT IN TIME.
YEAH. WE CAN'T LET OUR GUARD DOWN, BUT NOW WE CAN GO TO *THAT PLACE*.
WE CAN GO TO CREATE A NEW *PROMISE*.

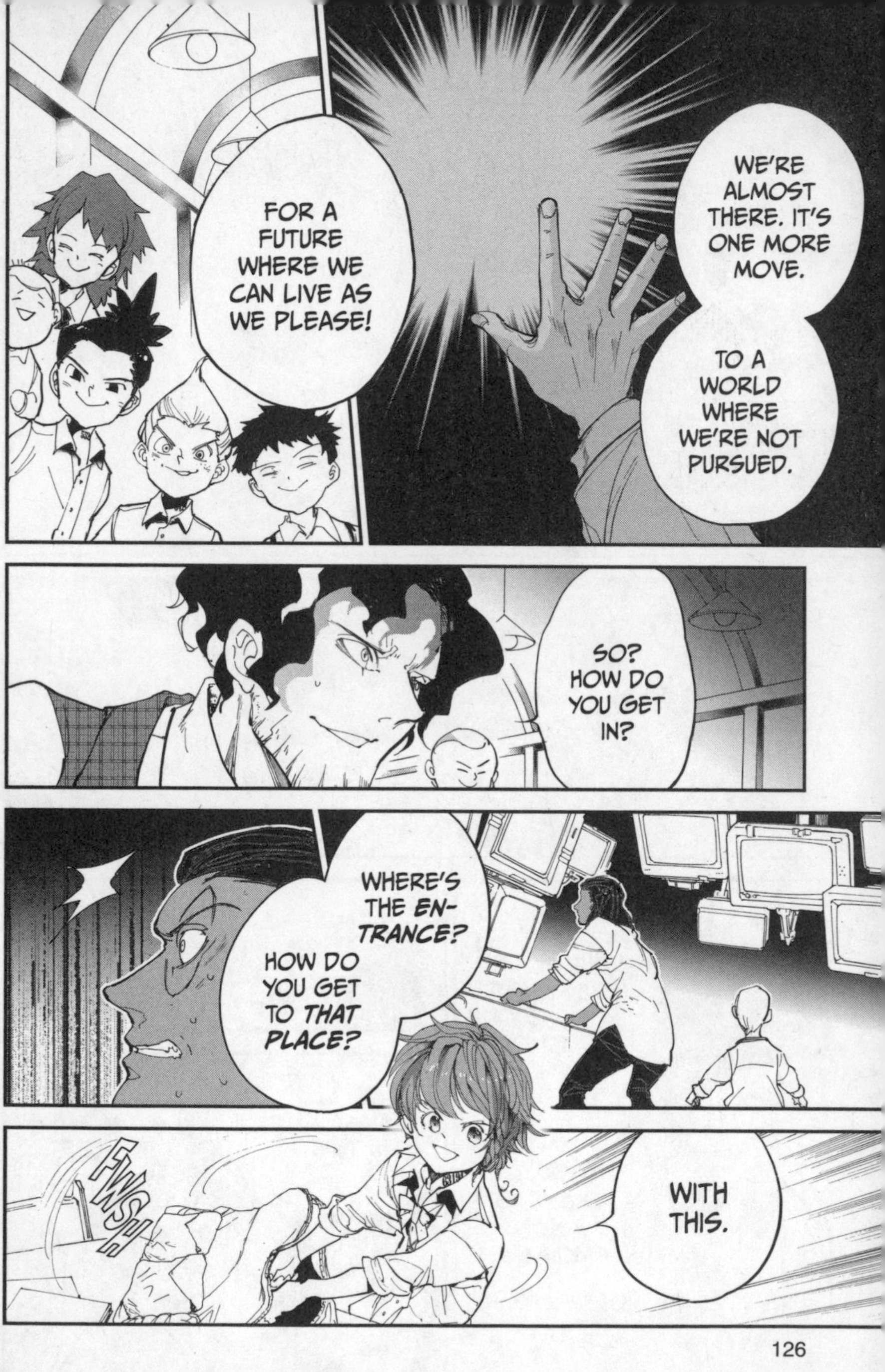
WE'RE ALMOST THERE. IT'S ONE MORE MOVE.
TO A WORLD WHERE WE'RE NOT PURSUED.
FOR A FUTURE WHERE WE CAN LIVE AS WE PLEASE!
SO? HOW DO YOU GET IN?
WHERE'S THE *EN-TRANCE?*
HOW DO YOU GET TO *THAT PLACE?*
WITH THIS.
FWSH

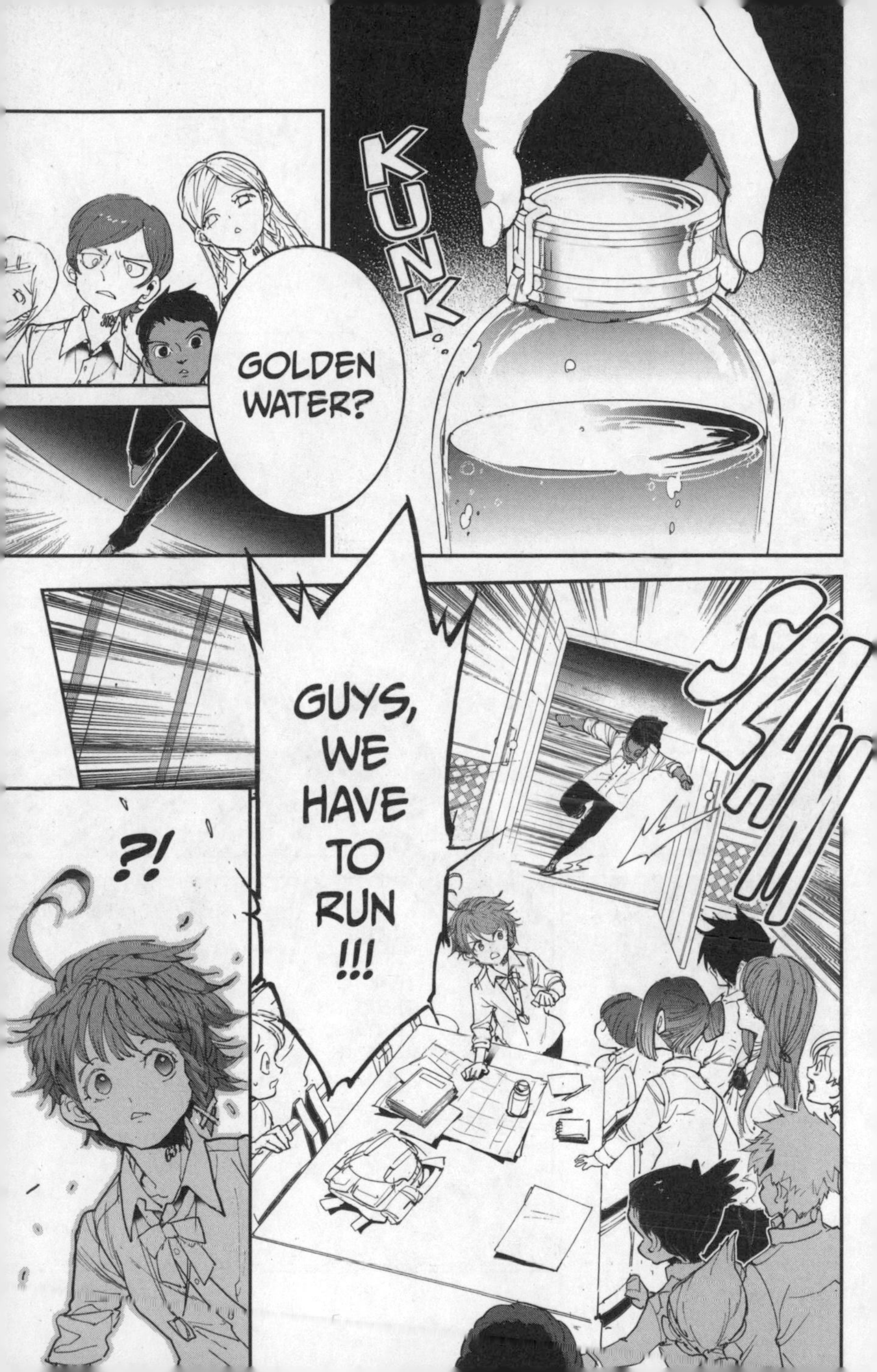
KUNK
GOLDEN WATER?
SLAM
GUYS, WE HAVE TO RUN!!!
?!

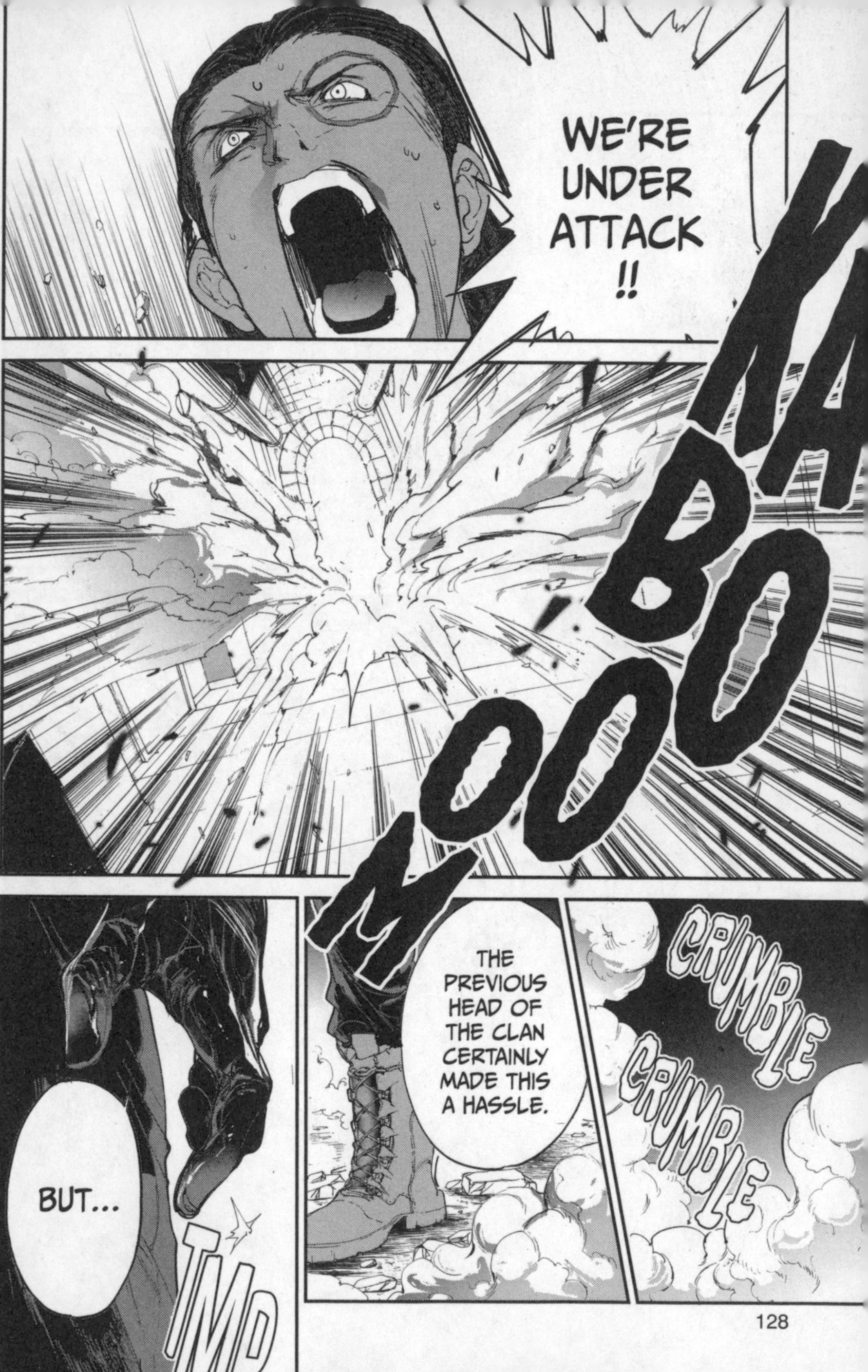
WE'RE UNDER ATTACK !!
KABOOOM
CRUMBLE
CRUMBLE
THE PREVIOUS HEAD OF THE CLAN CERTAINLY MADE THIS A HASSLE.
BUT...
TMP

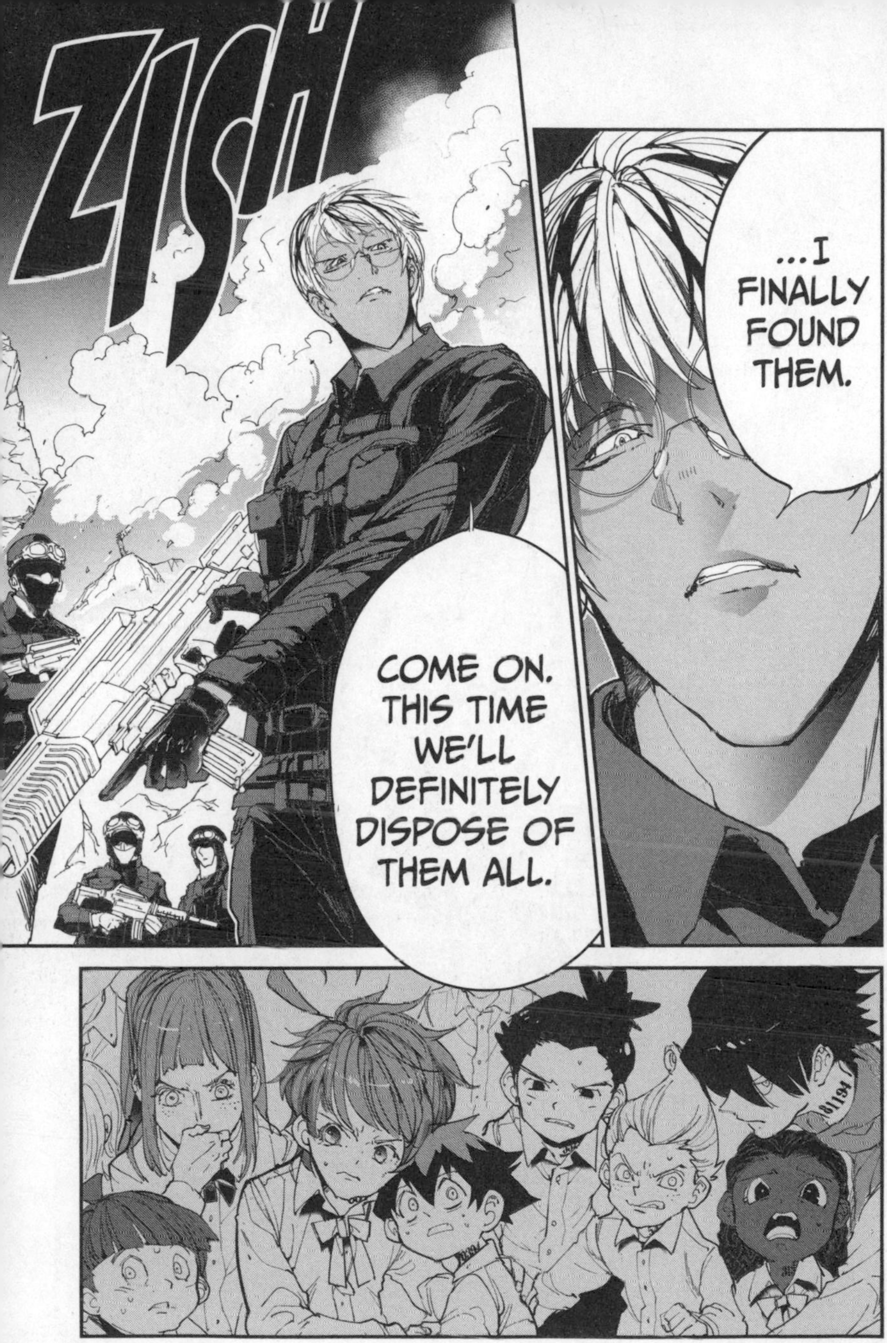
...I FINALLY FOUND THEM.
ZISH
COME ON. THIS TIME WE'LL DEFINITELY DISPOSE OF THEM ALL.

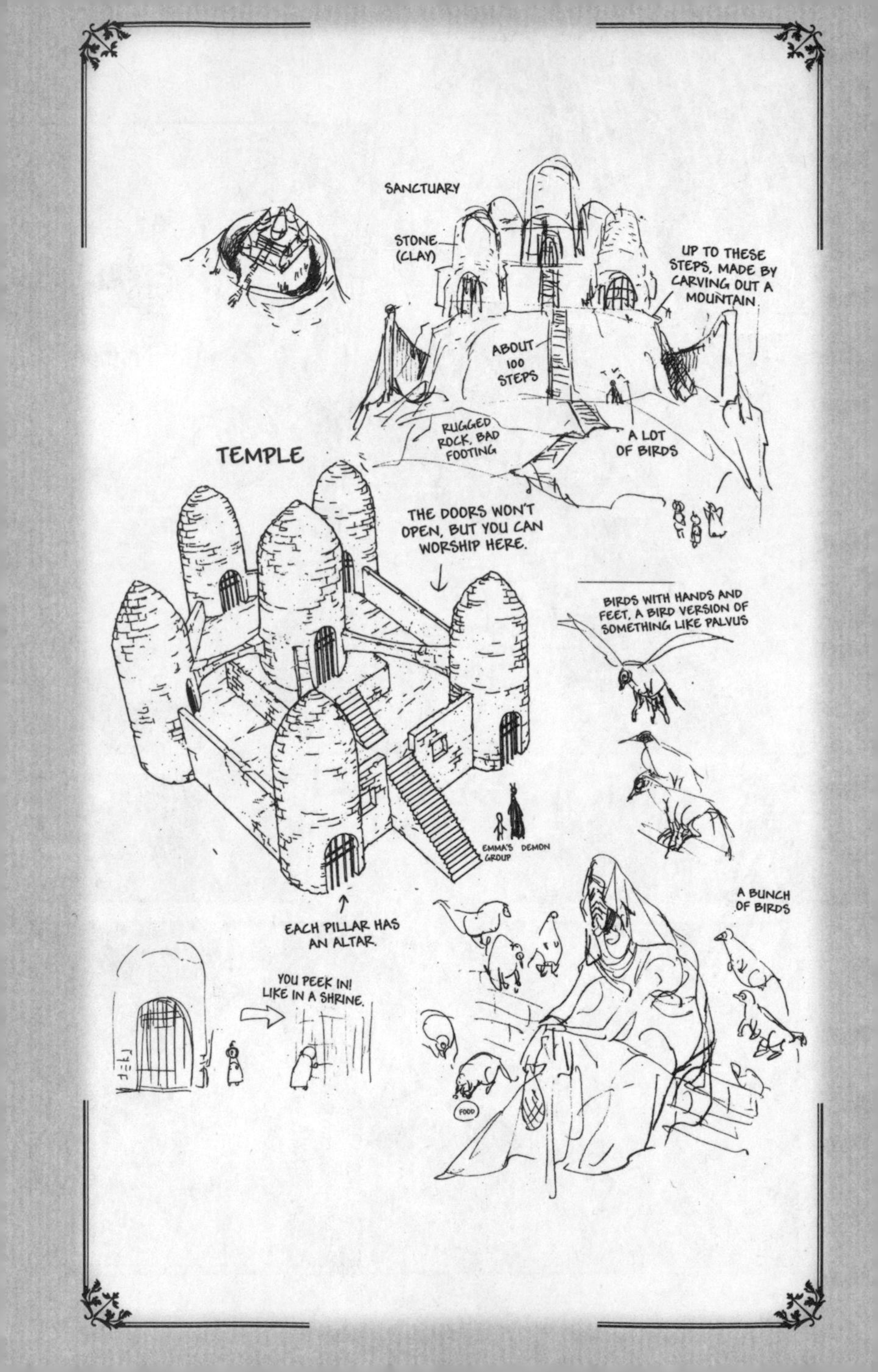
SANCTUARY
STONE (CLAY)
UP TO THESE STEPS, MADE BY CARVING OUT A MOUNTAIN
ABOUT 100 STEPS
RUGGED ROCK, BAD FOOTING
A LOT OF BIRDS
TEMPLE
THE DOORS WON'T OPEN, BUT YOU CAN WORSHIP HERE.
BIRDS WITH HANDS AND FEET, A BIRD VERSION OF SOMETHING LIKE PALVUS
EMMA'S GROUP
DEMON
EACH PILLAR HAS AN ALTAR.
A BUNCH OF BIRDS
YOU PEEK IN! LIKE IN A SHRINE.
FOOD

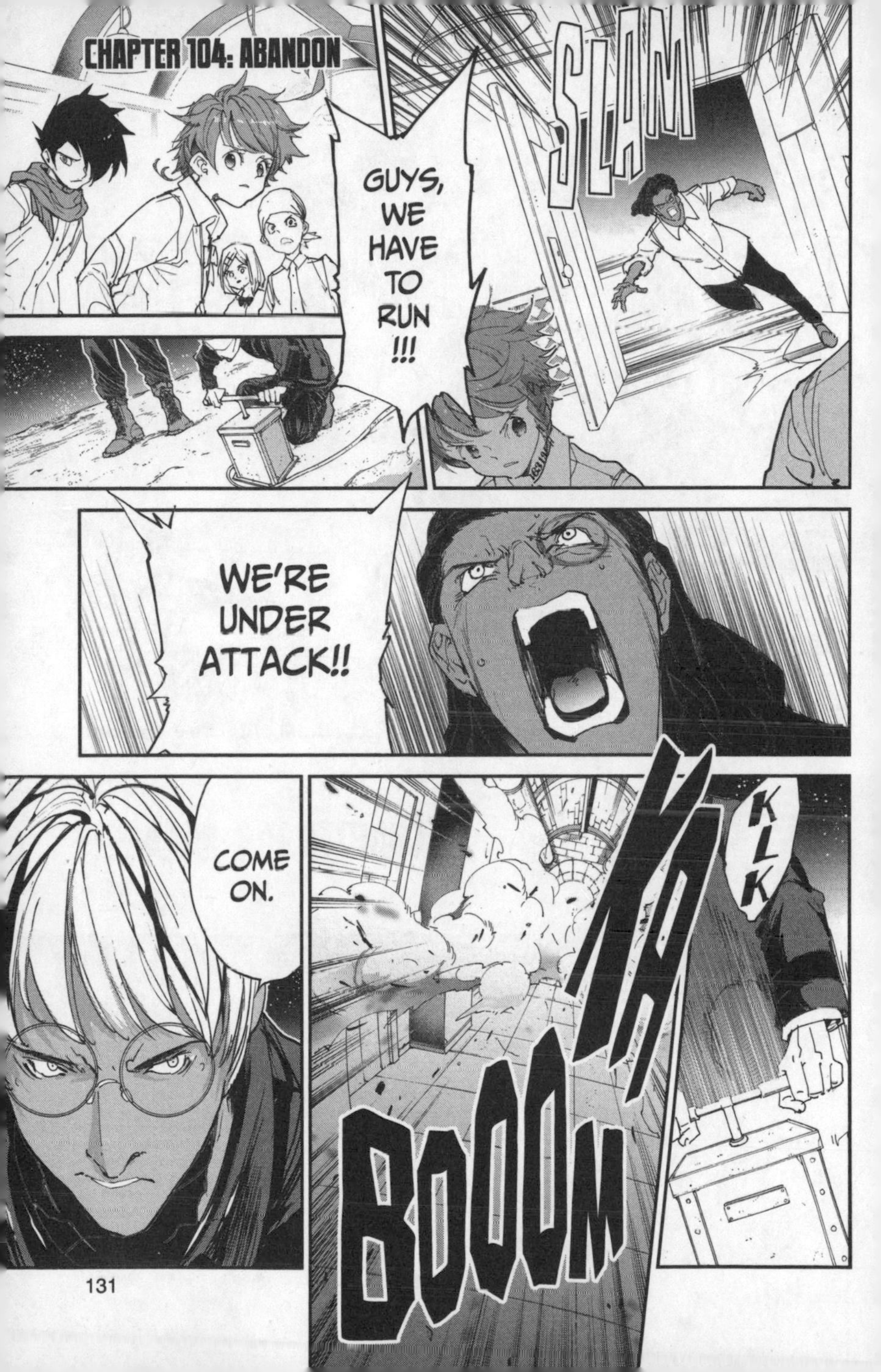
SLAM
GUYS, WE HAVE TO RUN!!!
CHAPTER 104: ABANDON
WE'RE UNDER ATTACK!!
KLIK
KA
BOOOM
COME ON.

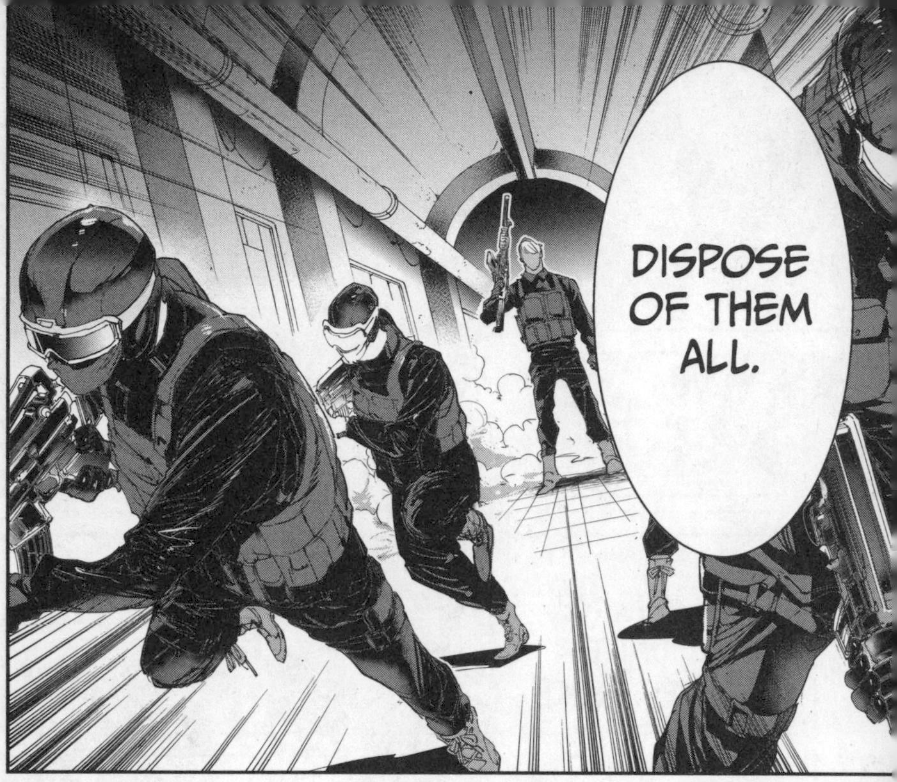
DISPOSE OF THEM ALL.

CHAPTER 104: ABANDON

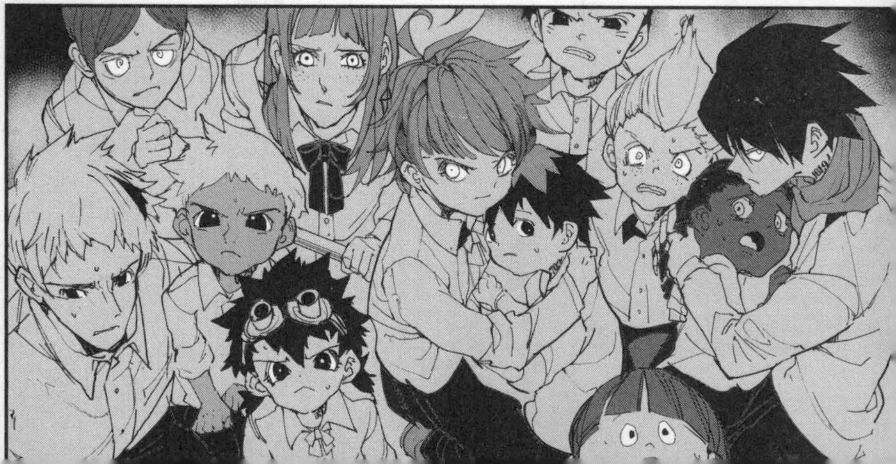

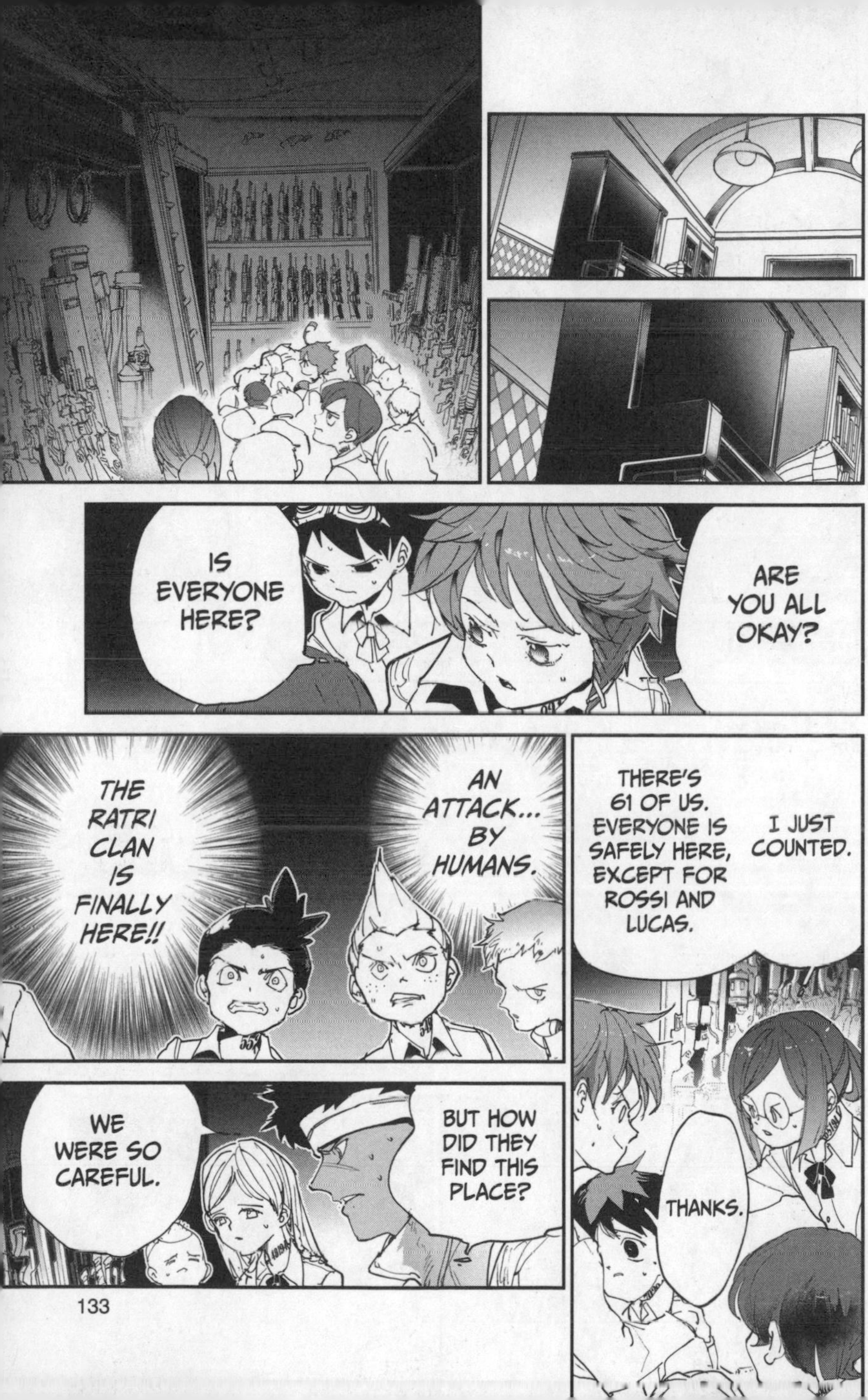
ARE YOU ALL OKAY?
IS EVERYONE HERE?
I JUST COUNTED.
THERE'S 61 OF US. EVERYONE IS SAFELY HERE, EXCEPT FOR ROSSI AND LUCAS.
THANKS.
AN ATTACK... BY HUMANS.
THE RATRI CLAN IS FINALLY HERE!!
BUT HOW DID THEY FIND THIS PLACE?
WE WERE SO CAREFUL.

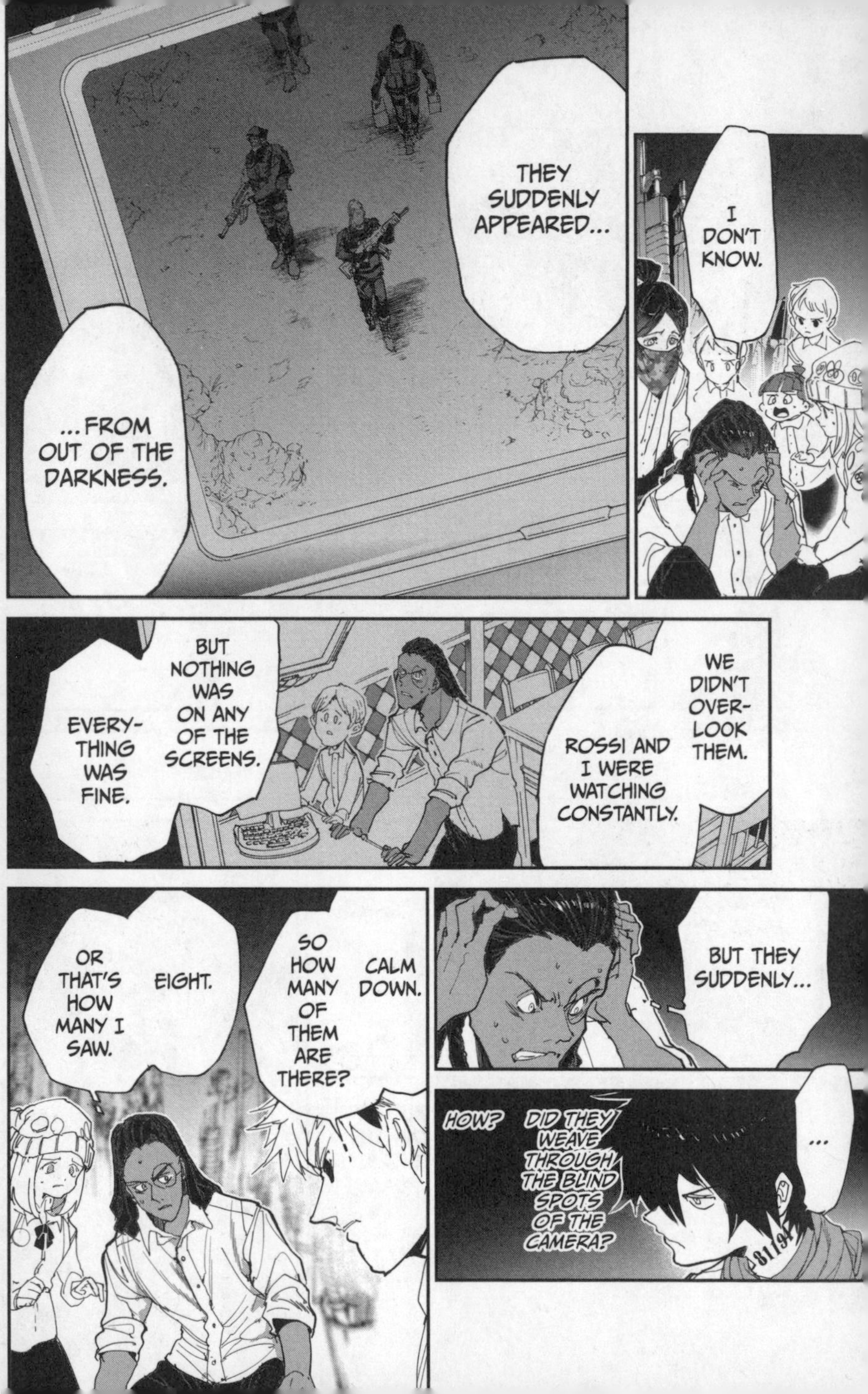
I DON'T KNOW.
THEY SUDDENLY APPEARED...
...FROM OUT OF THE DARKNESS.
WE DIDN'T OVER-LOOK THEM.
ROSSI AND I WERE WATCHING CONSTANTLY.
BUT NOTHING WAS ON ANY OF THE SCREENS.
EVERY-THING WAS FINE.
BUT THEY SUDDENLY...
...
DID THEY WEAVE THROUGH THE BLIND SPOTS OF THE CAMERA?
HOW?
CALM DOWN.
SO HOW MANY OF THEM ARE THERE?
EIGHT.
OR THAT'S HOW MANY I SAW.

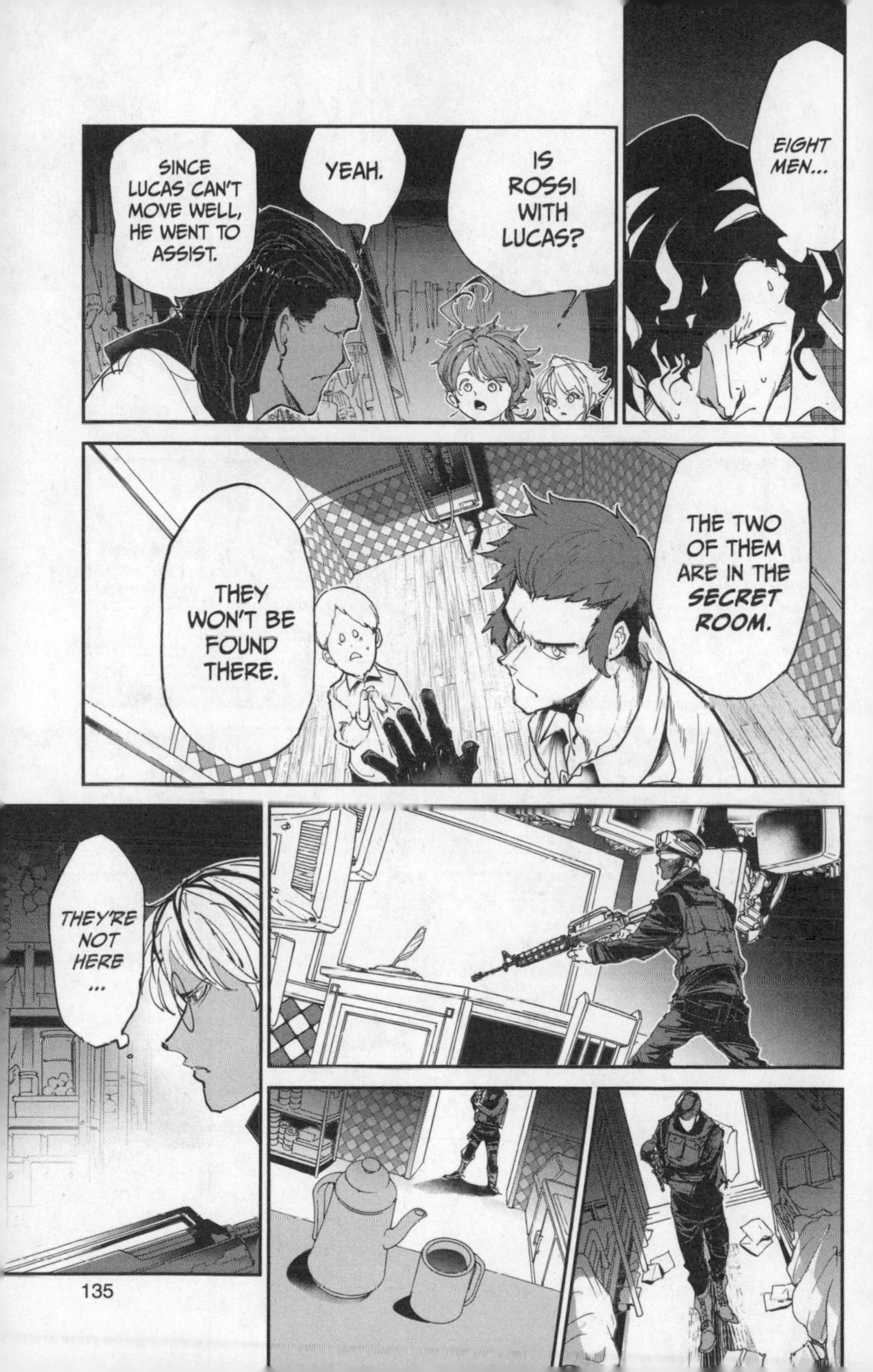
EIGHT MEN...
IS ROSSI WITH LUCAS?
YEAH.
SINCE LUCAS CAN'T MOVE WELL, HE WENT TO ASSIST.
THE TWO OF THEM ARE IN THE SECRET ROOM.
THEY WON'T BE FOUND THERE.
THEY'RE NOT HERE...

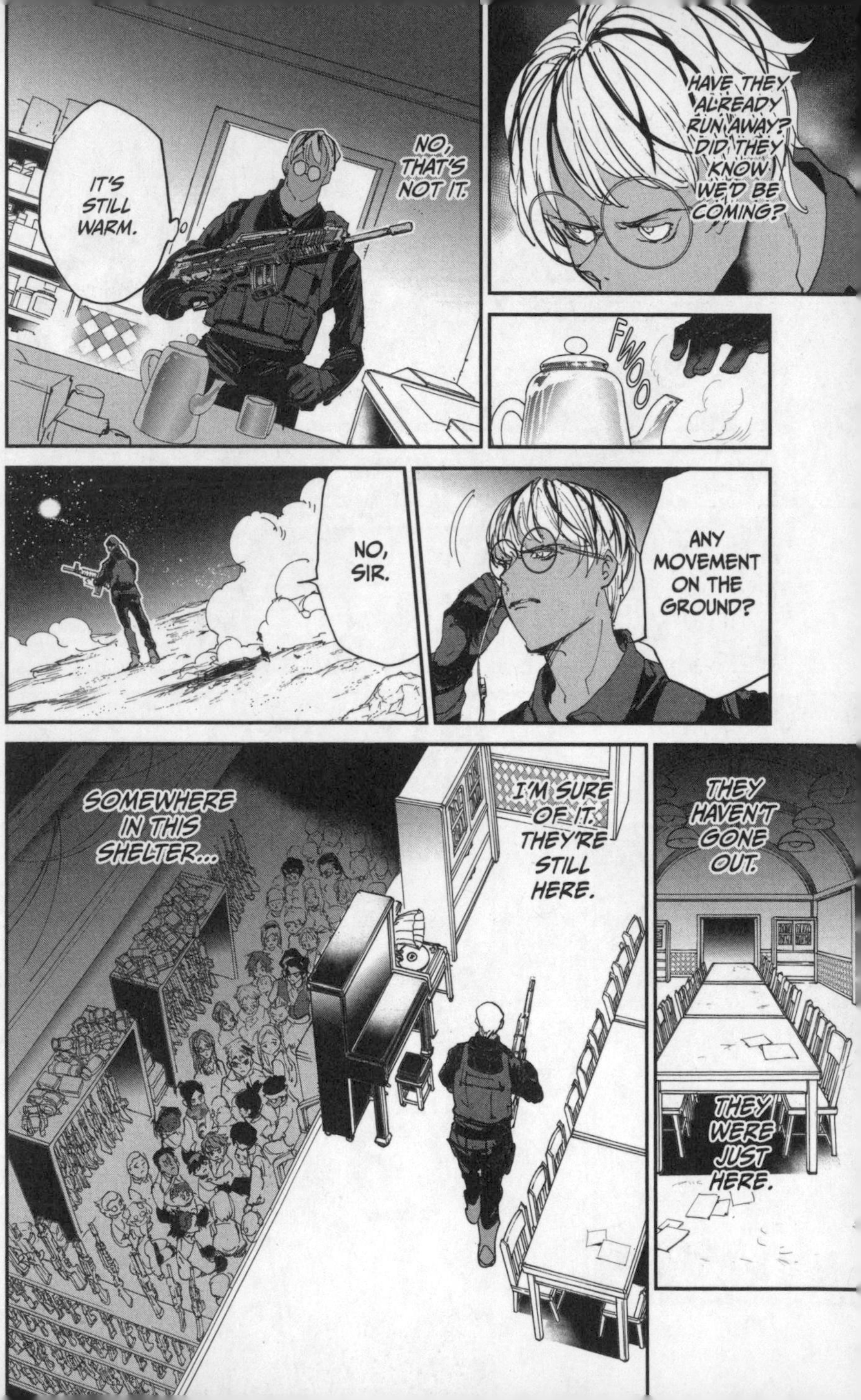
HAVE THEY ALREADY RUN AWAY? DID THEY KNOW WE'D BE COMING?
FWOO
NO, THAT'S NOT IT.
IT'S STILL WARM.
ANY MOVEMENT ON THE GROUND?
NO, SIR.
THEY HAVEN'T GONE OUT.
THEY WERE JUST HERE.
I'M SURE OF IT. THEY'RE STILL HERE.
SOMEWHERE IN THIS SHELTER...

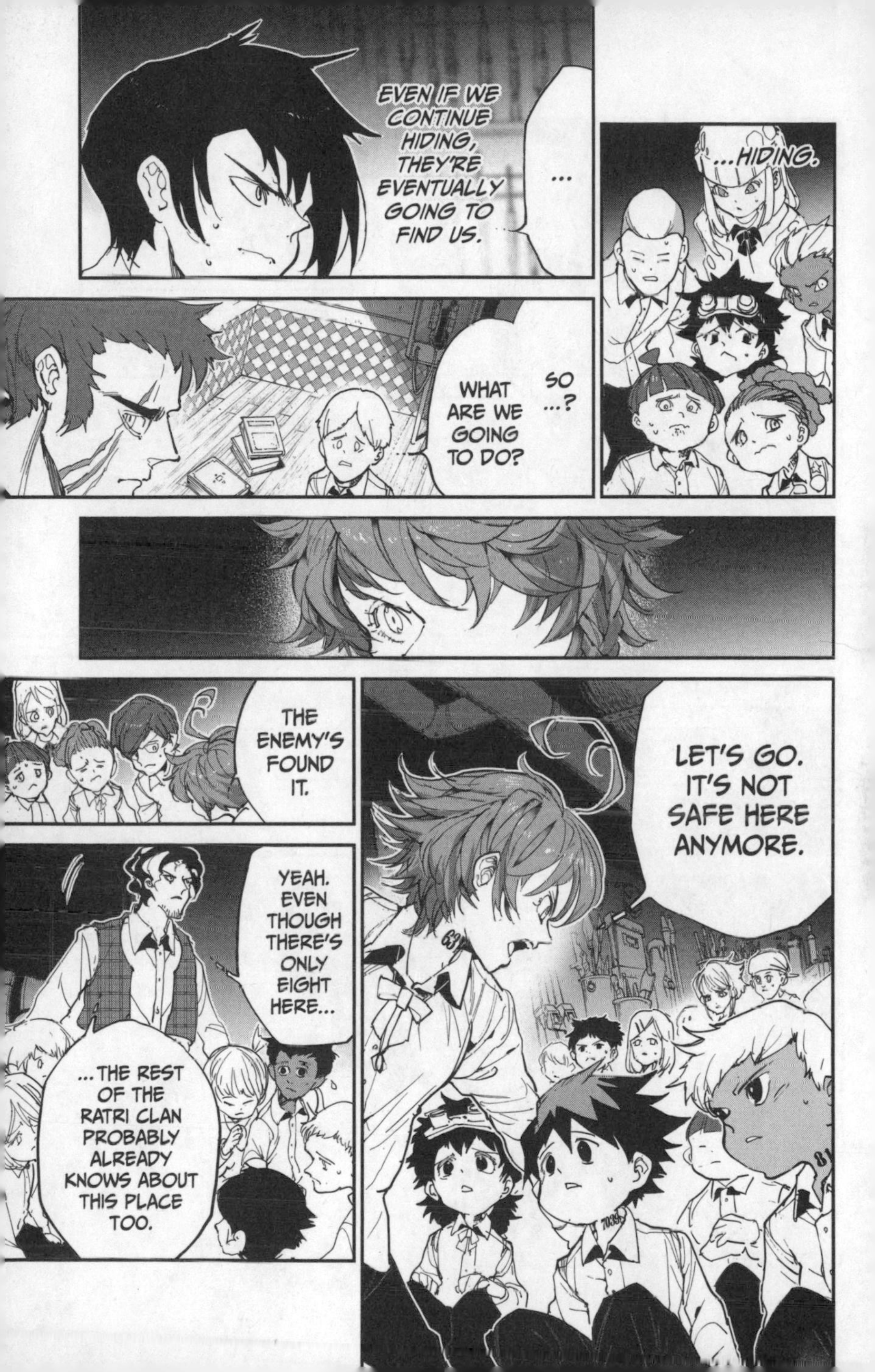
...HIDING.
EVEN IF WE CONTINUE HIDING, THEY'RE EVENTUALLY GOING TO FIND US.
...
SO ...?
WHAT ARE WE GOING TO DO?
LET'S GO. IT'S NOT SAFE HERE ANYMORE.
THE ENEMY'S FOUND IT.
YEAH. EVEN THOUGH THERE'S ONLY EIGHT HERE...
...THE REST OF THE RATRI CLAN PROBABLY ALREADY KNOWS ABOUT THIS PLACE TOO.

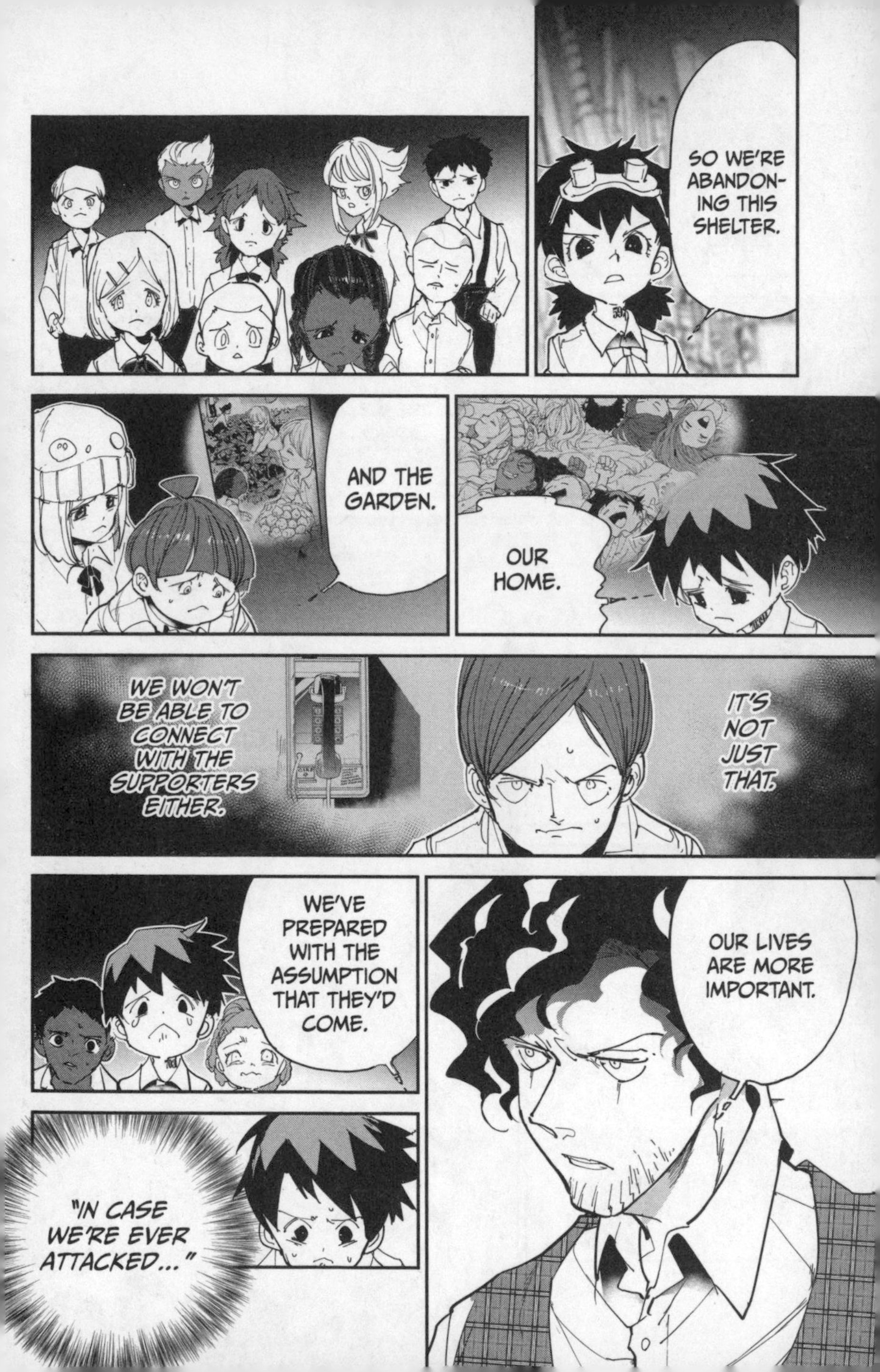
SO WE'RE ABANDONING THIS SHELTER.
OUR HOME.
AND THE GARDEN.
IT'S NOT JUST THAT.
WE WON'T BE ABLE TO CONNECT WITH THE SUPPORTERS EITHER.
OUR LIVES ARE MORE IMPORTANT.
WE'VE PREPARED WITH THE ASSUMPTION THAT THEY'D COME.
"IN CASE WE'RE EVER ATTACKED..."

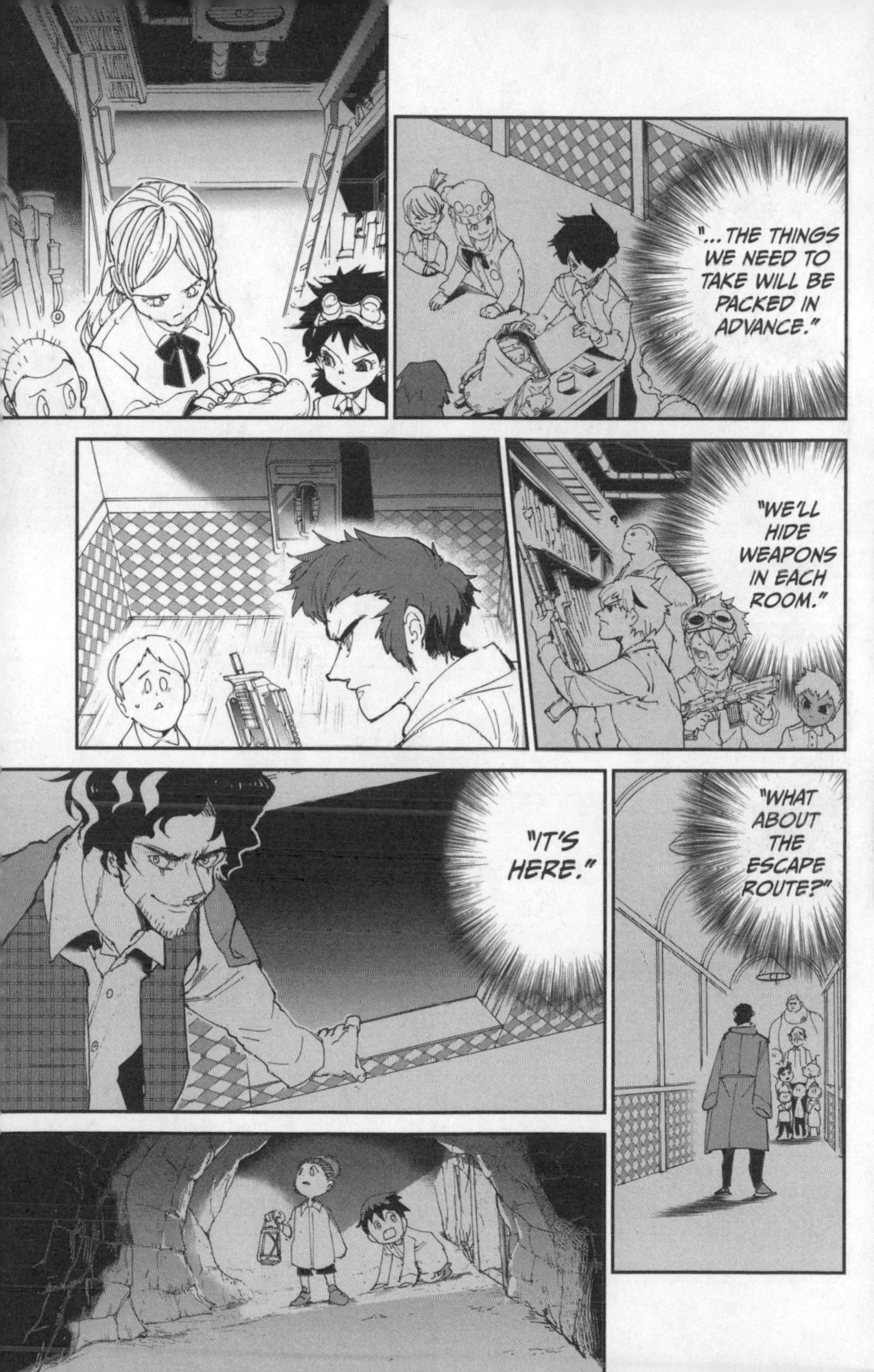
"...THE THINGS WE NEED TO TAKE WILL BE PACKED IN ADVANCE."
"WE'LL HIDE WEAPONS IN EACH ROOM."
"WHAT ABOUT THE ESCAPE ROUTE?"
"IT'S HERE."

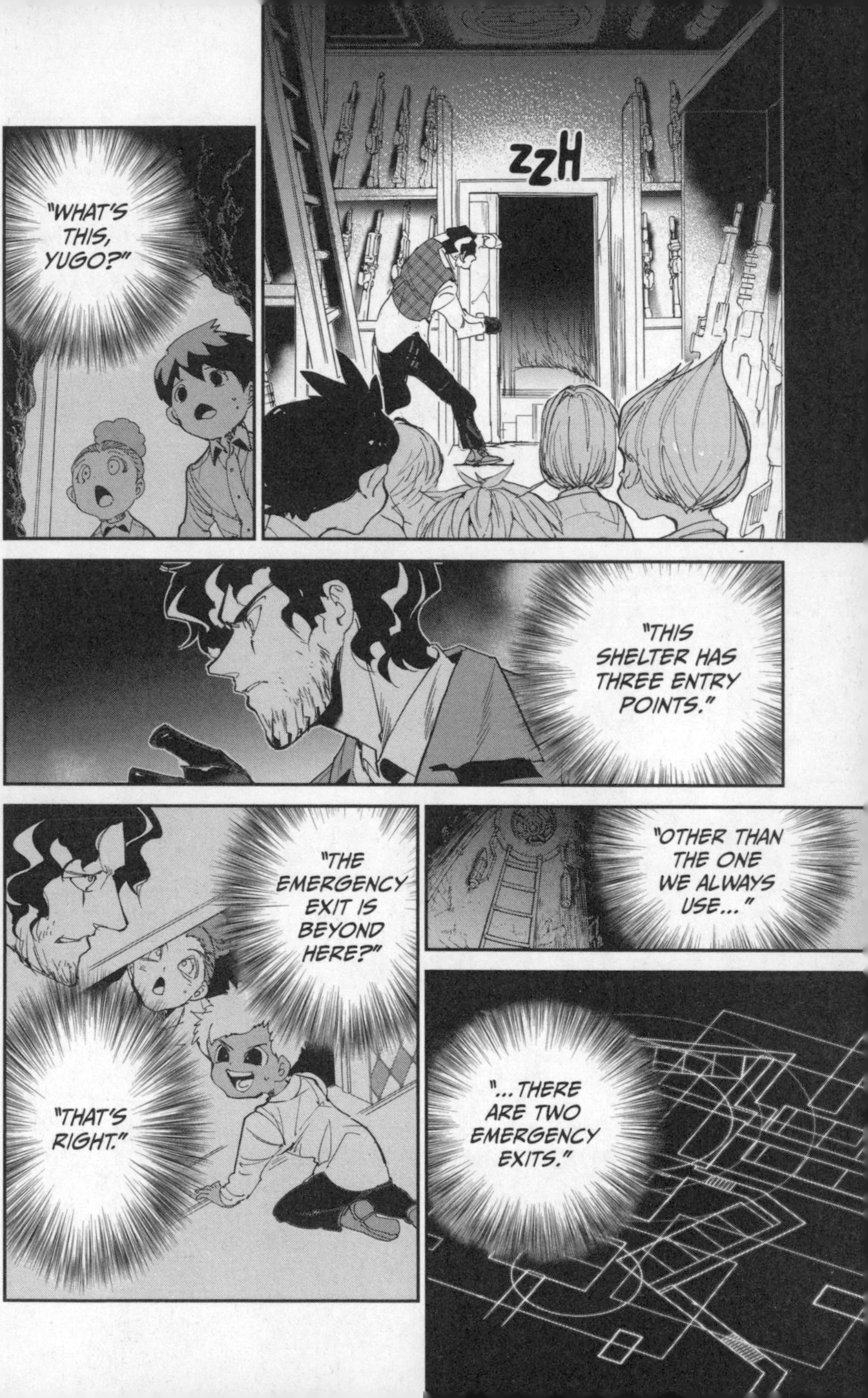
ZZH
"WHAT'S THIS, YUGO?"
"THIS SHELTER HAS THREE ENTRY POINTS."
"OTHER THAN THE ONE WE ALWAYS USE..."
"...THERE ARE TWO EMERGENCY EXITS."
"THE EMERGENCY EXIT IS BEYOND HERE?"
"THAT'S RIGHT."

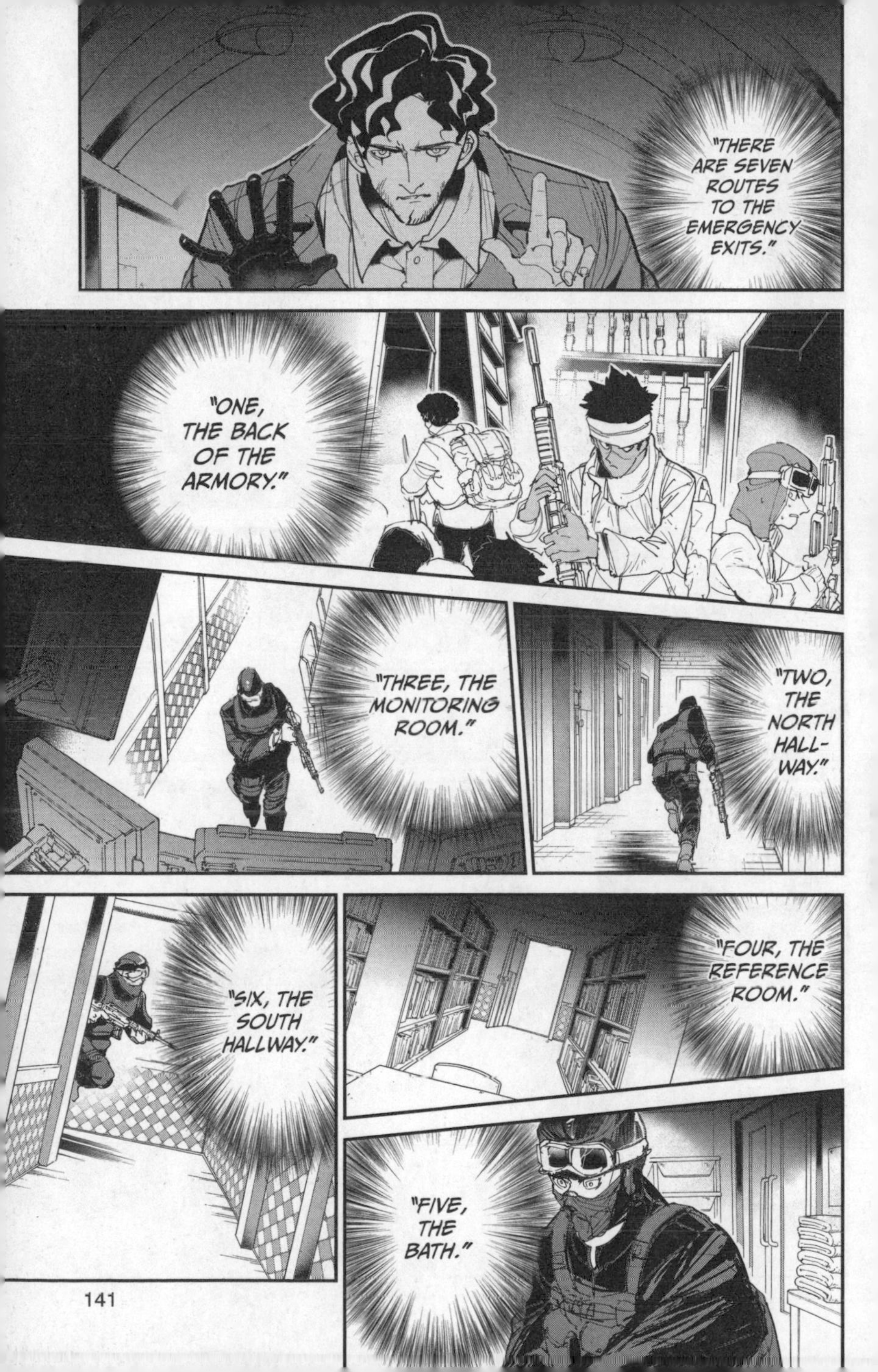
"THERE ARE SEVEN ROUTES TO THE EMERGENCY EXITS."
"ONE, THE BACK OF THE ARMORY."
"TWO, THE NORTH HALL-WAY."
"THREE, THE MONITORING ROOM."
"FOUR, THE REFERENCE ROOM."
"FIVE, THE BATH."
"SIX, THE SOUTH HALLWAY."

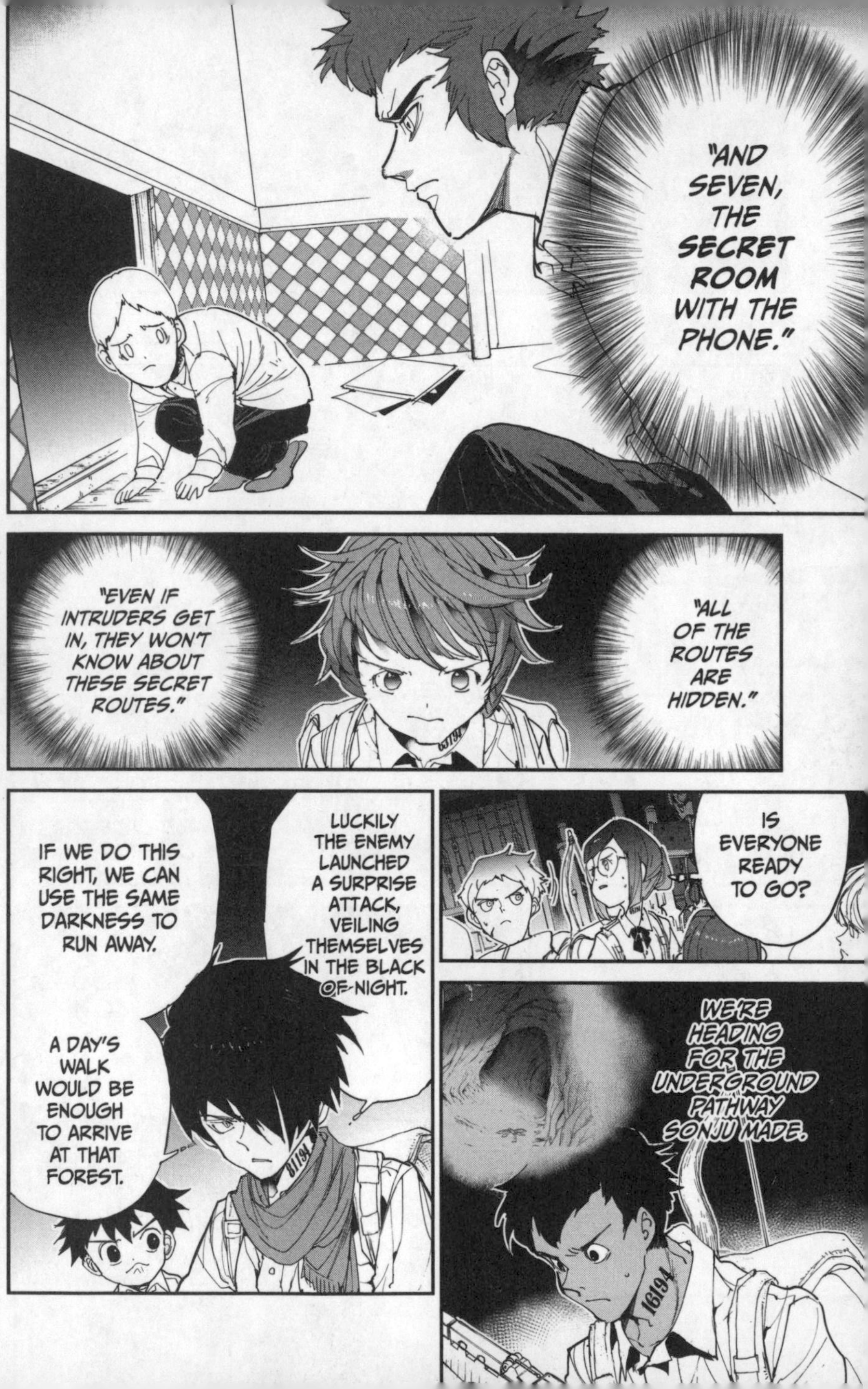
"AND SEVEN, THE SECRET ROOM WITH THE PHONE."
"ALL OF THE ROUTES ARE HIDDEN."
"EVEN IF INTRUDERS GET IN, THEY WON'T KNOW ABOUT THESE SECRET ROUTES."
IS EVERYONE READY TO GO?
WE'RE HEADING FOR THE UNDERGROUND PATHWAY SONJU MADE.
LUCKILY THE ENEMY LAUNCHED A SURPRISE ATTACK, VEILING THEMSELVES IN THE BLACK OF NIGHT.
IF WE DO THIS RIGHT, WE CAN USE THE SAME DARKNESS TO RUN AWAY.
A DAY'S WALK WOULD BE ENOUGH TO ARRIVE AT THAT FOREST.

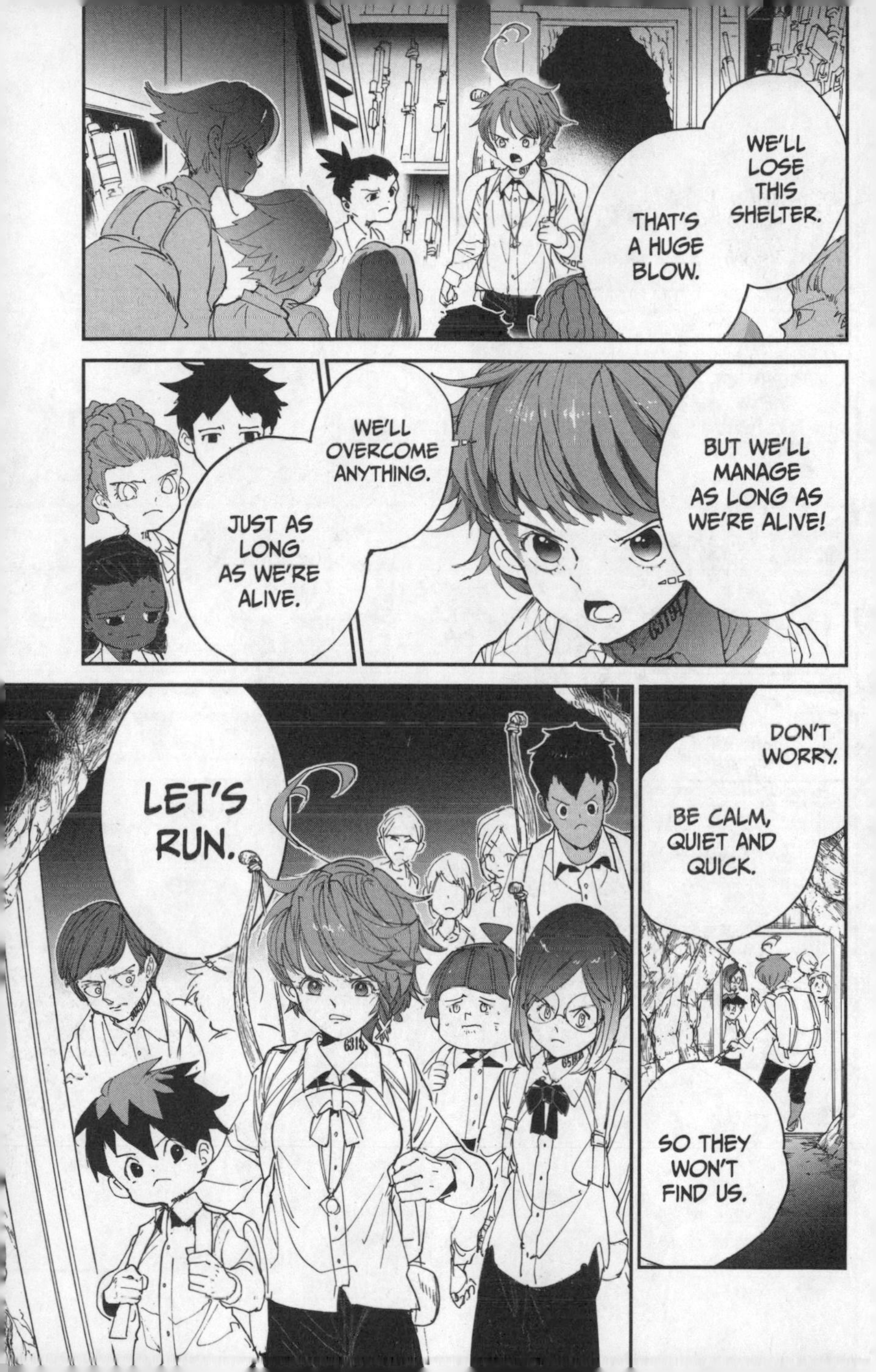
WE'LL LOSE THIS SHELTER.
THAT'S A HUGE BLOW.
BUT WE'LL MANAGE AS LONG AS WE'RE ALIVE!
WE'LL OVERCOME ANYTHING.
JUST AS LONG AS WE'RE ALIVE.
DON'T WORRY.
BE CALM, QUIET AND QUICK.
SO THEY WON'T FIND US.
LET'S RUN.

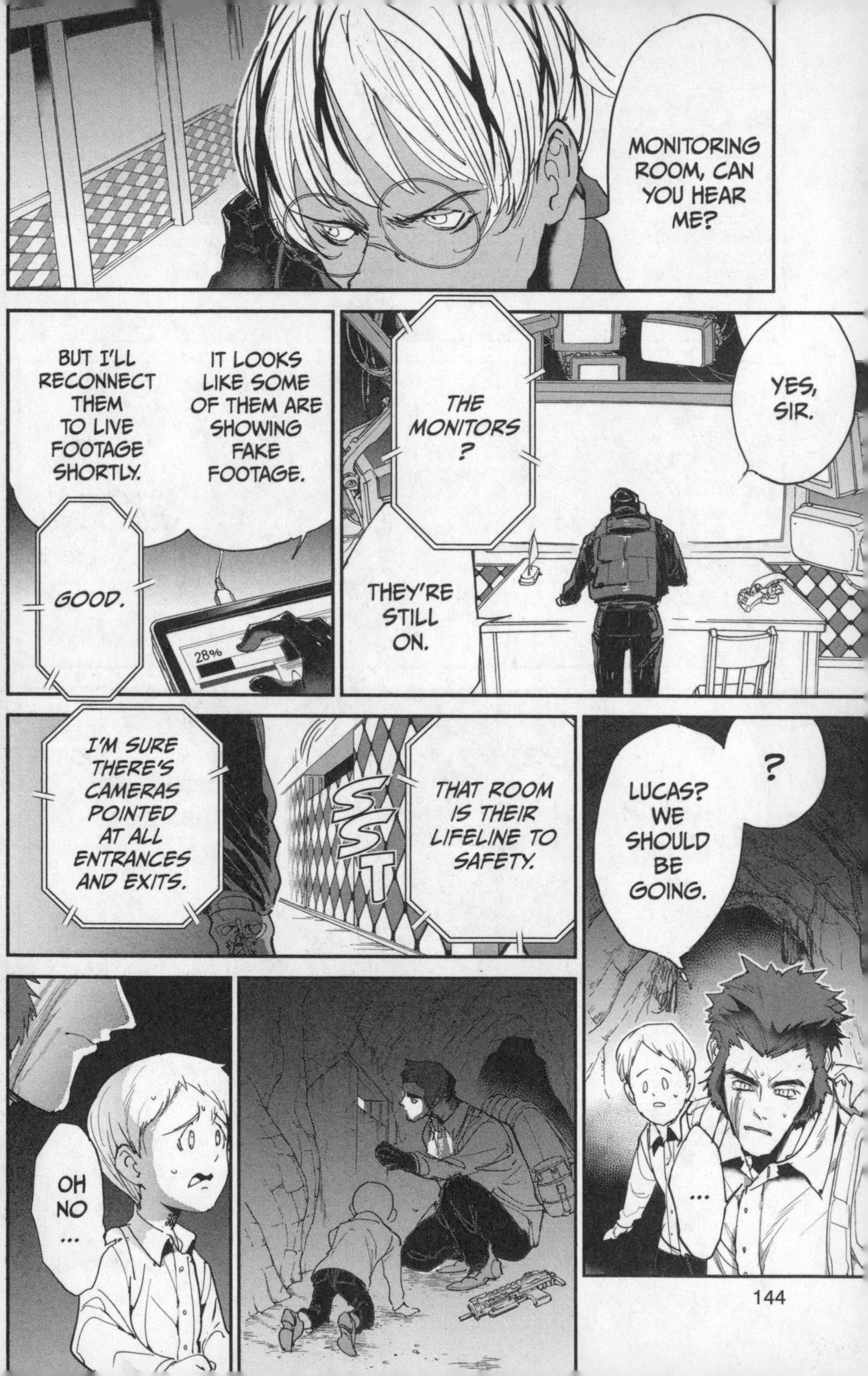
MONITORING ROOM, CAN YOU HEAR ME?
YES, SIR.
THE MONITORS?
THEY'RE STILL ON.
IT LOOKS LIKE SOME OF THEM ARE SHOWING FAKE FOOTAGE.
BUT I'LL RECONNECT THEM TO LIVE FOOTAGE SHORTLY.
GOOD.
28%
?
LUCAS? WE SHOULD BE GOING.
...
THAT ROOM IS THEIR LIFELINE TO SAFETY.
SSST
I'M SURE THERE'S CAMERAS POINTED AT ALL ENTRANCES AND EXITS.
OH NO ...

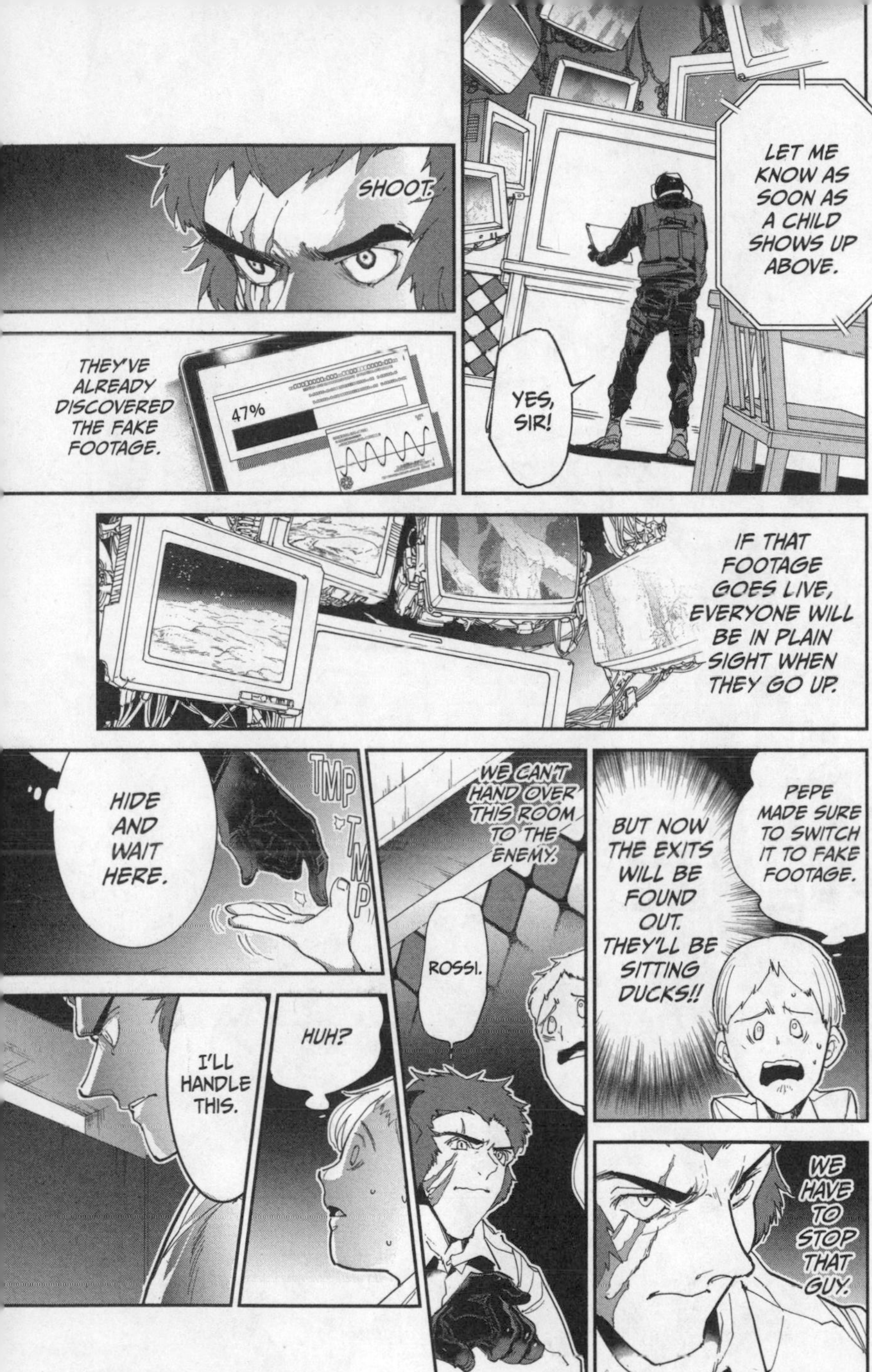
LET ME KNOW AS SOON AS A CHILD SHOWS UP ABOVE.
YES, SIR!
SHOOT.
THEY'VE ALREADY DISCOVERED THE FAKE FOOTAGE.
47%
IF THAT FOOTAGE GOES LIVE, EVERYONE WILL BE IN PLAIN SIGHT WHEN THEY GO UP.
PEPE MADE SURE TO SWITCH IT TO FAKE FOOTAGE.
BUT NOW THE EXITS WILL BE FOUND OUT. THEY'LL BE SITTING DUCKS!!
WE CAN'T HAND OVER THIS ROOM TO THE ENEMY.
ROSSI.
TMP TMP
HIDE AND WAIT HERE.
WE HAVE TO STOP THAT GUY.
HUH?
I'LL HANDLE THIS.

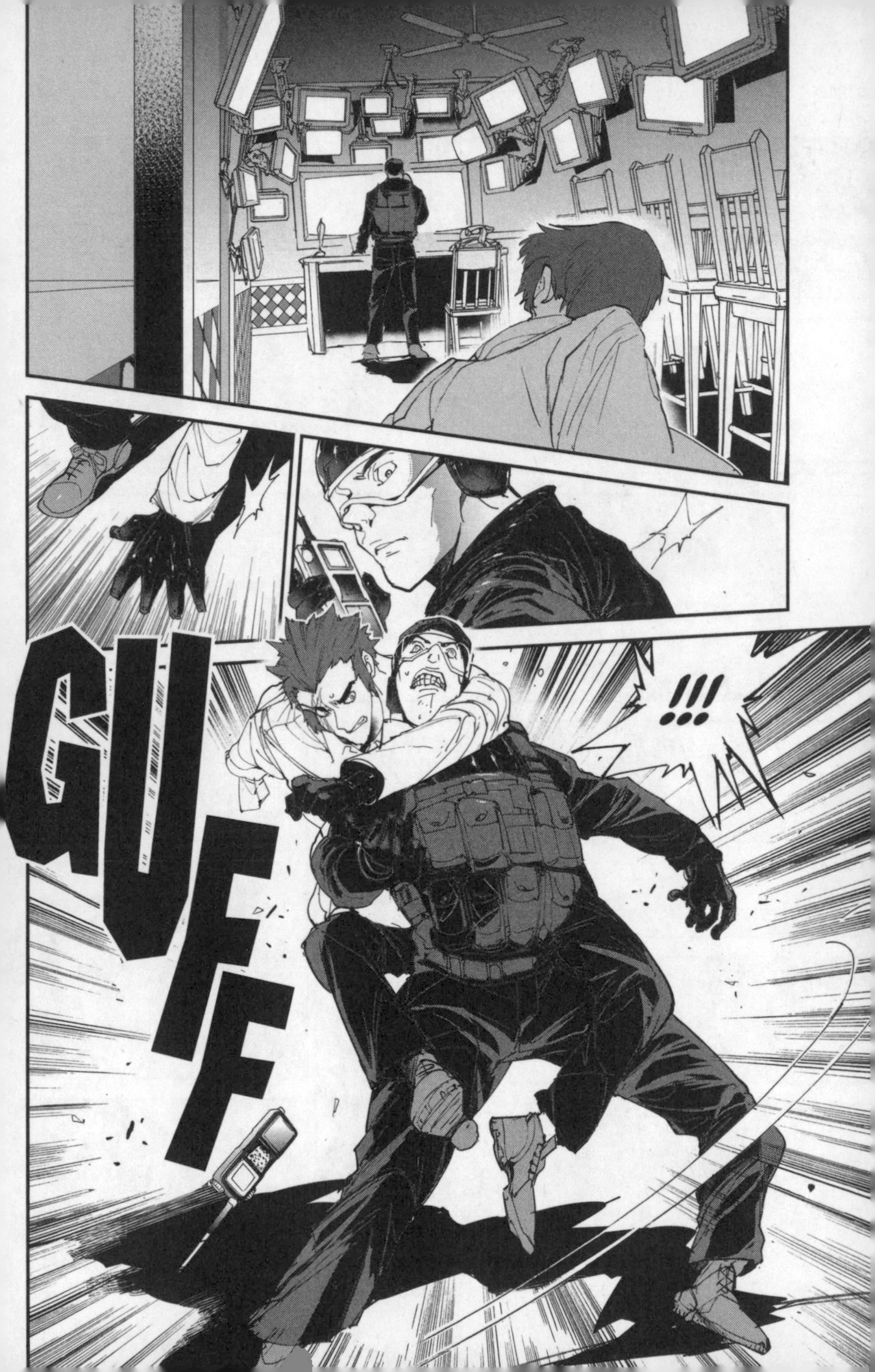
!!!
GUFF

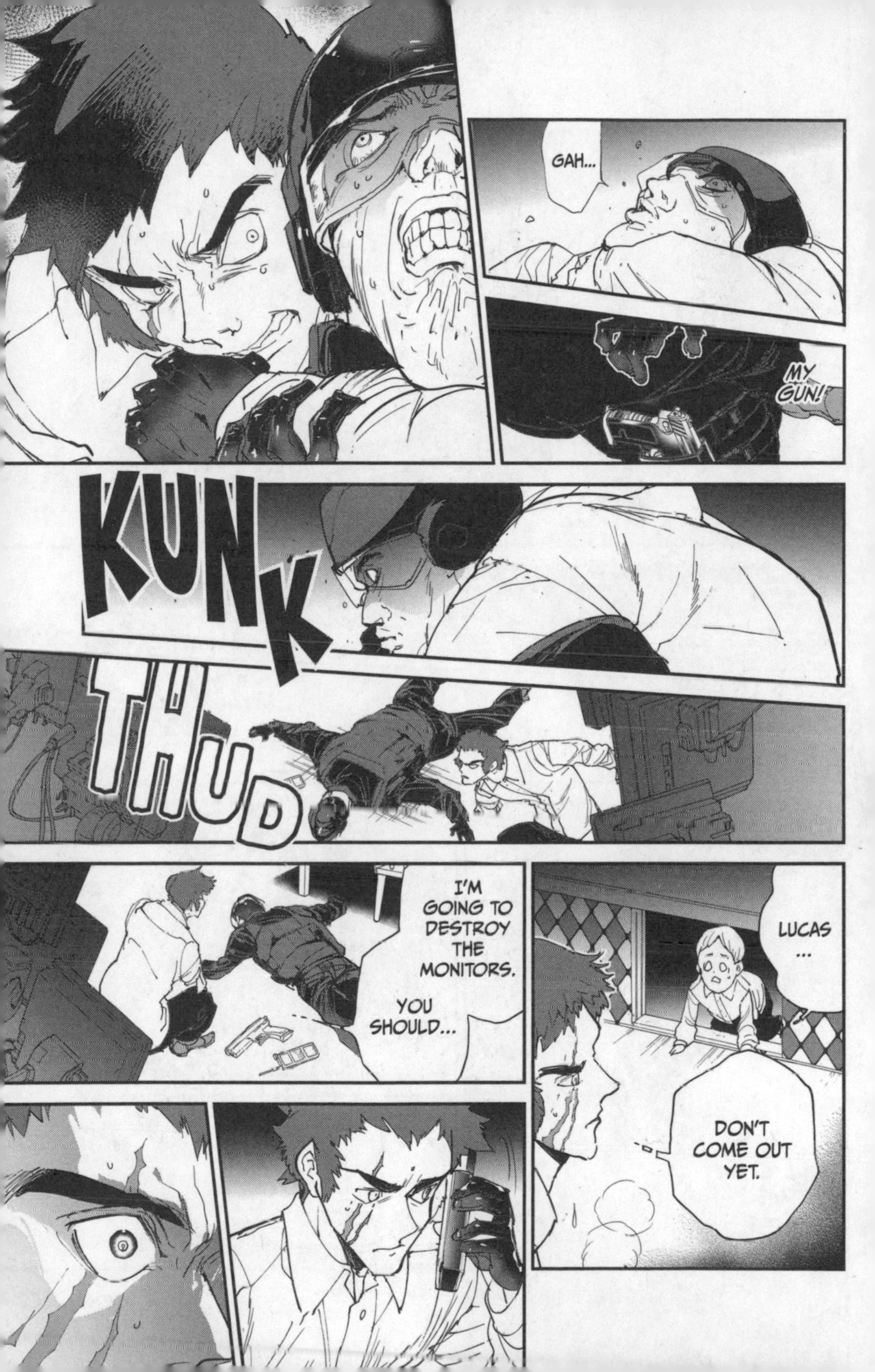
GAH...
MY GUN!
KUNK
THUD
LUCAS ...
DON'T COME OUT YET.
I'M GOING TO DESTROY THE MONITORS.
YOU SHOULD...

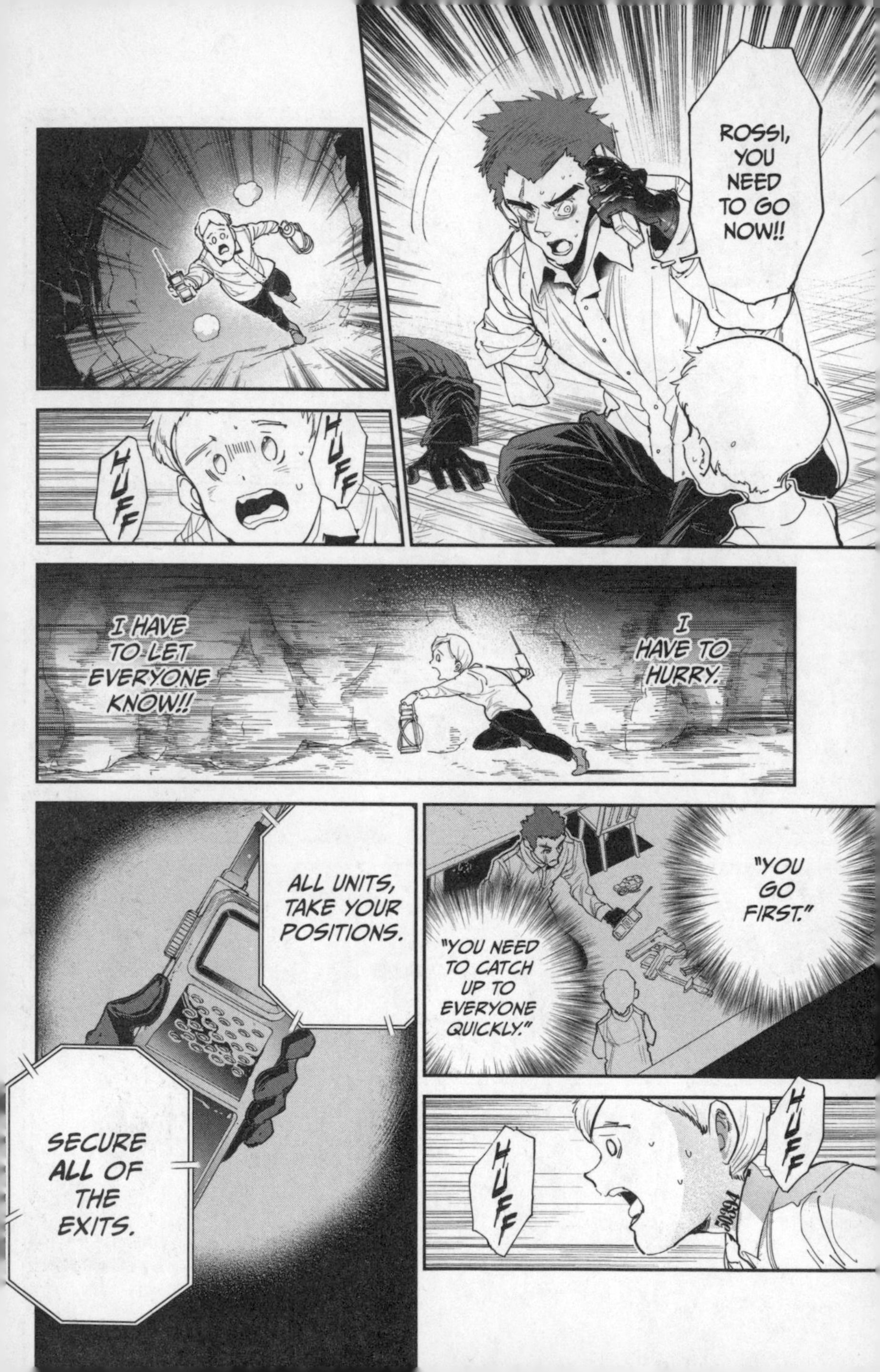
ROSSI, YOU NEED TO GO NOW!!
HUFF
HUFF
I HAVE TO HURRY.
I HAVE TO LET EVERYONE KNOW!!
"YOU GO FIRST."
"YOU NEED TO CATCH UP TO EVERYONE QUICKLY."
HUFF
HUFF
ALL UNITS, TAKE YOUR POSITIONS.
SECURE ALL OF THE EXITS.

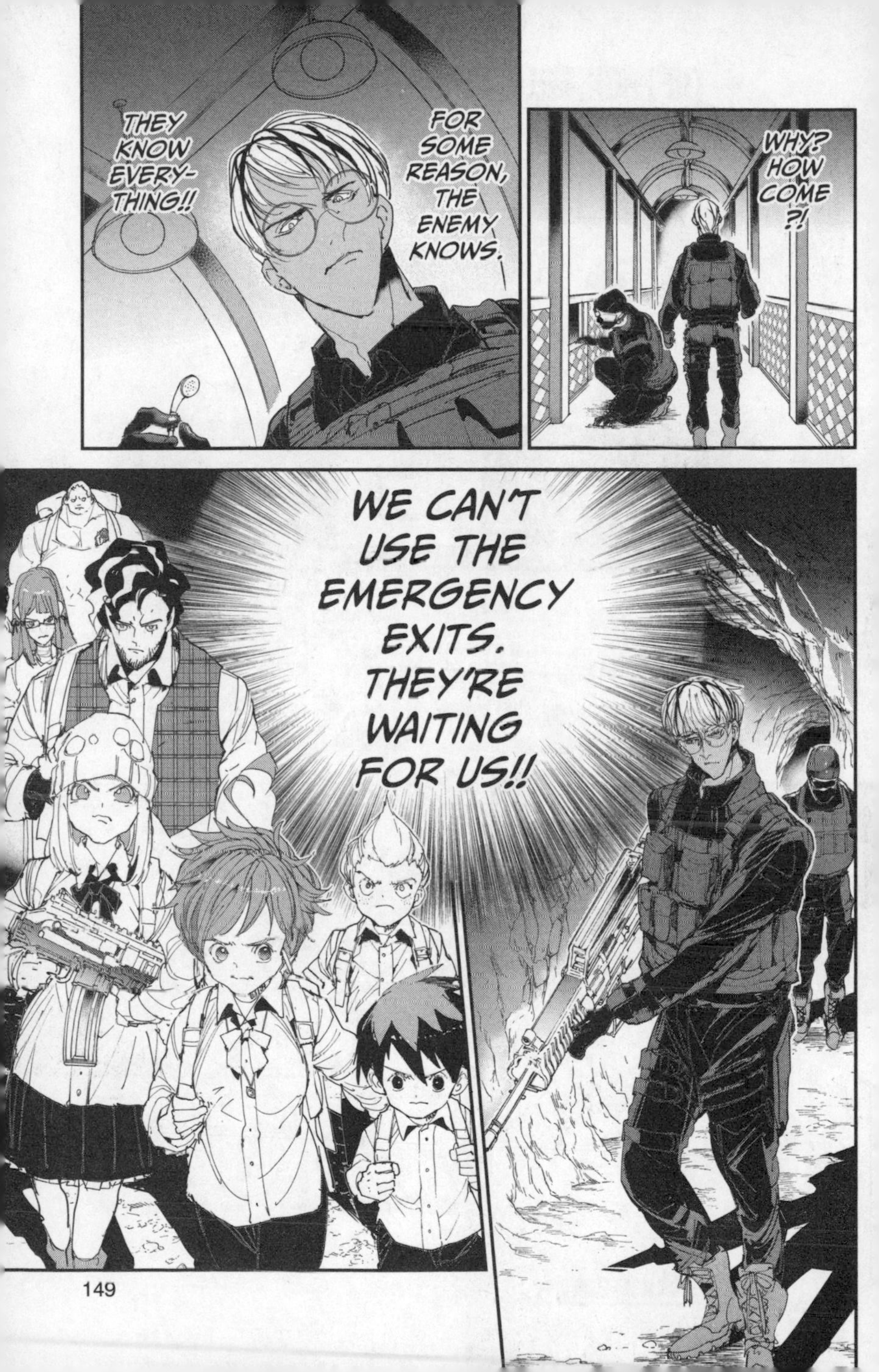
WHY? HOW COME?!
FOR SOME REASON, THE ENEMY KNOWS.
THEY KNOW EVERY-THING!!
WE CAN'T USE THE EMERGENCY EXITS. THEY'RE WAITING FOR US!!

THE PROMISED NEVERLAND SIDE SCENE 019-1

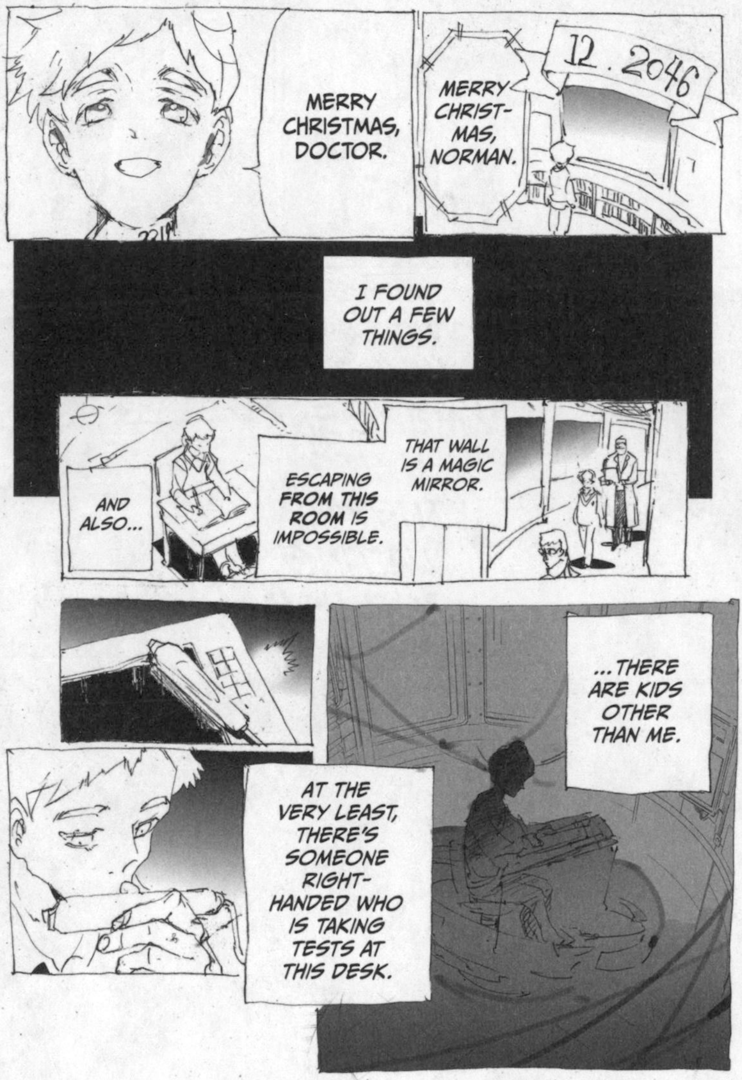
12.2046
MERRY CHRISTMAS, NORMAN.
MERRY CHRISTMAS, DOCTOR.
I FOUND OUT A FEW THINGS.
THAT WALL IS A MAGIC MIRROR.
ESCAPING FROM THIS ROOM IS IMPOSSIBLE.
AND ALSO...
...THERE ARE KIDS OTHER THAN ME.
AT THE VERY LEAST, THERE'S SOMEONE RIGHT-HANDED WHO IS TAKING TESTS AT THIS DESK.

TO BE CONTINUED IN SIDE SCENE 019-2

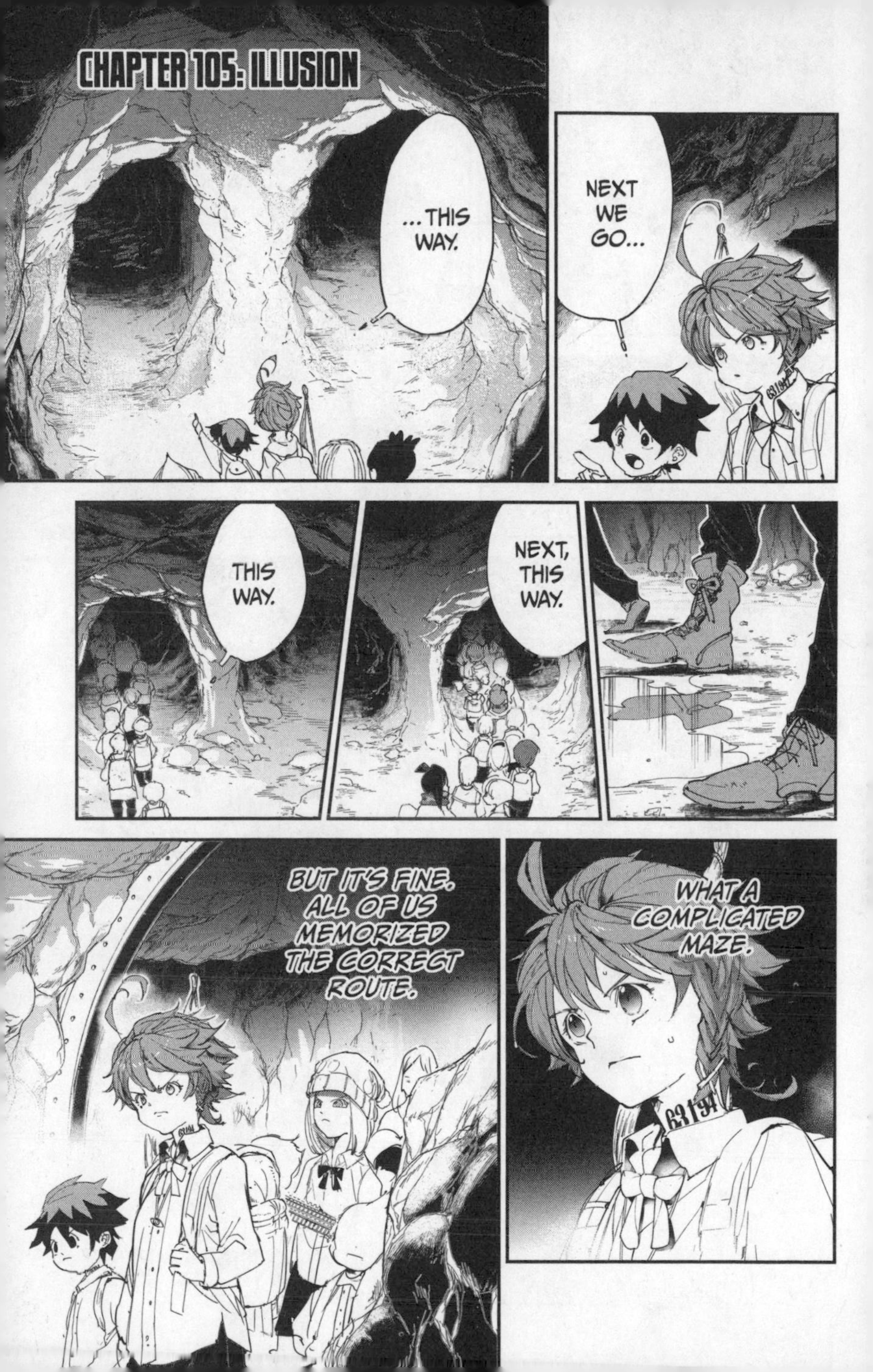
CHAPTER 105: ILLUSION
NEXT WE GO...
...THIS WAY.
NEXT, THIS WAY.
THIS WAY.
WHAT A COMPLICATED MAZE.
BUT IT'S FINE. ALL OF US MEMORIZED THE CORRECT ROUTE.

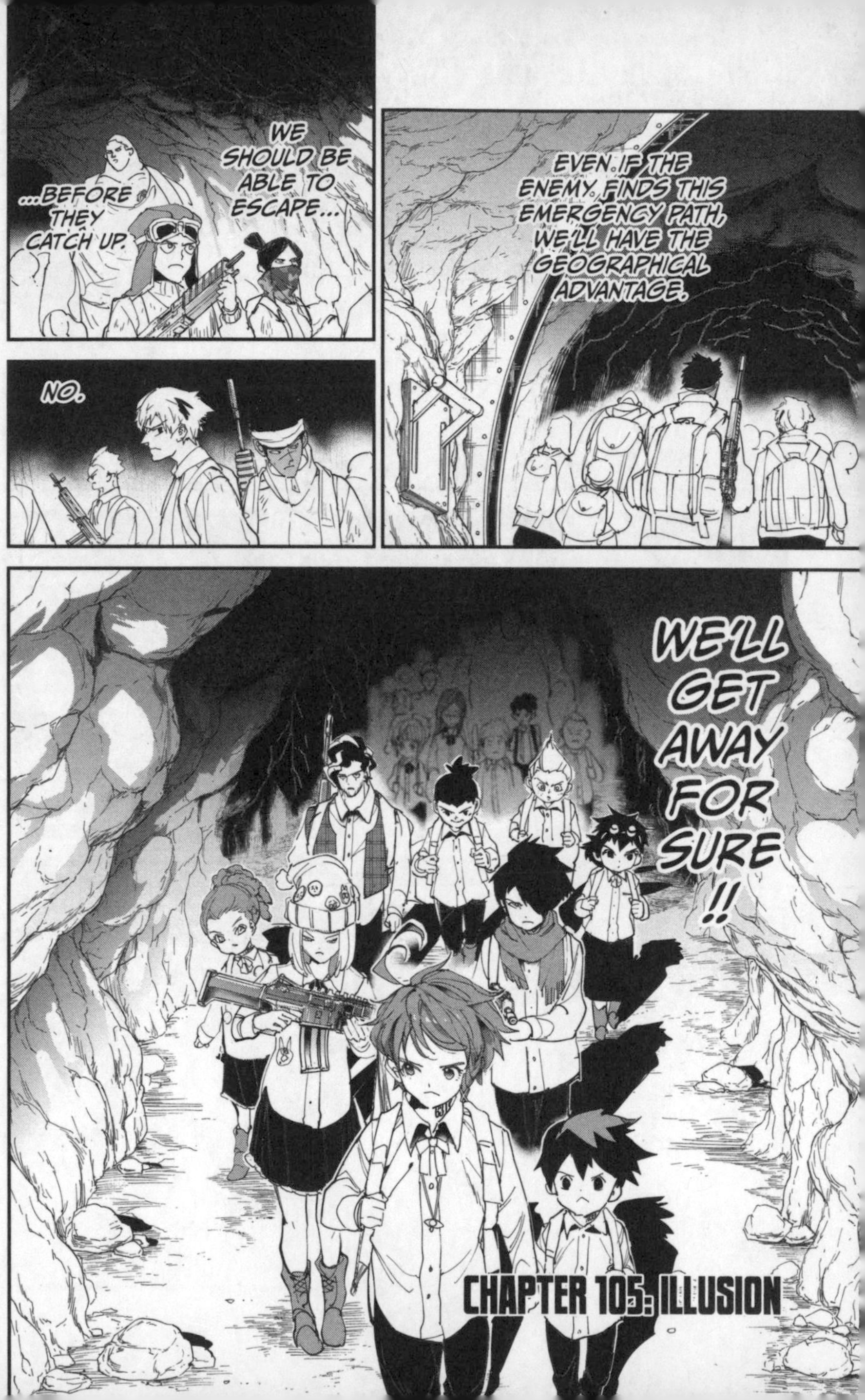
EVEN IF THE ENEMY FINDS THIS EMERGENCY PATH, WE'LL HAVE THE GEOGRAPHICAL ADVANTAGE.
WE SHOULD BE ABLE TO ESCAPE...
...BEFORE THEY CATCH UP.
NO.
WE'LL GET AWAY FOR SURE!!
CHAPTER 105: ILLUSION

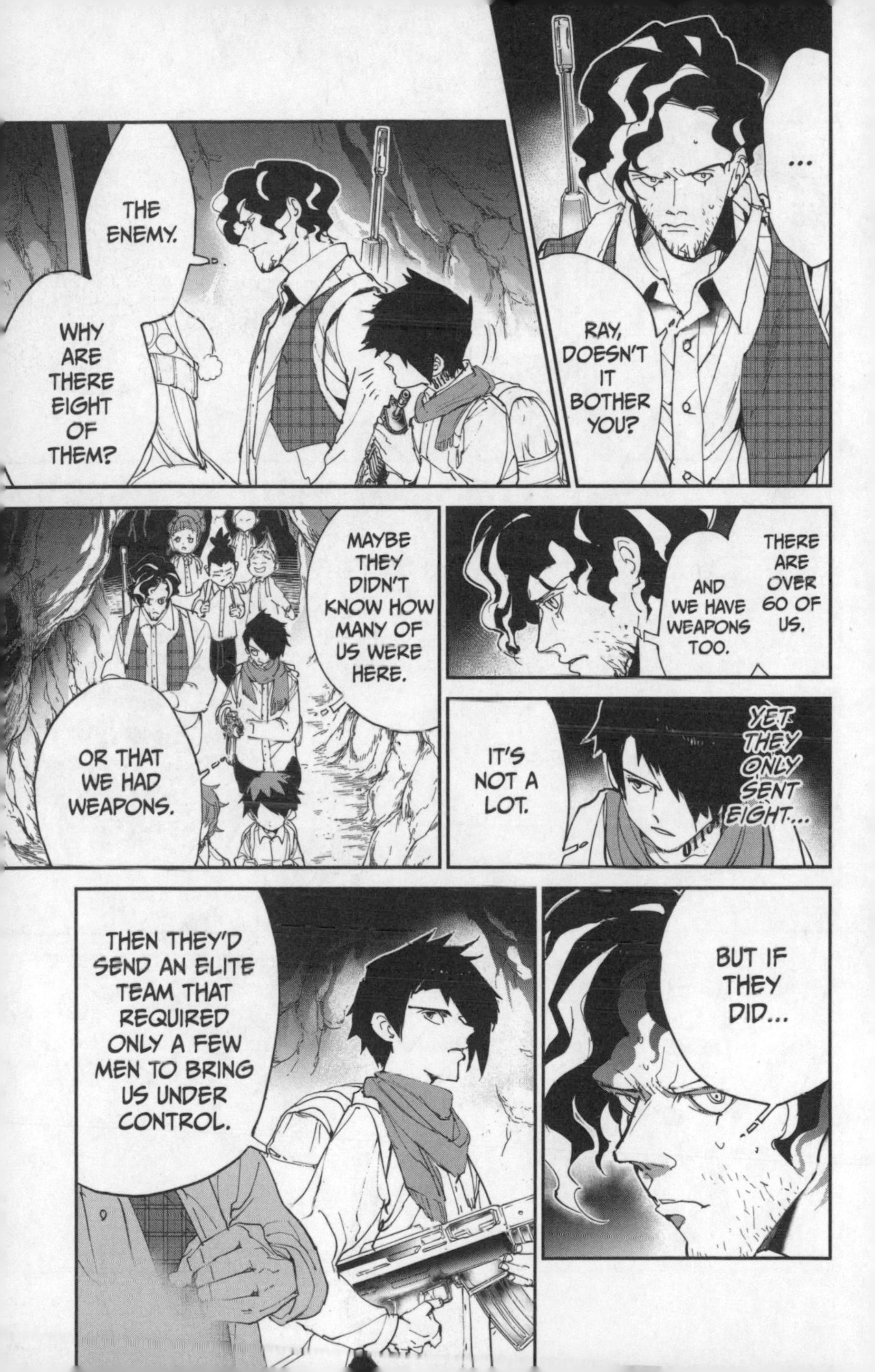
...
RAY, DOESN'T IT BOTHER YOU?
THE ENEMY.
WHY ARE THERE EIGHT OF THEM?
THERE ARE OVER 60 OF US.
AND WE HAVE WEAPONS TOO.
YET THEY ONLY SENT EIGHT...
IT'S NOT A LOT.
MAYBE THEY DIDN'T KNOW HOW MANY OF US WERE HERE.
OR THAT WE HAD WEAPONS.
BUT IF THEY DID...
THEN THEY'D SEND AN ELITE TEAM THAT REQUIRED ONLY A FEW MEN TO BRING US UNDER CONTROL.

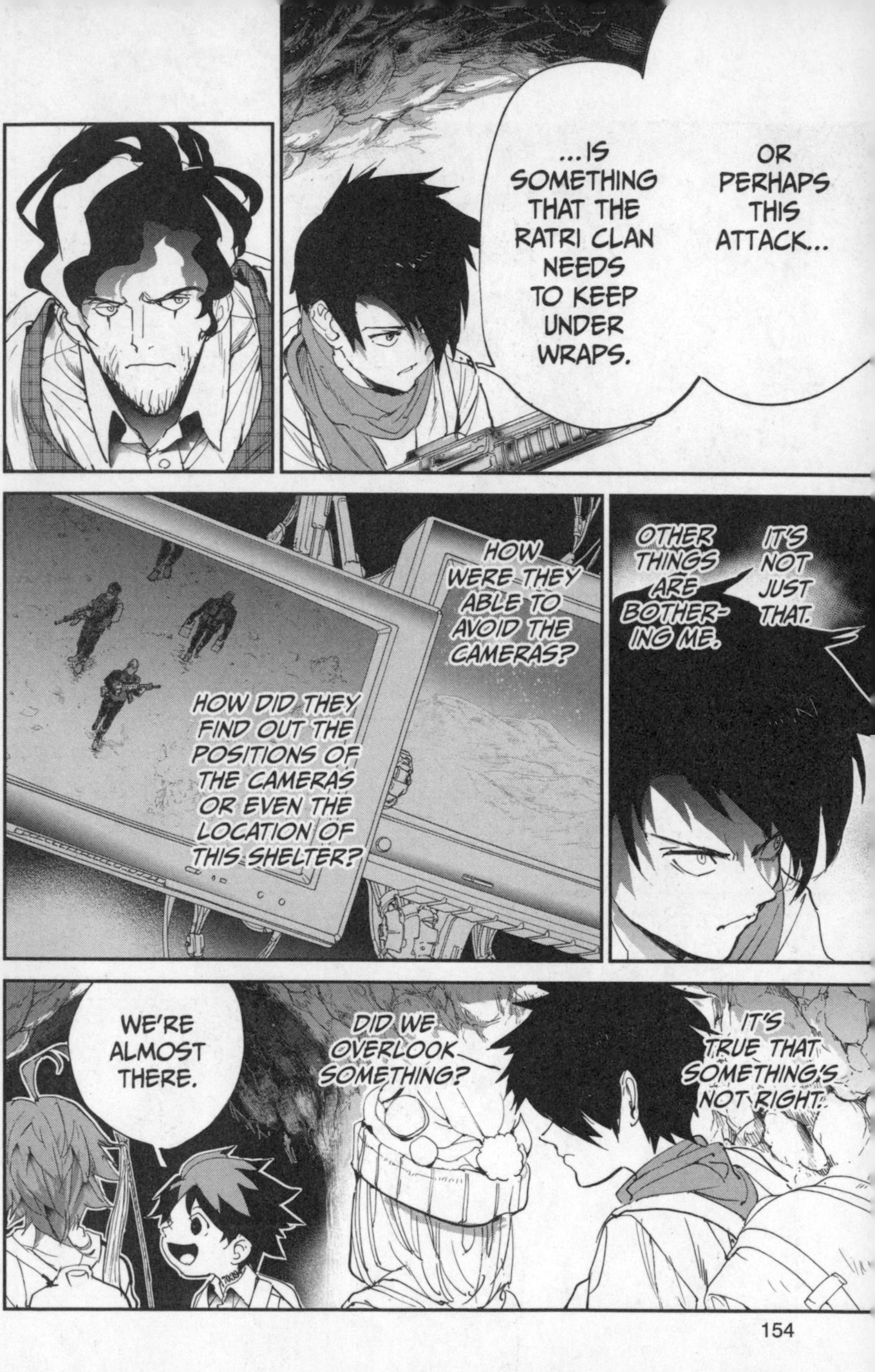
OR PERHAPS THIS ATTACK... ...IS SOMETHING THAT THE RATRI CLAN NEEDS TO KEEP UNDER WRAPS.
IT'S NOT JUST THAT.
OTHER THINGS ARE BOTHERING ME.
HOW WERE THEY ABLE TO AVOID THE CAMERAS?
HOW DID THEY FIND OUT THE POSITIONS OF THE CAMERAS OR EVEN THE LOCATION OF THIS SHELTER?
IT'S TRUE THAT SOMETHING'S NOT RIGHT.
DID WE OVERLOOK SOMETHING?
WE'RE ALMOST THERE.

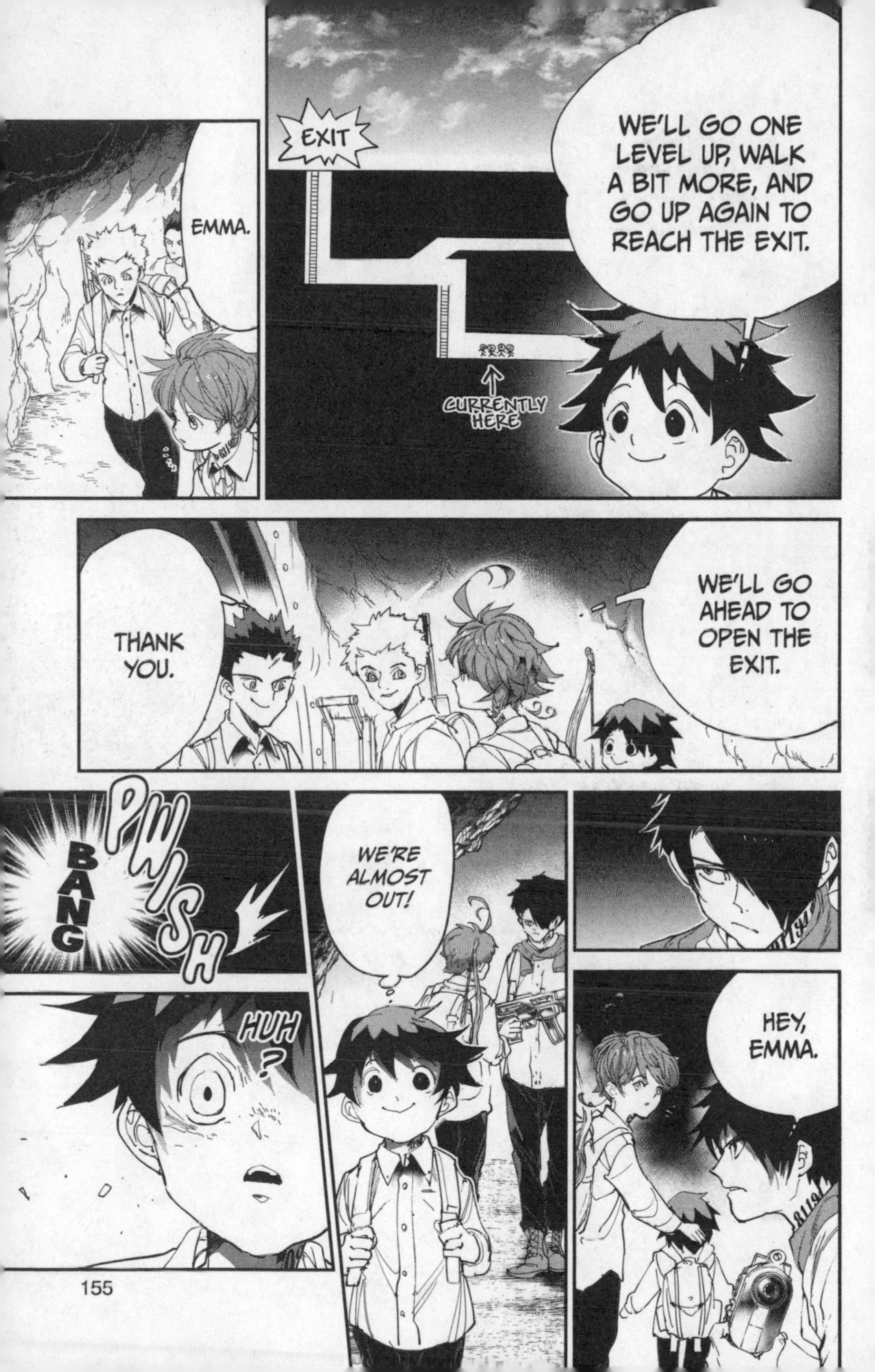
WE'LL GO ONE LEVEL UP, WALK A BIT MORE, AND GO UP AGAIN TO REACH THE EXIT.
EXIT
CURRENTLY HERE
EMMA.
WE'LL GO AHEAD TO OPEN THE EXIT.
THANK YOU.
HEY, EMMA.
WE'RE ALMOST OUT!
PWISH
BANG
HUH?

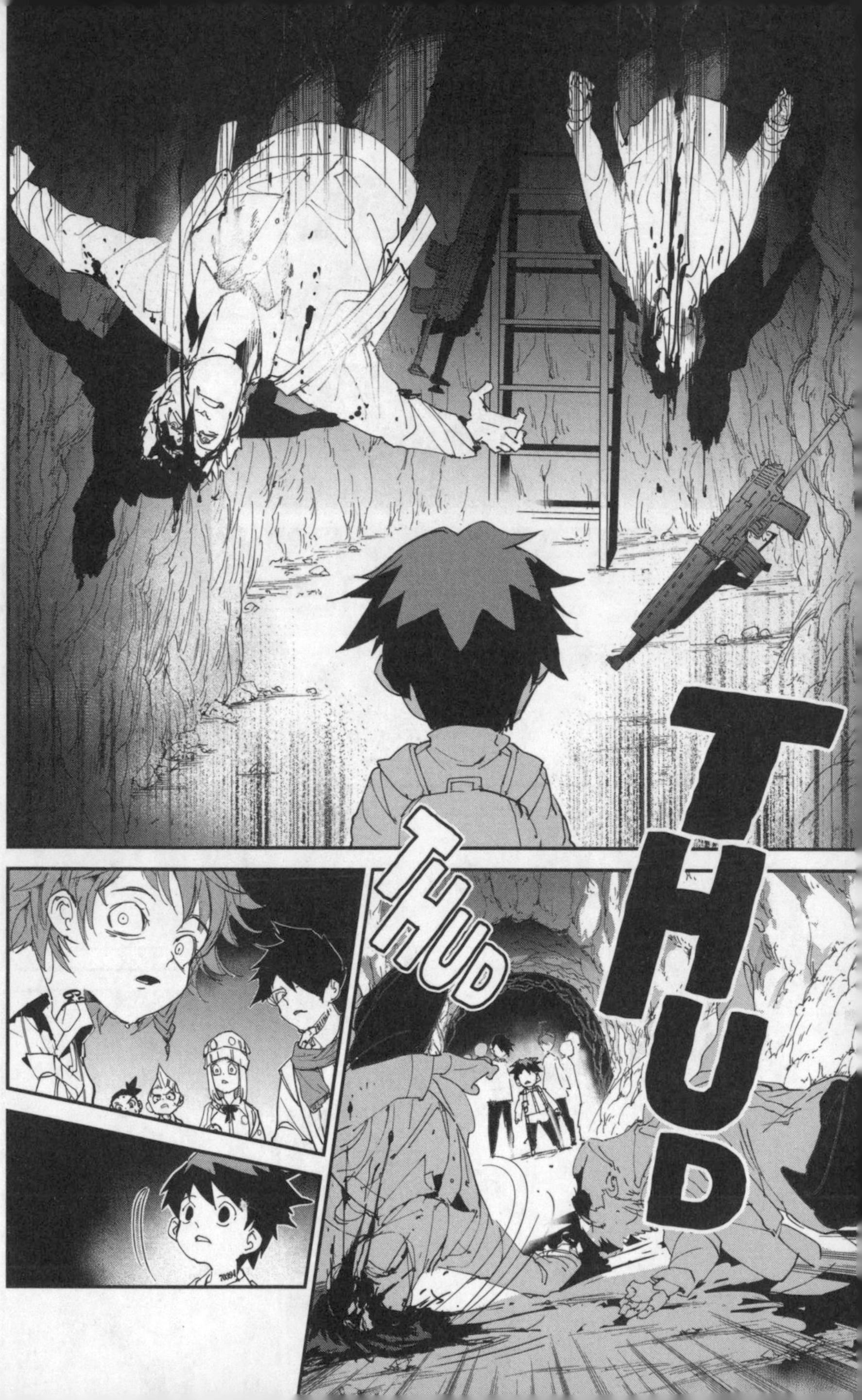
THUD
THUD

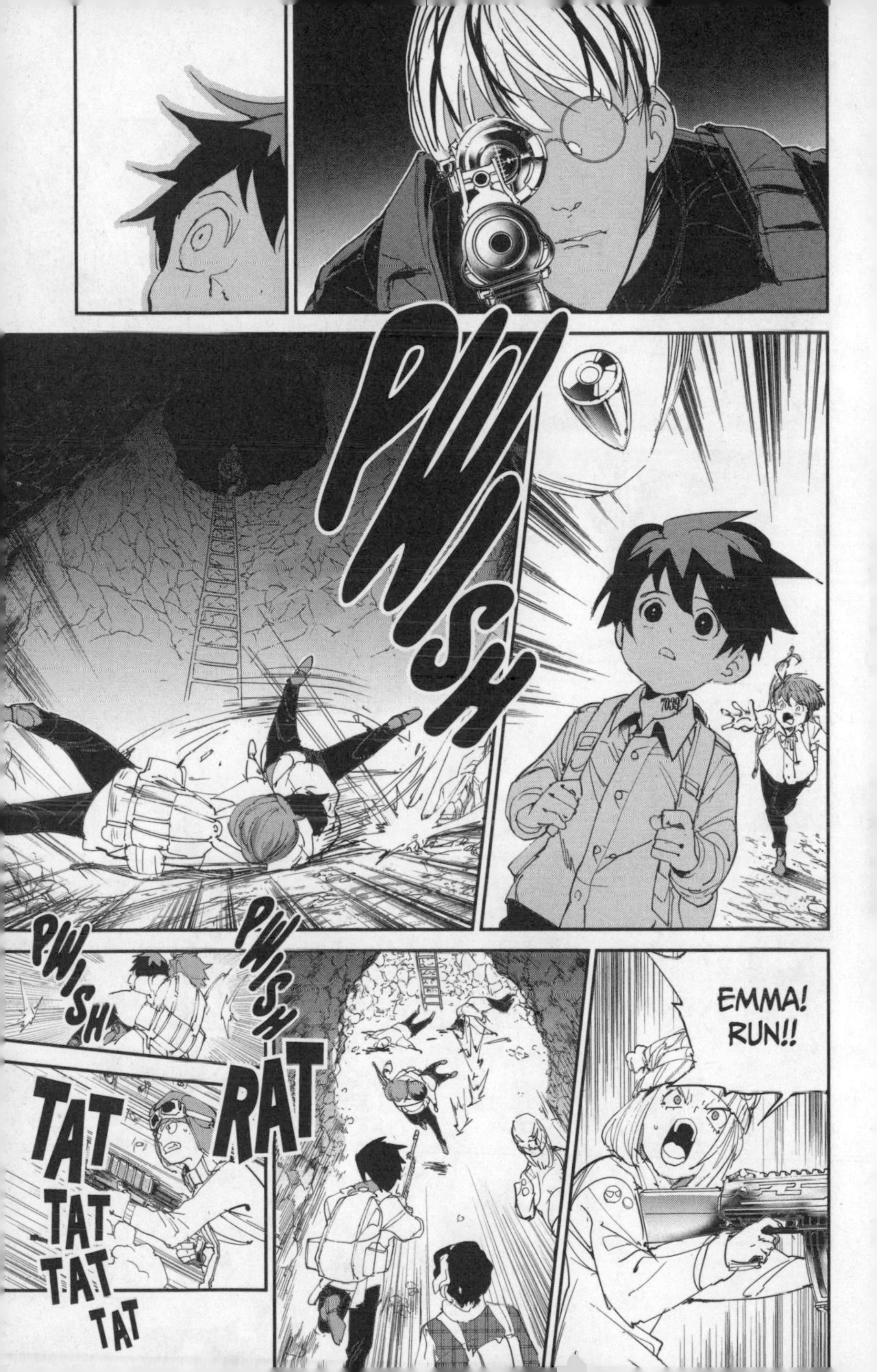
PWISH
EMMA! RUN!!
PWISH
PWISH
RAT
TAT
TAT
TAT
TAT

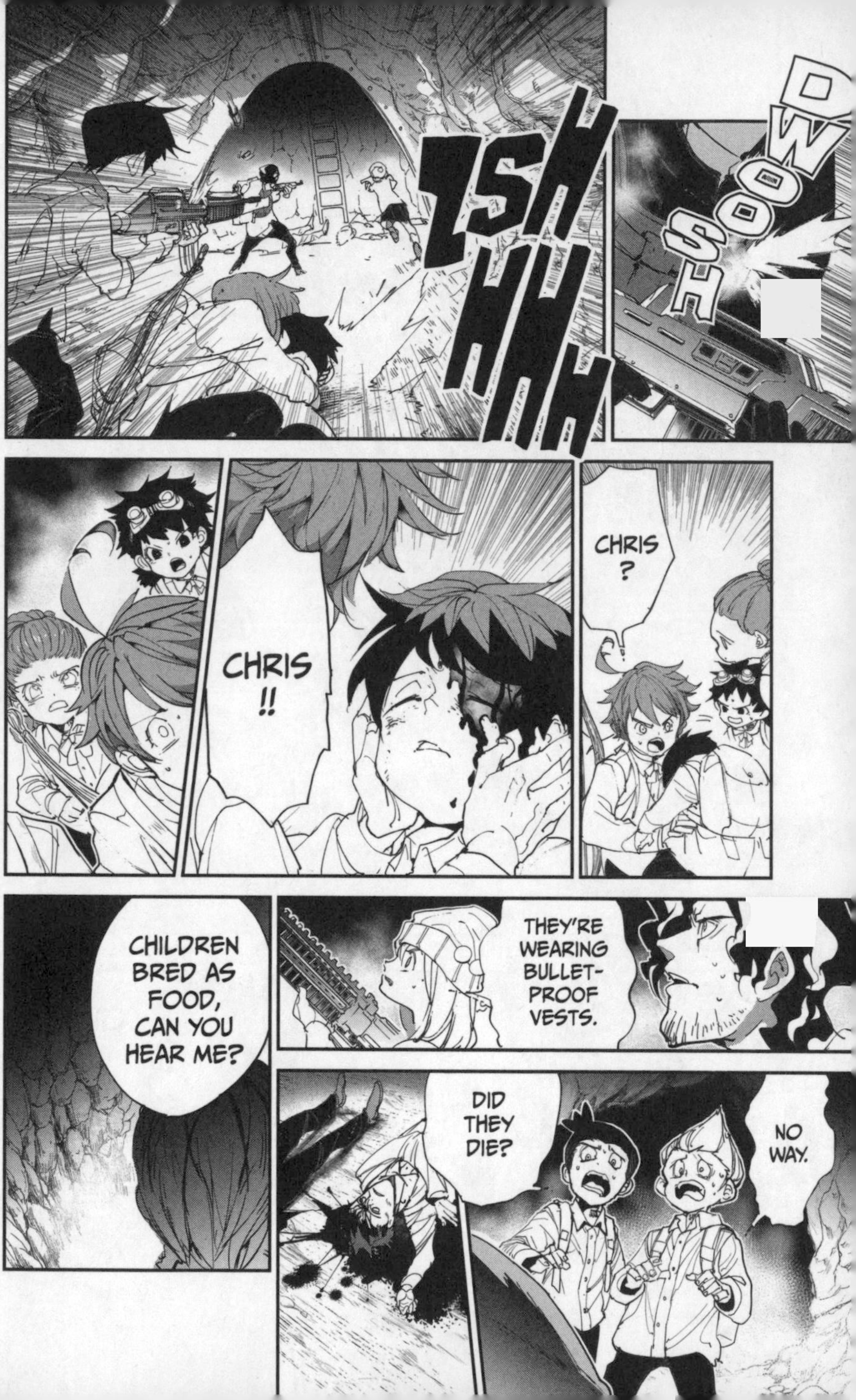
DWOOSH
TSHHHHHH
CHRIS ?
CHRIS !!
THEY'RE WEARING BULLET-PROOF VESTS.
NO WAY.
DID THEY DIE?
CHILDREN BRED AS FOOD, CAN YOU HEAR ME?

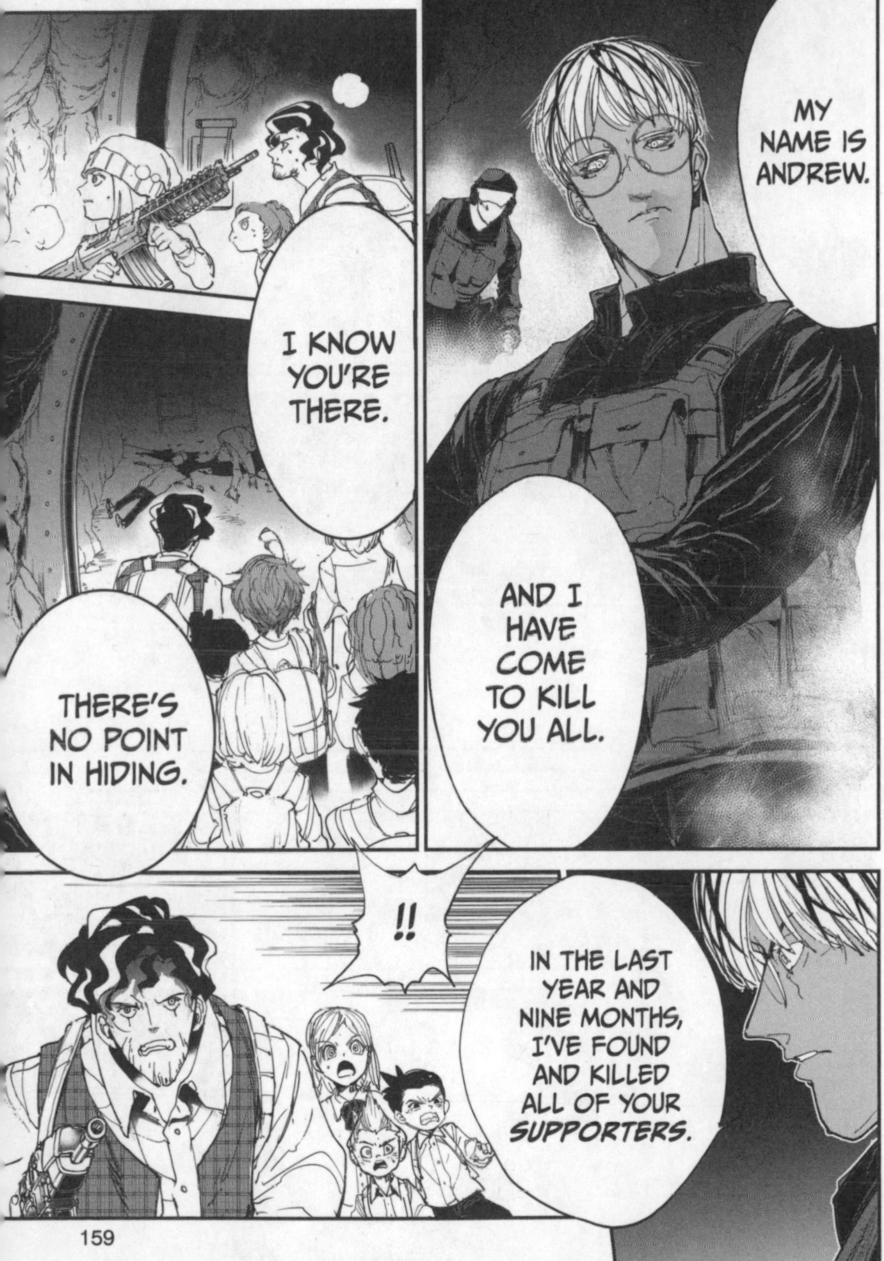
MY NAME IS ANDREW.
AND I HAVE COME TO KILL YOU ALL.
I KNOW YOU'RE THERE.
THERE'S NO POINT IN HIDING.
IN THE LAST YEAR AND NINE MONTHS, I'VE FOUND AND KILLED ALL OF YOUR *SUPPORTERS.*
!!

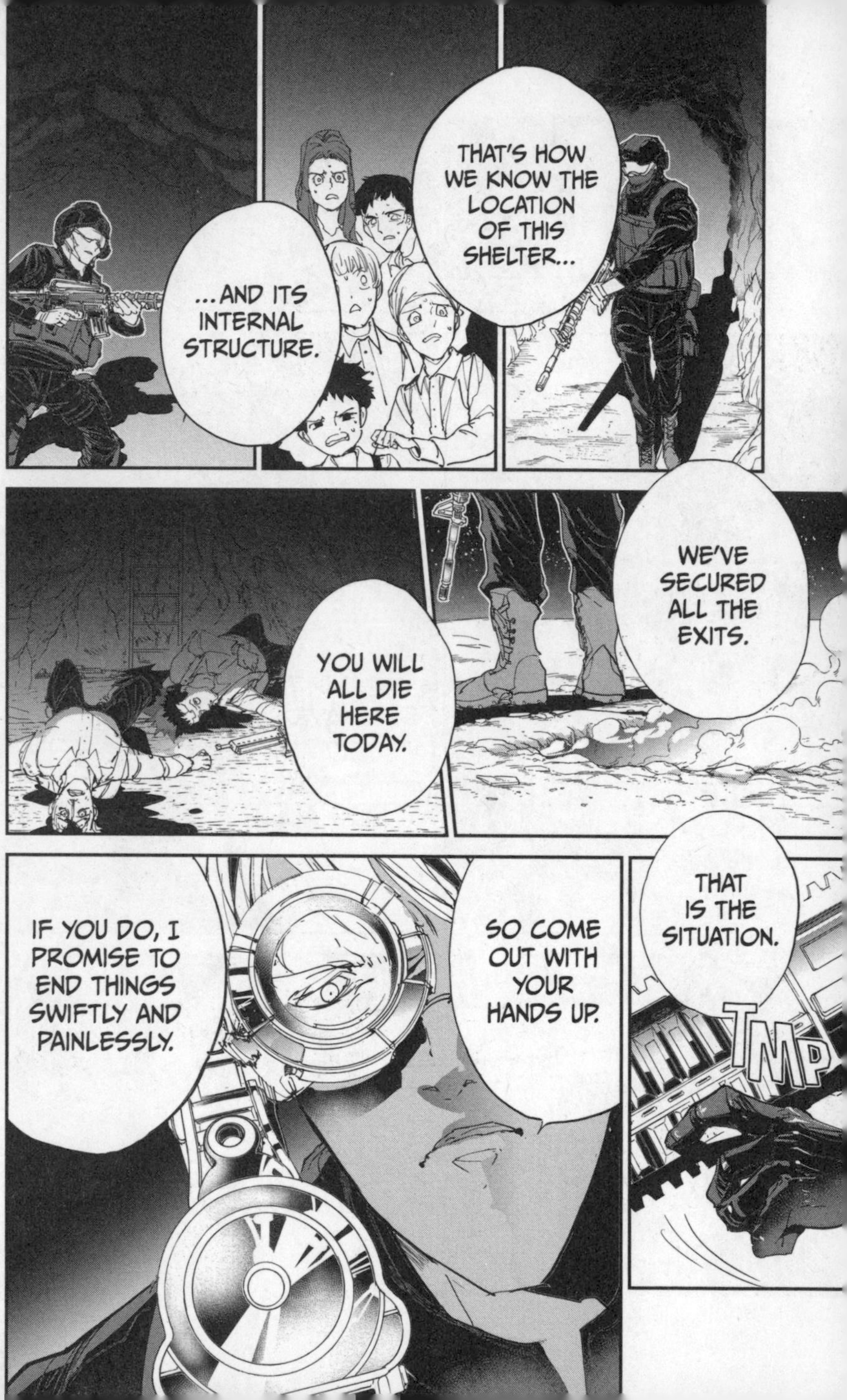
THAT'S HOW WE KNOW THE LOCATION OF THIS SHELTER...
...AND ITS INTERNAL STRUCTURE.
WE'VE SECURED ALL THE EXITS.
YOU WILL ALL DIE HERE TODAY.
THAT IS THE SITUATION.
TMP
SO COME OUT WITH YOUR HANDS UP.
IF YOU DO, I PROMISE TO END THINGS SWIFTLY AND PAINLESSLY.

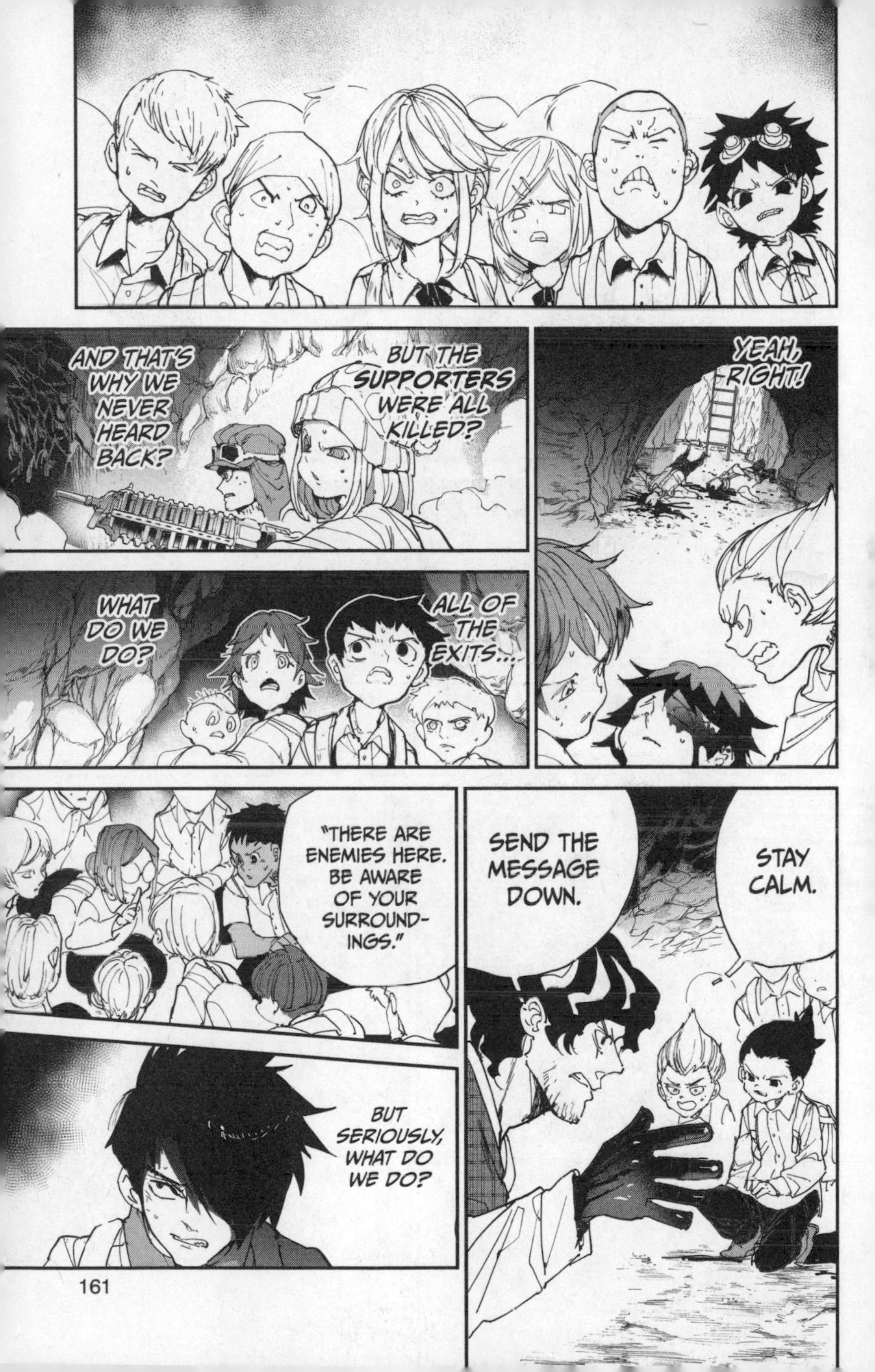
YEAH, RIGHT!
BUT THE SUPPORTERS WERE ALL KILLED?
AND THAT'S WHY WE NEVER HEARD BACK?
ALL OF THE EXITS...
WHAT DO WE DO?
STAY CALM.
SEND THE MESSAGE DOWN.
"THERE ARE ENEMIES HERE. BE AWARE OF YOUR SURROUND-INGS."
BUT SERIOUSLY, WHAT DO WE DO?

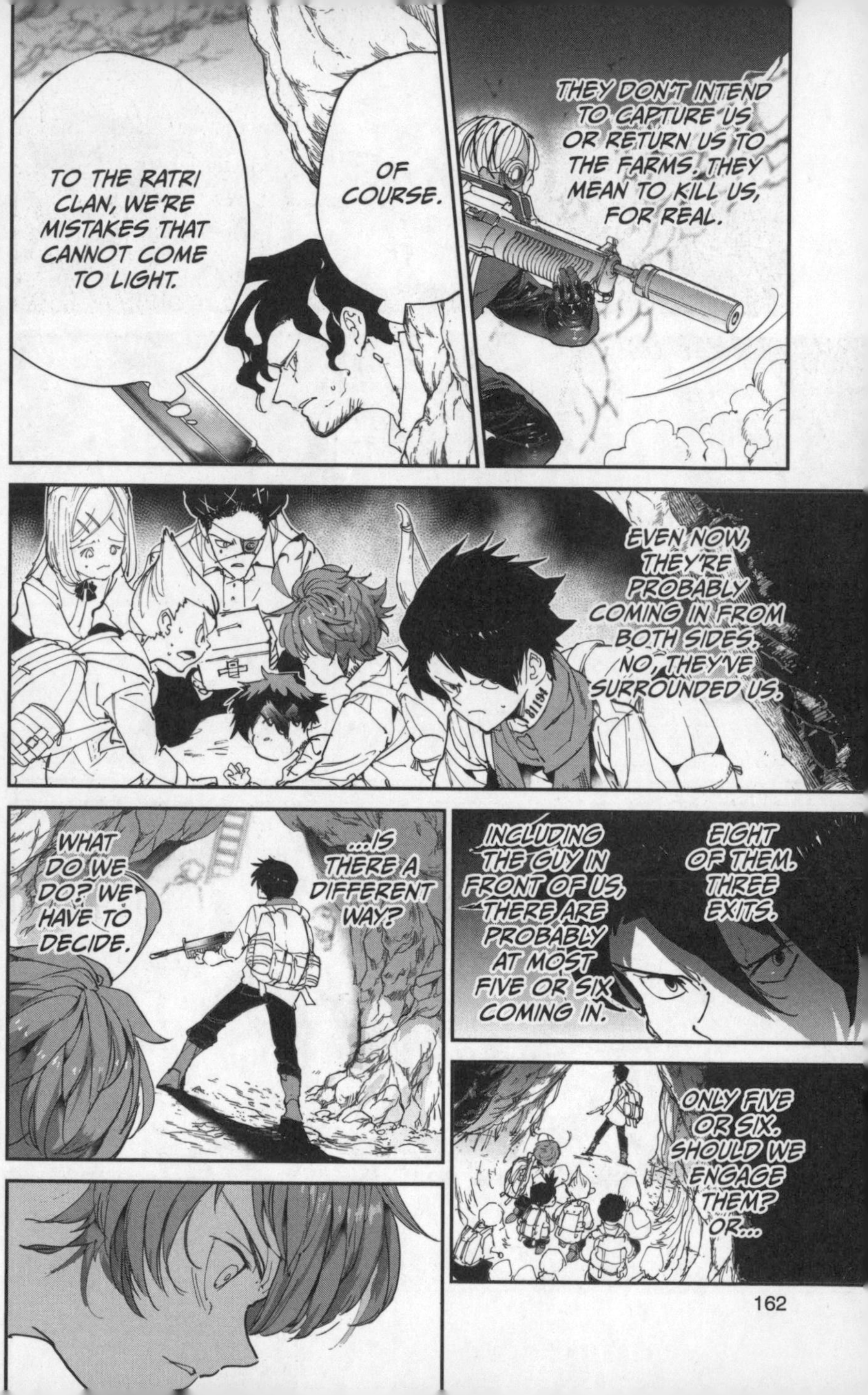
THEY DON'T INTEND TO CAPTURE US OR RETURN US TO THE FARMS. THEY MEAN TO KILL US, FOR REAL.
OF COURSE.
TO THE RATRI CLAN, WE'RE MISTAKES THAT CANNOT COME TO LIGHT.
EVEN NOW, THEY'RE PROBABLY COMING IN FROM BOTH SIDES. NO, THEY'VE SURROUNDED US.
EIGHT OF THEM. THREE EXITS.
INCLUDING THE GUY IN FRONT OF US, THERE ARE PROBABLY AT MOST FIVE OR SIX COMING IN.
ONLY FIVE OR SIX. SHOULD WE ENGAGE THEM? OR...
...IS THERE A DIFFERENT WAY?
WHAT DO WE DO? WE HAVE TO DECIDE.

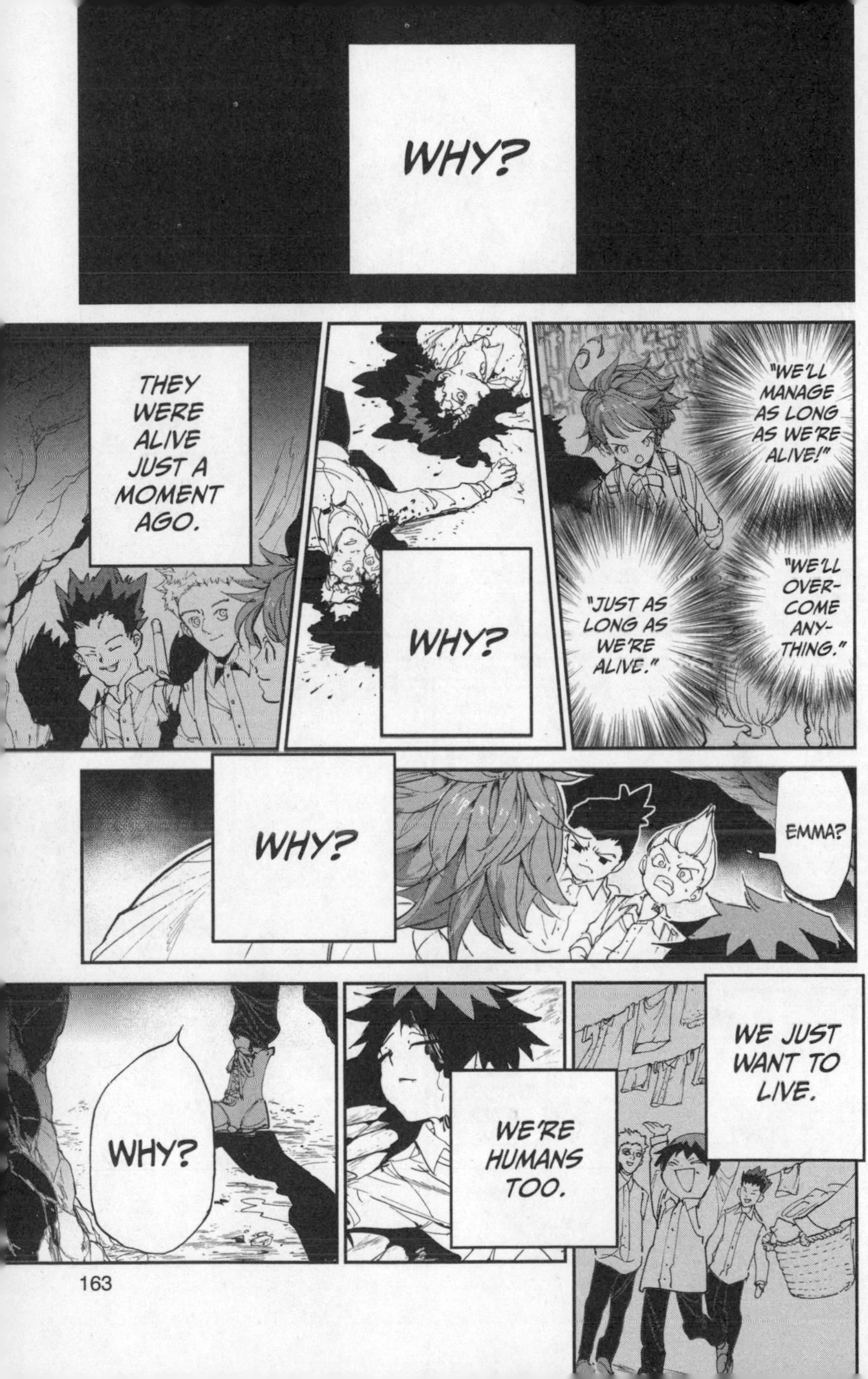
WHY?
"WE'LL MANAGE AS LONG AS WE'RE ALIVE!"
"WE'LL OVER-COME ANY-THING."
"JUST AS LONG AS WE'RE ALIVE."
WHY?
THEY WERE ALIVE JUST A MOMENT AGO.
EMMA?
WHY?
WE JUST WANT TO LIVE.
WE'RE HUMANS TOO.
WHY?

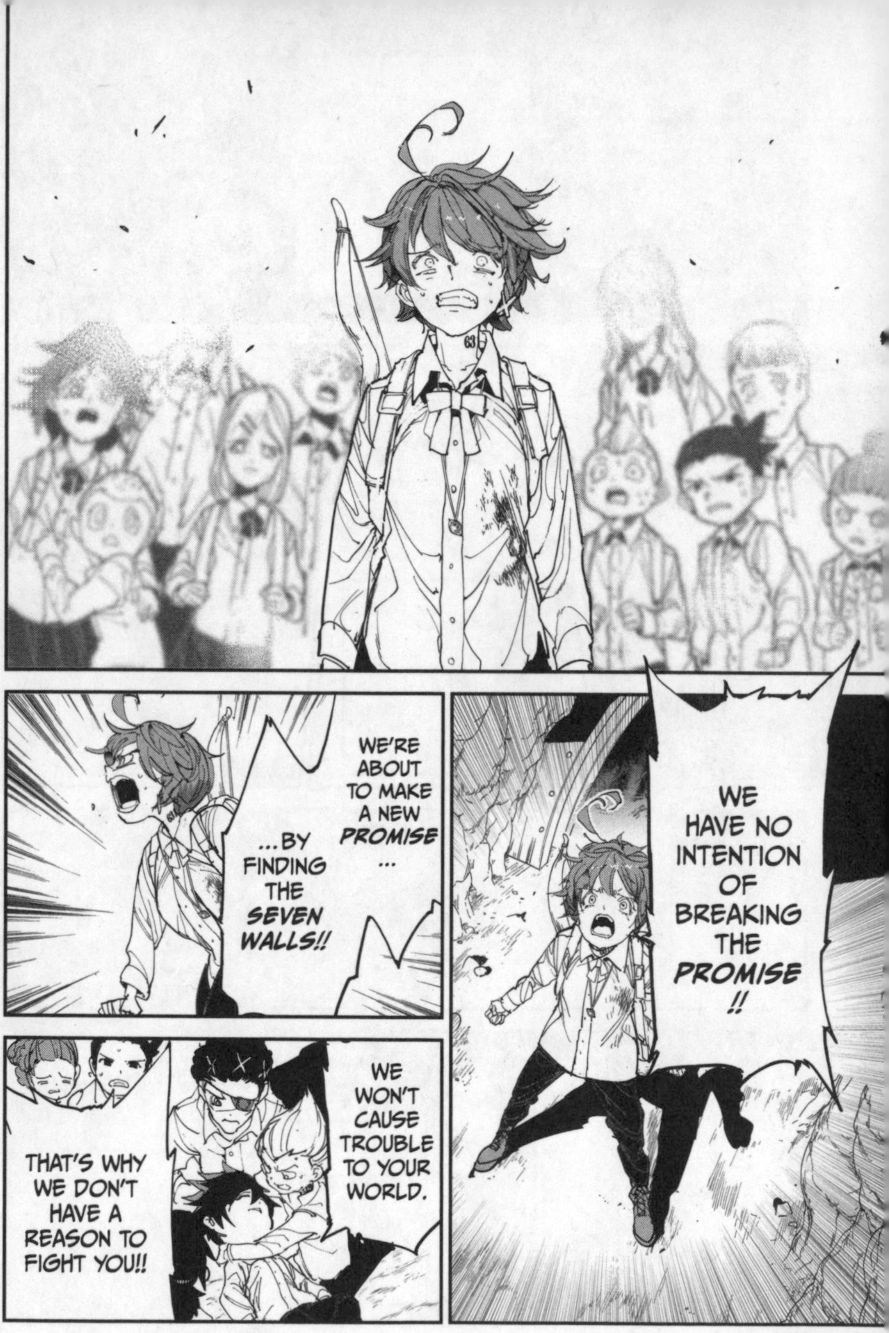
WE HAVE NO INTENTION OF BREAKING THE PROMISE!!
WE'RE ABOUT TO MAKE A NEW PROMISE...
...BY FINDING THE SEVEN WALLS!!
WE WON'T CAUSE TROUBLE TO YOUR WORLD.
THAT'S WHY WE DON'T HAVE A REASON TO FIGHT YOU!!

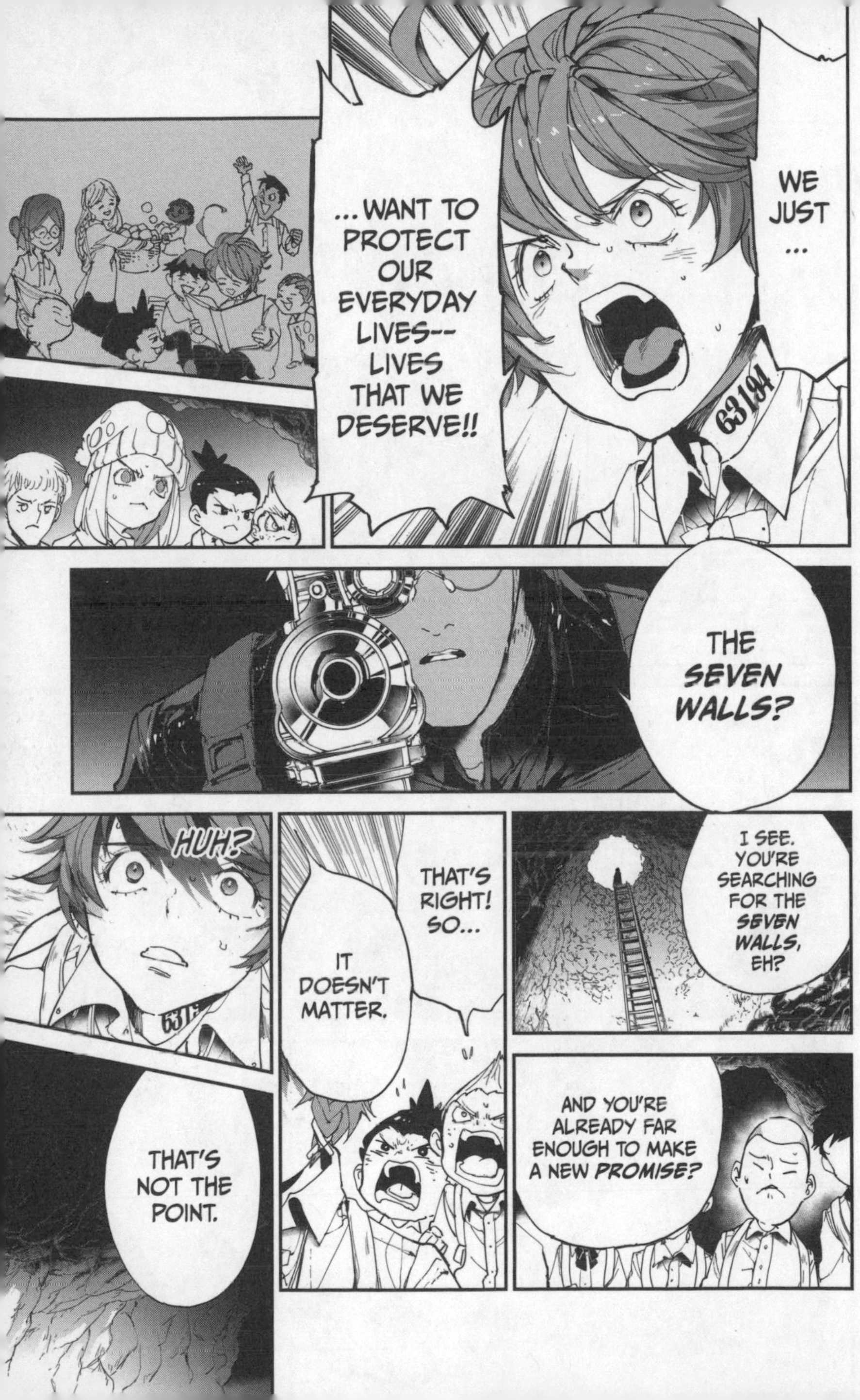
WE JUST ...
...WANT TO PROTECT OUR EVERYDAY LIVES-- LIVES THAT WE DESERVE!!
63194
THE SEVEN WALLS?
I SEE. YOU'RE SEARCHING FOR THE SEVEN WALLS, EH?
AND YOU'RE ALREADY FAR ENOUGH TO MAKE A NEW PROMISE?
THAT'S RIGHT! SO...
IT DOESN'T MATTER.
HUH?
THAT'S NOT THE POINT.

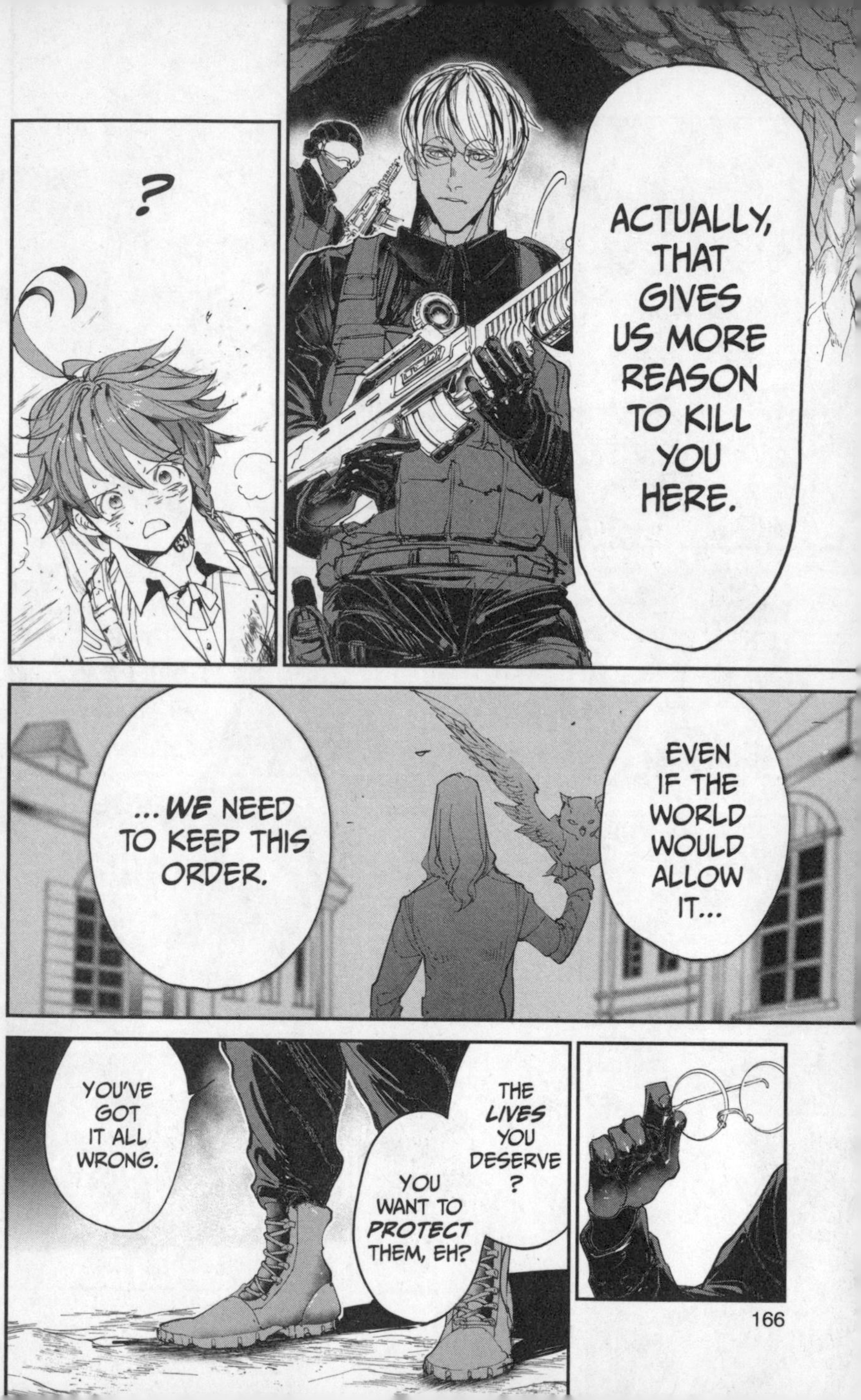
ACTUALLY, THAT GIVES US MORE REASON TO KILL YOU HERE.
?
EVEN IF THE WORLD WOULD ALLOW IT...
...*WE* NEED TO KEEP THIS ORDER.
THE *LIVES* YOU DESERVE?
YOU WANT TO *PROTECT* THEM, EH?
YOU'VE GOT IT ALL WRONG.

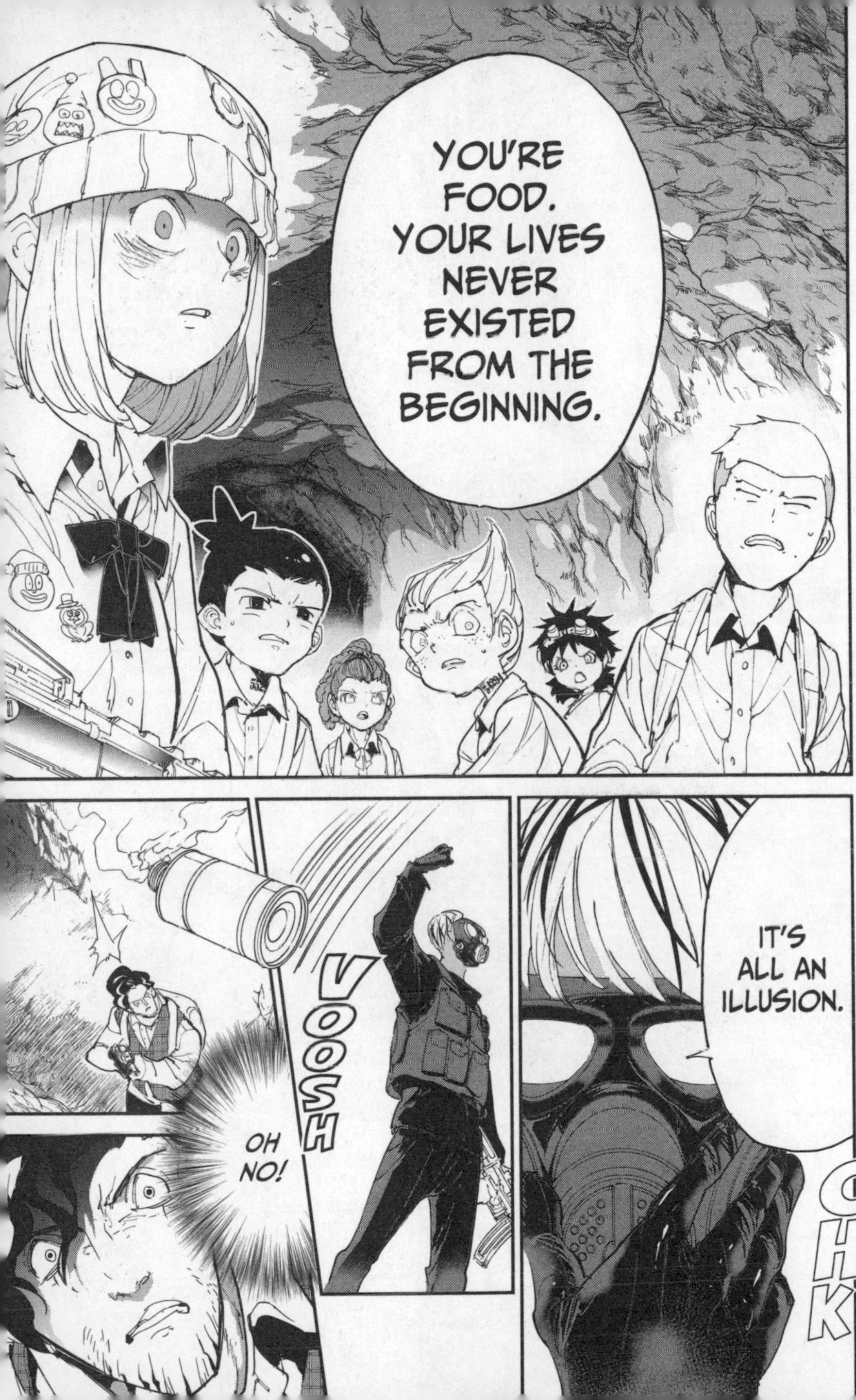
YOU'RE FOOD. YOUR LIVES NEVER EXISTED FROM THE BEGINNING.
IT'S ALL AN ILLUSION.
CHK
VOOSH
OH NO!

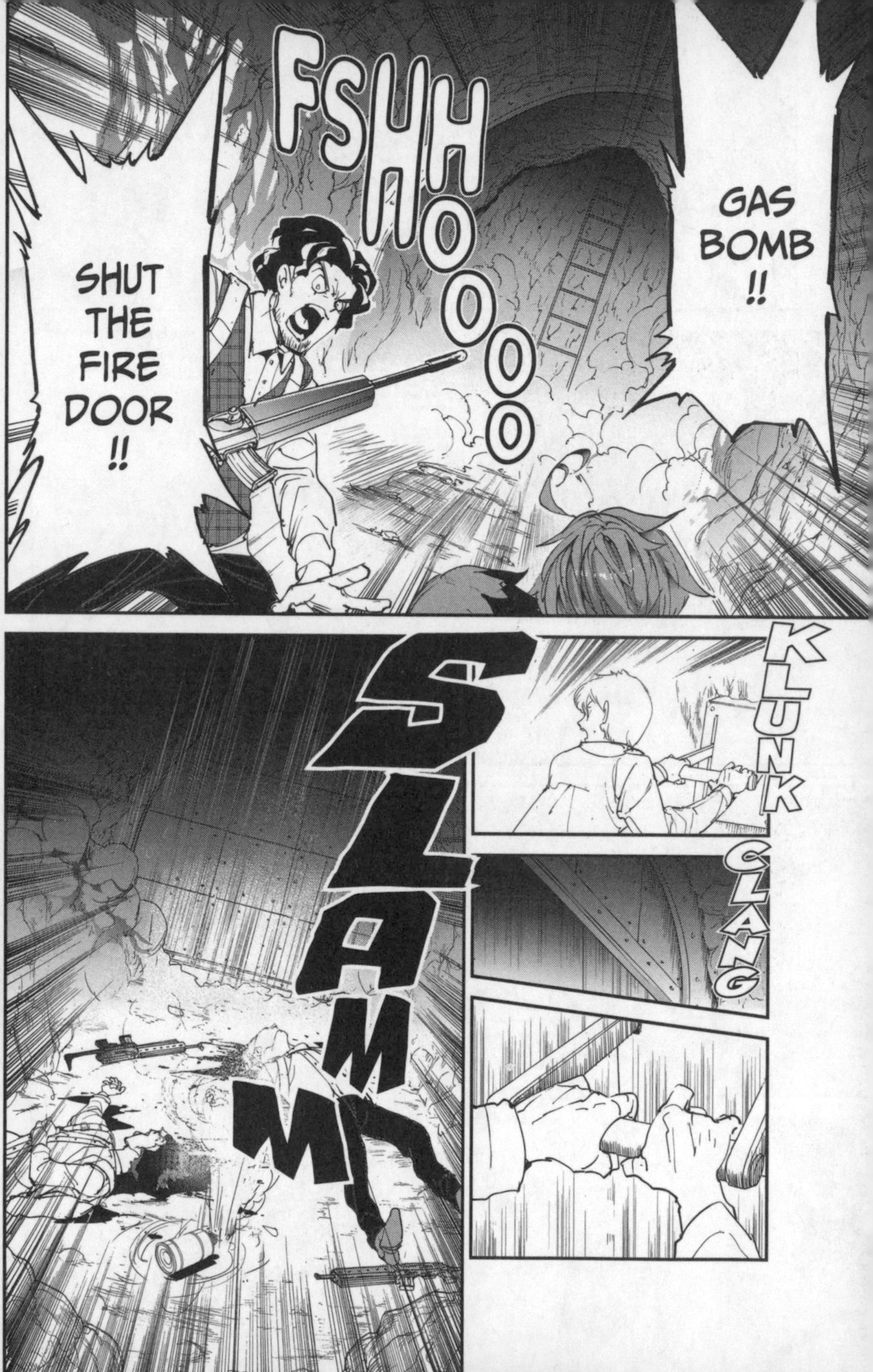
GAS BOMB!!
FSHHOOOOO
SHUT THE FIRE DOOR!!
KLUNK
CLANG
SLAMM

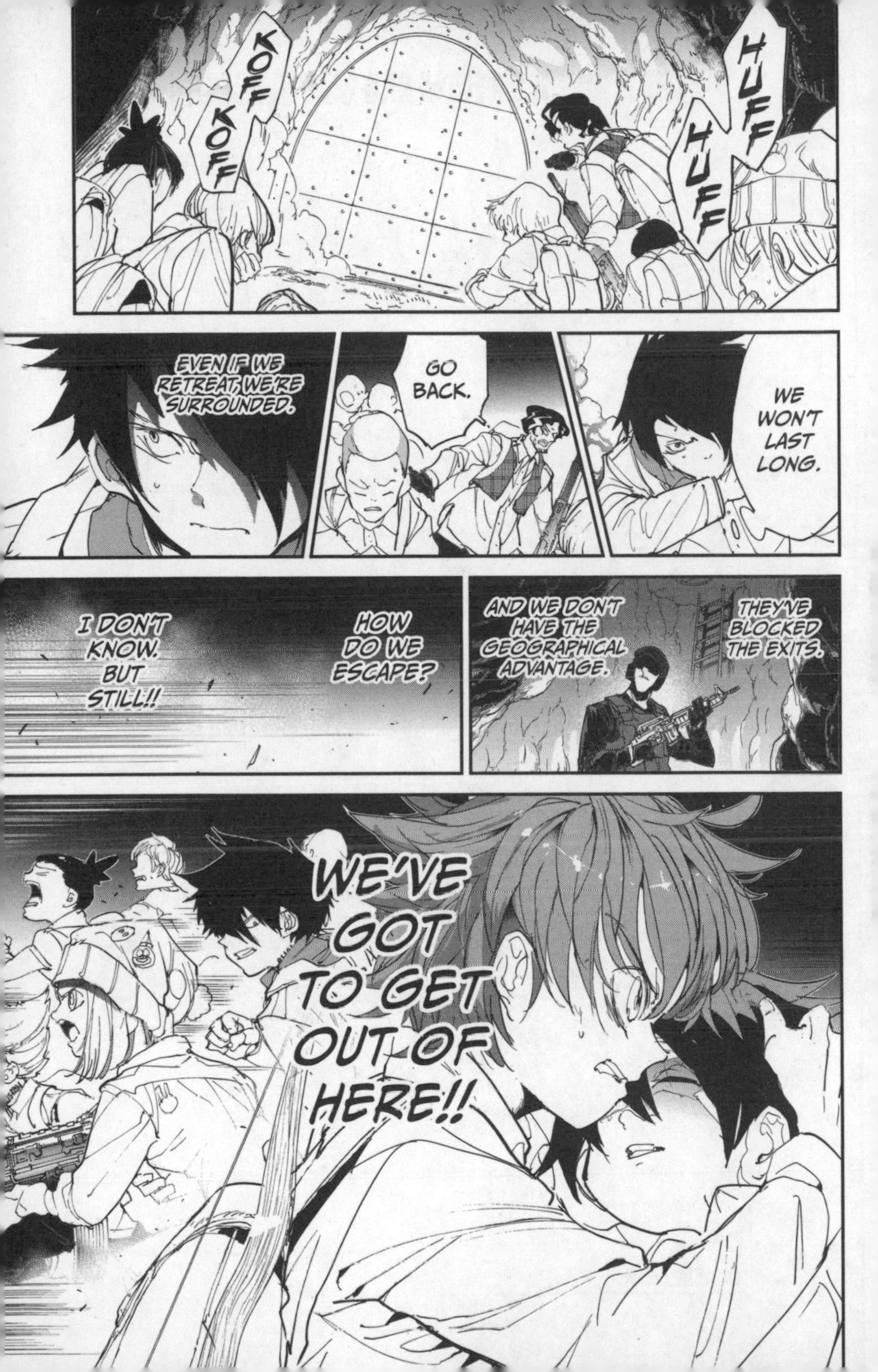
HUFF HUFF
KOFF KOFF
WE WON'T LAST LONG.
GO BACK.
EVEN IF WE RETREAT, WE'RE SURROUNDED.
THEY'VE BLOCKED THE EXITS.
AND WE DON'T HAVE THE GEOGRAPHICAL ADVANTAGE.
HOW DO WE ESCAPE?
I DON'T KNOW. BUT STILL!!
WE'VE GOT TO GET OUT OF HERE!!

THE PROMISED NEVERLAND SIDE SCENE 019-2

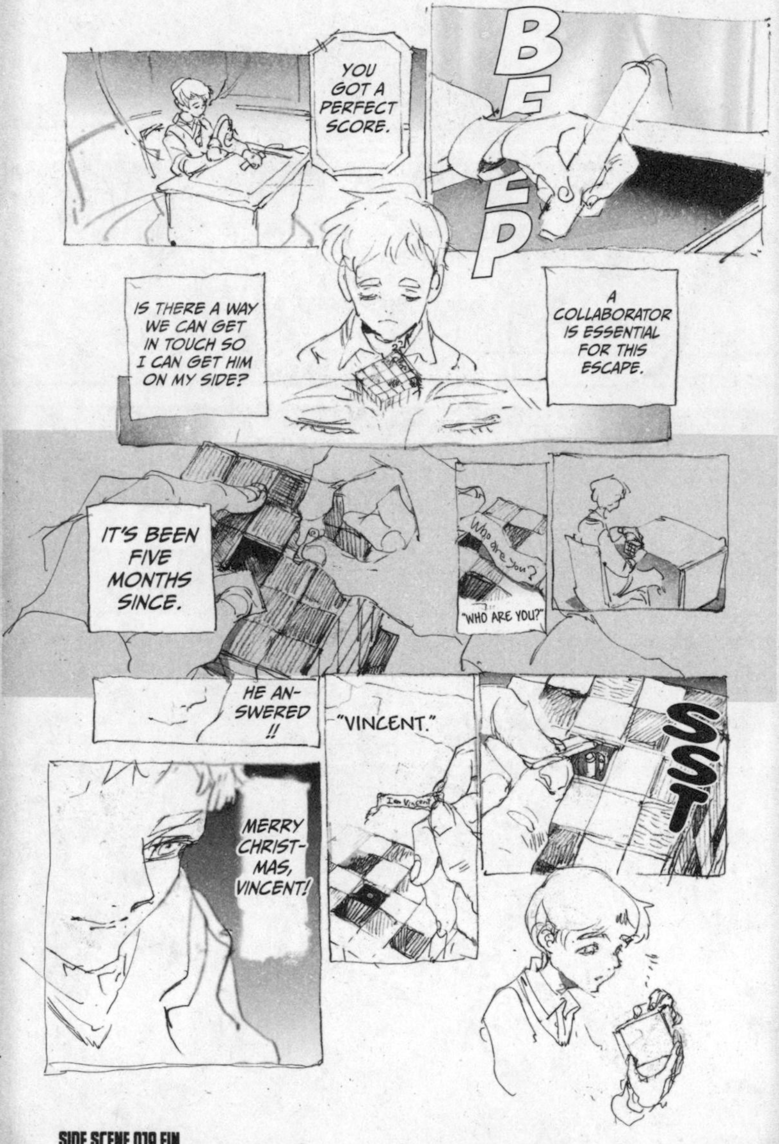
BEEP
YOU GOT A PERFECT SCORE.
A COLLABORATOR IS ESSENTIAL FOR THIS ESCAPE.
IS THERE A WAY WE CAN GET IN TOUCH SO I CAN GET HIM ON MY SIDE?
Who are you?
"WHO ARE YOU?"
IT'S BEEN FIVE MONTHS SINCE.
SST
"VINCENT."
HE AN-SWERED !!
MERRY CHRIST-MAS, VINCENT!

SIDE SCENE 019 FIN

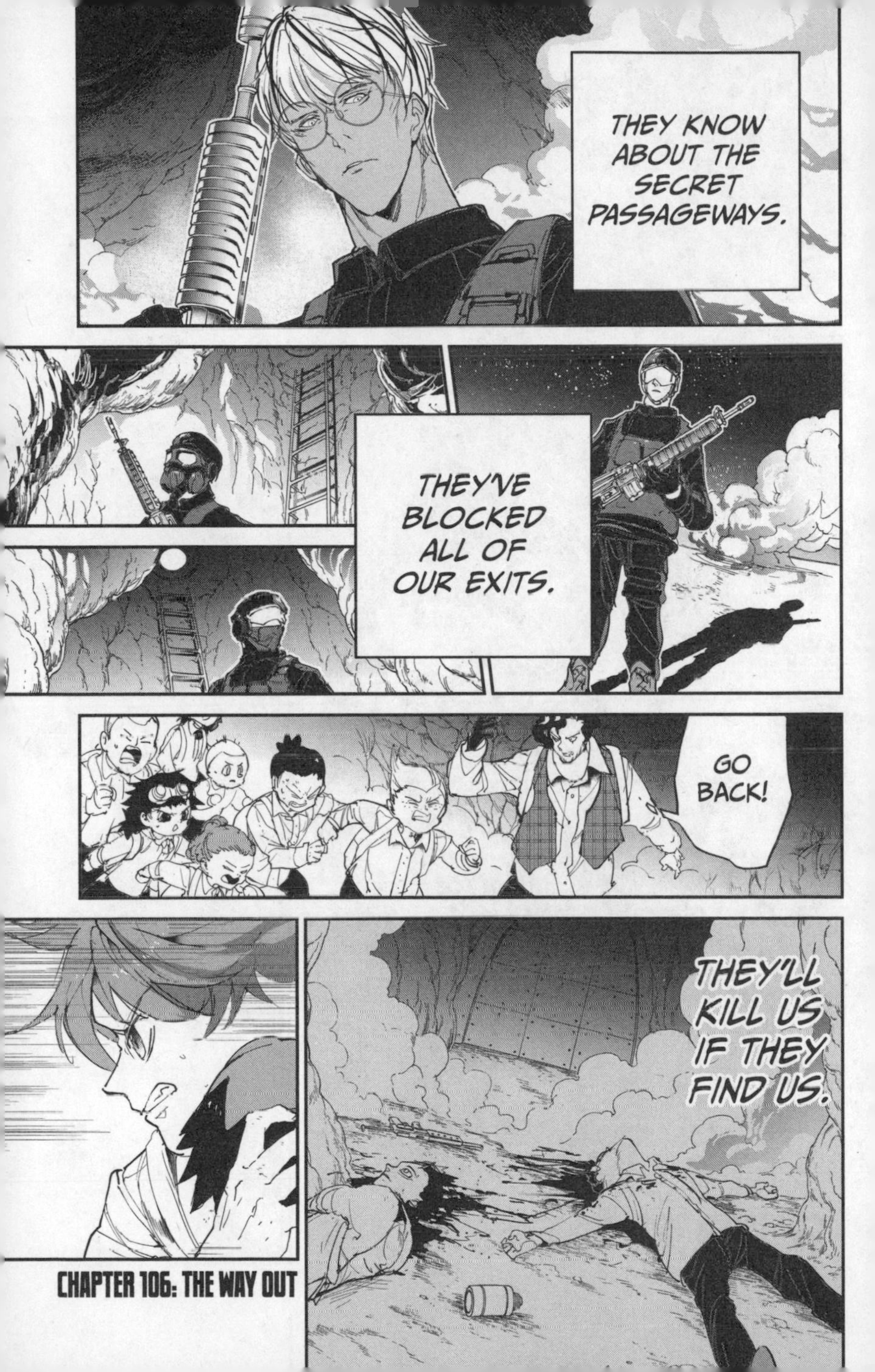
THEY KNOW ABOUT THE SECRET PASSAGEWAYS.
THEY'VE BLOCKED ALL OF OUR EXITS.
GO BACK!
THEY'LL KILL US IF THEY FIND US.
CHAPTER 106: THE WAY OUT

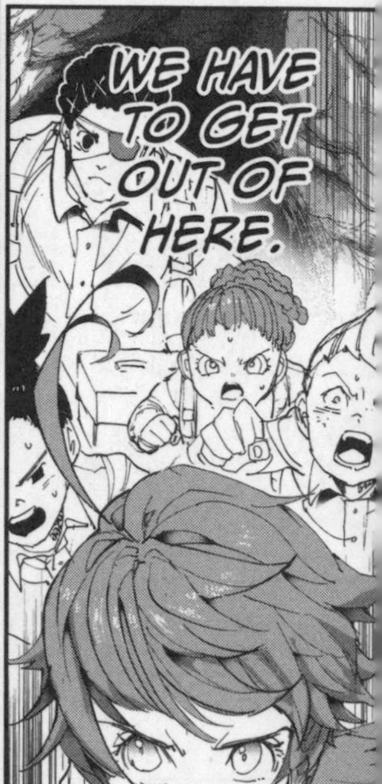
WE HAVE TO GET OUT OF HERE.

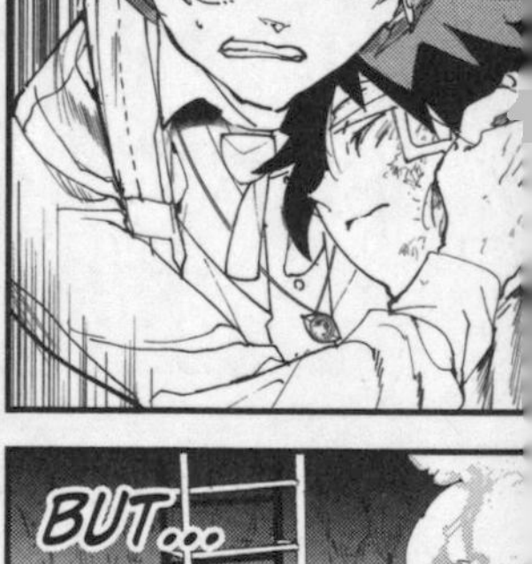
BUT...

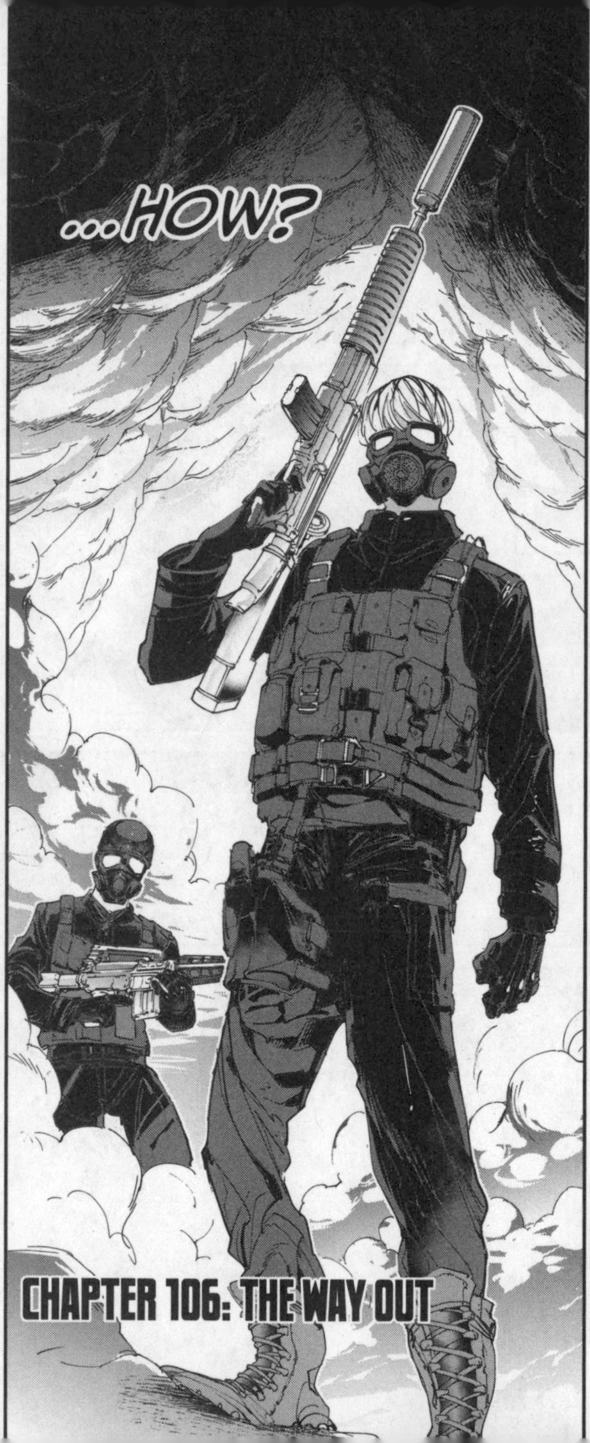
...HOW?
CHAPTER 106: THE WAY OUT

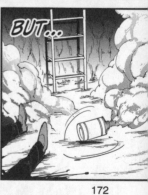

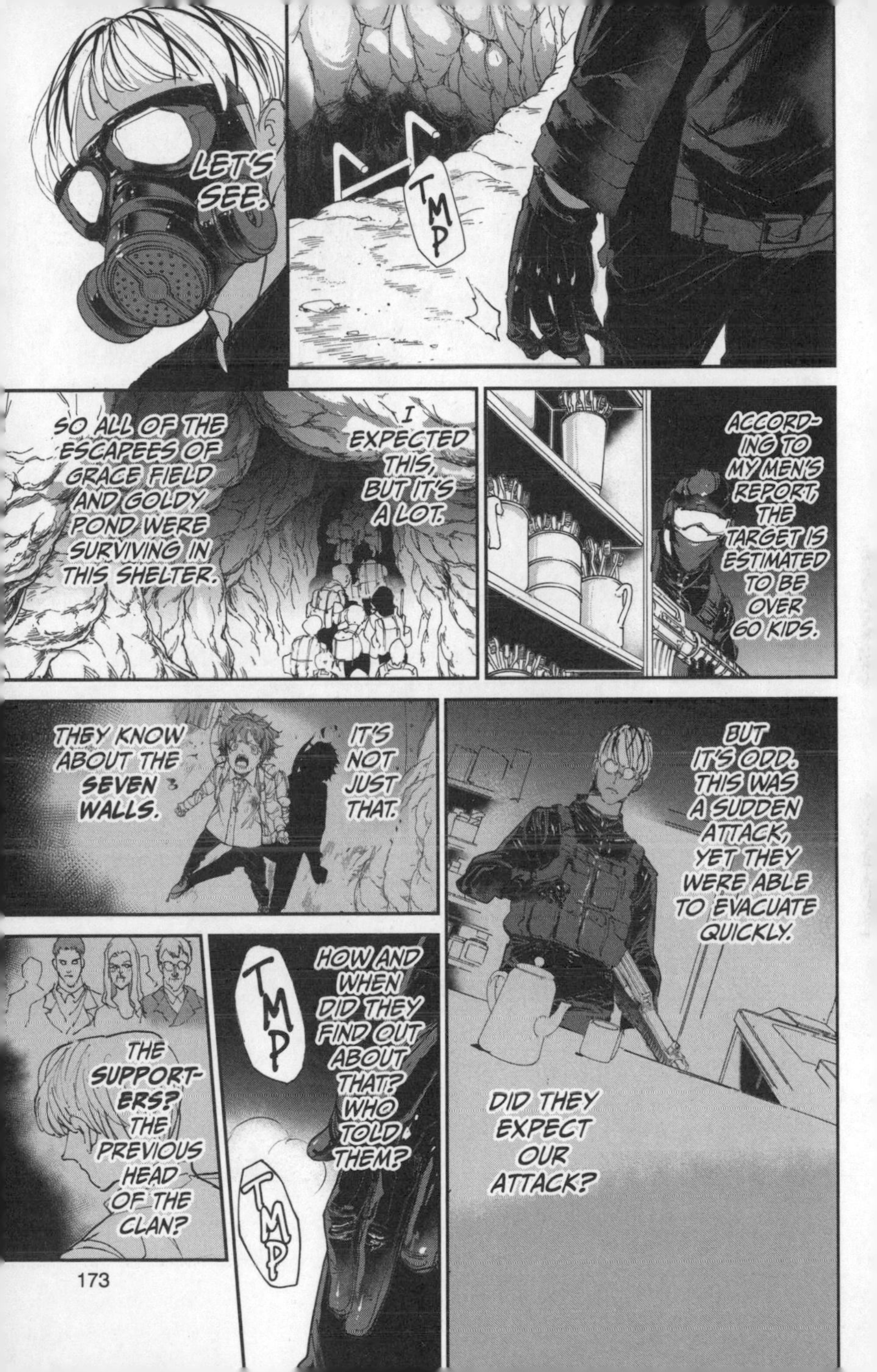
TMP
LET'S SEE.
ACCORDING TO MY MEN'S REPORT, THE TARGET IS ESTIMATED TO BE OVER 60 KIDS.
SO ALL OF THE ESCAPEES OF GRACE FIELD AND GOLDY POND WERE SURVIVING IN THIS SHELTER.
I EXPECTED THIS, BUT IT'S A LOT.
BUT IT'S ODD. THIS WAS A SUDDEN ATTACK, YET THEY WERE ABLE TO EVACUATE QUICKLY.
DID THEY EXPECT OUR ATTACK?
THEY KNOW ABOUT THE SEVEN WALLS.
IT'S NOT JUST THAT.
HOW AND WHEN DID THEY FIND OUT ABOUT THAT? WHO TOLD THEM?
TMP
TMP
THE SUPPORTERS? THE PREVIOUS HEAD OF THE CLAN?

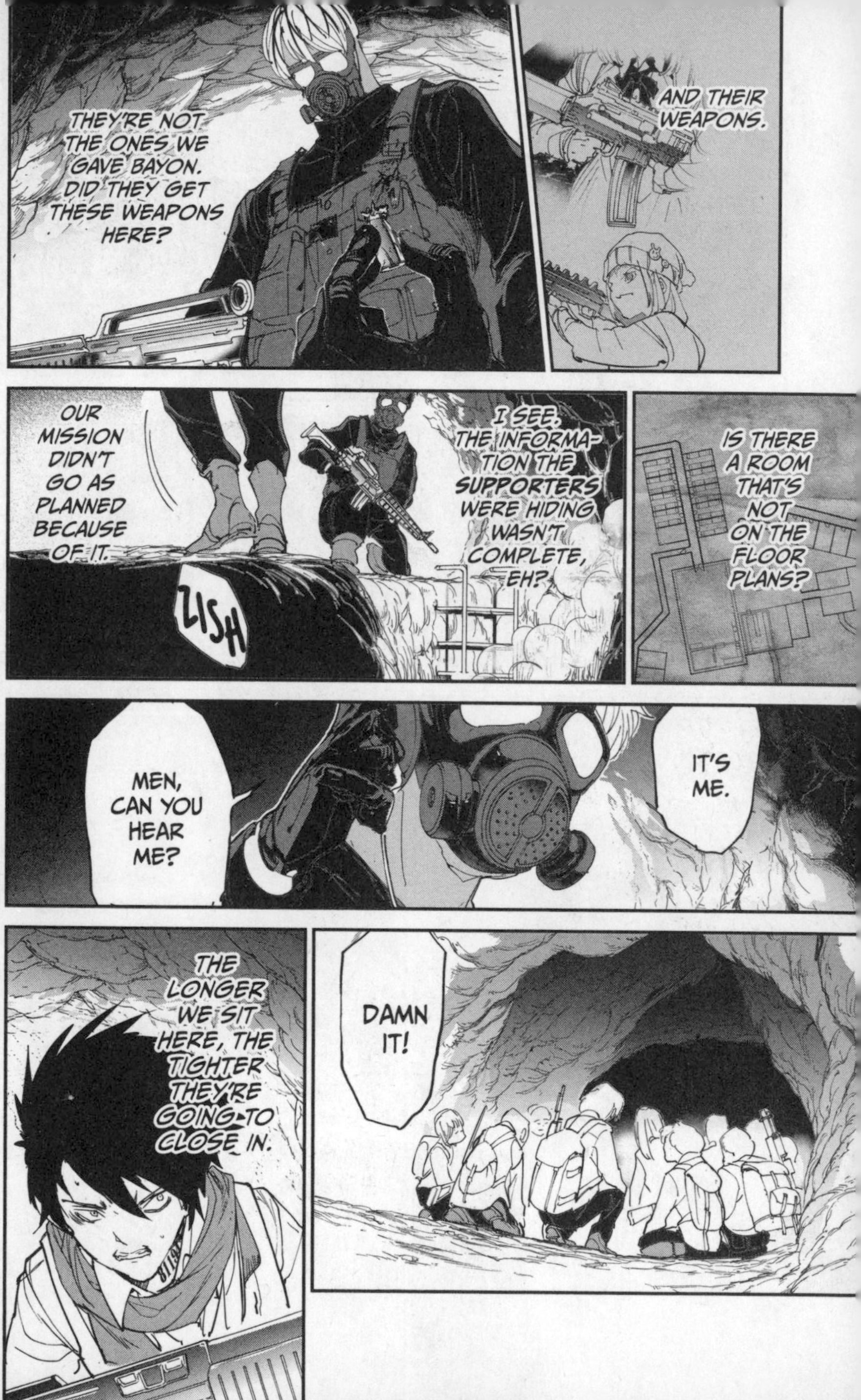
AND THEIR WEAPONS.
THEY'RE NOT THE ONES WE GAVE BAYON. DID THEY GET THESE WEAPONS HERE?
IS THERE A ROOM THAT'S NOT ON THE FLOOR PLANS?
I SEE. THE INFORMATION THE SUPPORTERS WERE HIDING WASN'T COMPLETE, EH?
OUR MISSION DIDN'T GO AS PLANNED BECAUSE OF IT.
ZISH
IT'S ME.
MEN, CAN YOU HEAR ME?
DAMN IT!
THE LONGER WE SIT HERE, THE TIGHTER THEY'RE GOING TO CLOSE IN.

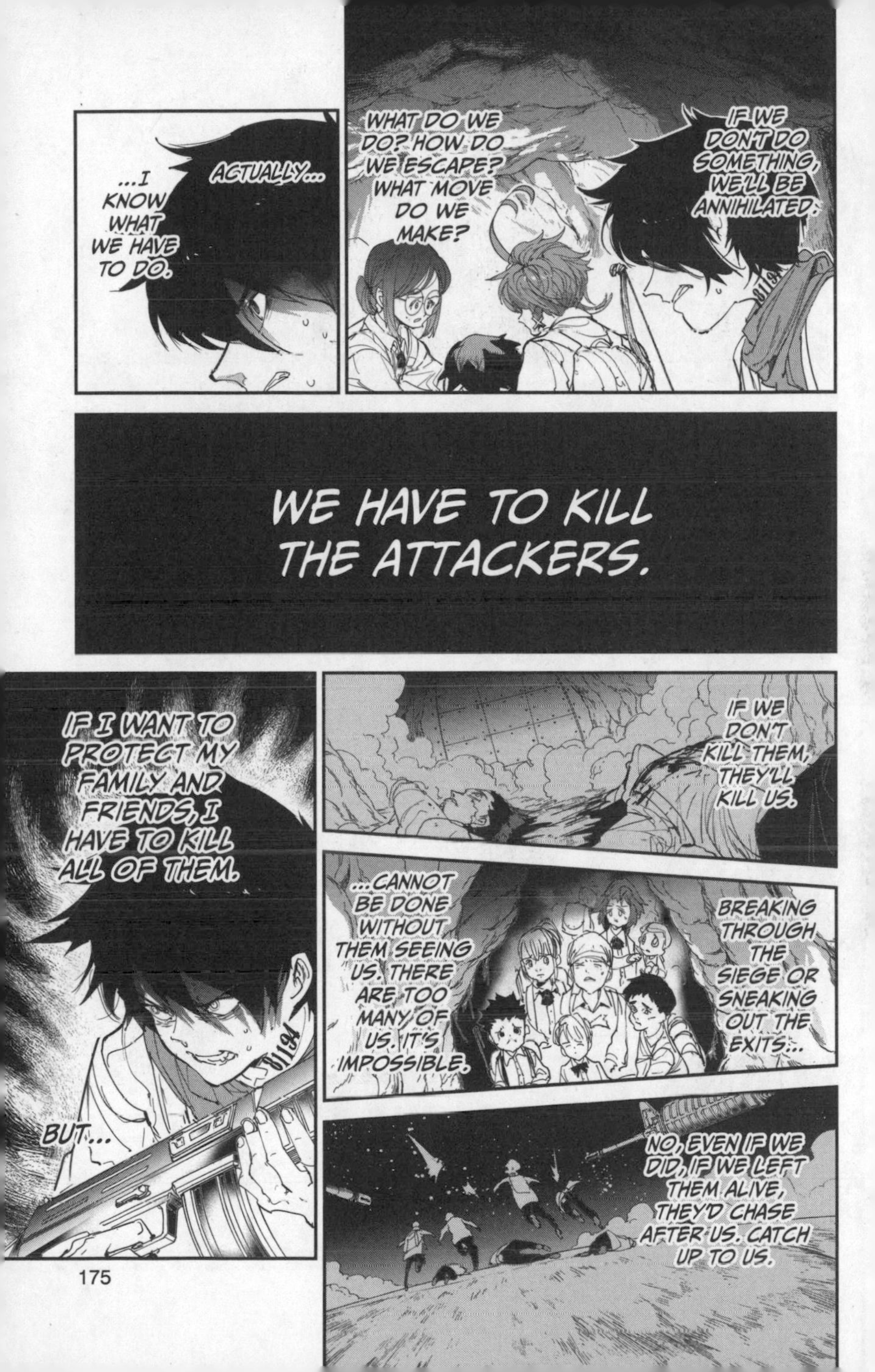
IF WE DON'T DO SOMETHING, WE'LL BE ANNIHILATED.
WHAT DO WE DO? HOW DO WE ESCAPE? WHAT MOVE DO WE MAKE?
ACTUALLY...
...I KNOW WHAT WE HAVE TO DO.
WE HAVE TO KILL THE ATTACKERS.
IF WE DON'T KILL THEM, THEY'LL KILL US.
BREAKING THROUGH THE SIEGE OR SNEAKING OUT THE EXITS...
...CANNOT BE DONE WITHOUT THEM SEEING US. THERE ARE TOO MANY OF US. IT'S IMPOSSIBLE.
NO, EVEN IF WE DID, IF WE LEFT THEM ALIVE, THEY'D CHASE AFTER US. CATCH UP TO US.
IF I WANT TO PROTECT MY FAMILY AND FRIENDS, I HAVE TO KILL ALL OF THEM.
BUT...

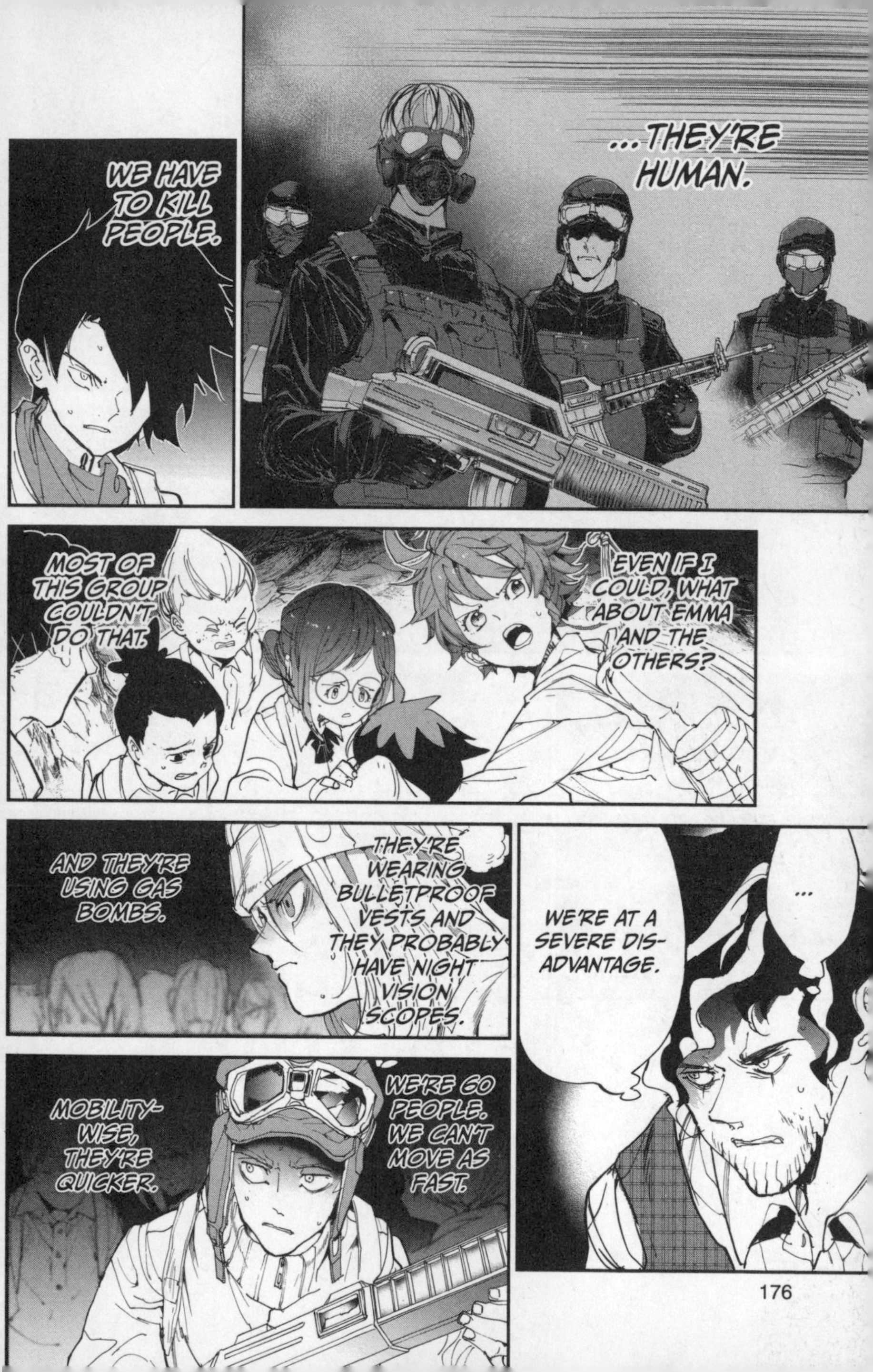
...THEY'RE HUMAN.
WE HAVE TO KILL PEOPLE.
EVEN IF I COULD, WHAT ABOUT EMMA AND THE OTHERS?
MOST OF THIS GROUP COULDN'T DO THAT.
...
WE'RE AT A SEVERE DIS-ADVANTAGE.
THEY'RE WEARING BULLETPROOF VESTS AND THEY PROBABLY HAVE NIGHT VISION SCOPES.
AND THEY'RE USING GAS BOMBS.
WE'RE 60 PEOPLE. WE CAN'T MOVE AS FAST.
MOBILITY-WISE, THEY'RE QUICKER.

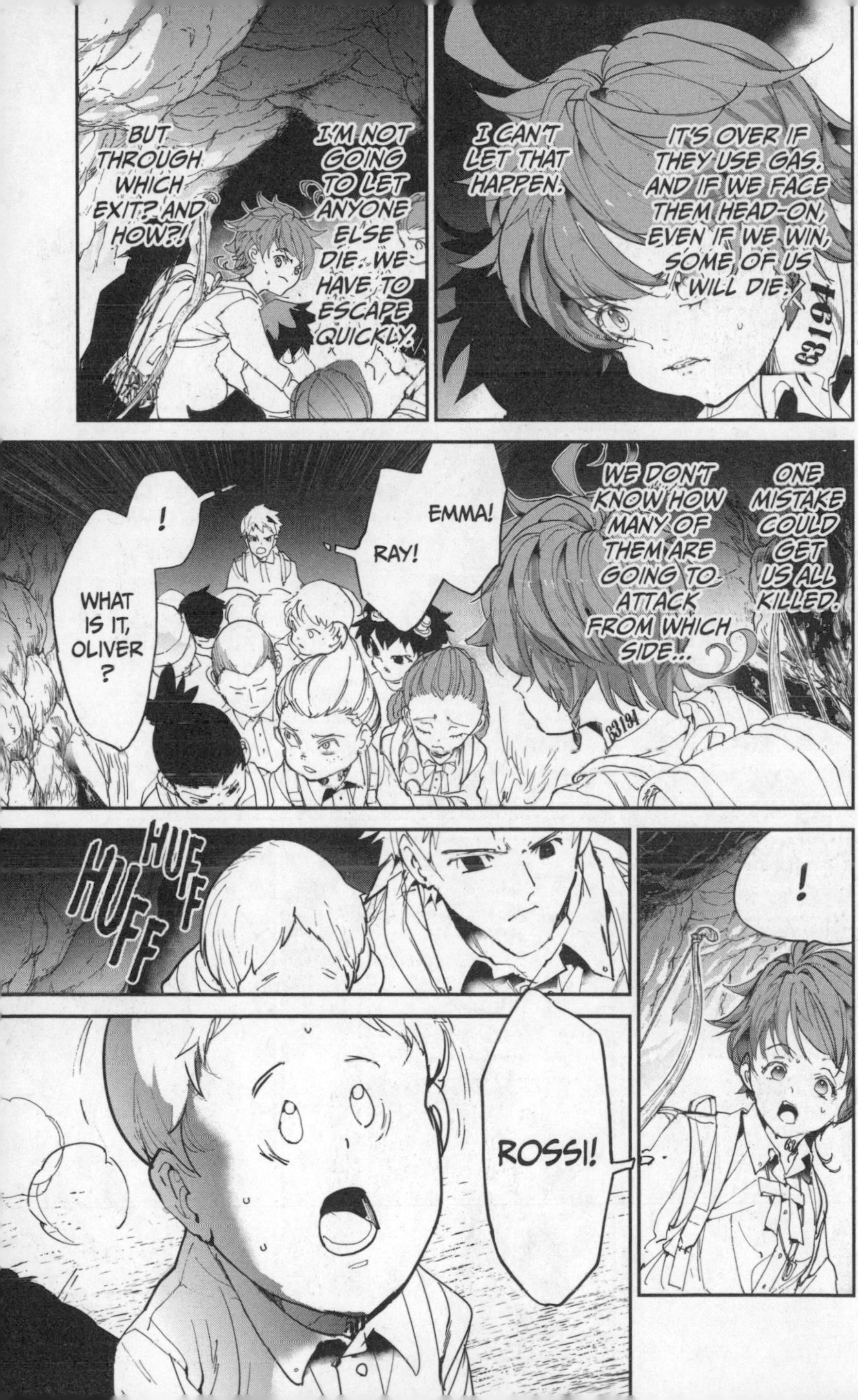
IT'S OVER IF THEY USE GAS. AND IF WE FACE THEM HEAD-ON, EVEN IF WE WIN, SOME OF US WILL DIE.
I CAN'T LET THAT HAPPEN.
I'M NOT GOING TO LET ANYONE ELSE DIE. WE HAVE TO ESCAPE QUICKLY.
BUT THROUGH WHICH EXIT? AND HOW?!
ONE MISTAKE COULD GET US ALL KILLED.
WE DON'T KNOW HOW MANY OF THEM ARE GOING TO ATTACK FROM WHICH SIDE...
EMMA!
RAY!
!
WHAT IS IT, OLIVER?
!
HUFF HUFF
ROSSI!

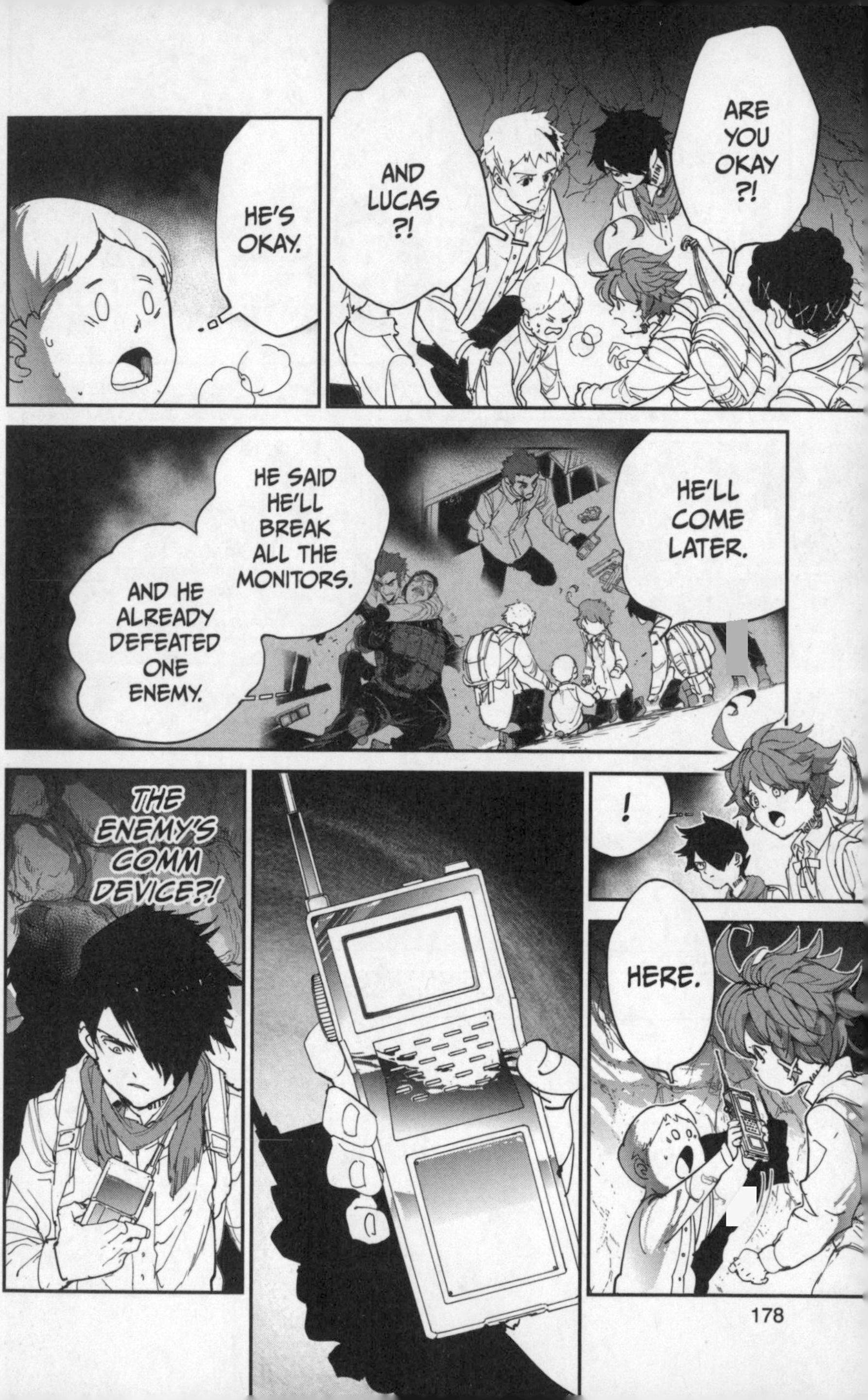
ARE YOU OKAY ?!
AND LUCAS ?!
HE'S OKAY.
HE'LL COME LATER.
HE SAID HE'LL BREAK ALL THE MONITORS.
AND HE ALREADY DEFEATED ONE ENEMY.
!
HERE.
THE ENEMY'S COMM DEVICE?!

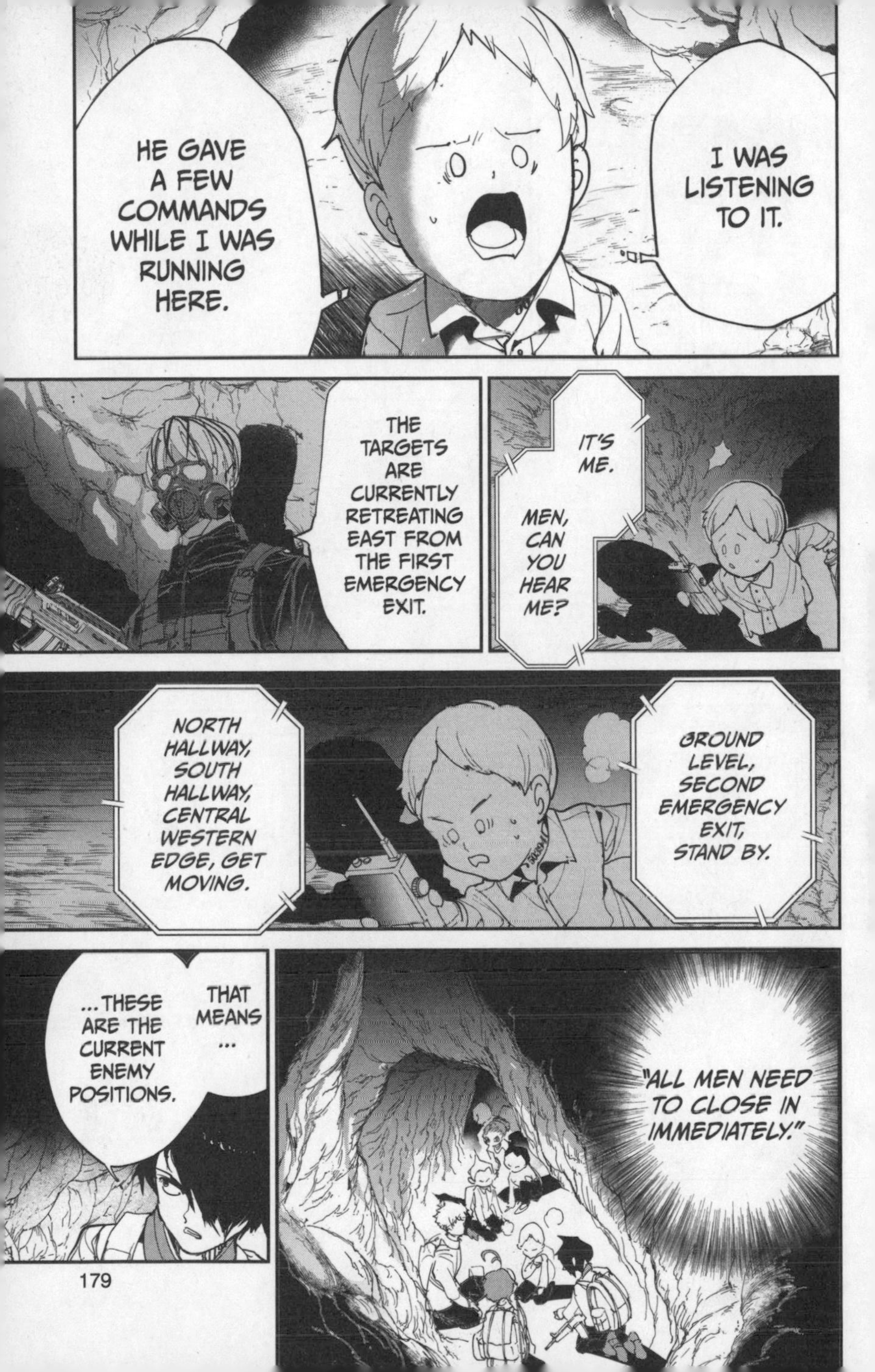
I WAS LISTENING TO IT.
HE GAVE A FEW COMMANDS WHILE I WAS RUNNING HERE.
IT'S ME.
MEN, CAN YOU HEAR ME?
THE TARGETS ARE CURRENTLY RETREATING EAST FROM THE FIRST EMERGENCY EXIT.
GROUND LEVEL, SECOND EMERGENCY EXIT, STAND BY.
NORTH HALLWAY, SOUTH HALLWAY, CENTRAL WESTERN EDGE, GET MOVING.
"ALL MEN NEED TO CLOSE IN IMMEDIATELY."
THAT MEANS ...
...THESE ARE THE CURRENT ENEMY POSITIONS.

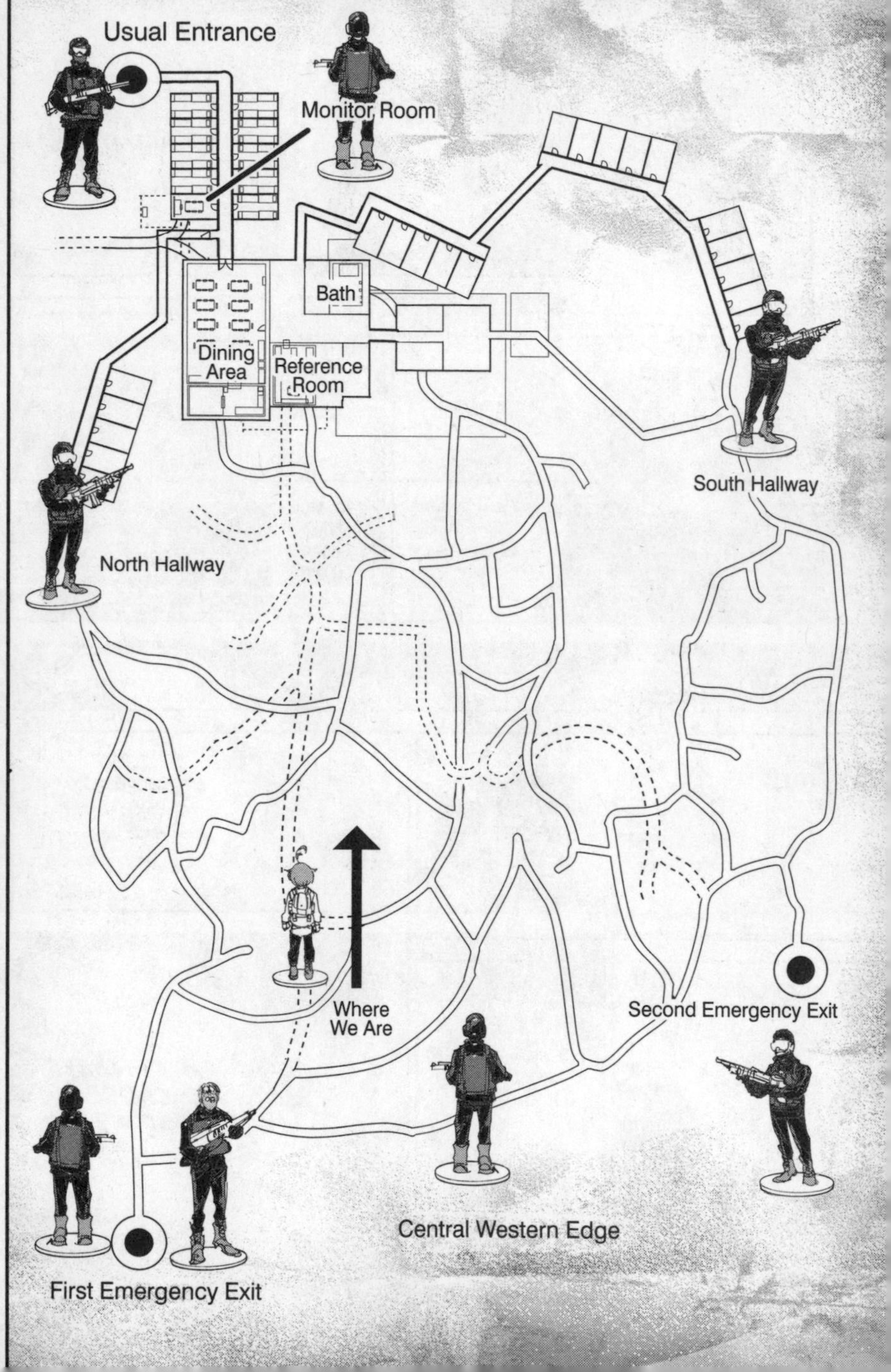
Usual Entrance
Monitor Room
Bath
Dining Area
Reference Room
South Hallway
North Hallway
Where We Are
Second Emergency Exit
Central Western Edge
First Emergency Exit

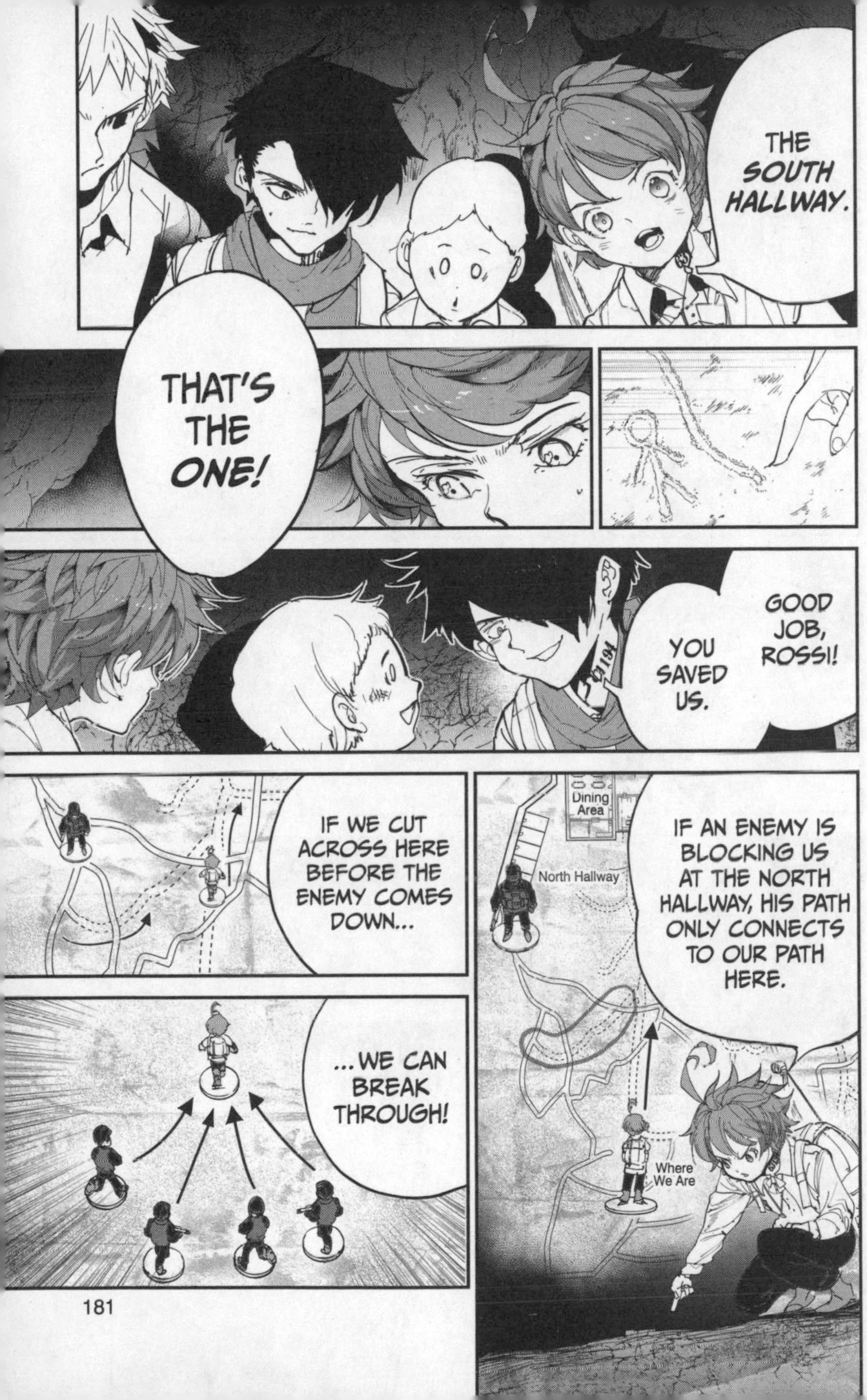
THE SOUTH HALLWAY.
THAT'S THE ONE!
GOOD JOB, ROSSI!
YOU SAVED US.
Dining Area
North Hallway
IF AN ENEMY IS BLOCKING US AT THE NORTH HALLWAY, HIS PATH ONLY CONNECTS TO OUR PATH HERE.
Where We Are
IF WE CUT ACROSS HERE BEFORE THE ENEMY COMES DOWN...
...WE CAN BREAK THROUGH!

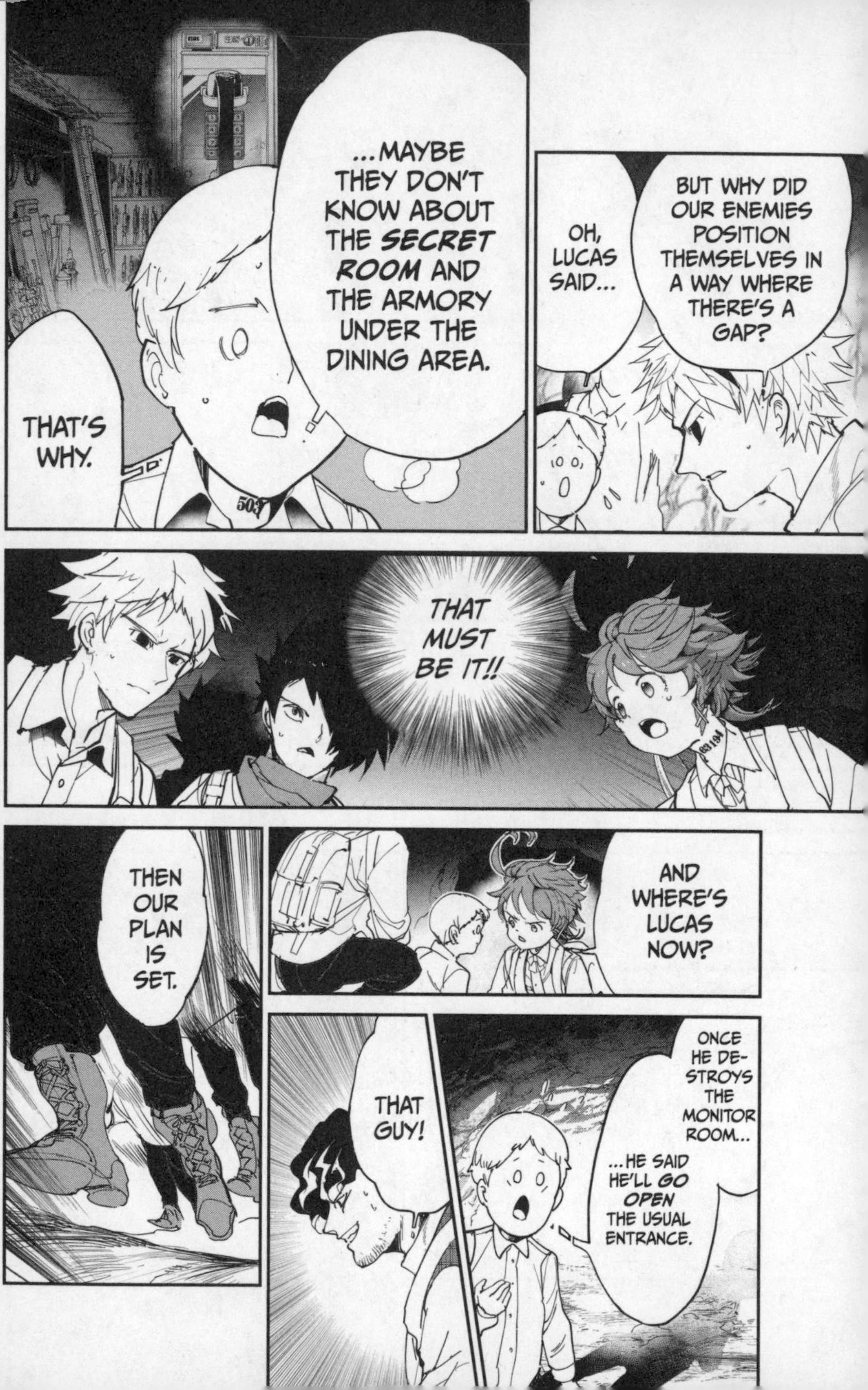
BUT WHY DID OUR ENEMIES POSITION THEMSELVES IN A WAY WHERE THERE'S A GAP?
OH, LUCAS SAID...
...MAYBE THEY DON'T KNOW ABOUT THE *SECRET ROOM* AND THE ARMORY UNDER THE DINING AREA.
THAT'S WHY.
THAT MUST BE IT!!
AND WHERE'S LUCAS NOW?
ONCE HE DE-STROYS THE MONITOR ROOM...
...HE SAID HE'LL *GO OPEN* THE USUAL ENTRANCE.
THAT GUY!
THEN OUR PLAN IS SET.

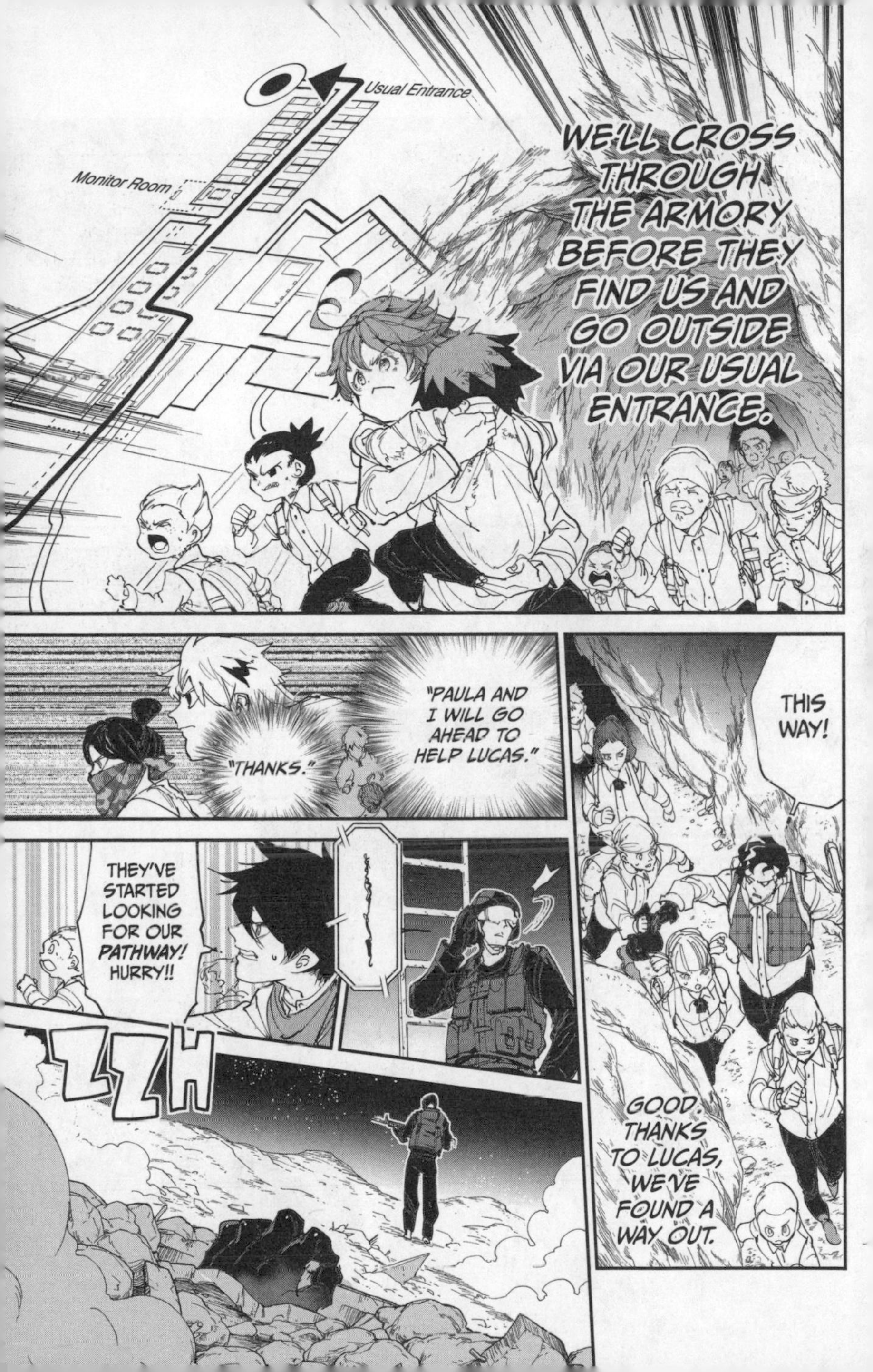
Usual Entrance
Monitor Room
WE'LL CROSS THROUGH THE ARMORY BEFORE THEY FIND US AND GO OUTSIDE VIA OUR USUAL ENTRANCE.
THIS WAY!
GOOD. THANKS TO LUCAS, WE'VE FOUND A WAY OUT.
"PAULA AND I WILL GO AHEAD TO HELP LUCAS."
"THANKS."
THEY'VE STARTED LOOKING FOR OUR *PATHWAY*! HURRY!!
ZZH

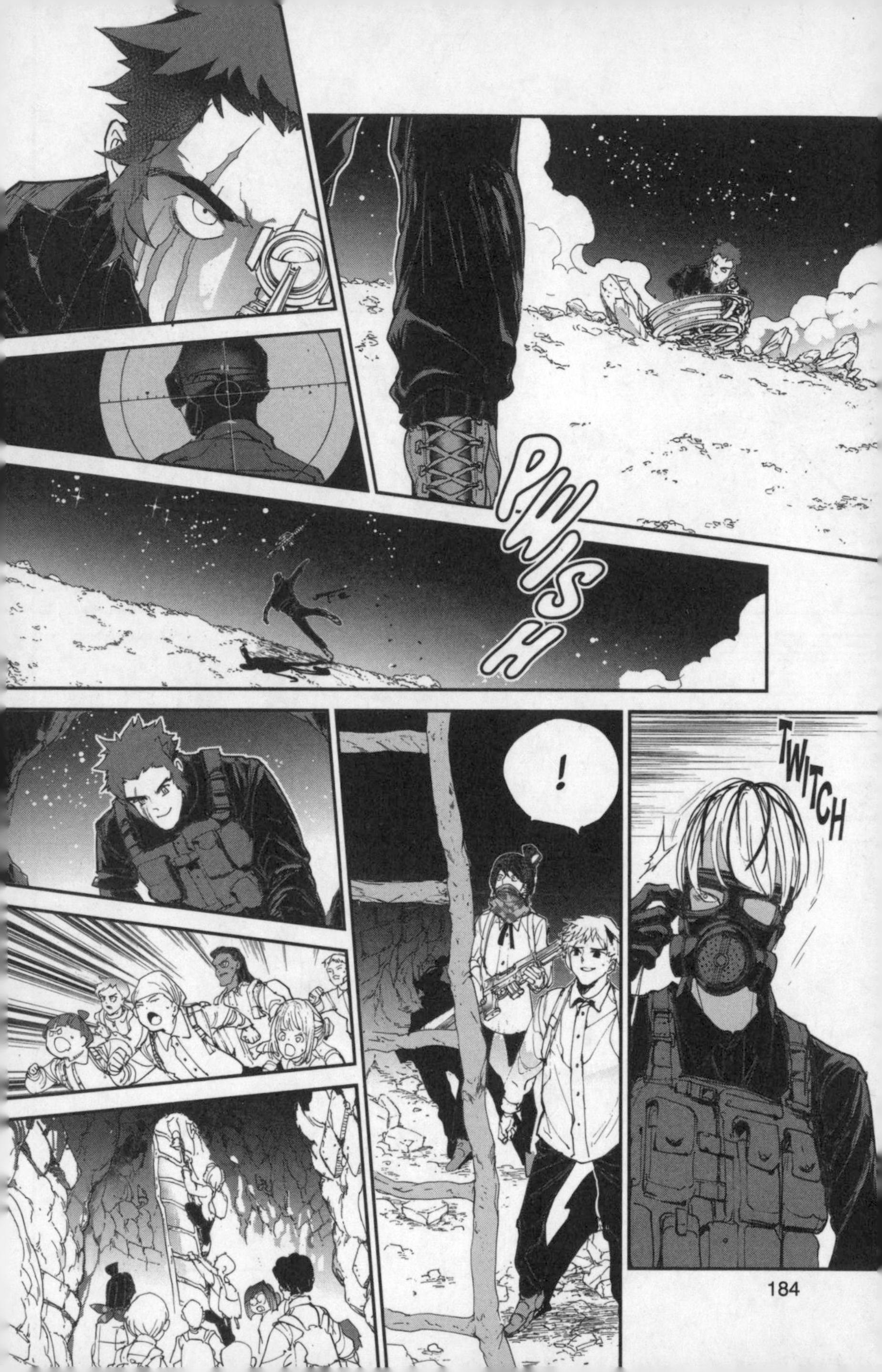
PWISH
TWITCH
!

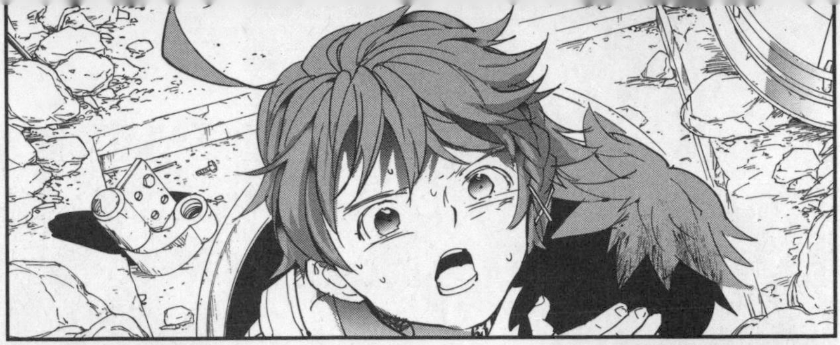
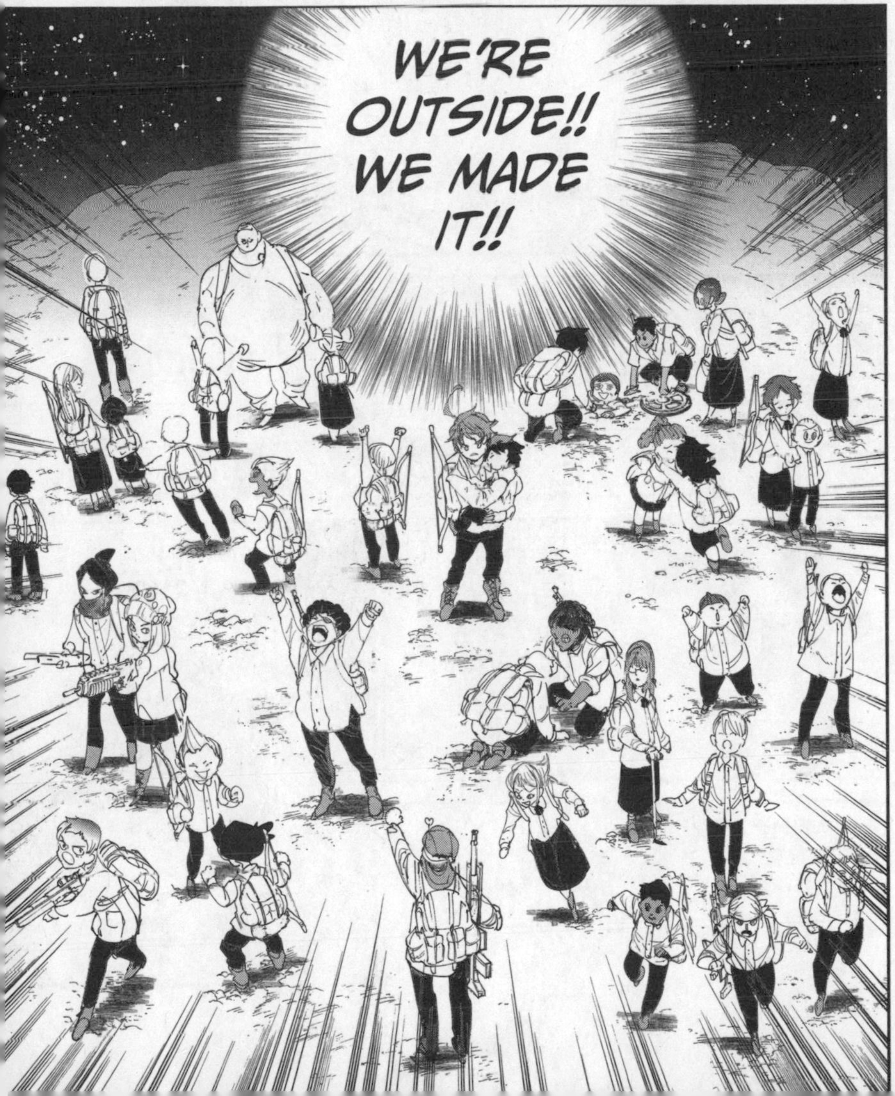
WE'RE OUTSIDE!! WE MADE IT!!

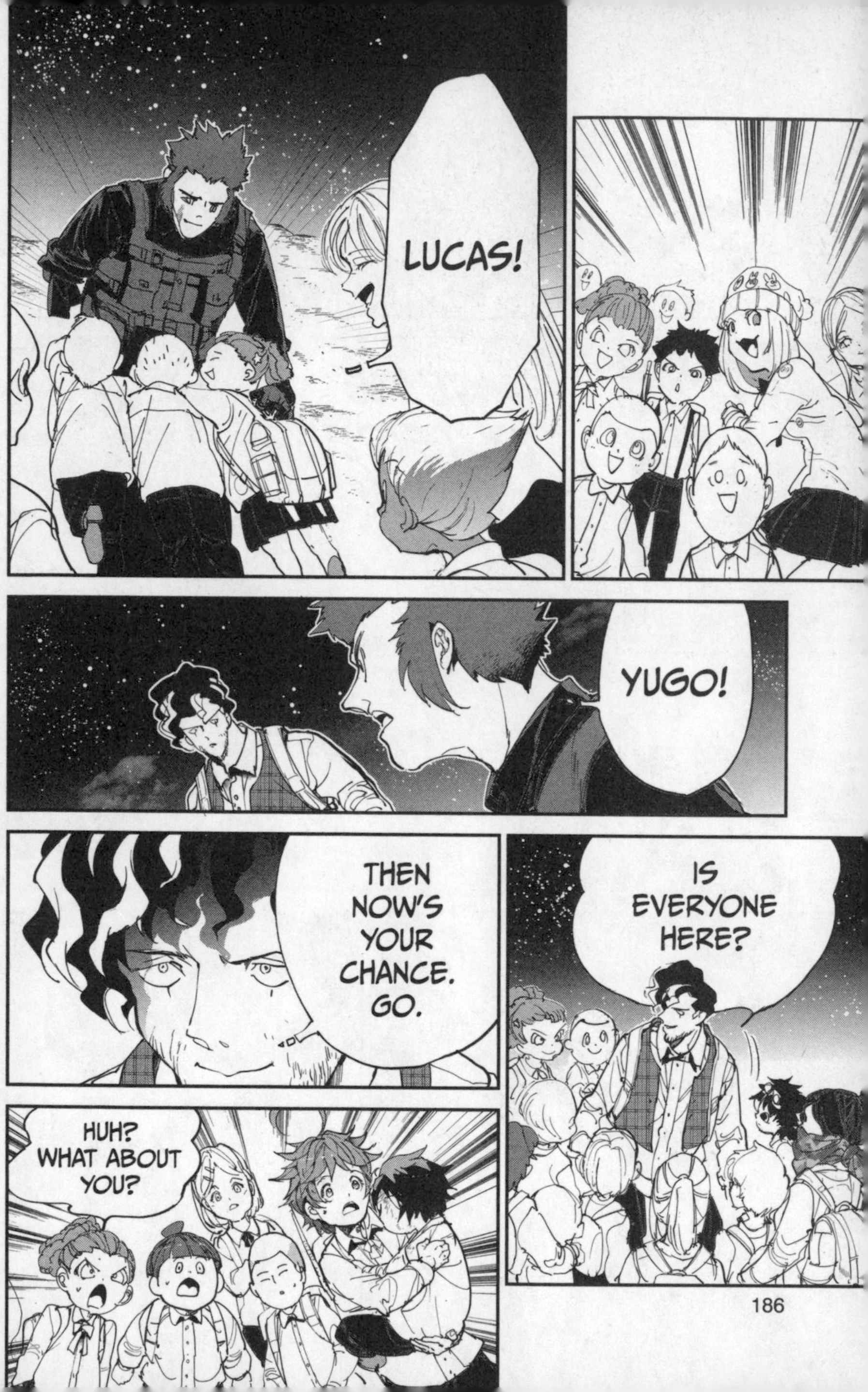
LUCAS!
YUGO!
IS EVERYONE HERE?
THEN NOW'S YOUR CHANCE. GO.
HUH? WHAT ABOUT YOU?

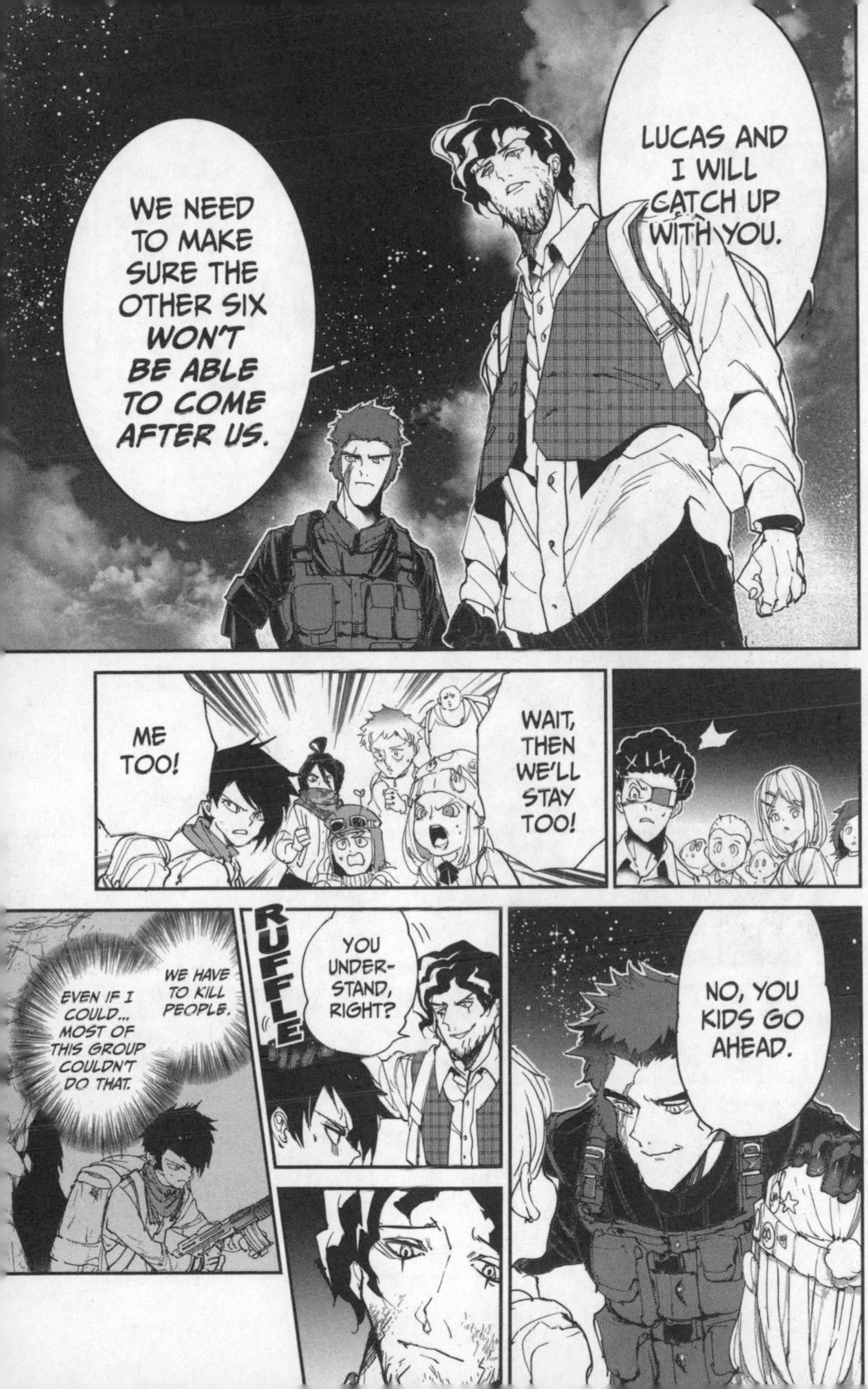
LUCAS AND I WILL CATCH UP WITH YOU.
WE NEED TO MAKE SURE THE OTHER SIX WON'T BE ABLE TO COME AFTER US.
WAIT, THEN WE'LL STAY TOO!
ME TOO!
NO, YOU KIDS GO AHEAD.
RUFFLE
YOU UNDER-STAND, RIGHT?
WE HAVE TO KILL PEOPLE.
EVEN IF I COULD... MOST OF THIS GROUP COULDN'T DO THAT.

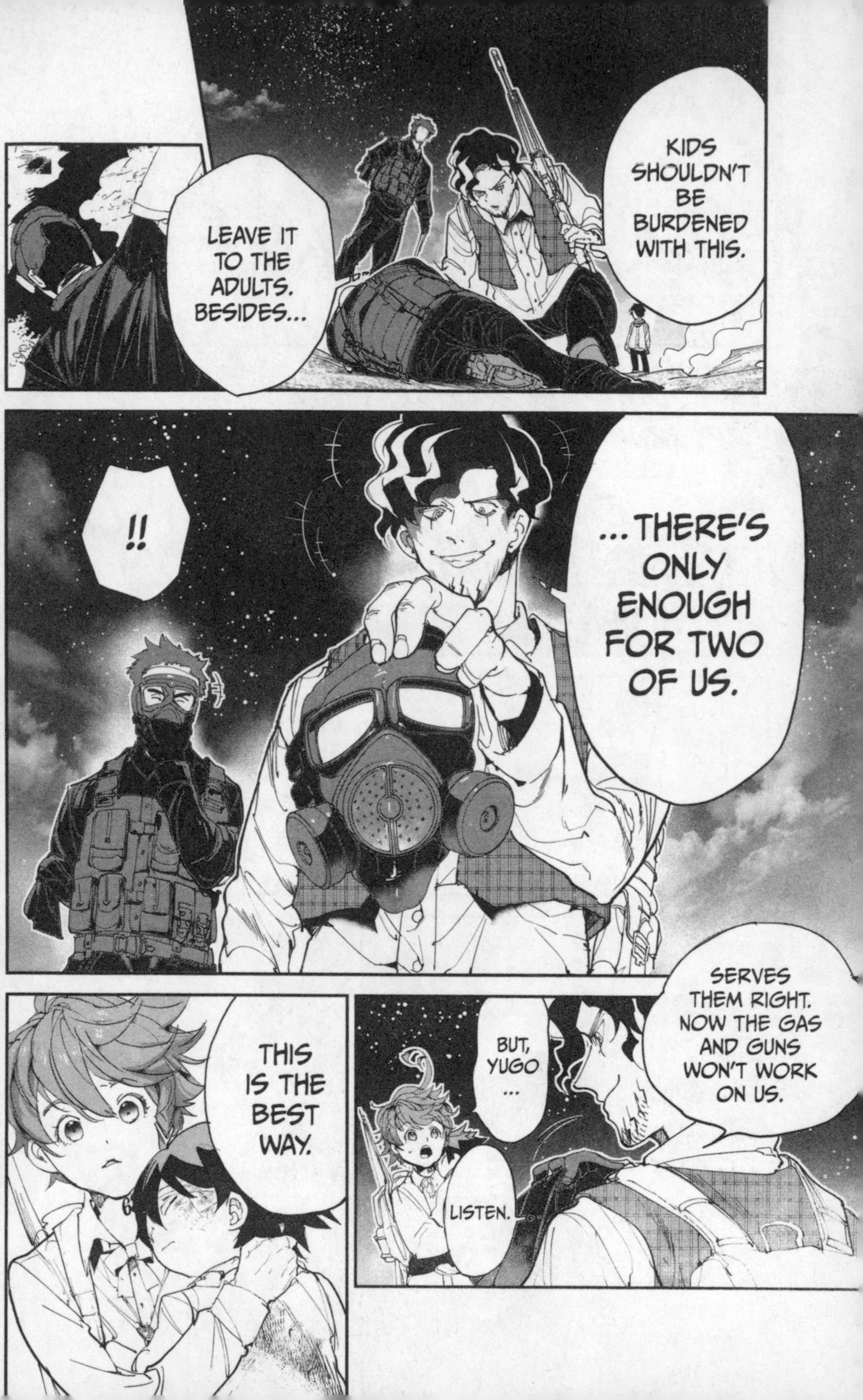
KIDS SHOULDN'T BE BURDENED WITH THIS.
LEAVE IT TO THE ADULTS. BESIDES...
...THERE'S ONLY ENOUGH FOR TWO OF US.
!!
SERVES THEM RIGHT. NOW THE GAS AND GUNS WON'T WORK ON US.
BUT, YUGO...
LISTEN.
THIS IS THE BEST WAY.

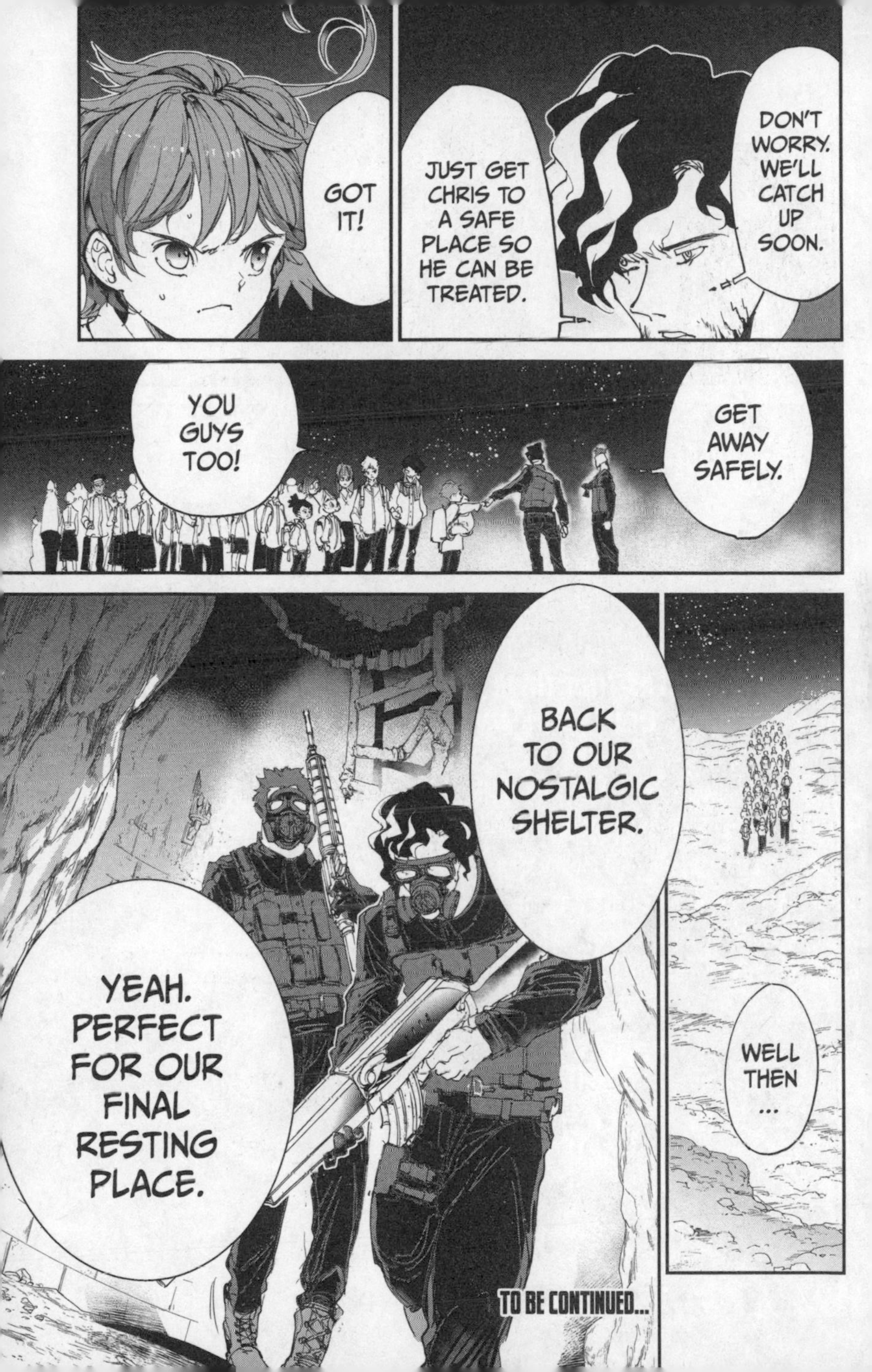
DON'T WORRY. WE'LL CATCH UP SOON.
JUST GET CHRIS TO A SAFE PLACE SO HE CAN BE TREATED.
GOT IT!
GET AWAY SAFELY.
YOU GUYS TOO!
WELL THEN ...
BACK TO OUR NOSTALGIC SHELTER.
YEAH. PERFECT FOR OUR FINAL RESTING PLACE.
TO BE CONTINUED...

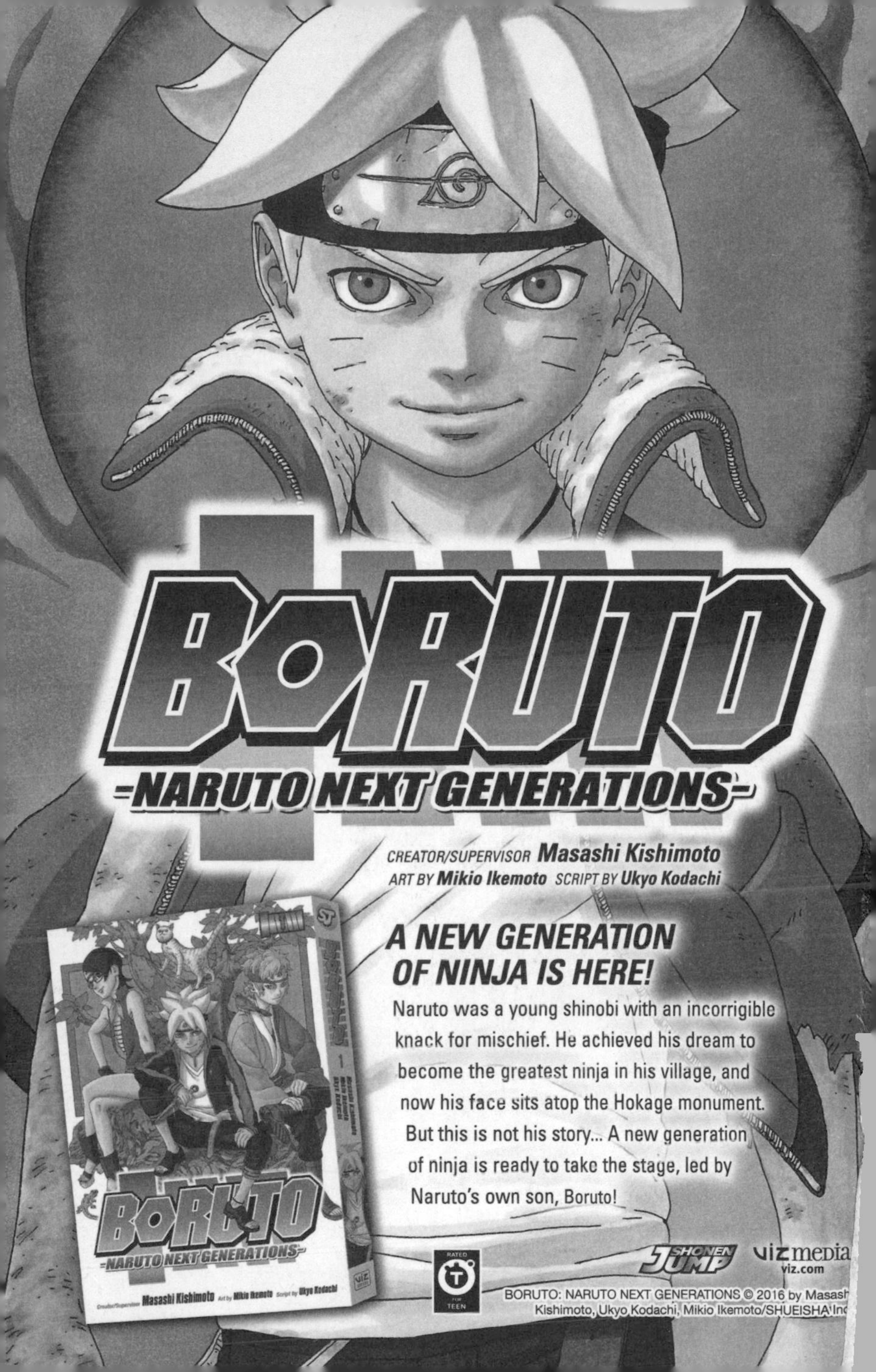
BORUTO
-NARUTO NEXT GENERATIONS-
CREATOR/SUPERVISOR Masashi Kishimoto
ART BY Mikio Ikemoto SCRIPT BY Ukyo Kodachi
A NEW GENERATION OF NINJA IS HERE!
Naruto was a young shinobi with an incorrigible knack for mischief. He achieved his dream to become the greatest ninja in his village, and now his face sits atop the Hokage monument. But this is not his story... A new generation of ninja is ready to take the stage, led by Naruto's own son, Boruto!
BORUTO
-NARUTO NEXT GENERATIONS-
Masashi Kishimoto
RATED T FOR TEEN
SHONEN JUMP
viz media
viz.com
BORUTO: NARUTO NEXT GENERATIONS © 2016 by Masash
Kishimoto, Ukyo Kodachi, Mikio Ikemoto/SHUEISHA Inc

YOU'RE READING THE **WRONG WAY!**

The Promised Neverland reads from right to left, starting in the upper-right corner. Japanese is read from right to left, meaning that action, sound effects and word-balloon order are completely reversed from English order.